The Spirit of the Times

Women's Voices in Ukrainian Literature

The Spirit of the Times

Selected Prose Fiction

by

Olena Pchilka

and

Nataliya Kobrynska

Translated by Roma Franko
Edited by Sonia Morris

Language Lanterns Publications
1998

Canadian Cataloguing in Publication Data

Main entry under title:

The spirit of the times : selected prose fiction

(Women's voices in Ukrainian literature ; vol. 1)

ISBN 0-9683899-0-2

1. Short stories, Ukrainian--Women authors--Translations into English.
2. Ukrainian fiction--19th century--Translations into English.
3. Ukrainian fiction--20th century--Translations into English.
I. Pchilka, Olena. II. Kobryns'ka, Nataliîa, 1855-1920.
III. Franko, Roma Z. IV. Morris, Sonia V. V. Series.

PG3932.5.W65 S64 1998   891.793010809287   C98-920168-6

Series design concept: © Roma Franko and Sonia Morris
Translations: © Roma Franko
Portrait sketches: © Raissa Sonia Choi
Cover production and technical assistance: Mike Kaweski

© 1998 Language Lanterns Publications
    321-4th Ave. N., Saskatoon, SK, S7K 2L9
    Web site: www.languagelanterns.com

Printed and bound in Canada by
Hignell Printing Ltd., Winnipeg

Women's Voices in Ukrainian Literature

Lovingly dedicated to
our mother
Sonia Melnyk Stratychuk
whose indomitable spirit inspired this series

Forthcoming Titles in the Series

Introduction to the Series

The turn of a century marks a pause in time—a pause that impels us to take stock, assess the extent and significance of societal changes, and make sense of our individual and collective experience. When the end of a century coincides with the millennium, this need to engage in retrospective analyses is intensified.

The purpose of this series is to make accessible to English readers the selected works of Ukrainian women writers, most of whom have not been previously translated into English, and, in so doing, enhance our understanding of women's slow, difficult, and ongoing trek to political, economic and social equality—a trek on which women in Ukraine embarked over a century ago.

The works selected range from vignettes and sketches to novelettes and novels. Together they constitute an unsystematic but compelling social history of an era during which the mortar of social mores, religious beliefs, and gender distinctions began to crumble as successive political and ideological cataclysms wreaked havoc with time-honoured personal and societal relations.

The authors are not equally talented or skilled. What they have in common is an appreciation of the power of literature, be it as an avenue of self-actualisation or a vehicle of social activism. In addition to national, political, and educational issues, they address matters of gender which cut across ethnic and social divisions, and explore the power and often devastating consequences of social conditioning.

They do not, of course, speak with one voice. For some, women's concerns are overshadowed by larger issues of political freedom, cultural autonomy, and socio-economic reform. Their goals range from group emancipation to individual freedom, with many initially defining their emerging status in terms of a synthesis of traditional female roles, immediate community responsibilities, and more general humanitarian imperatives.

More importantly, whatever the subject matter, they observe and interpret experience from a female perspective. They intuitively understand that women forge their identities in the context of relationships, appreciate the power inherent in this need for connectedness and emotional wholeness, and demonstrate a keen sensitivity to both the promise and the human cost of change.

Their voices are loud and strong, what they have to say is worth hearing, and their impact should not be confined to one time or place. Translating their stories into English permits their message to transcend temporal and geographical boundaries.

The process of translation, in and of itself a formidable undertaking, was compounded, in the case of the earlier works, by archaic forms of Ukrainian; late nineteenth century stylistic conventions, paragraphing, and punctuation; texts that varied with the era in which they were published; and vexing problems of transliteration. Ultimately, it was the criterion of readability that informed the many and difficult decisions that had to be made.

A biographical note about each author anchors her writings in a social and historical context. No other analyses are provided; the works are allowed to speak for themselves.

Sonia Morris, Editor
Former Assistant Dean of the College of Education,
Former Head of the Department of Educational Psychology,
College of Education, University of Saskatchewan

Roma Franko, Translator
Former Head of the Department of Slavic Studies
and the Department of Modern Languages and Literatures,
College of Arts and Science, University of Saskatchewan

Contents

Olena Pchilka

1849-1930

Biographical Sketch

Olha Drahomanova-Kosach, known by her literary name of Olena Pchilka, was born into a privileged family of landowners in Eastern Ukraine—a family that actively opposed the oppressive political and cultural policies of the Russian Empire. Her father was a lawyer who tried his hand at writing poetry and short stories, while her mother pursued interests in Ukrainian literature, songs, folk tales, customs, and traditions.

Her older brother, Mykhaylo Drahomanov (1841-1895), an eminent scholar, historian, political publicist, literary critic, and folklorist, served as her mentor. After the death of their father, he enrolled her in an exclusive girls' school in Kyiv, where she studied world literature and mastered German and French. In her brother's home, she met the leading intellectuals of the day.

In 1868, at the age of nineteen, Olha married a lawyer, Petro Kosach. A devoted mother, she instilled in her children—two sons and four daughters—a fervent love of country, a passion for knowledge, and a special interest in the study of languages and literatures. Her eldest son, who became a mathematician and a professor of physics, wrote under the pseudonym of Mykhaylo Obachny; her eldest daughter, Larysa, using the pseudonym of Lesya Ukrainka, became Ukraine's greatest woman poet.

Despite heavy family responsibilities, Olha's favourable financial position enabled her to continue pursuing her intellectual interests. In 1872, she visited her brother in Bulgaria where he was a visiting professor and, a few years later, stayed with him in Geneva, where he had settled as a political emigrant. At this time, she travelled widely in Europe and established contacts with writers in Western Ukraine, among them Ivan Franko, a renowned author, critic, publicist, and political activist, and the feminist author, Nataliya Kobrynska.

The first focus of Olha's national consciousness was Ukrainian folklore and ethnography. During the years that the Kosach family lived in smaller centres outside of Kyiv, she collected local customs, folk songs, and embroidery samples, and began her career as a writer in 1876, by publishing articles about Ukrainian folklore.

In the course of her career, she translated literary works from several languages into Ukrainian and wrote original poetry, plays, short fiction, and stories for children. She also published biographies, essays of literary criticism, literary reviews, and commentaries on current affairs. In addition, she compiled and edited journals, books, and almanacs.

Certainly, her pen name "Pchilka," which in Ukrainian means "little bee," was a most felicitous choice, for she gave up a life of leisure and assiduously fostered the development of Ukrainian literature.

Her literary activities intersected with her involvement in the Ukrainian women's movement and her political activism in the cause of unifiying Eastern Ukraine (in the Russian Empire) and Western Ukraine (in the Austro-Hungarian Empire). In 1887, she joined forces with Nataliya Kobrynska from Western Ukraine to publish the widely acclaimed *Pershy vinok (The First Garland),* an almanac that took the bold step of featuring only women contributors.

When the Kosach family settled in Kyiv in the 1890s, Pchilka, by then a well-known writer, became an active participant in the capital's cultural life and delivered lectures about Ukrainian, Russian, and Polish authors. In 1901, the Ukrainian literary establishment celebrated the 25th anniversary of her writing career.

In 1905, Pchilka participated in a successful effort to lift tsarist bans (1863 and 1876) on Ukrainian-language publications in Eastern Ukraine. This same year, in the province of Poltava, she founded an organization which fought for women's rights and issued a manifesto demanding autonomy for Ukraine.

The next decade in Pchilka's life was marked by personal tragedy. Her son, Mykhaylo, died in 1903; her husband, in 1909; and her daughter, Lesia Ukrainka, in 1913. She also lost a number of her closest friends and political allies, including Mykhaylo Starytsky (1840-1904), a renowned author, and Mykola Lysenko (1842-1912), a gifted composer.

During the First World War, Pchilka edited newspapers in her native village of Hadyach in Poltava. In 1924, she returned to Kyiv, where she worked in the ethnographic, literary, and historical sections of the Academy of Sciences of the Ukrainian SSR. Even though she had been persecuted for her anti-Soviet views and activities, in 1925, in recognition of her many achievements, she was made a Member of the Academy. Despite her advanced years and frail health, she continued writing until her death in 1930.

In her thematically fresh depictions of the lifestyles and concerns of the upper classes, Pchilka was among the first Ukrainian authors to record authentically the speech patterns and conversations of the Ukrainian intelligentsia. A highly principled woman, she challenged deeply ingrained norms governing the status of women in society, played a leading role in the struggle for Ukraine's reunification and independence, and made a noteworthy contribution to Ukrainian literature and the enrichment of the Ukrainian literary language.

Fumes

(1886)

> Fumes penetrate unnoticeably, but
> swiftly. There is a throbbing in your
> temples, and your heart begins to beat
> violently; then the fumes make you feel
> dizzy, until you completely lose
> consciousness.
>
> *(From a book on home remedies.)*

On a Sunday, just ten days before Christmas, Madam
Zaborovska, the owner of an estate in the small suburban village
of Kopychyntsy, asked that the horses be harnessed. She had some
shopping to do in town, and she wanted to travel in broad daylight
while the road was in good condition for sleighs. The holidays
were approaching, and she had to purchase a number of household
items—flour and other groceries, including salt and spices for
curing meat, because early in the week she was going to have the
fattened hog butchered. Madam Zaborovska was not one of those
truly grand ladies who retain housekeepers, so she had to see to
everything herself.

When the lady was almost completely outfitted for her
departure—she was already dressed in her fur coat—the children
began begging her to buy a few things for them. Lena, the older
daughter, wanted a few yards of ribbon, some thread, and buttons.
Manya, the younger girl, and Yuras, the little boy, asked her to
bring back some brightly coloured paper—they wanted to make
little baskets and lanterns to hang on the Christmas tree.

"Oh, for heaven's sake, you're making me absolutely dizzy!"
the lady exclaimed. "It would be best, Lena, if you came with me
to buy all these trifles, for I swear I won't have time to bother
with such nonsense!"

"Oh, no, mummy!" Lena protested. "I don't like to go to town
when you have a lot of your own purchases and matters to attend
to. You have to go here, and I have to go there—it's just a bother
for both of us."

"Well, have it your way," the lady said, making her way from the large parlour to the porch.

Just then, little Yuras looked out the window and shouted: "Mummy, we have guests!"

"What kind of guests? Where?" Both the older lady and the younger one moved quickly to the window.

A pair of bay horses came into view from behind the fence and appeared in the gateway. There were several well-dressed figures in the sleigh.

"So much for that!" the lady cried. "I was just about to leave, and now this! Oh, my God!"

"Don't get upset, mummy!" Lena placated her, as she peered out the window. "It's Nina Pokorska, with her brother and Doctor Ivasevych. They won't interfere at all with your plans. You can go, and I'll stay here with them."

"Aren't there any older people with them?"

"No, there aren't. Just the three of them."

"Well then, I'm off! I simply can't stay. The hog's going to be butchered tomorrow, and I must have the spices. You'll have to entertain the guests by yourself."

The lady walked swiftly out of the house. The children watched through the window as she stepped from the porch, greeted the guests, spoke politely to them, and then went on towards the sleigh.

As the guests made their way into the house, Miss Lena greeted them in the entranceway. "Hello! Greetings! Please come this way, into father's study! Take your fur coats off in here—it's cold in the entranceway. Father isn't home; he had some business in Horodyshche."

"So you're home alone?" the young lady visitor inquired.

"Yes, all alone! And I'm very happy you've come to visit!" Lena said, as she started to help her girlfriend remove various layers of winter clothing.

But her assistance was not required. The young doctor, a blond, agile young man, was bustling around Miss Nina Pokorska.

"What stroke of good fortune has brought you to our place?" Lena asked the other young gentleman—Nina's slender, handsome brother.

"It was the good doctor and I who thought of it!" Nina broke into the conversation. "We got the urge to go for a drive—it's such a beautiful day, and the roads are so good—and, to have a purpose for our drive, I suggested we visit you." Then, pointing to her brother, she added: "And we took this lazybones along with us!"

Andriy Pokorsky, a dark-haired young gentleman, really did have a rather dispirited appearance, as if he were not a very willing participant in this threesome.

"Well, no matter how it happened, I'm delighted!" Lena gushed, leading her guests into the room. "Yuras!" she called out. "Run and tell Anton to light a fire in here immediately. In the meantime, we'll sit right here. Please be seated. This is my favourite nook."

Still talking, the little group arranged itself on the chairs and studio lounge near the fireplace. As it turned out, the doctor ended up sitting quite near Miss Nina Pokorska. And she was a young lady whose beauty was truly worthy of such neighbourliness. Slender like her brother, she had finely chiselled features, luminous dark eyes, and beautiful dark hair, now slightly dishevelled, which attractively framed her high, intelligent forehead and her delicately pale countenance.

There was only one jarring note in her appearance, a note with particular significance for the doctor who sat near her—the enigmatic smile on her face that was attentive, but somewhat mocking. It was with this smile that Miss Pokorska gazed at her suitor. Young ladies assume this look only when they are overly confident of the adulation of their admirer, and when they would not be too much grieved if they lost it. The doctor, a somewhat awkward young gentleman, with a ruddy complexion and a sparse blond beard, appeared oblivious to its meaning. He fidgeted nervously, spoke incessantly to Miss Nina, and took almost no notice of their hostess, despite the fact that he ostensibly had come to visit her.

To tell the truth, the hostess—a charming, vivacious blond—was not all that interested in capturing the doctor's attention. Seeing that this guest was quite taken with the lady sitting next to him and, being a gracious hostess, she happily turned to Pokorsky, the languid, but handsome guest with the pensive dark eyes.

"Master Andriy!" the hostess said to him. "Do you want to look at a Russian newspaper, or one from Kyiv? They're over here!"

Master Andriy moved closer to a table covered with books and newspapers. "So, what's interesting in this section?" he asked, picking up a newspaper.

"Here, read this," Lena said, as she peered at a column. "Just look at what's happening at the university!" She pointed at a news item, then rose to her feet, saying: "Well, enjoy your reading. I have to attend to some housekeeping duties." And she disappeared into the next room.

They could hear her clanging keys and giving orders to the servants. She evidently intended to receive her guests hospitably.

The visitors busied themselves with their reading. As they glanced through the newspapers, they exchanged remarks.

"Good Lord, where are we heading?" Andriy exclaimed when he finished reading the "news item" that Lena had pointed out to him.

"Or better—to what level are we regressing!" the doctor added.

"Just take a look at this letter!" Miss Pokorska said, passing her section of the newspaper to the doctor. "It should be of special interest to you. A village doctor is saying that a professional person who wishes to live in a village is simply not able to do so for any extended period of time. He says it's impossible to earn a living, or, for that matter, to eke out so much as a bare existence, because the peasants can pay virtually nothing for medical services."

"Of course, it's impossible to make a living!" the doctor replied firmly after skimming the letter. "What kind of payment can one get from peasants? You could perish on earnings like that!"

"Really?" Miss Pokorska interjected with a smile. "You're of the same opinion? Well, I think it all depends on the style in which one wishes to live. Of course, if one measures what one needs to live on in the thousands—and all of you won't even consider a position that doesn't pay in the thousands—then certainly one can't exist on what peasants earn! But this is what I think: if you're a populist, you should limit your needs—the same way that common people have to. You, however, would like to make 'a noble sacrifice' and live in luxury at the same time. In my opinion, it is this passion for luxury that corrupts everything, all great flights of the spirit, and all endeavours!"

"But just a minute! Who said anything about luxury? We're talking about the most basic, everyday necessities!" the doctor parried heatedly. "Just listen to this. In this same letter the man is saying that after working unstintingly for several months among the peasants, he received one hen in payment! Well, you must agree that no matter how small your appetite, it isn't possible for a single hen to satisfy your hunger for half a year!" The doctor laughed heartily.

The argument was interrupted by their hostess, who invited them into the adjoining room for lunch.

Continuing their discourse in a disjointed manner, the guests made their way into the dining room. There, on the freshly set table, a rustic meal awaited them—ham, butter, and scrambled eggs. There were also two bottles of liquor.

Without any formalities, they all took their places and began to eat. Yuras and Manya, sitting towards one end of the table, ate with them.

The hostess bustled about. "Lukiya!" she called out into the other room. "Bring in the liqueur glasses and some little plates!"

A young female servant dressed in simple peasant clothing, her black hair smoothly combed, came into the room and busied herself at the table. Despite the simplicity of her attire, the girl drew everyone's eyes. Her face, with its unusually fine features, its velvety eyebrows, and dark eyes that appeared even darker because of her long lashes, commanded undivided attention. In addition, it appeared that the girl was agitated, and a deep blush on her dusky cheeks enhanced the beauty of her delicate face.

"What a specimen!" the doctor whispered to Pokorsky. "Amazing!"

But Andriy Pokorsky did not reply; he appeared to be somewhat disconcerted. When Lukiya walked in, his pale face turned a flaming red, and he lowered his eyes in confusion. Nina glanced sideways at her brother, smiled lightly, and then addressed the girl calmly: "Why, hello, Lukiya! How are you? You've become even more beautiful!"

The girl did not reply. Blushing furiously and lowering her fiery eyes, she walked out of the room.

"Do you know her?" the doctor inquired.

"Of course I do!" Miss Pokorska replied. "She served at our place. She's a wonderful girl! Andriy and I really liked her. I'm very sorry mother took a dislike to her and dismissed her. Really, Andriy, hasn't she grown even more beautiful since she worked for us this summer?"

"I don't know," Andriy said. "Perhaps. She truly is a beautiful girl!"

Upon hearing these words, Miss Lena also glanced up at Andriy, but she looked at him more attentively than his sister. The conversation came to an abrupt halt after the doctor blurted out impetuously: "A most beautiful girl! Worthy of being captured on canvas!"

The hostess changed the topic.

"Can you tell me," she inquired, "what social events are being planned for the holiday season in town?"

"God only knows!" the doctor replied.

"Why is that?" Lena queried. "There must be some social evenings planned at the club."

"Oh! There's something strange going on in our club. They're all at odds with one another—the ladies and the gentlemen, the military personnel and the civilians. It seems quite likely that our club will fall apart completely! Some kind of deficits . . ."

"Well, it would be too bad if the club were to close," Lena observed. "I don't know where I'd go to borrow books."

"Oh, it's certain that even if our club is not shut down, cutbacks will be introduced to cover the deficit. And they will be felt first in the library; nothing will be ordered in the coming year!" the doctor said sardonically. "I, for one, am no longer going to rely on the club. I'm going to subscribe to one of the more important newspapers myself. I've even set aside the money for it."

"Well, one can get by in some fashion without books," Miss Nina gibed. "But how are you going to survive without card games if you're deprived of the haven of the club?"

"Oh, Lord!" the doctor cried out. "As if one had to worry about a place to play cards! Why, every home is open for that! And there's no lack of company. Card players have a sixth sense when it comes to knowing on whose table a deck of cards is going to appear in the evening! They show up there as if they'd sprung up out of the ground!"

"Is that true? Have you begun to play cards as well?" Andriy asked incredulously.

"Well, what is one to do?" the doctor protested. "I know all the people in town, and I'm invited everywhere—be it to someone's name day feast, or just for the evening. It's impossible not to go; and when you do go, what are you supposed to do? Are you going to pound your head against the wall, while everyone else plays cards?"

"What about the company of the ladies?" Lena asked with a smile.

"Oh, forget it! The company of the ladies!" the doctor replied bitterly. "This 'company' also plays cards all evening, or else it indulges in that idiotic game of lotto. Well, I swear that I prefer to play cards than to call out those stupid lotto numbers and cover them with little markers! The devil only knows what that's all about! Not even a mechanical-molecular movement of one's brain is required for that!"

Everyone laughed.

"But still, one has to do something for entertainment during the holidays," Lena, the hostess, started up again. "You know," she continued cheerfully, "I'm going to do something really interesting the first day of Christmas! For quite some time now—since last year—I've wanted to write down some of the local Christmas carols. So when the carollers come to our home, I'll jot down a few of the more interesting ones. And do you know what else I've thought of? To gain an understanding of this carolling tradition, I'm going to go carolling with the young village girls!"

"Well, I've heard everything now!" the doctor guffawed.

"Why do you say that? Why shouldn't I?" Miss Lena persisted. Her blue eyes shone with genuine happiness.

"You're only going to cramp their style!" Andriy remarked.

"Cramp their style? Not at all! Our village is small, and all the girls know me. I'll tag along with Lukiya, so how will I be bothering them? I'll sing a bit, observe everything, and when they go on to a neighbouring village, I'll come back home."

"But who will light our Christmas tree?" little Yuras asked.

"I'll have enough time to light the tree as well!" Lena assured him. "I'll light it, and then I'll go!"

"Are you going to trim a Christmas tree?" Nina asked the children.

"Oh, yes!" Yuras replied. "I'm going to make little lanterns!"

"And I'm making some tiny baskets!" Manya added proudly, nodding her head.

"Who'll be at your place for this occasion?" the doctor asked the children.

"I don't know," Yuras answered. "Maybe the priest's children will be here. And maybe the children of the medical assistant, as well."

"Here's an idea!" the doctor cried out half seriously and half jokingly, making the point with his finger. "Miss Lena, you should invite ordinary peasant children to the party."

"Why, yes!" Miss Nina stated. "If it's to be 'populism,' then let it be 'populism' all the way! Well? What do you think?"

"Why, yes! That's possible. In fact, it would be very easy!" Miss Lena agreed.

"Listen," she addressed the children, "invite the children from the Khvedosky and Lukash families."

"Great!" Yuras responded.

"I drink to the union of different social classes—at least in the village of Kopychyntsy!" the doctor announced.

He raised his brimming glass of cherry brandy and, merrily toasting the young ladies, the children, and Andriy, he made all of them drink to what he had said.

Happy and carefree, they laughed and joked. Lukiya entered the room with some glasses.

"O most beautiful Lukiya!" the doctor turned to her. "Allow us to drink to your health and to your carolling with the young lady!"

Lukiya did not reply. She only glanced up bashfully and smiled. Andriy had regained his composure long ago. This time he did not lower his eyes and looked at the girl with unrestrained delight.

"Andriy!" the doctor called out slyly. "May aesthetics and beautiful national specimens be considered sacred!" And, refilling his glass, he toasted Andriy.

Lukiya exchanged glances with Andriy and ran out of the room.

"Well, that's fine!' Lena spoke up. "But I want to return to the topic of holiday diversions in the city. Surely, Master Andriy, you don't mean to say that you won't be going to a social or looking for some kind of entertainment during the holidays?"

"Probably not," the young gentleman replied. "Are those socials really so entertaining? It's all just fumes! The guests have nothing in common, nor do they get any true enjoyment out of it. They simply whirl around like fools! It's truly just fumes—nothing more."

"Fumes!" Lena repeated laughingly. "So that's what you think! What about you, Nina, are you also not going to be 'fuming' in the evenings during the holidays?"

"I don't know!" Miss Pokorska replied with her enigmatic smile. "On the first day of the holidays we have to be at a name day feast at the Khvedorovych's—that's taken for granted! And then I really do intend to get at my work during the holidays."

"What kind of work?" Lena inquired animatedly.

"Oh, my Lord!" Andriy interjected. "Surely you must know that Nina has mustered up her courage to embark on a writing career! She plans to write a short story . . ."

"You're mistaken!" his sister corrected him quite calmly. "Not a short story, but a novel . . ."

"Well!" her brother snickered. "For a novel, one needs a great deal of courage! It's quite an undertaking!"

"Why is that?" Nina replied, gazing out into space. "I already have a theme, and I've thought it all through—a romance between a handsome young lord and a beautiful peasant girl . . ."

"You don't say!" Andriy forced a laugh. "What a tired old theme!"

"So what?" Nina defended herself. "As Heine said: 'Es ist eine alte Geschichte, doch bleibt sie immer neu!' and he spoke the utter truth—it really is 'an old but eternally new story!'"

"No," Andriy persisted mockingly, "it would be better, for example, to write a little story about the courtship of a liberally minded young lady by an intrepid colonel . . . It would probably be much more interesting! There would be more room for psychological analysis, for all sorts of intricate twists in the plot!"

"Well, we'll see which will turn out to be more interesting!" Nina said, and her pale face turned slightly pink.

Miss Lena chuckled quietly. But this turn in the conversation was evidently not much to the doctor's liking.

"May I smoke?" he asked the hostess, interrupting the conversation and pulling out his cigarettes.

"Please do. Go ahead and smoke," Miss Lena replied pleasantly. "There's no need to stand on ceremony."

"Well then, I'll also take advantage of your permission," Andriy said. "I'll go and fetch my cigarettes from the study; they're in my coat pocket."

He left the table and walked towards the study. When he reached the doorway, he stopped abruptly and hesitated. Lukiya was busily tidying up a table in the study. Glancing up at the young gentleman, she lowered her eyes, and once again bent over her work.

"Why, Lukiya! Greetings!" Andriy said, walking up to the girl. "I didn't know you were working here, in their home."

"I've been here since I left your place," Lukiya replied, without changing her position or turning around.

"How happy I am to see you! How beautiful you've become! More beautiful than you were before!"

"Beautiful? So what?" the girl responded somewhat bitterly.

"Why are you so unfriendly? Lukiya! Sweetheart! Listen! Of course, this isn't the way to see each other, just for a moment like this! But perhaps . . . Do you ever come into the city?"

"Occasionally . . . when they let me . . ."

"Perhaps you could come to our place sometime?" the young gentleman asked, gently touching the girl's shoulder.

"Why would I go to your place?" the girl responded in the same bitter tone.

"Can it be you've completely forgotten me?"

The girl remained silent, but her face became troubled.

"Listen, my dearest Lukiya! Come to our place during the holidays. Let's say, on the first day, in the evening. All our family will be at the Khvedorovych's name day celebration, but I'll stay at home. I'll be waiting for you . . . I'll put a candle in my room, in the study. I'll open the door for you myself—the main entrance one—as soon as you touch the bell or the window. No one will see! There's nothing to fear. You'll just stay for half an hour or so—and I'll gaze upon you to my heart's content, without interference from anyone—and then you'll be home in no time. It's not far, you know—less than three kilometres! Will you come, Lukiya?"

Loud laughter drifted in through the parlour from the dining room. Startled, Andriy cried out: "Oh, someone may come in!"

Lukiya wanted to flee.

"Will you come?" Andriy asked once more, embracing her with his arm as he stopped her for a moment by the closed door.

"I'll come!" the words flew out of Lukiya's lips, and she vanished from the room.

Andriy took his cigarettes out of his coat pocket and rejoined the group. Along the way, he glanced indifferently at some music that was lying open on the piano, and so, when he walked back into the dining room, he could cheerfully say to the hostess: "What new music is that on your piano? Perhaps you'll play it for us?"

"Oh, there's nothing much to it. It's just a new march," Lena replied. "And I haven't quite finished learning it."

"That's enough modesty, quite enough! Come along and play it!" Nina insisted, rising from the table.

They all moved into the other room. Miss Lena sat down at the piano, and Nina made herself comfortable by the fireplace. The fire had burned down, leaving only glowing embers, shot through, at times, by tiny flames. Nina looked so elegant, that the doctor, sitting on a little stool nearby, could not take his eyes off her.

Andriy, as if suddenly realising that he had been paying very little attention to his hostess, went over to stand beside her, leaned on the piano, and listened. After the opening march, the young lady played a waltz—an intricate and flowing piece of music—then an excerpt from an opera. Her white hands flitted ever so pleasingly over the keys.

"Don't you have any Ukrainian music?" Andriy asked her.

"I'll order some!" Miss Lena exclaimed, as she rose from the piano bench. "I've been thinking about it for quite some time now! The next time I'm in town, I'll send a money order. Perhaps I'll get the music by Christmas. Then I'll invite all of you to hear it!"

"I'll be very happy to come!" Andriy replied.

"Well, gentlemen, it's time to leave," Miss Nina said decisively, and she rose to say her farewells to Lena.

The hostess urged them to stay, but the guests continued to make their way out of the room. In the entranceway, they once again embraced and shook hands. It seemed to Andriy that Miss Lena was bidding him farewell a trifle too enthusiastically.

Throwing a kerchief over her shoulders, the hostess went outside to see the guests off. "Good-bye, good-bye!" she called out to them from the porch.

Lukiya was also standing on the threshold, waiting to close the door after the guests had left.

"Good-bye!" Andriy shouted from the sleigh. It was not clear if he was responding to the young lady's words or Lukiya's gaze.

On the street, not far from the lord's manor, the guests caught up with Yuras and Manya.

"Good-bye, my little ones!" the doctor shouted to them. "Where are you off to?"

"To the Khvedosky's and the Lukash's!" the children replied.

The children turned to the left and walked up to a low, wretched cottage. A towheaded boy was standing on the threshold.

"Why are you standing here, Stepan?" Yuras asked.

"Just because," the boy answered seriously. "I was watching the gentlemen ride away."

He stepped aside to let Manya walk past him into the house.

"You know what we're going to do at our place?" Yuras began to say, remaining outside with the young boy. "We're going to trim a Christmas tree, you know? We're going to bring it from the forest and decorate it. Come and see it on the first day of the holidays, in the evening!"

The little boy, Stepan, did not say anything.

"Do come," Yuras tried to convince him. "It'll be so much fun!"

Just then, Manya came out of the house; she was speaking rapidly with two little girls walking along beside her. "There will be candles burning on the tree! And golden nuts and apples will be strung on it!"

The little girls just stared at her and listened.

"Come, do come!" Manya chattered on. "Come and see it! Then we'll take everything off the tree, and we'll divide it up, and I'll give you some of everything. Make sure you're there! Come on, Yuras, let's go to the Lukash's now."

Manya and Yuras crossed the street to the next house. After whispering together for a moment, the Khvedosky children followed them.

II

Three days before the beginning of the holidays, a man who had taken a load of firewood from Kopychyntsy to the city brought Lena the following note from the young Pokorsky gentleman.

"My highly respected Miss Lena! My sister has asked me to tell you that there has been a major change in the entertainment planned in the city. The Khvedorovyches are putting off the celebration of their name day because there is going to be a social at the club on the first day of the holidays. All those who are interested are invited to attend and bring their children. A Christmas tree will be brought in for them, and there will be dancing and the like." Then there was only his signature: "Yours, Andriy Pokorsky."

"What does this mean?" Lena cried out, as she read the brief note. "They said there wouldn't be anything, yet now . . . At least if they had been clearer in what they wrote! This way it's hard to know what and how . . . That Nina is always playing the sphinx! Why didn't she write, instead of Andriy? He signed it: 'Yours, Andriy Pokorsky!' What does this mean? Does it mean a great deal, or not very much? I must drive over there and find out what's going on."

Within an hour, Lena—both troubled and curious—was on her way to town. Just to be on the safe side, she took along some money.

Invigorated and rosy from the cold, she dashed into the Pokorsky home, greeted Nina and Andriy, and asked: "What's going on? Is the club holding a social on the first day of the holidays?"

"Yes, it is," Nina responded. "The army personnel have got together with the townspeople, and a joint social will be held. The colonel came to our place today. He even invited me to dance the mazurka with him!"

"So, this means you'll be there?" Lena asked Miss Nina.

"Why, yes, I'll be there . . ." she responded indifferently. "Somehow it doesn't seem right not to go, so I informed you as well. I know how much you enjoy dancing. I also thought you might want to send along your two little ones, Yuras and Manya, because there will first be a social for the children."

"I don't know . . ." Lena replied. "It's up to mother. Will you be there?" she suddenly asked Andriy.

"I don't know," he replied. "I don't think so . . ."

"Of course he'll be there!" Andriy's sister answered for him. "What would he do at home all by himself? But why don't you take your coat off, Lena?"

"No, I just dropped in for a moment. I have to go into town. It's Friday, and it will soon be the Sabbath. Perhaps I'll stop by later. But why do you have your coat on, Master Andriy?"

"I was on my way to the post office."

"Well, if you like, I can take you there on my sleigh."

Andriy accepted the offer. Lena hurriedly said good-bye to Nina and walked out with him. They sat down in the sleigh and rode off swiftly down the street.

The transaction at the post office was completed in no time at all. Lena was alone in the sleigh for only a few minutes, and then Andriy was once again at her side.

"Would you like to go for a short drive in the fields?" Lena asked.

Andriy sat down.

"We'll go out into the fields for a while!" the young lady shouted at the coachman.

Once again the sleigh flew down the smooth, ribbon-like road. The air was fresh, the view pleasant, and the conversation merry. The young lady, sitting close to Andriy, chirped away like a bird. A blue veil, that left only her little white chin exposed, was fastened over her rosy face, which time and time again turned to Andriy.

"You most definitely have to be at the social!" the young lady said.

"But . . . of what use will I be? I don't dance very much!" Andriy said, trying to come up with an excuse.

"That's nothing! It would still be pleasant to be there with our own little group. I'd really like you to be there!"

"So you're definitely planning to go?" Andriy observed. "But what about your carolling? Remember, you told us . . ."

The young lady was disconcerted.

"Well . . ." she said, "that's the way things work out sometimes! But then, so what? I can write down the carols another time, and as for the carolling . . . well, after all, I'll still be around next year, won't I? I'll go carolling another time."

"Miss!" the coachman spoke up. "You wanted to go into town, so shouldn't we turn back? The Jews will close their stores soon."

"Yes, turn back, turn back!" Lena ordered.

The sleigh came to a stop in front of the best dry goods shop in town. Andriy helped the young lady down from the sleigh and went in after her.

"What an attractive figure she has," he thought. "She looks slim, even in a fur coat."

"Ah! My dear guests!" Surka, the renowned owner of the shop, welcomed Miss Lena.

"Quickly, Surka, show me your flowers!" Lena said anxiously.

"Right away, right away! Oh, I have such beautiful flowers that you won't find nicer ones anywhere! They're French flowers," Surka extolled their virtues as she reached for the box. "Maybe you need some gloves and ribbons, young lady?"

The young lady picked out some flowers, then some ribbons, and finally a pair of gloves. It was quite likely that the sum of money set aside for Ukrainian music was decreased considerably or, perhaps, spent entirely, on Surka's wares.

"What about you, young sir. Don't you need any gloves?" Surka turned to Andriy.

"No, I don't . . ." he said indecisively.

"Take a pair!" the shop owner insisted. "They're wonderful gloves! Everyone is buying them! And when they're all gone, you won't be able to buy any." She set out a variety of men's gloves.

"Well, fine. Give me this pair—the white ones!" Andriy said.

III

It could be said that the Zaborovsky family did not really celebrate the first day of the Christmas season, because the entire day was spent getting ready to attend the social at the club. The evening, especially, brought nothing but problems and confusion. Mr. Zaborovsky was dressing in his study, the older lady was in the bedroom, and the young lady was in her room with Yuras and Manya. Of course, there were the most problems in this room. In addition to Lukiya, who was busily rushing around, another woman, Melanka, had been called in to help wash the children and run various errands.

Whenever more water was needed, Melanka was sent to fetch some. The second time that Melanka came back, she was laughing: "Can you imagine!" she said. "Those foolish Khvedosky and Lukash children came to see a Christmas tree! They said: 'The young master and Miss Manya invited us.' I couldn't help laughing. There's no tree in sight, and here they are! I said: 'Go away! There's nothing here!'"

"There, you see, Yuras!" Manya attacked him. "Why didn't you tell them we wouldn't be trimming the tree today?"

"Why didn't you go and tell them?" Yuras snapped back.

"There now, that's all right," Miss Lena reassured the children. "They'll come the next time you decorate a tree, for the New Year."

"No, they won't," Yuras stated gloomily. "They won't come again. I could hardly convince them this time . . ."

"Stand still, my young man!" Melanka observed. "It's hard enough to do up these boots, and your jumping around doesn't help!"

In the meantime, Miss Lena went into the parlour, where there was a bigger mirror, to see how she looked. She was peering intently at herself, when the ringing voices of carollers resounded under the windows. They were singing:

> "Oh, wondrous birth
> Of God's own son;
> Today the Virgin Mary
> To Him has given birth."

Even though Lukiya was holding up a bright light near Miss Lena, a shadow crossed the young lady's face.

"Miss, may I go carolling?" Lukiya inquired.

"Yes, you may—after we're gone."

Lena went to her room and found some small change.

"Here, Lukiya," she said. "Go outside and give it to the carollers."

"So you don't want to invite them into the house?" Lukiya asked.

"Well really, how strange you are!" Melanka spoke in defence of the young lady. "How can we invite them in at a time like this?"

A short time later, a group of girls came and carolled under the window:

> "Oh, in the grove, the grove, on the golden sand,
>   May God bless you!
> Miss Lena is singing and circling in a dance,
>   May God bless you!"

But the girls were told that none of the ladies or gentlemen were at home; they had all gone to a dance in town.

Only Lukiya joined the girls. It was quiet, clear, and cold outside. The stars glittered ever so brightly . . .

IV

The club social in the district town was being held on a grand scale. Are you smiling, my dear reader, because you are from a bigger town? Well, there's no reason to smile! You must remember that everything in this world has its own significance and merit. The resident of the provincial capital may scorn the district social, but then again, the provincial social may seem like a joke to people living in the country's capital! Even in the capital city, not all socials are the same! There are different levels there as well . . . quite different!

So, for that small town, the club social was a brilliant affair. It was attended—as they say in capital cities—"by the entire city." There was a great crush of people in the hall: men in both civilian and military dress, and ladies in exquisite outfits. (Do you really think there are no seamstresses and no fashion magazines in district towns? Oh, you better believe there are!)

Everyone was assembled: the older people, the younger ones, and the children. "The cream of society" was on display. In the middle of the ballroom stood a large Christmas tree adorned with candles and all sorts of decorations—rumour had it that the decorations had been brought all the way from Kyiv. The children, in a well-behaved, colourful cluster, were circling the tree.

After some time, the stubs of the candles were extinguished, the treats and decorations were taken down and divided among the children, and the tree itself, which had served its purpose, was hauled away. The children's dances began. The older people were delighted to see that the children were behaving "just like adults!"

And truly, the little boys, smartly scraping their feet as they bowed, politely invited the little girls to dance with them. The little girls examined each other's attire, but they did this a trifle more openly than the adults; some little girls even used their fingers to touch the buttons or a pretty ribbon on another girl.

When the adults decided that the youngsters had "pranced around enough," and that everyone had had their "fill of delight" from watching them, they quickly removed them from the hall and sent them home with their little packages. Yuras and Manya were taken away by a servant of the Pokorsky family.

At this point, it seemed that the musicians began playing more spiritedly and enthusiastically, and the social for the adults began.

V

Lieutenant Zalotny whisked Miss Lena away in a dance, and as they disappeared in the whirlwind of a waltz, a ribbon from Miss Lena's gown fluttered past Andriy.

"Why have I come here?" he asked himself, as he stood in the doorway without any intention of dancing.

Just then, Miss Lena came up to him and interrupted his thoughts.

"How pretty she looks this evening!" Andriy mused.

And how beautifully the young lady was dressed! She was wearing a simple white dress adorned with flowers; a plait of forget-me-nots was pinned obliquely across her breast; a slightly rolled bodice revealed a delicate white neck; and dimpled elbows peeked out from under her short, transparent sleeves. And her blond hair was styled ever so simply and elegantly!

"What's wrong? Aren't you going to dance?" the young lady asked Andriy. "Really, then, why have you come? You could dance at least one dance!"

"Well, what am I to do?" the young gentleman said. "I don't know any of the ladies here!"

"Oh, so that's your excuse!" Lena exclaimed. "Am I supposed to invite you? Well, you may dance the cotillion with me, if you so desire!"

"Well then, let me invite you, if you will be so kind!" Andriy bowed before her.

"Yes, of course!" the young lady replied. "I'll just settle the matter with my partner." And Lena vanished briefly into the crowd.

In the meantime, Andriy went up to the doctor. The latter was standing in front of Miss Nina, and he was experiencing quite a different fate.

"So both the mazurka and the cotillion are taken?" he asked.

"Yes, they are," Miss Nina responded with a smile.

"With whom are you dancing the cotillion?"

"With the colonel."

"What? But aren't you dancing the mazurka with him?"

"Well, what of it? Both the mazurka and the cotillion."

"Really?" the doctor commented sarcastically.

At that moment, a stout gentleman with a grizzled beard tapped him lightly on the shoulder and asked: "What's this? Are you planning to dance?"

"I was planning to!" the doctor said, as if he were joking. "But what am I to do if the young ladies are unkind and don't wish to dance with me?"

"Well, so much the better! Let's go!" the gentleman urged him.

"Where to?" asked the doctor.

"What do you mean, where to? They're waiting for us over there. We're lacking a fourth person to make up our party."

"So you won't grant me even a single dance?" the doctor asked Nina once more.

"I assure you, I can't!"

"Well, come on then! Let's go!" the doctor's partner persisted.

"Fine, let's go!" the doctor muttered, moving away gloomily.

The gentleman led him away by the arm.

The ballroom resonated with fiery dances. Trumpets blared, and bows were tautly stretched as the stirring melodies of the most fashionable dances were played.

"*Grand rond! Chaîné! Deux ronds, s'il vous plait! Les dames en avant! [A large circle! A chain! Two circles, please! Ladies, come forward!]*" The master of ceremonies shouted, bursting with self-importance.

Then he gave a command: "*Saluez vos dames! [Bow to your ladies!]*"

After this, there was a brief intermission.

The ladies who had been dancing cooled themselves off with their fans, breathing heavily but contentedly. The ladies who had not been dancing sighed with relief and mingled with the rest of the group. Some went into the dressing room, others into the dining area.

Miss Nina entered the room set aside for the card players and walked up to the table where the doctor was sitting with cards in his hands. "Well? How's it going?" she inquired.

"Thank you ever so much for your attention and kindness!" the doctor quipped sharply.

"Oh, our doctor is playing very badly today . . . very badly!" the doctor's partner elaborated. Then he slammed down a card and said to someone: "Let me give you the queen of spades!"

There was an exchange of abruptly uttered words.

"Four of clubs."

"Come on!"

"Another face card."

"Diamonds."

Then a few cards were put down wordlessly, in a tense silence, under the intent scrutiny of the four players. At this point, the doctor must have made a grave error. His partner glared at him angrily and hissed through his teeth: "Yet another surprise that could have been saved for a more opportune moment."

The cards were all put down. Before they were dealt again, the doctor's partner spoke directly to him: "Why didn't you play hearts? Furthermore, I called for a spade!"

"It makes no difference," the doctor stated dejectedly.

"What do you mean, it makes no difference?" The gentleman with the grizzled hair was enraged. "It does make a difference! It could have been a closer game. But now it's really embarrassing, it really is—once again we're left without a pair. Come to your senses, for the love of God! What's wrong with you?"

"My head's aching for some reason," the doctor said, drawing his hand over his forehead. "There must be some fumes in here, or something."

"It could be fumes from the Christmas tree," someone from the group spoke up.

"But we didn't notice any fumes in the ballroom," Miss Nina, who was still standing by the table, interjected.

"That's because, along with the air, you're inhaling the delirium of the dancing," the doctor explained furiously.

Just then, the colonel walked up. He was a tall, sturdy-legged man who had not yet turned grey, and his moustache was curled like a young man's. His chest blazed with medals.

"Ah! Here you are!" he called out to Miss Nina. "I've been searching all over for you. The cotillion is about to begin. Please."

The colonel bowed and scraped his foot with such alacrity that his spurs jangled, and then, like a young suitor, with his arm bent jauntily, he led Miss Nina into the ballroom. And why should the colonel not view himself as a genuine young suitor? He was a widower and a very eligible bachelor. One could say he was the best catch in town.

As the reader is aware, Andriy was dancing with Miss Lena. They happened to be near the orchestra with the music blaring right over their heads, and they could not carry on a conversation. This amused them greatly and made them laugh. Whenever they spoke, they had to bend over closely to face one another. The long cotillion was over before they knew it. When the master of ceremonies concluded the dance by shouting: "*Remerciez vos dames![Thank your ladies!],*" they exchanged warm handshakes.

"You're not angry with me that I made you dance, that I invited you myself?" Miss Lena asked Andriy.

"No . . ." he said with a smile.

They walked to the other side of the ballroom, to a window. It did not seem quite as warm there. There were figures out in the street, curious people who were looking in through the windows of the one-story building. Some heads were visible . . .

Andriy suddenly remembered about Lukiya. What if she had gone to his home? What if she were waiting for him? A flood of hot blood scalded his heart . . .

"But no!" he thought. "She would have known from Miss Lena that all the plans had changed! Furthermore, even if she did come, she'd realise that I wasn't at home if I didn't answer the door, and she'd have found out in the kitchen that I was here. And she wouldn't expect me to come home early from the club! So the *rendezvous* will have to be postponed until another time . . . Well, that's that! To tell the truth, perhaps it's even better that it's turned out this way, that she didn't come, or if she did come, that she didn't find me at home. Yes, indeed. How would it all have ended? It's better, much better, to have it all end this way! And most of all, it's better for the girl herself."

Having placated himself with these thoughts, Andriy was ready to respond to Miss Lena when she tapped his elbow with her white fan and, turning her delicate white neck towards him, said: "Perhaps you could open one pane a little? It's so warm!"

After finishing their game, many of the card players came to watch the mazurka. Doctor Ivasevych, with his hands folded severely on his chest, stood in the doorway that led from the dining room into the ballroom. His face was much too sad. There were two reasons for this: to begin with, he had lost too much money that evening—he couldn't even contemplate subscribing to one of the larger newspapers now—at least not this month! The second reason for the doctor's anger was that, directly across from him, Miss Nina and the colonel were dancing the mazurka.

"There you have it! She won't part from him," the doctor concluded painfully. "The one—you know—who thinks she's a writer. She's doing research, getting to know an interesting military type. Some type he is! An oak log smeared with honey. Just look at his shiny pate. It's like a watermelon! And what can he be talking about to her, and at such length at that? And she's listening ever so attentively. You can see what a populist she is, what an opponent of 'luxuries!' Just look at the velvet corsages she's wearing, and the gold bracelets glittering on her arms. Well, of course! She'll marry her colonel, and then she'll have even more expensive baubles—this ascetic who could get by on a peasant's wages! Yes, I'm sure! Her tongue says all the right things, but in her mind all she sees is the colonel's income."

This was how the doctor mentally reproached his young lady. But when Miss Nina, dancing the mazurka, floated by the door, she cast him such an interesting and enigmatic look that the poor fellow forgot all about his reproaches and sank even deeper into thought, as he tried to decide how much tenderness there was in that look.

In the meantime, the colonel finally finished his proposal of marriage to Miss Nina. And he received from her a simple and clear answer—she was willing to accept both his hand and his heart.

Miss Lena was not conducting such weighty conversations with her partner during the mazurka, for she was dancing with a married man—a justice of the peace. Virtually ignoring her partner, she continued to turn her attention to Andriy.

The latter was not dancing the mazurka; he was sitting close to the spot where Miss Lena was dancing, and they were carrying on a conversation of sorts. There was nothing overly serious in their intermittent exchanges—just inconsequential remarks and trivial observations. At times, they choked with laughter as they observed the strange steps of some of the dancers, for it is well known that the mazurka is danced in the most colourful, innovative ways even in the larger cities in Russia, let alone in such a small town as this district centre.

Be that as it may, Miss Lena's little head kept turning time and again to Andriy, and time again she saw his delighted look fastened upon her. In the middle of the mazurka, a lady chose Andriy. He tried to refuse, but finally had to comply. He danced one of the figures rather deliberately, but gracefully.

"Aha! So you were pretending that you don't know how to dance the mazurka?" Miss Lena observed reproachfully.

"Well, what can I say? In my opinion," the embarrassed Andriy responded, "the only demand you can make of a non-Polish mazurka dancer is that his 'steps' not be comical."

"Well, well, just you wait!" Lena mused with a cunning smile.

Just then, the dance formation with the "champagne" began. The colonel started it with his betrothed, and he received from her a glass of the sparkling wine. A few people exchanged glances . . . and the hapless doctor swallowed a glass of bitter poison.

Then it was Miss Lena's turn to sit on a chair in the middle of the ballroom. A group of young men gathered about her, and the judge, Lena's partner, pulled Andriy over to join the group. Is it necessary to tell you that the glass went to Andriy? And Andriy, whether it was because he was delighted by his victory over all the other young men, or because he was animated by the wine, now danced the mazurka in a much more lively fashion with Miss Lena than he had the first time.

Andriy was not fully aware of when the dance ended, and when the social was finally over. He felt tired. His head was either hurting or buzzing slightly from the wine—he could not quite decide which it was. It really was very warm in the ballroom. Andriy and Miss Lena were no longer talking so animatedly; they spent more time exchanging meaningful looks.

It was late, very late, when our acquaintances drove home from the club. They all met in the confusion that occurs when people are finding their coats, hats, kerchiefs, and boots. The doctor heard the colonel say to Miss Nina in parting: "Please give my regards to your dear mother! I'll come tomorrow."

The elder Zaborovskys had gone to a hotel earlier on, and Nina had invited Lena to her house for the night. So the young ladies and Andriy got into the wide, peasant sleigh of the Zaborovsky family.

"Doctor!" Miss Lena called out to Ivasevych. "Sit down! We'll give you a lift!"

The doctor sat down by the coachman without saying a word. Then they all fell silent, as they abandoned themselves to their own impressions of the evening . . .

O you psychologists who know the human soul! Can you guess how it came to pass that the doctor—that scorned, insulted doctor—sat down at the front of the sleigh in which Miss Nina was seated? He sat with his back to the young ladies and, staring ahead in a quiet fury, did not speak to them. Nevertheless, he was driving in the same sleigh as Miss Nina!

They drove up to the Pokorsky manor that stood by itself at the end of a street. In front of it, there was a small enclosed yard with ornamental shrubbery, and in the pale light of the early winter morning, both the building and the shrubs were already quite clearly discernible.

"With your permission, I'll ring the bell—to have the door opened more quickly for you!" the doctor volunteered, and he walked on ahead of the young ladies.

Before reaching the porch, he stopped short and exclaimed: "What's this? There's someone's sitting here!"

The group drew nearer, and everyone saw a stooped dark figure against the white wall between the grey porch and the black window of Andriy's study.

"It's a woman!" the doctor said quietly, scrutinising the clothing.

Andriy heard these words, glanced at the figure—turned numb and froze . . .

"What's she doing here? Is she sleeping?" the doctor deliberated. Then, bending down lower to take a better look, he cried out: "Ladies and gentlemen! There's something terribly wrong here! She may be frozen to death . . ."

"Oh, Lord!" Lena screamed.

"What are you saying?!" Nina cried out. "Who is this woman? Why is she here?"

The doctor pulled back the kerchief from the head of the unmoving, bent figure. Lena peered at her and screamed: "My God! It's our Lukiya!"

"Yes, it is! And she's frozen to death!" the doctor exclaimed

Andriy came out of his trance, and an unearthly cry tore out of his chest: "Oh, my God!"

The doorbell began to ring insanely, lighted lamps appeared, people came running. They carried the motionless Lukiya into

Andriy's study and laid her down on the lounge. The doctor rolled up his sleeves and busied himself with her, demanding first one thing, then another. They rubbed Lukiya down and did their best to revive her.

"Oh, my God! Oh, my God!" Andriy kept shouting and wringing his hands.

"What a senseless tragedy," the doctor sighed. "Poor girl. What a pity! What a waste! She's such a beauty."

Lukiya was lying face upwards, deathly pale, but astonishingly beautiful. Her black hair was spread out on the splendid white cushions, and she looked like a magnificent statue.

"Maybe she inhaled some fumes?" the cook, who was helping the doctor, suggested. "You see, she sat for a while in the kitchen. She said she'd come to carol in town with the girls, and that she had a really bad headache. So, maybe she inhaled some fumes! God knows what happened to her. She looked so strange as she sat there. We talked for a while. She asked me about the masters, and I told her: 'They're not here; they've gone out.' 'All of them?' she asked. 'Yes, all of them,' I said. Well, then she went away. She seemed to stumble a bit as she walked . . . Maybe there were fumes in our kitchen, or maybe she left home feeling like that!"

The doctor spent a long time doing everything in his power to revive her. Finally, he shouted: "A pulse! There's a pulse! Her heart is beating!"

Everyone crowded around the doctor and the girl. The doctor held Lukiya in his arms, raising her. She slowly opened her eyes, and gazed about unseeingly, once, twice . . . then she peered intently at all the figures in their fine evening attire, and she understood everything—just as they understood it all.

"Why did you save me?" the girl cried out, and she burst into bitter tears . . .

The Girlfriends
(1887)

I

"So, tell me, Mariya Petrivna, are you actually going to let your daughter go abroad?"

"Oh, I don't know, Kateryna Panteleymonivna. I simply don't know what I should do."

"But what's there to do? Don't let her go, and that's that!"

"It's easy for you to say, Kateryna Panteleymonivna. But how can I stop her, when my heart aches just looking at her. Of course, it's not as if she's insisting, but I can see that all she can think about is going to Zurich—or whatever that city is called—and studying there."

"Yes, yes, that's it—Zurich, Zurich! They've all lost their senses over Zurich. Yesterday, my son, Kost, wouldn't stop talking about it. But then, it's one thing for a man—he can take care of himself anywhere. But it's not at all fitting for a young woman to wander off—who knows where and for what—to study to become a doctor of some kind. God knows what's come over them."

"You're right! That's what I think too, but I can't refuse Lyuba. I can see she's pining away, and sometimes she cries secretly. I'm afraid she'll come down with tuberculosis."

"Huh, as if she'd get tuberculosis just like that! God forbid! She'll mope for a while, and then she'll forget all about it."

"Oh, no, she won't! I'm afraid she might end up like my late sister. When they didn't let her marry a certain teacher, she pined and grieved, and then . . . the poor thing departed for the other world."

"Really now! What a comparison! After all, that was marriage, and this is studying. No one's ever heard of someone getting tuberculosis because of not being allowed to study!"

"Oh, don't say that, Kateryna Panteleymonivna! You don't know how much my Lyuba loves studying, and what her character is like; but I know her—she's been like this from infancy. She'll suffer in silence, but when she makes up her mind about something, she doesn't change it very easily. But, hush now; let's be quiet—she's coming. Please don't say anything to her about this matter."

"Well, it's not up to me to interfere! It's none of my business."

This was the tone of the conversation between two older ladies sitting in a living room, or, to put it plainly, in a small whitewashed parlour with three rather small windows. The room was generously furnished with outmoded chairs and end tables that made no pretence of being stylish. It is true that the couch, standing at the far end of the room with an oval coffee table in front of it, had a somewhat more pretentious look, with carved curlicues on top of its wooden back and curving rolls for its arms; however, even though the couch was showy and well-stuffed, it did not have any springs—that recent innovation—and so it was quite hard.

It was in this most elegant spot in the room that one of the women, Kateryna Panteleymonivna, was sitting. She was obviously the guest, because she was wearing a mantilla and a larger and more elaborate bonnet, while the other woman was dressed simply in a cotton house dress and a creased muslin cap trimmed with small circlets of lace.

The two ladies also differed greatly in appearance. The guest—if the truth were to be told—was quite a large woman, with a good-sized double chin, and even though some grey could be seen in the black hair that peeked out from under her bonnet, she had a healthy, rosy complexion, and the keen look of a younger person in her dark eyes. The other lady, the hostess, was a frail, thin woman with a small, faded face and greying hair that bore traces of its former blondness; she had thin lips, a long nose, and gentle grey eyes that seemed to have a preoccupied look, especially when she shook her head to emphasize what she was saying.

The conversation of these two ladies was interrupted by the arrival of Lyuba, the hostess's daughter. She was a slim young woman, dressed in a simple, thickly pleated gray skirt and a white muslin blouse with wide, gathered sleeves; her only adornment was a small brooch fastened at her neck. The slender shoulders and sharp features of the young lady were reminiscent of the hostess—insofar as an eighteen-year-old can resemble someone who is fifty.

She could not be considered beautiful—her features were irregular—but she was rather pretty. Her chestnut-coloured curly hair was cut short and gathered loosely in a crown above her forehead; her dark-grey, almost black, eyes were thoughtful, and her small, uneven, and somewhat dense eyebrows gave her face a charming appearance, as did two dark beauty spots—one on her lower cheek, and the other near her refined lips.

Removing her cape and hat, and absently patting her hair, the girl crossed the threshold and entered the room with a delicate, gliding gait. She walked up unassumingly to the table and, extending her hand, greeted the guest. In her other hand she was holding a large, thick, bound book.

"Where were you?" the guest inquired.

"I went to the library to exchange my book," the girl replied, seating herself near a window and leafing through the volume.

"That's quite a book!" the guest remarked. "Dear me, it's such a hefty size. It must be a novel, right?"

"No, it's not a novel," the girl responded smilingly.

"Well, what could be written in a book of that size?" the lady continued, shaking her head.

The girl wrinkled her brow, as if she were pondering what she should say, and then stated calmly: "It's a scientific book."

"Scientific!" the guest repeated in a strange tone. The hostess, noticing that there was a dangerous note to the guest's voice, glanced worriedly at her, but the latter, without paying any attention to her, looked sharply at the girl and asked, apparently quite innocently: "Lyuba, my dear, please tell me—is it true that they're now writing in scientific books that human beings are descended from monkeys?"

The hostess was now gazing in open alarm at the guest; but the latter replied with a look that said: "Why are you alarmed? This isn't at all what you think it is!"

In response to the guest's question the girl smiled and, without lifting her head from the book, said: "Well, there's not much point in my saying anything! You wouldn't believe me anyway."

"Why wouldn't I believe you?" the lady rebutted defensively. "Just prove to me what and how things are, how it's stated there, and I'll believe you. Why wouldn't I?"

"Well, you see," the girl said, "it would take a lot of explaining and a lot of listening to prove it properly—because at first, it does, of course, seem somewhat strange . . ."

"Tell me! I'm listening!" the lady interrupted firmly.

"You see, it all depends on the point of view with which you approach this question. If you think that a human being is a completely distinct creation, and that his nature 'is not of this world,' then, of course, how would it be possible to be convinced that he resembles any other creature on this earth? But, if you assume that a human being lives on the earth just as all other creatures, that he has a living body just as they do, that for this body he requires everything that other creatures—let's say animals—require for theirs, then why wouldn't there be similarities between the body of a human being and that of an animal? Why aren't we surprised that one species of animal is similar to another? For example, a wolf is similar to a dog, and yet, despite these similarities, the wolf and the dog have their own distinctive features."

"But, after all, one's a wolf, and one's a human being!" the guest interjected; her tone, however, was not antagonistic.

"A human being is an animal as well—only more intelligent," the girl continued in a more animated manner. "And no one is taking this away from him; quite the contrary, let him take pains to become even more intelligent, but let him know what he is, and what his place is in the order of living things! There is no insult to human beings in the fact, that at one time, our race was more like that of an animal than it is now; that it was very similar to a breed of monkeys which, even today, remains to some degree similar to and related to humans. Why be offended that monkeys have hands, that their skulls are similar to ours, and that it was from this breed—which resembles humans most closely—that the human race first descended, and then kept developing and became far more perfected?"

Tilting her head to one side, the lady listened attentively. A genuine curiosity was evident in her eyes. Finally, she said: "The devil only knows what those monkeys are, what they're like! I can't say that I've ever really seen one. I did once see a monkey being paraded through the market in Poltava, but I was so worried about other things at the time, that I hardly noticed what it looked like. Who the devil knows—maybe they do resemble humans!"

"Wait just a moment; I'll show you some in a book!" the girl smiled, stepping into the adjoining room.

"Really, Kateryna Panteleymonivna, what a thing to be interested in," the hostess whispered softly after Lyuba left.

"What's the matter?" the dark-haired woman retorted, making no effort to lower her voice. "I want to know! What's wrong with that?"

The girl brought back an illustrated book and, seating herself by the guest, began showing her various breeds of monkeys. The lady peered at them with a curiosity that she apparently did not want to fully reveal; however, from time to time, she burst out with brief exclamations: "Oh, so it's like that!" "Just look!" "You don't say!" and so on. Then, pointing at one of the monkeys, she spoke excitedly to the hostess: "Look, Mariya Petrivna! This one looks just like Luka Vasylovych!"

"Oh, there you go, Kateryna Panteleymonivna! You're always coming out with things like that!" the hostess replied, waving her hand in disgust and evincing no interest in looking at the book.

"But, just take a look—and see if it doesn't look like him! It's the spitting image of Luka Vasylovych! The head's the same, and the nose is identical. Exactly like Luka Vasylovych. And look—it's even supporting itself with a stick. Amazing!"

The girl laughed and, leaning her elbows on the table, briefly explained the illustrations. Her mother went into the adjacent room and began bustling about with the samovar that had been brought in. A short time later, tea was served, putting an end to the guest's zoological studies. The book—the most interesting parts had already been looked at—had to be cleared away, because the hostess and the servant, Tetyana, brought in a tray with cups of tea, sweet pastries on little plates, buns, and fresh butter.

As they began eating, the theme of their conversation changed of its own accord. When the older women began deliberating where it was better to buy crystallised sugar for baking—at Bihun's or Yudka's—the young woman, quickly finishing her cup of tea, picked up her library book and walked out of the room.

Stepping out on the unpretentious porch, with its two weathered wooden posts, the girl sat down on the steps that led into the quiet yard, bent her head over the book, and began reading intently.

The yard was spacious; in addition to the main building there were two storehouses, a few outbuildings, and a smaller cottage. Everything was in order and well-maintained. The roofs were thatched, grass grew in patches in the yard, and moss was visible on the earth that covered the roof of the ice-house.

The residence was on the very edge of a level plateau on a hillside and, immediately past the most distant outbuildings, the plateau ended abruptly with a fairly steep drop. Standing by the storehouse, under the wild pear tree at the edge of the declivity, you could see the other hillsides in the town, dotted with the residences of the nobility and townspeople, and small orchards dissected by ravines and valleys.

The hillsides sloped into a wide valley, and a rather large river—along with its tributary, the Brun, and smaller streamlets—flowed in freakish twists and turns through green meadows and white, sandy shoals. To the left, beyond the Brun, one could see nearby villages woven into a cheerful panorama, with the glittering crosses on their churches illuminated by the setting sun.

Immediately beyond the river valley, a lengthy strip of dark pine forest blocked the landscape, and behind it, still other villages disappeared from view. The forest, which accommodated within its mysterious walls the winding stately course of the river, loomed like a mighty, haughty giant, its top ridge silhouetted sharply against the clear blue of the sky.

The view from the yard was magnificent, but at the moment no one was enjoying it. The yard was deserted, and only a servant occasionally ran across it, carrying something from the house to the smaller cottage. No one interfered with the young woman's reading. She was sitting on the bottom step of the porch, quite close to the gate leading into the street, which was also deserted and quiet. It was a remote street at the edge of an obscure district town, and no one was riding or walking by.

At times, the girl tore her eyes away from her book and let them rest on the wide expanse between the buildings where the blue forest and the edge of the river valley, flooded with sunlight, were visible. Her gaze, however, rested unconsciously on the view, taking no delight in it. Her eyes reflected the deep thoughts that, having passed from the book into her young head, were stimulating vigorous mental activity. Then, she once again bent over her book and became absorbed in it.

She was sitting like this, completely caught up in her reading, when the gate opened, and a young man walked through it. The girl did not see him until he was quite close to her. She looked up with a start, shut her book, smiled, and said, in some confusion: "Oh, it's you!" And she extended her soft, slim hand to the guest.

"You're so engrossed in your reading that you don't see anything else," the young gentleman greeted her in a refined, resonant voice. "Well, it's really strange how things turned out. After arriving with my mother and finding that you weren't at home, I set out to look for you—and in the meantime, you returned."

"Our paths didn't cross!" she responded, her face flushing with joy. "I just selected a book and came right back home."

"So, you're reading," the guest said, sitting down beside her and peering—with a welcoming smile and half-closed eyes—both at her and the book.

"Yes, I'm reading! And you know," the girl added, turning her head aside in confusion, "recently—the more I read, the more I realise how little I know!"

"That's quite a paradox," the guest said, smiling again.

"No, really! Sometimes I pause over things that would be perfectly comprehensible to others. And, even what I do understand right off seems to be so new, so unexpected. It's as if a completely different world were opening up to me."

"Well, that just makes it all the more interesting."

"That's true; it is interesting." The girl's eyes shone, and her face became animated. "As I recall, the novels I read earlier with such enthusiasm did not excite me nearly as much as these books. The novels were filled with imaginary wonders, while these books focus on the actual sphere of the earth, with its familiar phenomena and strange laws. It's so fascinating to explore the operation of those laws, the meshing of the facts. It's so tempting to apply them!

"Yesterday, I finished reading Lewis's *The Physiology of Everyday Living*. What a marvel! It captivated me! You know, when all is said and done, it's this field that attracts me the most. What could be more interesting than to understand the processes that govern our lives. Oh, I'm getting all tangled up in my own words; I can't express my thoughts adequately."

"I understand you. Indeed, your sentence would suit the speech of an eloquent orator. Well, anyway, if that's how you feel, pick this field as your speciality. After all, you're going away to study medicine."

"I'm going away, going away," the girl repeated slowly in a worried tone. "It's still all up in the air. Oh, but I'd really like to go!" she added, shaking the curls on her head. "I'd study so hard and apply myself so diligently, that I'd just have to understand everything; I'd learn everything I wanted to!"

The door to the porch opened, and Tetyana, the young serving woman, announced politely: "The mistress says that you're to come and have tea."

"Oh, I forgot all about tea! I just rambled on and on! Come!" the young lady said to her guest, scrambling to her feet.

The young gentleman also rose automatically and, without breaking off the conversation, continued speaking as he followed her: "Well, just don't give up on your wishes, and you'll go! You simply must go. I'm confident that Mariya Petrivna will not stand in your way."

As they sat at the table and drank their tea, the young man spoke little with the older ladies, despite the fact that the dark-haired lady kept turning to him with various questions.

"Kost, did you see the justice of the peace? Did you speak with him?" she inquired.

"No, I didn't stop in to see him . . ."

Kateryna Panteleymonivna, who had travelled with her son from the village with the express purpose of having him look after a few of her matters in town, was most unhappy to hear his answer. She obliquely cast sharp, penetrating looks at Kost; he kept giving her curt, almost automatic, responses, while carrying on a conversation with the young lady, who was also paying far more attention to him than to the older ladies.

And truly, it was not difficult to pay attention to such a young man! His face was wonderfully handsome and intelligent. His regular features were artistically refined; his thoughtful dark eyes, emphasised by black eyebrows, seemed to be lost in dreams; his chestnut hair, cascading in waves down his back, was combed off his face, revealing a high forehead and a delicately sculpted profile. His pale face, however, was not lifeless—it had a hint of colour in it, and his lips called to mind the full red lips of his mother, Madam Kateryna; but the expression on his lips, which peeked out from under a silken moustache, was completely different from hers, as were his slender, delicate hands and gentle manner. Kost—or, as the hostess referred to him, Konstantyn Mykhaylovych—had a calming effect on his mother; in his presence, Madam Kateryna spoke more softly, and her tone was less strident.

It did not even occur to the two older ladies to disagree with the young gentleman when, gazing through the window at the quiet street and green orchards on which the evening shadows were already settling, he said: "Lyubov Vasylivna! Let's go for a walk. It's so splendid outside!"

"Go ahead, Lyubochka!" Madam Kateryna encouraged her. "Why sit in the house? I'll stay here with Mariya Petrivna."

Lyubochka rose to her feet, threw her black cape over her shoulders, put on her grey hat with its modest feather, and walked out with the young gentleman. Madam Kateryna followed them with her dark eyes and, turning her head, glanced at them surreptitiously as they walked past the window. Mariya Petrivna was sitting quietly; her gaze, which seemed to be troubled, was lowered, and she was staring at the floor.

After entering the street, the young couple first walked beyond the residential area and stopped on a promontory at the edge of a slope from where the expansive landscape—with which we are already familiar—could be seen. The riverbank was bustling with activity; people had come to the river to bathe or wash clothes. On the dam by the mill, a long line of loaded wagons—probably a carter's caravan—had come to a stop.

On the horizon, the meadow and pine forest were perfectly still. Between the distant banks the water stood like a mirror—calm, and almost motionless. Young willows admired their reflections in a tributary of the Brun, while the Brun itself wound its way like a ribbon through the green meadows, past the villages enveloped in a diaphanous mist.

"What are you gazing at so intently, Lyubov Vasylivna?" the young man inquired.

"I love this landscape!" the girl replied, and she fixed her delighted gaze even more intently on the panoramic view.

"You'll see still more beautiful landscapes! Over there!"

II

The young couple turned back and, conversing animatedly, strolled through the town. They walked down the length of the square with its attractive brick church, two rows of fairly elegant shops, and a few stands set up by women peddlers. There was little activity in any of these businesses and, in the side streets, with their single-story buildings and broad, shaded yards, empty and deserted, a lazy lassitude prevailed. The two young people then entered a wide street that was considered aristocratic because several taller, grand looking mansions with ornamental trees stood on it. It was quiet here as well; the unpaved street was covered with a thick layer of fluffy dust and, next to the buildings, narrow, well-trodden paths stretched through green lawns.

"Let's drop in to see Rayisa!" the young lady suggested to her admirer.

They were approaching a lord's manor with a brick veranda that, graced by two thick white columns and a balustrade, looked out on the street. Through the open window, the sound of singing, accompanied by a piano, drifted out into the street. As they drew nearer, they could make out the words of the song that a fine, but no longer youthful, soprano voice was performing:

"I've lit the lamp and picked some flowers,
Come to a rendezvous of love!"

"Vira Nykolayivna is at the Brahov's; it's her voice," the girl said, as she and the young gentleman entered the house through the veranda.

In the parlour, with its outdated but aristocratic furnishings, they found an entire party of people. A tall brunette with slightly faded features, her white gown adorned with crimson ribbons, was standing by the piano; it was she who had been singing. At the piano sat a younger and fresher brunette in a fairly simple percale dress that was, nevertheless, elegantly sewn, and adorned with a string of large, black beads.

By the table sat a thin, ungainly blonde in an indifferent dress, and a middle-aged gentleman with a round, shiny face, cheerful grey eyes, and reddish hair combed to one side. His bright woollen suit, set off by a wide blue tie, unmistakably suggested the condition of bachelorhood. A little to one side, an attractive young officer sat in an unassuming pose, holding a book in his hands.

When the young couple arrived, the singing had just ended. There were greetings all around. It turned out that they were all acquainted.

Miss Lyuba, exchanging kisses with the brunette seated at the piano, said: "We came to get you, Rayisa—to see if you would go for a walk with us; we didn't know you had guests."

"There's nothing to hinder us," Rayisa replied, rising from the piano. "We can all go." Then she moved forward to greet Kost, speaking to him in a firm, friendly voice: "Ah! Konstantyn Mykhaylovych! I'm very pleased you've come! I haven't seen you for a long time." Then, mindful of her duties as the hostess, she added: "Do sit down, ladies and gentlemen."

But there was no time to sit—a little girl entered the room and, curtsying deeply, stated: "Mother invites you to have tea."

"Let's go, ladies and gentlemen," Rayisa called out, interrupting the reddish-haired man's flirtatious conversation with Vira Nykolayivna, the lady who had just been singing. Then she turned to the officer: "Monsieur Bohdashevych! Leave Karl Fokht in peace, and let's go have tea."

The officer smiled in embarrassment, set the book down on an end table beside a stack of other books, and rose to his feet. Lyuba and Kost, despite their protestations that they had already had tea, were persuaded to join the group.

In the dining room, presiding over a table covered with a white linen cloth, sat a lady advanced in years—even though she did not want to appear old as yet—with an elegant black head-dress on her dark, stiffly combed hair. Sitting erect, with a customary but conscious propriety, her long nose at a haughty angle, she solemnly greeted the newly arrived guests and, in a dignified manner, invited everyone to tea. They all settled in around the table that was set in an elegant, but somewhat less than lavish, fashion. The entire group felt constrained.

It was only Miss Rayisa who seemed to wish to appear bold and unoppressed, even here. She spoke forcefully, firmly, and more than anyone else. Seated as she was, beside Lyuba, the difference in their appearance was striking. Rayisa had quite a sturdy build, with shiny black braided hair and regular features. A fresh, rosy hue suffused her full cheeks, her dark brown eyes were keen, but not very large, and her bold black eyebrows contrasted sharply with her pale, smooth forehead.

Miss Rayisa was truly beautiful. Nevertheless, the gleam in her eyes had something cold about it, and the smile on her beautiful lips seemed to be arrogantly self-assured; her movements were bold and a trifle abrasive, and her voice, despite its freshness, had a metallic ring to it. But if one did not care about tenderness, sincerity, and warmth, and attached more importance to external beauty, energy, and self-confidence—then one would have to concede that Miss Rayisa was attractive and pleasing to the eye.

Sitting between Rayisa and the songstress, Vira Nykolayivna, the reddish-haired man in the bright blue necktie—referred to by the others in the group as Petro Stepanovych—gazed at Rayisa from time to time with a tender expression on his face; but the terse, somewhat mocking words which she occasionally directed at him appeared to confuse and alarm him. Uncertain how to reply, he turned to his neighbour, Miss Vira, whose refined smile on her pale lips was less intimidating.

"Petro Stepanovych, I'm glad you came to town today," Rayisa said. "I'm going to commission you to write a petition for me."

"A petition?" the gentleman repeated, now truly alarmed.

"Yes, indeed, a petition to the governor, asking him to issue me a passport."

"Whatever for? Where is Rayisa Pavlina planning to go?" Petro Stepanovych inquired of the hostess, without taking his eyes off Rayisa.

"Rayisa is going abroad," the lady answered in a dignified manner, placing a great deal of emphasis on the word "abroad" and giving it a decidedly Russian pronunciation.

"Yes, I'm going away to university," the daughter added. "Yes! We're not allowed to enroll in universities here, so I'm going abroad. That's even better! When we return, people will bow and scrape even more before doctors from abroad."

"Are you so sure you want to become a doctor?" Kost inquired.

"Of course," Rayisa replied. "Why else spend the time? Lyuba and I are determined to do it."

Lyuba smiled gently and, raising her eyes, caught a smile on Kost's lips as well.

"So you're going as well, Lyuba?" Miss Vira inquired. "You're so fortunate!"

"I don't know yet," Lyuba responded, blushing.

"It will be difficult for you," the hostess remarked. "It's another matter where Rayisa is concerned, with her knowledge of foreign languages."

"They're all going, all of them! They're abandoning us!" Petro Stepanovych interjected, half worriedly, half jokingly.

"What do you mean, all of them? Many are staying behind," replied Rayisa, glancing at Petro Stepanovych's other neighbour.

"Besides, if you're so concerned, pack your bags and come to Zurich with us!"

"That's not very likely," Petro Stepanovych replied in utter confusion, smoothing back his shaggy hair.

"But you know, Rayisa," Lyuba said, "we actually do have a companion for our travels—Konstantyn Mykhaylovych is also going."

Rayisa glanced at the young gentleman in delighted surprise. "Yes, I'm going. It's definite!" he responded to this glance. "And I'm ready to assist my compatriots in any way I can."

Rayisa was genuinely happy when she heard the news about Master Konstantyn. "Oh, that's marvellous!" she said with true feeling. "It's wonderful! And I knew nothing about it!" Her eyes shone with a warmer light, "Well, come on, we'll discuss all the details—when we'll leave, how, and what! Ladies and gentlemen! Am I right in assuming that you've finished your tea? Let's go for a little walk."

She rose abruptly, and all the others, after bowing to the hostess, enthusiastically followed her out of the room. The young ladies started dressing for the walk—Rayisa in her own rooms, and Miss Vira in the parlour; the latter put on a hat with a wide rim and adjusted it in front of a large mirror. A short while later they made their way out of the house. They exited as a talkative group, but because the pathway was narrow, they had to break up into pairs.

"You're coming with me," Rayisa said to Kost, and she took him away with her to lead the procession.

"And we're left together," Vira said simply, as she paired up with Petro Stepanovych; the latter eagerly continued their conversation, but made it clear that the emphasis was on the "left together," and not on the "we."

Lyuba and the tall blonde walked in the company of the young officer. But the blond lady ended up being a silent partner in this situation as well. Lyuba and the officer, recalling their chance meeting in the library earlier in the day, began talking about books they knew from their reading; both had borrowed them from the public library. The young officer spoke softly and was somewhat embarrassed; after a while, however, he became excited and stated his ideas forthrightly and passionately. They were both speaking like neophytes, hastily and fervently, but their conversation was natural and sincere, because they did not have to restrain themselves in any way, as they would have felt compelled to with a more authoritative, learned interlocutor.

"Hartvig did not appeal to me!" the officer said, shaking his head with displeasure. "He's so obscure; there's something mystical in his writing. Moreover, he always strings a line of facts around some previously conceived idea, and that's not the way it should be."

"Nevertheless," Lyuba argued, "I think it's difficult for a deep thinker to refrain from expounding the main idea that gave rise to his actual search for the facts. The work would be too dry, too objective. In my opinion, learning that is not warmed by a leading thought—I'd even say, sincerity—would not interest us as much."

"I'm not speaking of fervour, of honesty in a learned work; it's the facts, what they reveal, perhaps even unexpectedly, to the investigator—that's what's most important of all! Take Darwin, for example—there's no one better. He didn't have a preconceived notion, and that's why he didn't write any nonsensical phrases—just the plain facts. But the picture that arises out of them is so clear, so eloquent, that the deduction has only to be noted. And that makes it even clearer for the reader, because he could draw the same conclusion himself."

The young man was coming out as the victor in the conversation, because his last few assertions had silenced Lyuba; after a moment, however, she once again picked up the subject: "It's a dark, inexplicable circle with those inductions and deductions."

The interchange was increasing in volume. Kost glanced back at the conversationalists and slowed his pace to walk beside them. They came to a quiet open field enveloped in the whitish light of the bright night; deep shadows fell from the tall embankments along the path. The words of the speakers rang out clearly in the silent expanse. On a break in the embankments, near a windmill stretching its wings like a giant in the field's wide open spaces, the group sat down to rest.

The conversations became sporadic as the young people joyfully inhaled the clean air and delighted in the unobstructed view of the residences, veiled by dark clumps of trees, that slumbered on the distant, outlying edges of the town. An occasional, pensive poplar stood silhouetted against the clear starry sky. Suddenly a star fell, streaking brilliantly across the heavens to the horizon. Kost watched the star and whispered softly:

"A star streaked across the western sky,
Farewell, my golden one, good-bye!"

"Ah, Konstantyn Mykhaylovych! You're infatuated with poetry!" Rayisa said, laughing merrily and casting a familiar look at the young man. "Why bid farewell to that star? Is it really vanishing? It's just changing its position in the worldly expanse."

"Where would poetry ever find a home if everything were examined?" Kost replied. "Poetry is a human being's subjective view of the objects and phenomena of nature."

A fervent conversation was begun again; however, the debaters could not come to an agreement. Kost found a supporter in Lyuba.

Finally, they rose to their feet and started walking back. Before long, Rayisa's boisterous laughter was resounding by her home, where the young people parted company.

"Farewell, poet and poetess," Rayisa shouted after Kost and Lyuba who had started off for home in the company of the young officer.

Saying little to one another, the trio reached Lyuba's house.

"Good night," the officer said, as he bid farewell to Lyuba by the gate. "Pleasant dreams! You should have delightful dreams," he added with a smile, "because you're such an idealist. Pleasant dreams to you!"

"Thank you. But why do you think that idealists would necessarily have delightful dreams?" Lyuba flung out in reply. The officer had moved quite far away already, and only his laughter, hearty but amicable, could be heard.

Lyuba and Kost entered the yard. Walking quickly across the veranda, Lyuba stepped into the unlocked house. On the couch where Madam Kateryna had been sitting in the evening, a bed had been made up for the visiting young gentleman; a partly burned candle lit the deserted room.

"Good night," Lyuba said, returning to the veranda where Kost was leaning on a post in a thoughtful pose. He was in no hurry to part with Lyuba who, flooded by moonlight, was standing before him with lowered eyes and extended hand.

"Mother will be waiting up for me. She never sleeps until I come home," the girl said quietly, in response to his look which she could feel on her. And, releasing her hand from Kost's, she hurried through the yard to a side porch that led to the utilitarian back rooms of the house.

Here she was engulfed by oppresively warm air. The first room did not have a window, and the moon's rays from the doorway lit the path for Lyuba past the sleeping Tetyana. In the next small room Lyuba stopped by a small, simple couch where a bed had been made up for her; she glanced through the open doorway into the neighbouring bedroom that was faintly lit by a small lamp under the icons in the corner. There, in Lyuba's usual spot, Kateryna Panteleymonivna was snoring in her sleep; the bed of the hostess was made up, but it was empty. Mariya Petrivna was kneeling and praying in front of the icons; her white nightcap was bent down low. Glancing at Lyuba, who had begun to undress quickly, Mariya Petrivna bowed her head still lower and whispered the words of her prayers with even greater fervour. Lyuba, settling into her bed, glanced at the crouching figure lit by the lamp's rays and sighed.

III

My dear readers are probably asking me when and where all this was happening. I think that, in large measure, you've already guessed the answers to both these questions.

The action took place in the mid-eighteen sixties in a small district town in the province of Poltava in Eastern Ukraine. Miss Lyuba Kalynovska came from a petty noble family. Her father had worked for a while as an electoral officer, but, tiring of the problems connected with this position, he retired and settled on his suburban estate which, although not large, assured him of a peaceful, but not boring, existence.

Mr. Vasyl Kalynovsky was a fairly well-educated man for his day. He subscribed to almanacs and a newspaper, and had an exceptional liking for the works of Hohol [Gogol], spending many hours reading them under the shade of a pear tree in his orchard.

The neighbours considered Kalynovsky to be a learned man. It was probably because he respected learning that, even though he had only daughters, he wanted them to be educated. In the initial stages he himself instructed them in the basics of Russian and French, and then, to ensure that their studying would assume a more diligent character, he turned to other people.

The older daughter, who was taught by a neighbour, a teacher in the local school, fell in love, not only with her studies, but with her instructor as well; she married him, and they moved to the city of Poltava, where he obtained a better teaching position. The middle daughter was sent to an Institute in Poltava where, it was said, she became "homesick" and died.

That left the youngest one, Lyuba. When Kalynovsky was still alive, she had been sent to study in a boarding school run by two upright ladies in their home town. In this school they taught Russian grammar, French, and music—that is, instruction in playing the piano. When an older German woman became attached to the school, those girls who so desired could study German, as well.

The instruction proceeded quite nicely. The girls studied and, because of the proximity of their homes, did not pine too greatly for them. When Lyuba came home to visit, she studied her lessons, while her mother sat and knitted beside her, or Tetyana, singing happily, worked away at her sewing.

"The Ural Range, the Ural Range," Lyuba repeated over and over again, but all the while she was thinking: "Why is mother's face so sad? Is she still grieving for poor Manya who's buried in Poltava, or for daddy? Poor daddy! He caught a cold so suddenly, on the Feast of Epiphany, and died so quickly." All the sad and solemn activities on the occasion of her father's funeral surfaced in Lyuba's mind; then her thoughts moved on to other matters. Tetyana was singing:

"Oh, what runs without a bridle,"
What grows without a root?"

Lyubochka knew this song—water runs without a bridle, and a stone grows without a root; but how could a stone grow without a root? How did it grow? Lyuba pondered this, but could not come up with an answer.

She shook her closely cropped hair, and recalled that she had to learn some French words. "*Le rossignol—solovey [nightingale],*" Lyuba recited distinctly. "*Rossignol*—that's a pretty word," she thought, "but it just doesn't seem to fit. *Solovey, soloveyko.* As is said in one of our songs: 'Oh, *solovey*, little bird, do not warble as you soar on high! Do not disturb the morning dew.' In Bakay's orchard and on our farmstead, the nightingales sing so charmingly . . .

"And, beyond the farmstead, the cuckoo also calls out gloriously: 'Cuckoo, cuckoo!' How can a cuckoo guess how many years you have left to live? But perhaps it isn't true that a cuckoo can guess? How could a bird know? But why do people say things like that?" Lyuba fell deep into thought once again. There was no one she could ask to get definitive answers. She would be ridiculed if she raised such questions in the boarding school.

Lyuba was maturing . . .

Occasionally, as her mother sorted spools of thread and other delicate objects in the storage room, Lyuba would peer curiously at a chest filled with books. If she picked one up, her mother immediately said: "Don't touch them, Lyubochka, don't touch them; they're daddy's books, and they're not suitable for children." And Lyubochka would move away from them.

As time went on, however, Lyubochka dared to take those books out of the storage room into the light of day. The books had a musty smell to them, and some of their pages were stuck together. Lyubochka first read the titles, then entire pages. She began visiting the chest with the books more and more frequently. She found much to read there—entire runs of journals, and interesting novels that described strange adventures. In some of the stories very ordinary events were portrayed so mournfully that Lyuba, reading the books in the orchard under the mulberry tree, wept over them.

One day, Lyuba went to the chest and pulled out a humorous book written at the end of the eighteenth century by a Ukrainian author, Ivan Kotlyarevsky. It was a marvellous travesty of Vergil's Aeneid. At first she could not believe her eyes! What was this? It was written so straightforwardly! On the very first page appeared the words:

> "Eney [Aeneas] was a clever lad,
> And every inch a kozak [Cossack] bold,
> Born in mischief to excel,
> More cunning than vagabonds of old."

What was this? Lyuba's eyes shone with delight. "Mother? Where did this book come from? Is it also daddy's?"

"Yes, it's daddy's, sweetheart, it's daddy's. He used to read out loud from it . . . It's such a funny book!"

Lyuba also laughed when she read it, and she kept on laughing even after she had finished it. She read a bit of it to Tetyana, and the latter also understood everything and had a good laugh or two; and the next time Tetyana saw Lyuba, she asked her: "What happened next in that story?"

Lyuba did not find any more unusual books of that kind. One time, however, in her wanderings through the authors, she did come across such clear, accessible language again. Her sister and brother-in-law from Poltava came for a visit, and they brought with them a small collection of deeply moving poems; some of the lines and phrases were imprinted forever in Lyuba's mind: "Like a writhing crimson serpent, the river Alta bears the bloody news of battle," "To bring at least my heart, tortured and gnawed by grief, to Dnipro's hilly banks, and there to lay it down to rest."

She was told that these banned verses, copied surreptitiously by hand, were written by Taras Shevchenko, a Ukrainian poet with peasant roots, who defiantly wrote in ordinary language like that—in *Little Russian [Ukrainian]*. He was now living in exile, banished by the tsarist regime for his writing.

Lyuba told her school friend Rayisa Brahova about this poetry and recited an entire section of it to her, but Rayisa said that it was composed in the language of peasants and, as such, she found it indecent! The young ladies in her family—Rayisa was the eldest—spoke French.

Rayisa, you see, was a grand young lady. Well, not all that grand, but her family put on airs and pretended they were aristocrats. At one time, Rayisa's grandfather, the elder Brahov—or *Braha [home-brewed beer]*, as the peasants called him—was truly very rich and respectable; he was even elected as a Marshall of the nobility. However, his son, Pavel Brahov, a military man, did a good job of "rubbing open the eyes" of his patrimony. He squandered everything—mortgaging and remortgaging his property until there was more debt on it than the property itself was worth. Nevertheless, because he was of noble lineage and had married a woman from one of the more important families, he remained a member of the aristocracy. He was even elected to important government positions—as a judge, and as a deputy of some sort—and so, in general, life in the family went along in a lordly fashion.

Everything would have continued in this manner if the serfs had not been freed. This was the final undoing of the Brahovs. Lord Brahov, after settling the debts on his property, disappeared somewhere—supposedly to serve on some relative's estate; but some people said that there were family reasons for his departure. Be that as it may, Lady Brahova remained in the small town with her children and had to make do with only a portion of their former property. And yet, despite all this, the lordly tradition and the arrogance remained. Her greatest desire was to give Rayisa, who was maturing, "a proper education," but it was difficult!

As things turned out, Rayisa had to be sent to the same boarding school that Lyuba Kalynovska attended. And it was strange that even though many girls in the school were richer—the daughters of petty lordlings or merchants—Rayisa Brahova was considered to be the grandest young lady of them all, and she viewed herself in this light as well, having heard from her mother that she must remember the lineage from which she was descended. And so, sometimes glancing askance at each other, and sometimes enjoying a close friendship, first as children, and later as young ladies, the two girls completed their studies at the boarding school and were immediately swept up into a vibrant wave of life!

It did not matter that the little town was obscure and parochial; the new life of those years flowed into it in powerful streams. The old foundations of community life, of thinking, of taste, broke up like river ice in the springtime and, crushed to pieces, they swirled away, driven by a warm, free current. Something very fresh and very young was in the air. Old hands and heads—surprised, dejected, stunned—were lowered, while young ones rose boldly and confidently, diligently seeking vocations. Young people looked with shining eyes directly into the rising light of justice and freedom, without ever thinking that the light could fade.

Lyuba no longer had to search for books in her father's old chest—it was as if books now found her and other young people like her. Who could say how it came about that a group of amateurs began to put on plays to raise money for a library in the town. Where had it been born—this library! And, just like Lyuba, Rayisa also found food for thought there—ideas that opened a new world for both of them.

It is difficult to say who first uttered the words: "Let's go abroad to study." The idea was drifting around on its own. Time and again, there was talk about young people who had already gone abroad and about those who were making plans to leave. Only one question remained: how was it possible to break out of the family nest whose hold—even though its authority had been shaken—was still significant. Lyuba caused her mother much grief when she first told her about her desire to go abroad to study.

"My Lyubochka is all I have left now; she's the baby in the family," Mariya Petrivna thought, her eyes filling with tears. "How am I to remain alone? How can I let her go so far away? But how can I not let her go? How can I not find the means to expedite her trip, if she's so eager to go? And she says she won't be gone for long. Perhaps the Lord will allow me to live a few more years, so I can see her again—my dearest little dove. Yes, I must find the wherewithal for Lyuba to travel and live there. Well, I guess it should be possible to arrange things somehow—the land has been rented for a definite amount each year; and I'm old already, so how much do I need? Besides, I'd give Lyuba most of the money that comes in yearly, anyway—so I could still give her just as much, or even a little more, for that Zurich—the devil knows where it's sprung up from!"

And what about Rayisa's mother? How was she reacting? Well, for most mothers, the thread of control over the fate of their children—especially such strong-willed ones as Rayisa—had already been broken! And, after all, she was not an only child; praise God, Lady Brahova had a rather large family—four children in all.

What was Rayisa to wait for in this godforsaken place, especially without the financial means suitable to her pedigree? But if she went abroad, upon her return she would be someone special among the rest of the young ladies, a learned person—this was in style now—and who knows, perhaps Rayisa would find her good fortune in this way. And so, in the final analysis, Lady Brahova not only proudly informed her acquaintances about Rayisa's intention to travel "abroad," but also, to a large degree, began using her eldest daughter's anticipated career to plan the future careers of her younger daughters.

IV

There was bedlam in Lady Brahova's house. Servants and children were racing back and forth, Rayisa was rapidly issuing orders, and even Lady Brahova was not her usual composed self. Rayisa's baggage was being tied, and small bundles were being prepared. This was the day that Rayisa was setting out on her travels.

The plan was that she, Lyuba, and Kost Zaharovsky were to travel together. First, the three of them had to go to Kyiv, and to get there, they either had to hire a coach and driver, or use their own horses. After considering what would be best, it was decided to hire the best coachman in the whole town; it was not to be a Jew with a rickety covered wagon—oh no!—but an upstanding townsman, Semen Moroka, who had a troika of horses and a covered carriage of good quality. It was Madam Kalynovska who engaged Moroka.

"I don't want them to pick me up here, mother," Rayisa said. "Their mothers might decide to come with them to see them off, but you're not acquainted with them, and it would only be uncomfortable for everyone. It will be better if I pack my things and meet them at their place. I've made all the arrangements."

Lady Brahova thought the matter over for a minute and said: "You're right. You can ride there in our droshky."

Rayisa, attired in a light grey travelling outfit and wearing her mother's watch on a fine gold chain, was in good spirits, and she only occasionally glanced around worriedly to see if she had forgotten anything. Lady Brahova was leaning her head on her hand; tears welled up in her eyes, and she quietly lifted a fine handkerchief to her face.

"Now, mother," Rayisa said, as she drew closer to her. "I'm not permitting any crying! It's bad luck. Why worry?" Her own voice, however, sounded unnatural, strained.

"The Kalynovskys have sent a message inquiring if the young lady will be ready soon," a servant said, entering the dining room.

"Are they ready to leave? Is Master Zahorovsky there already?" Rayisa asked with a start.

"Yes, he's there. And the horses have arrived."

"Fine! Tell them that I'll be there shortly. Well, mother dear, it's time for me to go."

They all rose to their feet. Once again, confusion filled the rooms. The luggage was carried out and placed on Petro Stepanovych's buggy. He was personally attending to the stowing of the baggage. Rayisa, accompanied by Vira Nykolayivna and her admirer, was going to travel on the Brahov's droshky.

Everyone was seated in the dining room. Flushed, and mopping his perspiring brow, Petro Stepanovych entered the room. "We're ready!" he announced.

Rayisa, her face serious, approached her mother. "Farewell, mother," she said quietly.

Lady Brahova rose to her feet and stood without moving, clutching her kerchief with fingers adorned with gold rings. Her black eyebrows were contracted with suffering, and many fine wrinkles—which Lady Brahova detested—appeared on her forehead. She controlled herself long enough to bless Rayisa; then she burst into tears and hugged her tightly. Rayisa kissed her hand without saying anything.

"May God bless you," Lady Brahova continued, and tears flooded her face again as she whispered, softly and brokenly: "And daddy . . . daddy isn't here . . . he didn't come to see you off." Her pale hands were spasmodically clutching Rayisa's shoulders. The sound of bitter weeping filled the house.

"Don't cry, mother dear," Rayisa urged her quietly. "Don't grieve so much. Everything will be fine. Take care of yourself."

"Write! Write to us!" her mother said.

"I will. I'll write immediately." Rayisa kissed her mother's hand once more, parted from her, and then kissed her two sisters who, their eyes filled with tears and their lips trembling, were standing together, tightly holding on to each other's hands.

"But where's George?" Rayisa asked about her brother. They called the little boy, who was playing by the carriages, clambering first on one, and then on the other. Rayisa forced herself to be cheerful. "Good-bye, George," she said, kissing the boy's animated face. "One day you'll also go away to study, to become a professor. Good-bye!"

Her farewells with her aunts were rather perfunctory . . .

"Farewell, farewell. Till we meet again!" Rayisa called out to all and sundry as she walked out of the house. On the threshold, her mother once again embraced her. The buggy and the droshky were ready.

In the meantime, the Kalynovsky home was filled with its own bedlam. Mariya Petrivna, after getting almost no sleep, rose very early. Lyuba, who had finished her packing quite late, slept in. When she awoke, she could hear that her mother's orders were in full swing.

The *pyrohy [turnovers]* were prepared early. And the morning meal was soon ready as well. With trembling hands, Mariya Petrivna wrapped food for the road—*pyrohy* and baked chicken. She was pale, without a speck of colour in her face, and she appeared to have grown still thinner and older in the last twenty-four hours. Her eyes were red—visible proof of her sleepless night. She said little, and when she did speak, it was in a lowered, constricted voice; however, she did not stop seeing to everything that had to be done for her Lyubochka, who was going away. She would take care of one matter, shake her head, draw her hand over her eyes, and then rush off to look after something else.

Her nearest neighbour dropped in, and then some more distant neighbours who were close friends came by, and finally, Lyuba's aunt and the Zahorovskys arrived. Lyuba greeted them on the veranda. With a flushed face and a warm sparkle in her eyes, she extended her hand to Kost.

"Well, are you ready to leave?" Kost inquired with an engaging smile. Lyuba returned his smile.

Kateryna Panteleymonivna walked into the house and greeted everyone. Madam Kateryna did not look her usual self. Even though her eyes were as lively as always, they were darting around uncertainly, as if trying to prevent others from noticing their worried expression. Having enjoyed a rosy complexion all her life, it was difficult to rid herself of it completely; nevertheless, Madam Kateryna's face was not blooming as it usually did—it was a trifle paler, and any colour that did appear showed up in spots.

Lyuba and Kost were left alone on the veranda. Even though it was an autumn day, it was warm and clear.

"Let's go into the orchard for a moment," Lyuba said.

Their orchard was not very large, but it did have a few rows of flowers planted without any artifice. The mignonettes and brown-eyed Susans were still blooming luxuriantly. Lyuba picked a few of the brown-eyed Susans.

"I'll take them as mementos," she said to Kost with a gentle smile, and her preoccupied gaze wandered involuntarily over the familiar scene. "It's sad, so very sad, to part with these vistas," Lyuba said. "It feels as if something is breaking my heart. And I have a feeling that when I return I won't be the same. No one knows what the future holds!"

"You'll return an even better person than you are now," Kost observed, gazing into Lyuba's thoughtful, troubled face.

They returned to the house. The rooms were filled with clamour and confusion. Suddenly a bell chimed. It was the coachman with the carriage. Mariya Petrivna turned still paler; her heart fainted, and she stood as if petrified. Lyuba's heart also began to race. She would be leaving soon, very soon.

They had their meal in an even less orderly manner than the Brahovs. No one felt like eating. Mariya Petrivna sat silently, with clasped hands and lowered head; she lifted her face to fasten her mournfully tender gaze on her dearest Lyuba, and then she lowered it again, for tears were clouding her eyes.

They finally got through the meal. It was almost time to leave. Mariya Petrivna was sitting on a chest near a window in another room, weeping bitterly and stifling her sobs. Lyubochka came into the room, sat down beside her, and gently nestled against her shoulder. Mariya Petrivna pressed her face into her hands and sobbed even more loudly. Then she embraced Lyubochka.

"My dearest little dove! My sweetheart!" Mariya Petrivna gasped through her tears. Lyubochka was also crying.

Just then Tetyana came in and said: "Madam! Moroka is becoming annoyed; he says it's time to leave."

And so they sent a message to Rayisa. She arrived with Vira Nykolayivna and Petro Stepanovych, and brought with her a more lively mood; she was in high spirits and joked with Kost. Bohdashevych, the young officer, dropped by to wish them a safe journey. He wanted to speak jovially to Lyuba, but there was uncertainty in his voice and eyes—more tenderness than jocularity.

"Please write to tell me how you're getting along," he begged Lyuba, pausing over his words.

"I will, I will," she replied. "And, if anything happens here, write and tell me. I'll be very happy to receive your letters, because mother doesn't write long ones."

Her mother could no longer hear anything. She did not hear what Vira Nykolayivna and Petro Stepanovych were saying to her, and she did not hear the din that filled the house.

The belongings of all three passengers were packed away; the baggage of the young ladies was stowed in the luggage box, and Kost's was placed directly opposite.

"Well," Kost said, rising to his feet. "Farewell, mother"

The embracing and the tears began. Mariya Petrivna was awash in tears. Lyubochka bid everyone farewell.

"Good-bye, Tetyana! Good-bye, Ulyana!" she whispered tearfully, as she exchanged kisses with them.

On the veranda, Mariya Petrivna once again clasped Lyubochka to her heart and froze in that position. If it had not been for the tears rolling down her cheeks, you might have thought she had turned to stone. And so, Mariya Petrivna hardly saw how Rayisa, Kost, and her dear Lyubochka settled in the carriage; indeed she hardly saw the world for her tears.

"Good luck! Go with God! Good luck! May God guide you! Good luck!" Petro Stepanovych shouted.

The young officer silently waved his cap to Lyuba, who was gazing out of the carriage at her mother.

The carriage could no longer be seen. Only the bell could be heard in the distance.

V

As has been stated, Semen Moroka was a well-built man and an upstanding coachman. His horses and carriage were well looked after, for he believed, as the saying goes, that horses are needed more than once. So the travellers relaxed and enjoyed the countryside.

The fields were slowly unfolding before them, and the woods and the valleys were drawing nearer; an isolated farmstead, shaded by fruit trees, and with a well under a willow tree, came into view, and then there were fields once again, fields without end. On the edge of the horizon a village, looking as if it were half-sunken into the ground, shimmered in the distance; thatched roofs and the green dome of a church glimmered indistinctly on the horizon. In the middle of a black, dormant ploughed field, a large, melancholy half-excavated grey mound conversed with the wind.

And now there were fields of rippling grain, a small ravine, another one, and then a crest, from which one could see the village of Verbivka scattered around a pond. Even though the sun had not quite set, the travellers were to have their first stopover here. Now they were on the embankment of a dam with willows planted on both sides; the rough road tossed the young ladies about in the carriage— but they just laughed. A canoe was tied near the bank; on a footbridge quite close to it, several young women, their skirts tied back, lowered their washing beetles for a minute and stared at the travellers.

Now they were in the village itself. At the crossroads stood a large wayside inn, but Moroka did not stop there. As they went along, men doffed their hats in greeting, while in the street, towheaded children stood at the gates or clambered up on stiles, staring intently at the travellers. The carriage continued on its way, past yards, wells, and winding fences. In a bend just before the square, Semen Moroka reigned in his horses by another hostelry. "We'll stop here," he said.

The young ladies looked out, climbed down, and went into the guest area, where they and Kost were greeted by two small rooms crowded with dark furniture. The travellers removed their dusty outer clothing; they were a trifle tired, but still ready to laugh at the couch that stood like an ancient "fossil" in the room and at the twisted samovar carried in by the Jew's servant. Later, this servant brought them a teapot decorated with fantastic blue flowers and some dubious-looking glasses on a round, chipped tray.

Digging out the provisions brought from home, the young people made a meal of them and drank some tea. They talked and joked— for now they were truly on their way! They were travellers! After lunch, they went for a walk beyond the village.

The village grew livelier as the sun began to set. Young women were fetching water from the well, and their animated chattering and the creaking of the pulley on the well resounded far and wide. Cattle and a flock of sheep raised a cloud of dust as they went by, and their cries echoed down the street: "Meh-eh-eh-eh! Beh-eh-eh-eh!" Men were returning home from the fields with wagons loaded with sheaves. One of the householders who was walking alongside his oxen greeted them as he drew up beside them: "Good evening!"

Kost bowed, and Lyuba responded quietly: "Good evening."

Rayisa laughed and remarked: "What a strange greeting! What on earth for?"

"Just because . . . out of politeness, by way of a greeting," Kost replied. "You, Rayisa Pavlivna, are a lady, and so you don't know your own people—neither their customs, nor their character."

"And I don't want to know," Rayisa retorted. "Of what use is such knowledge to me? None of the common folk can, to my way of thinking, evoke more interest than a vegetable. They lead a purely vegetative existence."

"Vegetative? Do you really think so?"

"Of course! Just look at the little boy and girl on top of that wagon—how do they differ from the sheaves on which they're lying? They're motionless; their eyes are vacant. Or, take the man with whom you just exchanged greetings; he could be best compared to his ox; they have the same functions in life—both physiologically and intellectually."

"Rayisa, you're greatly mistaken," Lyuba broke passionately into the conversation.

"Yes, greatly mistaken!" Kost repeated.

"You say I'm mistaken, mistaken!" Rayisa continued heatedly. "Prove to me that I'm mistaken."

"There's nothing to prove!" Lyuba replied. "Find out for yourself what those children are thinking, what that man can tell you."

Rayisa laughed mockingly: "Oh, please! What he could tell me! Ha-ha-ha! Ha-ha-ha! What a conversation that would be!"

"Well, it may not be what you think." Lyuba responded with a calm smile. "You might find it very interesting."

"Moreover," Kost added, "if we think that the world view of these people, their intellectual powers, are lower than ours, not as well developed, then it is our obligation to raise them, to develop them."

"Develop them?" Rayisa repeated slowly and mockingly. "Thank you very much! The work is too difficult and too thankless. Moreover," she added after a moment, "if we were to choose that path—it would mean stopping progress."

"How's that?" Kost asked in surprise.

"It's like this," Rayisa replied with an audacious look. "It would mean arresting the progress of those few people—the minority—who are moving forward; instead of letting at least them move on and attain their goal, you want to sentence them to halt half way there and concentrate on chewing over once again what has already been attained, to chew it over along with the oxen, with the unthinking masses!

"Masses cannot progress; they simply can't," the girl continued. "According to the natural order of things, people in the human community can't all be equally strong—some are weaker and less capable, while others are stronger, more capable; so, without talking about an impossible comparison of strength, let those who can, move ahead."

"Yes, let those, who are able to, move ahead," Kost stated passionately. "But let them take by the hand and lead those who have fallen behind, who have temporarily grown weaker."

"If they don't," Lyuba added, "then those individuals who have gone on ahead alone may leave a chasm behind them."

"Let them!" Rayisa retorted with a stubborn smile.

"It doesn't make any sense," Kost observed. "The head would be cut from the body! Why should that chasm be allowed to grow larger, so that even you, some day, will fear to look into it—because if you did, your head would spin?"

"Stand farther away from the edge! Don't gaze into the abyss; always look ahead! Find a suitable position for yourself. But then, if someone has the desire to construct footbridges over an abyss, let them! They're free to do so! But I think that for a person who has already moved on ahead to the other side of the chasm, there is no turning back," Rayisa added resolutely. "He can only fall off the footbridge and smash his head, or sink in the mud!"

"But perhaps he won't smash his head!" Kost said with a smile. "And if he does fall, perhaps it won't be into the mud!"

Talking loudly, they reached the end of the street. The cottages thinned out and were interspersed with gardens and meadows. Off to one side, a group of girls and youths, sitting on logs under some willows, were singing; the words resounded clearly in the still air:

"Oh, an oak over a birch its leaves did unfurl!
O young *kozak*, why do you sit and worry?"

Kost turned his head in delight towards the singing executed spiritedly, almost exultantly, by rich, youthful voices.

"Well? Is your heart rejoicing?" Rayisa asked Kost smilingly, casting a quick glance at him.

Kost did not respond immediately, as he was listening to the singing. "No, you tell me," he said, when they had passed the logs, "can it really be that this singing doesn't speak to your heart?"

Rayisa raised her eyebrows uncertainly and did not say anything. The singing rang forth, washing over them in waves. Its echo could be heard as far as the village gates. The old gatekeeper, his head bowed, sat beside his hut listening intently. It grew dark in the field, and stars ignited in the sky. On the western horizon a spreading cloud was fading, darkening, and blending in with the evening shadows. It was tranquil on the road—only a tardy wagon was rumbling in the distance. Returning from their long walk, the young people quietly approached the hostelry. It was time to think about getting some rest. Rayisa began unpacking her baggage, hoping to make up a half-decent bed for herself. Kost was concerned that he find a spot where he would not be in the way of the young ladies. Lyuba, leaning on her elbows at the open window, gazed at the starry sky.

Some village girls, coming home from a *vulytsya [party]* or, perhaps, just hastening to one, were singing as they walked by:

"O my dark night, O my bright star!"

VI

"Grünerberg! Zwei Minuten!! [Grunerberg! Two minutes!] *Grünerberg! Zwei Minuten!"* the conductor was shouting as he ran down the aisle, the length of the train. *"Grünerberg! Zwei Minuten!"* The sound was coming now from the vestibule at the end of the passenger cars.

Where is this? What is this? It seemed as if they had just left Verbivka, and here they were already in Grunerberg! Yes, that's how it is! Verbivka was left far behind, long ago. And it has been a while since Semen Moroka, haven driven the young people to Kyiv, set off for home with a letter from Lyuba to Mariya Petrivna—a letter she will sprinkle with tears of joy. And the Kyivan highway, Brest, and Warsaw have long since been left behind. Borders were crossed, and European cities passed by as in a dream.

The face of the earth kept changing, delighting the eye with the most marvellous wonders of culture, with the most captivating beauties of nature. Was it possible that castles such as this really did exist—not just in fairy tales? And that green, rugged mountains, such as those in the Rhine country were not found only in paintings? God! How wonderful! How beautiful!

The young ladies could not tear their eyes away from the landscapes. Over there, vineyards cloaked an entire mountainside, and down below there was a city—but no, it was called a *Dorf [Village]*—crowded with tall red-roofed buildings, and crowned by a church with a tall steeple; all the land was cultivated, green, and beautiful—not a spot was lying waste. And, on the very top of a lofty green mountain, stood a castle—sheer and fantastic. How could people build it way up there? How could they climb up there with the stones, with everything! It was as if a magical hand had placed it there, long, long ago!

And down below, a river wound its way; hemmed in by the mountains, it bounded in silvery waves over its stony bottom as it flashed by. Once again there were only mountains and exquisite valleys. But now, the passengers were saying that the Rhine river would be next! The German neighbours of the travellers stood in the coaches and pressed closely to the windows, watching for the approaching river with rapt faces.

"*Sieh! [Look!]*," an elderly German said triumphantly to a little girl, most likely his granddaughter, who probably had not yet seen "Father Rhine" in her short life. And the grandfather pointed a finger without saying another word. A wide, mighty expanse of water appeared. The Rhine! The river before which mountains part—mountains wrapped in vineyards and wreathed with centuries-old pine trees.

Beyond the Rhine, the mountains towered higher and crowded in on one another. And, farther away, still loftier mountains with white ridges on their tips could be seen. Green pine forests grew on their slopes, and villages and chalets clung to them; streams cascaded downwards, and a railroad wound its way through narrow mountain passes. On the curves, astonishing panoramas followed one after the other. And, above it all, the sky was blue, so very blue . . .

The travellers were talking less and exchanging glances— glances in which both joy and anxiety were reflected. But then their eyes fastened once again on the unfolding vistas.

The sun was in the west. A mist, rolling in over the deep valleys, rose ever higher in broad swaths. And, above it, the setting sun bathed the mountains in a luminous glow and painted them in magnificent colours. It would be impossible to capture all those hues—from deep blue to the delicate pink of a rose blossom. The sun set, and the mountains darkened and pressed in from all sides in the misty twilight, like unknown, mysterious giants. Here and there a star glimmered. Darkness settled more densely on the mountains and the breathtaking vistas.

Even in the dark of the night, one could see that a large city was drawing nearer; there it was—glimmering lights at the foot of the mountains. The train, descending into the valley, emitted a sharp, shrill whistle, once, twice—and approached the station in Zurich.

Hearts fluttered in trepidation, and hands trembled anxiously as belongings were collected.

Now the city itself came into view—a new city with huge factories, black chimneys, and vertical stacks of flickering lights that dominated the landscape. There was evidence of so much human labour here, labour united with the mighty power of steam! What was that? A bridge. Stars flashed in the water below. The train crossed to the other side of the bridge, wound its way past a whole section of the city, and came to a stop at the station. It was not possible to see the station from the coach, but the conductor could be heard shouting, as he unlocked the coach: "Zürich! Zürich!"

It was of no concern to the three travellers how long a stopover other passengers had here; they stepped down from the train—they had arrived!

The hubbub in the big station swallowed them. Messengers were shouting the names of hotels, inviting people to stay in them. The three newly arrived travellers placed themselves in the care of one of them, and soon they and their baggage from Poltava were being transported to a hotel. As they passed unfamiliar buildings and strangers in carriages, they began talking, joking, and laughing. Then there was a troubled silence once again—like the silence in a theatre before the curtain is raised.

VII

The hum of excited young voices filled the wide corridors of the university. Not all the students behaved in the same manner; some waved their arms about and carried on heated conversations; others were calm—they spoke quietly, without laughing, and their gait was unhurried, peaceful; but they also had bright, happy faces, and there was an intense, fervent gleam in their eyes.

"Greetings, Kalynovska!" a young lady—blond, with large, bright grey eyes, and so delicate that she swayed like a blade of grass when she walked—called out to Lyuba. "Well, how's it going? Do you have your registration forms yet?"

"Yes, I do."

"And I've already bought the anatomical atlas they told us to get. Come over to my place, and we'll take a look at it! We can go right after classes are finished, if you'd like to."

"Good! I'll be sure to come!" Lyuba replied.

"May I come too?" A short young man, carelessly dressed, unexpectedly joined the young ladies.

"Of course!" the blond young lady replied with a smile. "Do come!"

"You know, I wanted to buy that atlas myself—I even dashed over to the bookstore—but there's no way I could buy it. It's devilishly expensive! Only princesses can afford it."

"Why only princesses? Princes can afford it as well," the young lady rejoined with a thin smile.

"Well, you see, a prince needs a lot of money for restaurants and the like; but princesses—they have it made! But that's neither here nor there. Tell me, where do you live?"

"On *Raemi Strasse [Raemi Street],* Number —"

"Should I ask for Princess Biloselska when I get there? What's princess in German? It's *Fürsten,* right? The devil take it. It sounds ponderous in every language."

"Kuzmenko!" someone shouted at the youth who was doing the talking. "Why weren't you at the physiology lecture?"

A group of students, including Rayisa, came up to them. Looking very fit and happy, she laughed as she listened to a young gentleman, leaning over to her and gesticulating with his hands. The young man walking on her other side was also a participant in the conversation. Just ahead of them were the students who had shouted to Kuzmenko.

The couples and groups met and regrouped, and the young people struck up both serious and jocular conversations. Then, all at once, they broke away and rushed off to their classrooms; all that could be heard was the echo of their footsteps and the sound of doors opening and closing.

And so, Lyuba and Rayisa were at the university in Zurich. They were students, no less! At the outset, some obstacles had arisen—

something about their not arriving at the time when students were normally admitted—but it had all worked out. True, it had taken these inexperienced newcomers some time to find their way around. They made their first mistake immediately upon their arrival.

They had registered, you see, in the hotel "*Bourg au Lac [Village on the Lake]*. Well, who could have foreseen it would be a problem? It certainly was very comfortable, and the view was spectacular—but it did not suit their pocketbooks at all! So they quickly moved to houses on the other side of town. They rented rooms nearer the university on a street called *Künstlergraben*; their landlady, *Frau [Madam]* Piltz, dampened their spirits somewhat with her exhortations to be exceedingly careful not to damage the walls and furniture, but still, to some degree at least, they began to feel at home.

The girls eagerly unpacked their belongings and settled into their new quarters; they set out their books and various other things— some from home, some purchased here. From their window they could see the river Limat with its bridges and banks, the "Old Town," and splendid mountains that dazzled their eyes. The wonders of nature enraptured the girls; not only Lyuba, who did not conceal her delight, but even Rayisa—who claimed she did not have a sentimental disposition in this regard—fell under the spell cast by the magnificent Swiss scenery.

The girls were no less amazed, and their intellects were no less enthralled, by the wonders that their lessons—which they approached with great diligence—were revealing to them. Having read a lot at home, they were familiar with what they were learning—but it was the familiarity of a dilettante, superficial and disjointed. Now, as they became acquainted with their chosen field of study in an orderly fashion, they saw in the professors' lectures the full significance and benefits of these studies, and the newly discovered world looked still more wonderful to them.

Even the instructional specifics—things they already knew— seemed completely different when they were clearly demonstrated. The zoological lab, the anatomical models, and the physical and chemical experiments impressed them so profoundly, so palpably, that their eyes fastened on all of them as on something extraordinary, unexpected. And then, there was the microscope, that small instrument which revealed—equally to them and to true scientists, the princes of learning—a new, boundless world. How marvellous! How many wonders—all of which could be investigated, understood.

Oh, they had to know everything, absolutely everything! They had to study and study! And they did study, eagerly, conscientiously. But, there was a slight problem—the lectures were delivered in a foreign language and difficult to understand. There were times when they wanted to stop the lecturer and say: "Just a minute, *Herr [Mr.]* Professor! What was it you said? We didn't quite understand it." But, of course, they did not stop the professor. They continued to listen carefully, and later tried to figure out the meaning of obscure passages from what they had written down. Little by little, they learned the language—both to understand it and speak it. Oh, they listened so carefully to the lectures; they listened without letting their attention stray for even a moment, until their heads grew weary; and when they came home, they had to go over the lesson once again, using their notes and texts, until their heads spun.

It did not matter that their heads spun; they had to sit over their books—and they wanted to. More than once, they studied well into the night. Even after Rayisa said: "That's enough!" and went to bed, Lyubochka often continued reading, either at the table or in bed, until the morning star, glinting on the mountains, glanced in through the window.

VIII

There were many students in the classroom, and almost all the seats were occupied—the professor was due to arrive at any moment. Lyuba made her way to a spot at the edge of a bench where she liked to sit. Oh, what a pity! The place was taken—an unfamiliar blond student was sitting there. She had made a beeline for it, and now she stood there, confused, not knowing where to find another spot; without realising it, she blurted out something in Ukrainian.

"Sit down!" the blond student called out, moving over and making room for her. Lyuba sat down. The student watched her attentively as she busied herself with her papers, but he did not engage her in conversation, even though the hum of voices, restrained but audible, surrounded them.

The professor walked in, and an air of expectancy filled the room. In the sudden silence, the professor began his lecture. Speaking in the measured tones of an elderly man, his voice conveyed conviction and concern. At times he left the podium and walked to the blackboard, where he drew explanatory diagrams clarifying what he was saying.

The lecture concluded. It was the last one that morning, and the students dispersed. Only Lyuba was left by the blackboard, pondering something as she studied the drawings on the blackboard and the paper she held in her hand.

"Is there something you haven't understood?" asked the student by whom she had been sitting. He was one of the last to leave and had noticed her intense concentration.

"Yes . . . there's something here I didn't understand initially, and I still can't figure it out," Lyuba replied. From among the drawings of the circulatory systems of various creatures, she pointed at the blood-bearing system of one of the amphibians. "Both the gills and the lungs are here, so how is the process of blood purification conducted? How do these two systems branch out?"

"Well, it's like this," the student began to explain.

Just then, however, his friend Kuzmenko glanced in the doorway and shouted: "Korniyevych! Where are you? Come on!"

"Right away," Korniyevych replied calmly, continuing with his explanation.

"Thank you! Now I understand," Lyuba said.

"In a word," Kuzmenko, who had come up and listened to the explanation, added: "you, my fellow countrywoman, should know that it would suffice if this worthless gilled-and-lunged entity had only gills for oxygenating its blood; its lungs were given to it just so that it could perplex and annoy our brother, the ignorant student."

The students laughed and moved away from the board. As they left the university, they realised they were going in the same direction; Korniyevych and Kuzmenko were on their way to the same restaurant as Lyuba.

As they walked along, Kuzmenko did most of the talking.

"Tell me," he said to Lyuba, "in which part of the province of Poltava do you live?"

"But how do you know I'm from Poltava?" Lyuba inquired, smiling. She was surprised that she could speak so easily to Kuzmenko, as if she had known him for a long time.

"Oh, dear God!" Kuzmenko replied. "How could I not know? And when I heard what you said in German to the watchman, I could tell right away that a fellow countrywoman was speaking."

"Aha, so that's it! Are you from Poltava as well?"

"Of course! Korniyevych and I are right on the boundary between the province of Poltava and Slobodian Ukraine—I'm on the Poltava side, and he's on the Kharkiv side . . ."

Carrying on a conversation in this way, they arrived at a small restaurant crowded with students. Dishes were clattering, and young people were chatting noisily.

Making her way to the table where Rayisa and Kost were sitting, Lyuba sat down in the chair they had saved for her. Korniyevych and Kuzmenko settled in close by, and the latter quickly became acquainted with Rayisa and Kost, joking and laughing with them.

Kost, looking closely at Lyuba's flushed face, took advantage of the noise at the neighbouring tables to ask her: "Lyubov Vasylivna, why haven't I seen you for a couple of days? I've really missed you."

"Who's to blame? I've missed you too," Lyuba responded, smiling happily.

"But I tried to see you! Yesterday you went somewhere with your girlfriends, and today, when I stopped by to walk to the university with you, you were gone! If only we could go for a walk somewhere together, or something!"

"Well, why not? Let's go!"

"Where to?" Kuzmenko intruded into their conversation. "It's a great idea. Let's go, ladies and gentlemen! After all—the devil take it—we're in Switzerland! Are we going to spend all our time moping over those proteans and tritons? May they all perish! Am I right, my fellow countrywoman?"

Lyuba just laughed at his barb—she felt so happy! "Let's go, let's go somewhere!" she called out.

The group of Ukrainian students walked out together. They came to the terrace in front of the polytechnical building, from where there was a view of the city and the mountains, flooded with sunlight.

Korniyevych suggested going to the *Hohe [Upper]* Promenade. "With those poplar trees, it's the most *kozak*-like promenade here!"

"Oh, it's Slobodian Ukraine that's speaking now," Kuzmenko hooted. "But those poplars really do have something reminiscent of the *kozaks* about them."

The entire group set out and turned into *Raemi Strasse*. Before they reached the *Hohe* Promenade, they met Princess Biloselska. She was walking with another young lady and carrying a basket of grapes.

"Ah, your Highness!" Kuzmenko greeted her. "Where are you coming from?"

"We were just at the market, buying some grapes."

"You see what a democracy we have here! Well, when are you going to show us your anatomical atlas?"

"Why didn't you come before? Please, come right now," Biloselska replied graciously. "My home is quite close by, near the *Hohe* Promenade."

"Why, we were just going there. Let's drop in, shall we, ladies and gentlemen?" Kuzmenko invited the others.

"Come, please come! We'll have some grapes, and then we'll go to the *Hohe* Promenade. I'll gladly go with you." Saying this, the slender princess walked on ahead, leading her guests home.

Her apartment consisted of two rooms—a bedroom, and a "little parlour" with a round table in the middle and attractive furnishings. There was a mirror on the wall, and a few Swiss landscapes—the mountains, the Rhine rapids, and Shilyon Castle. On the balcony opening out from the parlour were pots of tall flowers.

When the princess entered the room, she kissed Lyuba, saying: "Welcome, my dear." She invited the others to sit down and gave Kuzmenko the atlas; then, she and her roommate rinsed the grapes, set them out in a nice basket, and passed out fine china plates.

The young women preparing the grapes were very different in appearance, even though they were of the same "colouring"—they were both blondes. Biloselska was very slender, pale, and delicate; her pure blond, fairly long hair was pinned back on both sides and cascaded in waves down her back; her large, greyish-blue eyes and thin lips had a refined expression. Her features were not quite regular, but her round face, with its large eyes, fine eyebrows, and soft little chin, was quite attractive and pleasant; her tall figure was supple, and her clothing—expensively simple—fitted her in a most pleasing manner.

Pestsova, as Biloselska called her friend, was short and plump; she had a thick neck, and her shorn, thick, clayish-coloured hair did not do much for her wide, ruddy face with its small grey eyes; but her features had a tender kindness about them, and her eyes reflected affability and a keen intelligence. The eyes of the viewer, however, involuntarily passed from that "kind, Russian face" to the figure of Biloselska . . . even though her eyes were more alluring than thoughtful.

"Ladies and gentlemen!" Biloselska invited everyone to have some grapes. "Monsieur Kuzmenko! Leave the atlas; come join us."

"Don't call me 'monsieur,'" Kuzmenko replied, applying himself to the grapes. "Choose whichever name you want—either Apollon, or Mykyta—but not monsieur."

Everyone laughed as they looked at the youth. "What do you mean?" Biloselska and Lyuba asked simultaneously. "Apollon or Mykyta!"

"It just so happens that I can narrate a very instructive story," Kuzmenko replied, pinching off some grapes. "You see, my dear mother is of the nobility—the Rabaza family; well, when she brought forth her beloved first son—namely me—she came up with the idea of calling him Apollon. It does have a nice ring to it, doesn't it? Apollon Stepanovych Kuzmenko. My father, an ordinary dweller of the steppes, took a strong dislike to this appelation; he laughed at my mother's whim, but she stuck to her guns: 'Oh, yes! Apollon—it has to be Apollon!' The time for the christening came. The godparents and guests arrived, and everything was progressing as it should. Until I was christened, however, my mother—in keeping with tradition—stayed at the back of the church.

"Well, they christened me, started passing out the wine, and carried the newly-baptised child to its mother. She blessed and kissed it, saying: 'Oh, my darling Apolloshenka!' And the godparents said: 'Apolloshenka? The boy was given another name.' 'What do you mean, another name?' So, they began telling her that Stepan Artemovych—my father, that is—told the priest to christen the child as Mykyta. Oh, that father of mine! My mother screamed: 'Mykyta!' and collapsed on the pillows in a fit of hysteria. But, then, what could she do? A christening can't be undone. So, the name stayed! My mother tried to make the best of it by giving me tender pet names—'Koko,' 'Totok,' and the like. But my father really liked me as Mykyta. He used to laugh whenever he introduced me: 'This is Apollon, christened as Mykyta!' And so you too, my noble young lady, may choose whichever you wish—Monsieur Apollon, or Mykyta Stepanovych!"

"Well, that's all very fine, Mikita Styepanych," Pestsova called out in Russian. "But don't throw the seeds around—you know that kind of behaviour is not looked upon kindly here."

"Oh, the devil take them, these Swiss! I always forget their ways of doing things. They've really got to me! Yesterday, after the rain, I walked across the room in my galoshes, and my landlady, *Frau* Froelicher, ran after me and almost licked the marks off with her tongue! The deuce take them! A most unpleasant people. They're always scrubbing everything—they've almost scrubbed away their human face! It's all so restrictive, so indecent!"

"That's true," Korniyevych observed. "The students here are also a trifle strange—pathetic, in fact."

"But it's very evident that they're Europeans. No, really, with every step you take, you feel you're in Europe," Kost stated. Rayisa supported him, saying that, in any event, relationships among the Europeans were more civilised.

"So what's so special about Europe! In my opinion, it's better to be a rough human being than a polished log," Kuzmenko pronounced.

The argument continued unabated.

"We're still supposed to go to the *Hohe* Promenade, ladies and gentlemen," Kuzmenko reminded them.

"Let's go! Let's go!" There was a general commotion as they left. Before long they were on the Promenade. It was magnificent—a wide walkway with poplars planted on either side. The trees, ancient and luxuriant, cast a dense shadow. Down below, there was a striking view of the lake; the water glittered, and white sails gleamed.

"Good health to you, O poplars!" Kuzmenko greeted the meditating trees that softly rustled their leaves in the breeze. Occasionally a leaf floated to the ground.

"They say the view is exceptionally beautiful here in the morning," Biloselska said.

"Let's come here tomorrow morning, just the two of us," Kost said softly to Lyuba. "Ring my doorbell, and I'll come out to meet you. Will you?"

"I . . . Yes, I will," Lyuba, hesitating slightly, replied, and then she rejoined the group.

Kost was left alone, leaning against a poplar. Biloselska came up to him, saying: "What are you thinking about so intently?" She knew how to be gracious to everybody, but it was easy to see that the handsome Kost was most to her liking.

Kuzmenko was conversing jokingly with Rayisa, and even managed to quarrel with Pestsova, taunting her that she had probably never seen poplars before in her life. Korniyevych was gazing intently at Lyuba's face, as if he wanted to guess what the expression on it meant.

"Well, ladies and gentlemen, it's fine to stroll about, but it's time to go home, to put our noses to the grindstone," Kuzmenko finally decided, as he moved away from a statue of Neheli—an ideal spot from which to enjoy the view.

They slowly made their way back. It was quite late already—a pleasant, gentle evening was descending. The princess and Pestsova were seen home first, and then Korniyevych and Kuzmenko turned off to their living quarters.

"That Kuzmenko is a strange fellow," Rayisa said, as she strolled alongside Lyuba and Kost.

"Well, I like him. He's frank, and it's very easy to talk to him," Lyuba defended Kuzmenko.

"I find nothing attractive in that frankness," Rayisa continued. "He clowns around and prattles away, spouting all sorts of nonsense. He really is a crafty Mykyta!"

"Did Korniyevych appeal to you?" Kost asked Lyuba.

"I don't know," she responded, turning away. "I haven't figured him out yet; he's so reserved."

They came to the young ladies' residence. Rayisa went on ahead to ring the doorbell.

"So you won't forget about the *Hohe* Promenade?" Kost softly asked Lyuba.

"No," she replied.

IX

Lyuba sat up late that evening—she had to make up for the time she had lost during the walk. But she woke up early, very early—and something stirred in her heart. Why was it beating like that? Was there something extraordinary in store for her today? Well, she would go for a walk with Kost Zahorovsky—but so what? It wasn't as if it were a date. Back home, she had walked alone with him many times. There was nothing different now. But a troubled flush crept into her face, and her hand trembled slightly as she dressed.

Rayisa was still sleeping. Well, it didn't matter! Lyuba was not hiding the fact that she was leaving the house; if Rayisa woke up, Lyuba would tell her that she was going for a walk on the *Hohe* Promenade. But Rayisa continued sleeping soundly, and Lyuba was not going to awaken her just to say: "I'm going already." Let her sleep if she wanted to.

Lyuba put on her coat and hat in front of the mirror—why were her eyes shining like that?—and, forgetting that there was no reason to conceal her actions, she walked out quietly, closing the door softly without locking it. The outside door would be locked by *Frau* Piltz

It was no longer summer, and so it was a trifle fresh outside—but still quite pleasant. It was early, and there was no one in the streets; Lyuba, her heels tapping sharply on the cobblestones, came across only a boy who was carrying bread in a large basket.

Here was Kost's residence. How quickly she had made her way here. She should ring the bell. But perhaps he was not up yet? She should wait for a while. But why should she stand here like this? Someone was coming down the street, and he might think that . . . Well, what could he think! Lyuba rang the doorbell—not even very softly. Did they hear it in the house? They heard it, and were opening the door. Oh! It was Kost who opened it!

"Greetings," he said joyfully. "I was beginning to think you wouldn't come!"

"But why wouldn't I come?" Lyuba blushed and looked embarrassed. "I was slightly delayed because I had to gather up my books; I'm going directly to the university from there."

Lyuba regained her composure and chattered on. Kost, who was ready to go, put on his black hat. The landlady, shutting the door after Kost, glanced askance at Lyuba, but she had no reason to do so. Lyuba and Kost strolled along casually, talking about the most ordinary matters—and quite loudly, at that. It was evident that there was nothing untoward about this walk; it was just that both of them were happy and felt joy in their hearts. What was wrong with that?

They reached the *Hohe* Promenade with its rows of tall, thick poplars that enclosed the deserted street stretching between them. It truly was sublime here in the morning! The sun's rays, breaking through the branches, settled on the walkway in broad swaths among the tree trunks, while farther on—oh, how splendid it was! The edges of the lake glittered with gold and, from a distance, the water was very clear and reflected a deeper colour than during the day. All the vegetation on the bank was fresh, green, and lush, as if it were springtime. The distant mountains were being transformed by delicate, shifting hues.

"Let's sit down," Kost said after they had spent some time revelling in the view. They seated themselves and suddenly fell silent. Lyuba turned her head away and gazed intently into the distance. Kost looked attentively at her books and her soft, slender hands.

"How are your classes coming along?" Kost inquired after a pause. "I don't know anything about them."

"Well, if you'd enrolled in the faculty of medicine, you'd know," Lyuba replied, in a gently joking manner.

"Medicine isn't what interests me. Its sphere of knowledge, its outermost limits do not satisfy my intellectual needs. I feel a need for broader perspectives, more space."

"For your fantasies?"

"For my thoughts," Kost responded, after a moment's silence.

"No, it's for your fantasies," the girl stated emphatically. "The precise framework within which a naturalist works does not suit you; you want to indulge in a free association of thoughts, flights into the past and the future that can be divined in their own way, as you wish, sometimes according to your own ideals. Of course, for this kind of thinking there's more freedom in your area, with all that history and philosophy."

"Perhaps you're partly right in what you're saying. But even in what is certain—what is known, as you have said, in its precise framework—there is more than meets the eye. It's more interesting to learn about the varied manifestations of the human soul, of thought, than about the soulless nature of a human body, contemplated purely as a collection of material elements governed by either physical or chemical laws."

Lyuba smiled: "So, you want to exist outside of the material world and its laws? It's too bad that it's impossible to do so. In any event, I see that you are a great idealist. How limited and base our realm of knowledge must seem to you. Especially the studies of insignificant students like us—like me, for example."

"Oh, no! Not at all! Study, learn, if you want to! This desire on your part is also a manifestation of your soul, of the powerful impulse of your thoughts!"

"This is some kind of metaphysics!"

"No, it's not metaphysics! And I want this elevation of your soul, these impulses of your intellect to save you from the trifling, soulless memorisation of facts in which petty minds become lost forever. I want you to see a transcendent goal beyond your work."

"I do see it."

"I'm convinced of this; that's why I asked you with sincere interest about your studies. And you shouldn't conceal anything from me; regardless of how different our work is, you must remember that I'm your closest friend. Just recall how, not that long ago, we played together in our childhood, when you called me Kost, and I called you Lyuba."

"But that was quite some time ago! Now, I can't understand how it was possible," Lyuba said, and she rose to her feet.

"Really? That means you've distanced yourself from me."

Lyuba wanted to deny this, but she could not think of a reply.

"You shouldn't distance me," Kost said softly once again, as he walked alongside Lyuba.

They continued strolling down the promenade, having forgotten all about the beauty of the morning and the landscape. People of leisure began to make their appearance on the promenade—Englishmen with books in hand, and others. The day had progressed noticeably. Lyuba and Kost walked casually to the street and, conversing quietly, headed for the university. As they parted, Kost silently pressed Lyuba's hand and followed her delicate, slender figure with a tender look. The girl felt so peaceful, so lovely, so complete. Only a slight flush on her face betrayed her recent anxiety. She sat down in her favourite spot that Korniyevych was saving for her.

X

Korniyevych was often Lyuba's neighbour now, and they became friends. They conversed often, but always in a reserved manner, and only about the lectures, their notes, or books. He dropped by Lyuba's place several times and, one time, finding her home alone, he sat for quite a while and drank some tea with her, but their conversation did not assume either a more intimate or jocular tone.

Lyuba calmly observed his good looks—straight, thick, blond hair combed simply to the back, with a single strand falling on his wide, pale face that had a little furrow between the eyebrows; intelligent, calm dark eyes; a thin, energetic mouth, with the lower lip protruding slightly; and a *kozak* chin. Broad shoulders, a powerful chest, and a fresh face gave Korniyevych the appearance of a strong, healthy man—he even seemed older than the rest of the students. This strength—both physical and intellectual—was noted by Lyuba; it impressed her and, at the same time, distanced her from him. It seemed to her that his strong character was overly confident and cold.

Lyuba felt uncomfortable whenever she noticed Korniyevych looking intently at her with his large, calm, penetrating eyes—it always seemed to her that a condescending smile might appear on his face at any moment. And, sitting beside her on the bench, he did watch her quite often, gazing at her curly head and her soft, slender neck, as she sat bent over her writing. More than once, Lyuba would stealthily lift her head, catch his look and, bending down still lower, write even more diligently.

A couple of times, Korniyevych accompanied Kuzmenko when the latter stopped by to see the young ladies. In strong contrast to Kuzmenko's humorous demeanour, Korniyevych seldom relaxed and rarely said anything; in general, he preferred to observe others rather than draw attention to himself. Lyuba was happier when Korniyevych came with Kuzmenko—the latter did not oppress her, and when he was around, she was a cheerful and frank friend, and a rather bold one at that, responding, in kind, to all of his jokes and provocations. She feared Kuzmenko's loud roars of laughter less than she feared Korniyevych's slightest smile.

"Well, my fellow countrywoman, have you dissected frogs yet?" Kuzmenko asked.

"Yes," Lyuba replied. "You've seen my lab specimens."

"And then you soap your hands three time when you wash them?"

"Four times!"

"But can you cut off the head of a live frog?"

"No, I can't."

"Yech! That's the kind of dissector you are! There you have it—a woman's soul, and a young lady's to boot! But oh, they're ever so keen! As the saying goes—the blacksmith forges, and the frog sticks out its leg, as well."

But Lyuba, unoffended, flung out in reply: "There, there now! Just make sure that you're keen!"

"We'll see, we'll see! I'll bring a frog to your quarters. What will you do with it? In a laboratory, of course, you do what's expected of you; you want to impress the lab technician and the other students, and so the courage born of despair supports you. But what will it be like at home?"

And the next time that Kuzmenko came with Korniyevych, he actually did bring an aquatic frog in a jar, and under his arm he had a little board and a box with a good microscope.

"This is for you. Here!" Kuzmenko said, placing the jar on the table. "And I've brought along a little board, because your German landlady would hang herself if she saw something like this happening on her table. Well, Miss Experimenter, please!" With these words, Kuzmenko took Lyuba jokingly by the hand and led her to the table. She was laughing happily.

"It's wonderful that you've brought all this," Rayisa said, as she bent over the table. "I have to do an experiment."

"Do it, do it!" Kuzmenko urged her, almost smirking.

Korniyevych was also smiling a bit as he looked at the girls. He reached into a box for the galvanised battery he had brought. "I'll demonstrate the experiment I told you about," he said to Lyuba.

"Fine, that's good!" she replied like an obedient schoolgirl.

"Well, Madam *Rana temporaria [temporary frog]*, if you please," Kuzmenko joked, pulling the frog out of the jar. The animal stirred; then, with ridiculously bulging eyes, it sat without moving, as if it were a lifeless mass.

The students examined and discussed it. Korniyevych explained to Lyuba, in great detail, the important effect nerves had on blood vessels—how a bigger or smaller strain on the nerves constricts or expands the blood vessels and causes a change in the flow of the blood. Using the microscope, he showed her the ending of the arterial nerve.

Lyuba watched his strong hands perform the tasks, noted how easily he spoke, and thought: "He knows so much, and he does everything so dextrously." And, folding her arms, she listened seriously to him, as she would listen to a professor—she did not want him to think that he had a frivolous audience, and that it was not worthwhile to explain things to her carefully.

Kuzmenko tried to get her attention with a joke, but Lyuba just smiled and did not budge—Korniyevych was looking at her seriously with his dark eyes.

"Well, is the lecture over, Slobodian Ukraine?" Kuzmenko inquired. "Let's put the demonstrations away now. Just leave Miss Rayisa a leg, so she can dissect it at her leisure."

The table was half cleared off when the doorbell rang. Kost entered and exchanged greetings with everyone. Observing the look of revulsion on his face when he glanced at the remains of the demonstration, Lyuba hurried to clean the table up as quickly as she could. Kost sat down at another table without saying anything.

"Well, Konstantyn Mykhaylovych, how are you?" Rayisa hastened to engage in conversation the always welcome guest. "I haven't seen you for a long time. When are you going to deliver us a lecture?"

"It would be a good idea, it really would," Lyuba's voice rang out effortlessly, "because we're so busy here that we don't know anything about the fate of the human race."

Lyuba had hardly finished saying this, when the doorbell rang again, and Biloselska and Pestsova walked swiftly into the room.

"The girls are really hot on the trail of that Zahorovsky chap," Kuzmenko said to Korniyevych, picking up his microscope. "Let's get our things together, and away we go!"

"Come along with us, Apollon Styepanych!" Pestsova called out. "We're going to the mountains."

"Ah! Diana herself is calling us! We have to go! What is your patronymic? Diana Makaryevna or Terentyevna?"

"Ilyichina," Pestsova replied laughingly.

"Ah! Ilyichina! Wonderful! Well, Korniyevych, there's still hope for us—they're inviting us as well. Let's go, ladies and gentlemen! My dear fellow countrywoman, Rayisa Pavlivna—or rather, Militrysa Kirbityevna—let's go!"

They walked down the street. Kost was in the lead; Rayisa's little black hat bobbed up and down on one side of him, while Biloselska's blue muslin shawl drifted over his other shoulder.

XI

The days passed by. While it was still warm outside, everything was fine, but then the cold began to set in. If you dashed outdoors lightly dressed, the cold went right through you—especially if the hateful wind was blowing. It was also cold in the house, the devil take it!

Of course, it was cold—there were no double windows and no stoves with large brick ovens; the windows were large and had only single panes, while the tiny stove—as Kuzmenko put it—was "a pitiful mockery" of a brick oven-stove; the little pipe-like thing in which coal was burned stood in the room like a post for placards in the street—small and miserable. You could only warm your hands by it—if there was enough coal!—but you could forget about heating a room up properly. It's true that the winter was not long, and there were no heavy frosts; nevertheless, it was vexing! So the students suffered from the cold, especially at night and first thing in the morning, before they warmed up a little by walking around outdoors.

But the work of the students at the university was coming along as it should. They studied, worked, and met from time to time. Now, however, they felt lonelier for their kin and for everything back in their native land. They avidly read newspapers and journals from Russia whenever they came across them. And, as for letters from back home—well, it goes without saying how much they appreciated them!

Both young ladies received many letters from their mothers. Lady Brahova wrote more, even though she rarely had anything cheerful to say. Mariya Petrivna wrote shorter letters, but she never complained about anything, and only pleaded with Lyuba to write more often and tell her how she was doing. But these uncomplaining letters always brought grief and sorrow to Lyuba— she would fold them silently, and sigh.

And so, life slowly went on. Even though their desire to do well in their studies had increased the pressure on the girls, and they appeared to have lost a lot of weight, things would not have been all that bad if they had not run out of money. They had never had to live on a budget before, so they did not know how to apportion their money to meet their needs. At first, they had spent more; it was understandable, of course, because they had to settle in—but there had also been more money then! Later, there was barely enough to meet their daily needs. And now, they were running short of money to buy coal, so they had to use it sparingly. Actually, things were even worse than that! If one of them did not receive money from home quite soon, there was no telling what might happen; they both had only a few francs left, along with some small change.

And so, one day, having returned from the laboratory to their cold quarters, the girls were feeling a bit depressed. Lyuba, her legs tucked under her, was reading a book, while Rayisa paced the room rapidly, looking intently at a piece of paper and reciting quite loudly from it.

At that moment, Kuzmenko unexpectedly dropped by. "Greetings!" he said. "This weather is fit only for dogs! It's been blowing now for three days and nights. Brr . . . Do you know why I've come?" he asked Lyuba.

"Why have you come?" Lyuba repeated his question with a smile.

"To warm up! It's so devilishly cold at my place that dogs would freeze there. Perhaps you're thinking that I'm speaking in a figurative sense—that I want to warm myself in the presence of tender girls, next to their warm souls? No! I simply want to warm up in a warmer room!"

Lyuba smiled, and Kuzmenko took off his plaid cape.

"Well, what are you forging, Militrysa Kirbityevna?" Kuzmenko inquired, approaching Rayisa and peering into her notebook.

"Oh, leave me alone Kuzmenko, spare me your silly remarks," Rayisa retorted in annoyance.

"Ah! She's memorising some chemistry," Kuzmenko said. "That's why she's so shrewish! Well, carry on with your studying, carry on! It's commendable!" And he walked over to where Lyuba was sitting.

"But you know," he said, after talking with Lyuba for a while, "it's not all that warm at your place either! By God, it's really cold!" And he bundled himself up in his plaid cape once again. "Why don't you light a fire in the stove?"

"We've already lit one today," Lyuba responded.

"Oh. Well, that's all right then," Kuzmenko said, glancing at Lyuba's lowered head. "Listen to me for a moment, my fellow countrywoman. I have something to ask you. Would you be so kind as to lend me some money?"

"How much do you need?"

"About five francs."

"No . . . I can't lend you that much," Lyuba said, and she blushed. "I can give you two, if you'd like . . ."

"Ha-ha-ha! My poor fellow countrywoman! She's sitting there with two francs. Ha-ha-ha! Oh, the poor dear! Oh yes, I can see it now—she's sitting there with her legs tucked under her! Ha-ha-ha!"

"Why are you laughing?" Lyuba asked in confusion. "We're not down to just two francs."

"Well, then, perhaps three! Ha-ha-ha!"

"There's absolutely nothing to laugh at! Even if we didn't have any money, so what? Both Rayisa and I are expecting some from home any day now . . ."

"It's not enough to expect some. I'm expecting some too."

"Well, that's good. In the meantime, take these two francs and that's the end of the matter. Go ahead, take them."

"Well, God be with you," Kuzmenko, still laughing, replied. "Do you think I'm a highway robber? That—may God have mercy on my soul—I'd snatch your last *kopiyka [penny]* from you? What are you thinking? Oh, my dear fellow countrywoman! Ha-ha-ha!"

Lyuba, angry and troubled, was ready to cry. "Well, if you don't want them, it's up to you." She blushed furiously.

"Well now, don't be annoyed, my dear Lyuba! Don't be annoyed!" Kuzmenko took Lyuba by the hand. "Oh, my God! How cold your hands are. I didn't notice it at first. My poor, dear child! That's what it's like—living in a foreign land!"

"Oh, go away!"

"I'm going, I'm going! Farewell, my dearest dove!"

"Won't you take the money?" Lyuba shouted after him.

"No," Kuzmenko replied. He smiled and walked out of the room. The next day, Kuzmenko ran in once again. He greeted Rayisa and Lyuba cheerfully, and said: "It's hard to believe how things work out sometimes! Yesterday, I was living in poverty, but when I came home there was a notification for me—my money had come. Today, I rushed as fast as I could to the post office. And now—may the devil perish—we're rich! Permit me, my fellow countrywoman!" Kuzmenko placed ten francs in front of Lyuba.

"What's this?" the girl asked in amazement.

"Take them! It means that I'm lending them to you."

"But why? I don't need them . . ."

"Oh my God! Is it fitting for such highly enlightened maidens to be broke? I'm telling you—take them! When you receive your money in the mail you can return them. Well, I can't tarry here any longer—not even with two beautiful fellow countrywomen; I must be off to the university! Farewell!" And he dashed out of the room.

Kuzmenko was telling the truth, but not the whole truth; he had received some money, but not through the mail. After coming home from his visit with the girls, he had gathered together some of his belongings and taken them to a pawn shop. Not only had he managed to get some money for himself "for coal," he had also been able to help his poor little fellow countrywoman.

XII

Spring! It was spring! In distant Poltava snow still lay on the fields, but here, violets were already blooming. The joyful sky turned blue, and the nearby mountains adorned themselves in bright green tapestries. Only their eternally white tops were still covered with snow—and even it was melting around the edges under the caressing eyes of enchantress-spring. From white-clad mountain tops, swiftly flowing streams rushed noisily into green valleys, refilling blue lakes into which the bright spring sun was gazing, scattering its rays. On the verdant highlands, bells tinkled, and the shepherd's horn sounded different, happier! Echoes resonated in the clear air.

The young people were intoxicated by it all. They had never greeted such a spring. They needed to study, to stay at home with their books, but it was impossible to do so; they were drawn to the bright azure expanses. They had gone walking yesterday, and the day before yesterday, and they were preparing to go into the mountains tomorrow as well—this time, somewhere farther! An entire group of them was assembling.

"Oh, there's just no time; it's terrible! I don't think I'll go," Lyuba said to Kost, who had stepped in to invite her to come along.

"Please come, I'm begging you. If you don't go, then I won't go either," Kost said.

"Well, what am I to do? I'll go, then," Lyuba agreed.

The lively party left the city behind and entered the mountains. Quite a few young people—as youthful as spring itself—had congregated. Among them there were a few new faces, as well as the familiar ones—Korniyevych, Kuzmenko, "Diana" Pestsova, and Princess Biloselska in a new little hat with a long white muslin veil.

"How pretty Biloselska looks today!" Lyuba said to Kost.

"She's more refined and slender than pretty," he responded.

"She flaunts herself and puts on too many airs," Rayisa added.

They all gathered into a noisy, joking, laughing cluster, and began unpacking the food and drinks they had brought along. After a brisk walk in the fresh air, everything was appetising.

"Mikita Styepanych! Do you want some beer?"

"Yes, I do, I do," Kuzmenko replied, as he accepted the bottle of beer held out to him by Pestsova. "But how are we to drink it? Or should we drink it right out of the bottle? Share and share alike!"

"Of course! No need for ceremony here!" Pestsova called out. "Do you want some cheese?"

"Why wouldn't I? Give us some cheese as well."

"Aha, Mr. Mykyta. I've noticed something," Lyuba said softly. "Diana seems to be wooing you."

"Why shouldn't she? Do you think that no one is supposed to woo me?"

"Did I say that?"

"It's only you who does not like me," Kuzmenko continued.

"Who told you I don't like you? I like you very much!"

"Uh-huh, very much! If you hadn't added these words, it would have been better."

Lyuba was a trifle embarrassed. "Well, if you don't want the 'very much,' then there's no need to like you at all."

"Aha! Now she's taking it back! Fine! That's enough about wooing, the devil take it! Right? I'll go and fetch you some food. Oh, but I see that Korniyevych has already done that. Just look at what he's bringing you! I say, there, how dare you look after my lady?" Kuzmenko said jokingly to Korniyevych, who really was bringing Lyuba something to eat.

"But how can she be yours," Korniyevych responded, "if you don't take care of her? As you can see, I also want her to be mine."

He sat down by Lyuba and passed her some food.

Lyuba found it strange to hear Korniyevych say something like that—and he had said it so forthrightly.

And then, along came Kost. Having managed to disengage himself from the attentions of the princess, he was now heading towards Lyuba: "Do you want some wine, Lyubov Vasylivna? Here's a glass for you."

Kuzmenko stood up in a pathetic pose and declaimed:

"Before the Spanish noble lady
Stand three chivalrous knights!"

"It's true, it's true! There are too many of them around one lady," said the small, dusky Kropotova, sitting down beside Kuzmenko, and exhaling thin streams of smoke from her cigarette. Through the haze, her eyes shone lovingly.

In a short while, the young people regrouped and started out again. They spread over the mountain and moved on to another valley.

"Oh, my God! Just look at all the violets!" Kuzmenko shouted. "Hey, everyone! This must be an illusion—the ground is completely covered with violets!"

And truly, for eyes that hailed from the steppes, there was an immeasurable host of delightful alpine spring violets in this valley; the grass was a sea of blue. Some of the young people picked the flowers, while others, their hands stuck in their pockets, trampled over them arrogantly; everyone moved farther into a valley that wound quite narrowly between the mountains. Off to one side, the loud gurgling of a fairly large stream could be heard as it cascaded down the mountain.

And then, everyone reached the summit and gazed at the mountains shimmering in the distance. The sun was setting, and the Alps were afire—the sun could no longer be seen, but its golden glow was gleaming on the mountain tops. The colours fluctuated, merged, glowed—pale rosy-yellow, gold, pink, hot yellow—then they burned more brightly, like coals in a huge fire without any flames. One could look at this spectacle forever. Then, it slowly began to fade—the hues modulated once again, but more gradually, gently, delicately. Light shadows crept into the rosy tones, struggled with it, and wrapped the mountainous distance in a dark-blue mist. The fire was dying.

"Do you want to cross over to the other side?" Kost asked Lyuba. "Give me your hand; let's go."

They descended lower into the mountain pass, coming to a foot bridge made of two unsteady boards placed over a foaming stream. The water, cascading down the mountain, jumped over the rocks, showering the boards. Kost took Lyuba's hand and led her across the little bridge; laughing happily, Lyuba gingerly followed him. After they crossed the stream, Kost could have let go of her hand, but he continued holding it, leading her down a small path on the other side of the pass.

"We'll sit down here for a while. It looks so inviting under that tree," Kost suggested.

"The others will be here soon," Lyuba said. She sat down, off to one side, over by the mountain path, and stretched out her legs. Why was Kost sitting so close to her? Why were his eyes filled with such tenderness?

"Are you tired?" he inquired, taking her by the hand. "Are you tired, Lyubochka?"

"No, I'm not tired," Lyuba replied, freeing her hand and deeply inhaling the mountain air, in which a touch of evening coolness could already be detected. "How would it be possible to become tired during such a pleasant walk? It's truly beautiful here."

"It's enchantingly beautiful! My soul soars when I gaze at nature here. No, regardless of what anyone says, nature is a powerful force, and it has a great influence on one's soul. It's impossible to agree with the newest theory that a poet's delight in nature is a petty feeling to which a thinking man should not submit. It's untrue! This feeling is not petty and base—it elevates us above the trivialities of life; it tunes one's soul to what is great and good."

Noise and laughter could be heard; the rest of the group was approaching. Lyuba rose to her feet. "Let's go," she said.

"Yes, let's go! This path will lead us to the valley where we were all sitting. Let's go on ahead!" Kost took Lyuba's hand and placed it on his arm, but Lyuba did not lean on it; she walked quietly, aware of the closeness of Kost's heart . . .

"Lyubochka! Darling!" Kost said when they reached the valley. He stroked her trembling hand and kissed it lovingly, sensitively. His eyes misted over, and he wanted to draw closer the supple figure that was pulling away from him.

Then a shout was heard quite close to them: "Zahorovsky! Where are you? Zahorovsky!"

"Aha! Look where they are already! They arrived here sooner than we did," Pestsova said, as she entered the valley with Kuzmenko.

The others followed them. Rayisa, strolling arm in arm with a tall, blond young gentleman, was laughing animatedly, making it clear that she did not consider herself to be part of an intimate couple, and that she was simply walking like this for a lark. Lyubochka was embarrassed. She hardly dared to look up—and when she did, she met Korniyevych's penetrating gaze. It seemed to her that he sensed her discomfiture, and she once again lowered her eyes.

The shadows were falling thickly now. It was growing late and dusk was falling. By the time they drew near the city, it was completely dark. Zurich sparkled with fires; far away, like stars in a darkened heaven, lights were visible on the wide lowlands of the hills that stretched on both sides of the Limat.

"This was what it was like when we first rode into Zurich," Kost said to Lyuba. "Do you remember?"

She remained silent. Kost's voice seemed to have changed and deepened.

"Are you angry with me, Lyuba?" Kost inquired softly. "Forgive me, my darling." Yet Kost was ready to do once again what he was asking forgiveness for!

XIII

Time flowed on. The months went by, and then entire semesters. The students were now familiar with all the seasons of the year. There is no point in hiding the fact that they had some "romances"—are there young people anywhere who do not?—but they also applied themselves to their studies.

The young ladies were now real students; they no longer felt themselves to be insignificant pupils. Oh, no! There were even some male students they could outdo and outperform, not only in discussions about what they were learning, but also in the practical work.

The professors praised highly the ability of the *"Russky [Ukrainian]"* female students. They were amazed by them—could they have expected anything like it from descendants of Sarmatians?—and delighted in their excellently executed dissections. They wrote about them in journals, defended them from the sharp tongues of reactionaries, and testified to the seriousness of women's academic pursuits. All this, of course, encouraged the young ladies.

Rayisa was the one who rose head and shoulders above the others; Kuzmenko even said that she had "turned up her nose." Her behaviour was the most serious, her voice the most assertive. She learned to talk in the tone of a person who knows everything, even in situations where she did not know very much.

She ingratiated herself into working under the supervision of a certain professor, *Herr* Stockmann, known in Zurich not only as a scholar, but as a practitioner. *Herr* Stockmann was a middle-aged, self-made man; he was a hard worker from a bourgeois family, and he valued individual striving and determination to attain one's goal. He began to look with respect at *Fräulein [Miss] Bragoff*, who sat so attentively in his laboratory. The expression in his colourless, almost glassy eyes, merged harmoniously with her hard look and demeanour.

Herr Professor praised Rayisa's work, directed her studies for a short time, and once even gave her a couple of books to read from his own library. There was no ulterior motive in the attention that he paid the beautiful Rayisa, although it is true that when Stockmann's young blue-eyed assistant spoke highly of the beauty of his special student, Stockmann said: *"Ja, sie ist sehr schön [Yes,*

she's very beautiful]." But the words were said with a total lack
of emotion, as if the conversation were about a figure embroidered
on a pillow, or a mannequin made out of plaster.

After beginning to study with Stockmann, Rayisa flaunted
herself even more. Her tone irritated her modest friend and
roommate. The truth is, however, that there was still another
reason for the difficulties and hostility that arose between the two
girls; it had not caused an open rift as yet, but it could be felt all
too plainly in their conversations and interactions.

For a long time, Rayisa had been turning her gracious attention
to Kost Zahorovsky. Up to now, however, Kost had been
completely taken with Lyuba, his childhood friend, and so, when
Lyuba became aware of Rayisa's attentions to Kost, she simply
dismissed the situation, and when she saw that it was becoming
more evident, she concealed a mocking smile.

God only knows when the matter took a completely different
turn. Kost no longer avoided Rayisa, as he had in the past, and
Rayisa's voice became more confident when she addressed Kost,
and, for that matter, Lyuba as well. It may be that Kost
Zahorovsky, who at first was repelled by Rayisa's strident
character, began to fall under the sway of her imposing appearance
and the respected position she had gained for herself among her
peers. Seeing Rayisa's great self-confidence, and hearing about the
remarkable erudition with which she distinguished herself, he
began to see in her "a great, feminine, intellectual power," "an
energetic type of woman," and so on. And finally, Kost fell into a
trap set for him.

Rayisa came up with the idea of taking a little trip—one that
had some scholarly merit. She decided to explore the lake in
Zurich during her leisure time and gather molluscs in a remote,
quiet inlet, where, she said, there were interesting varieties. She
did not invite Lyuba to join her, because the latter was not feeling
well and was unlikely to come along. Just at that time, she met
Kost, presumably accidentally, and asked him to accompany her.
Kost had not been out on the lake beyond the lakefront in the city,
so he agreed with pleasure—it was only a four-hour trip, and there
was a steamer going back in the evening.

They arrived in the suburb of Kusnacht, a pretty little spot,
where the inlet was quite calm. While Rayisa searched for
molluscs, Kost delighted in the beautiful landscapes. They were

supposed to return to Zurich that same day, but they just happened to miss the steamer on its return trip past Kusnacht and had to remain until morning. Well, in the evening, the two of them strolled around for a while and gazed at the view over the lake; the night turned out to be a starry one, filled with moonlight. Well, there was a moon, and an attractive young woman on a secluded walk. No one knows if Rayisa caught many snails at Kusnacht, but Kost was partially entangled in her net.

At first, Lyuba did not notice the new relationship, and even if she had, the friendship of their childhood years need not have been affected. Kost did not avoid their home; but Lyuba began to notice that he no longer came to see her. He would arrive, greet her, look around—not unpleasantly, but indifferently—and then ask: "Isn't Rayisa Pavlina at home?"

"No, she hasn't come home yet."

"Will she be here soon?"

Lyuba was amazed by this turn of events. At first, she just looked on in astonishment, then her face began to betray both her hurt and her contempt. But she never said anything explicit about it to Kost, and, most certainly, not to Rayisa. She remained silent and kept her distance, giving Kost and Rayisa the opportunity to be alone.

In time, not unexpectedly, the two girls ended up living in separate quarters. Rayisa found a room closer to her place of work with Stockmann and took up residence in it alone; Lyuba accepted Pestsova as a roommate, because the latter begged her to. Lyuba guessed why Pestsova wanted to move in with her, but she pretended that she did not suspect anything.

Kuzmenko, as usual, was a frequent visitor in Lyuba's living quarters; Korniyevych also dropped by occasionally, and even though he did not come over more often than before, he behaved more warmly; Kost came to see Lyuba only when he was with someone else—he never came to see her by himself.

XIV

"Have you heard that Brahova is going to give a public lecture on Wednesday?" a tall, scrawny student asked Korniyevych.

"No. What research has she done?"

"Oh, something very interesting—about the lungs and their functioning."

"Have you heard that Brahova is going to present the results of her investigation in the lecture hall? And the general public is going to be admitted as well!" Kroptova told Lyuba.

"No. What research has she done?"

"Oh, they say it's something very scholarly and well-done— something about the lungs! Stockmann himself has praised it and is arranging for the lecture."

This news resounded throughout the university.

Wednesday arrived. Students bustled about, casually conversing in the corridor outside the lecture hall. Individuals hurried in, and entire groups of people shoved to get by. Everyone was talking about this special event: "Well? Will it be soon?" "Has Brahova arrived yet?" "Do you know the contents of Brahova's lecture?" "Oh, of course, it must be very interesting!" and so on.

"Well, tell me, Kuzmenko—isn't this an important moment? For the first time within the walls of the University of Zurich, a woman is going to give a public lecture. What do you say about that, eh?"

"Nothing! I'll listen to the lecture, and then I'll tell you."

"Well, you're allowing your scepticism and your analytical bent to encroach on everything!"

Yes, indeed, a small opposition to the lecture could also be discerned. Princess Biloselska had a sceptical expression on her usually pleasant lips. She had never considered herself a friend of Brahova; whenever she had visited Rayisa and Lyuba in their quarters, she had bestowed her warm benevolence only on Lyuba.

Kost showed up as well, flinging back his long hair with his pale, elegant hand. He had grown a beard during his years in Zurich—a very silky one—and his features had become still finer and more sharply sculpted. His head seemed to be in the clouds. Today, in particular, Kost appeared to be troubled, as if he were slightly dazed; he exchanged greetings without looking at people or saying anything; he just walked along and looked straight ahead.

"Where are you going in such a hurry, Konstantyn Mykhaylovych?" Biloselska asked him as his rapid stride brought him face to face with her. "It won't begin for a while yet."

"Ah!" Kost said. Bereft of his quick wit and feeling a bit embarrassed, he followed Biloselska.

She smirked slightly and was silent for a moment; then she began speaking with her enchanting smile: "It's doubtful whether you'll find the lecture interesting! You're not a medical student."

"It doesn't matter! The topic is of no concern here! What is interesting is the fact itself—it's the achievement that has great significance. A woman is assuming the right to place her foot on the lecturer's podium!"

"Her 'little foot,'" Biloselska corrected him.

"Let it be 'a little foot!'" Kost agreed, smiling. "But in any event, *to do it*! And it is this fact that has such an immense meaning—a societal meaning, if you will; it's the full recognition of women's rights in such an important, elevated sphere as science. It's proof that an intelligent woman can break out from the routine forms and demands of living that have, for so long, kept her from the light and, more importantly, from independent, scholarly pursuits. It's proof that our women are able not only to listen, but to expound the scientific word from a podium."

"You're a very eloquent defender of our cause! God grant us more people like you!" Biloselska observed with the same smile. "But, looking at the fact personally, there's no reason to be too happy about it or to make too much of it—who knows how taxing this research was for the lady lecturer, and how soon she could make public the results of another investigation."

"I'm not taking a personal perspective. All the same, I think that if Brahova has the energy, initiative, and erudition to appear in public with a scholarly lecture, then there is personal merit in it as well."

Biloselska caught Kost's dispirited look; turning her head towards him, she smiled cunningly and fluttered her long eyelashes. Kost's eyes fastened on the poised and supple figure swaying beside him like a blade of grass—a figure which he had not noticed before. Biloselska took out a delicate handkerchief and wiped off a sleeve she had brushed against the white walls; the fragrance of the refined perfume "Ilang-ilang'y" wafted through the air.

"Where does she get such fine perfume?" Kost thought. "And she really knows how to dress—the modest clothing of a student always look so alluring and elegant on her."

While Kost was observing Biloselska, Lyuba and Korniyevych walked by. Coming abreast of Kost, Lyuba began conversing more animatedly with her companion, as if she did not see Zahorovsky and the princess.

"Greetings, Kalynovska," Biloselska called out, as she and Kost caught up to them.

Lyuba responded to their greetings. In the last while she had grown a trifle paler. Today, she looked thinner, as well; but her eyes were lively, and there was a smile on her lips.

"Why are you in such a hurry?" the princess inquired. "Come along, we'll chat for a while. You won't be offended if I take your lady away from you Korniyevych, will you?"

"My companion is free, her own person! She may go with anyone she wants to," Korniyevych replied.

"Well, then, come along, come along," Biloselsksa said amiably, wanting to link arms with Lyuba.

"No," Lyuba responded, meeting Korniyevych's look. "It's awkward to walk three abreast." And, moving on with Korniyevych, she could be heard saying: "No, I still think that Brahova's lecture will be of great significance—she's worked very hard. In any event, she will have the honour of being the first woman to present her scholarly work at a public lecture."

"Well, this fact in itself is not of great merit," Korniyevych replied. "In fact, it imposes an even greater need for congruence between the value of the work and the courage of the lecturer. For if you decide to make such a presentation, then it must convey something significant. Because there's no point in just putting on a show—that's more shameful than praiseworthy."

Suddenly everyone stirred: "Brahova's coming!" "It's Brahova!" "Where is she?" "There she is, walking in with Stockmann! See?" "Come on! Come on!" Everyone moved noisily into the lecture hall. Silence fell.

Rayisa stood at the podium. She did not look as courageous as might have been expected; it was apparent that she was somewhat apprehensive, after all.

The public—it is a terrifying word! Most of the audience was known to Rayisa, but even so, gathered together in a large assembly that was hushed with anticipation, they seemed far more intimidating than at an ordinary get-together. Besides, in addition to the students, there was a sizeable group of professors and some members of the public—that completely foreign public. Excited by the news from the university that there was to be a "lecture by a woman," they had also come to listen; and even those who were totally indifferent to the content of the lecture prepared themselves to listen and wondered: "Well?" "What will it be like?"

Everyone was looking at Rayisa's figure in her black dress, cinched at the waist with a shiny belt, and adorned with a little white collar and a gold brooch. A fine gold watch chain on her chest rose and fell in time with her anxious breathing; her pale face stood out clearly against her black attire and her dark, smoothly combed hair. In her hands she held a small notebook from which she was about to read.

First, however, with a serious mien and shining eyes, she looked into the expanse filled with expectant heads and made a few extemporaneous comments. Then she began to read what she had written. As she went along, she regained her composure and read freely, in a somewhat monotonous and muffled voice. The members of the audience, not entranced by the content of what, at first, they had listened to with rapt attentiveness, slowly began to exchange remarks and look around in all directions.

The lecture, however, was brief. The lecturer was already finishing it in a completely calm, deliberate voice. She pronounced the final words almost too firmly and loudly.

Rayisa stepped down from the podium to the sound of enthusiastic applause. People surrounded her on all sides; they were congratulating her and shaking her hand. She became animated, the colour returned to her face, and her voice took on its usual tone. Laughing happily, she responded to some of the remarks, made her way to the exit, and disappeared. *Herr* Stockmann, contentedly stroking his grey whiskers, walked away with the other professors, talking about his "learned creation."

Kroptova ran up to Lyuba, saying: "Listen! Some of us have decided to hold a party. It's only fitting! We'll invite Brahova because it's mostly in her honour. We really should honour her! Do come! We'll be meeting at our place." And she ran off into the crowd.

As the audience dispersed, Lyuba fell behind and became parted from her friends. She came home alone. Her head was aching, and she could not collect her thoughts. But she had to decide—should she go to the party, or not? She paced the room, thinking it over.

Her thoughts bored through her mind and flip-flopped, but she could not make a decision. She would say to herself that she really should go, because if she didn't Rayisa would think that she had truly caused her so much pain that Lyuba could not be a witness to her triumph, or that she, Lyuba, was purposely making a point with her absence. Rayisa might even think that she was jealous. She had to go! They had invited her because they considered her to be in Rayisa's inner circle of friends.

Then, her thoughts flipped once again in her head, and she decided not to go—why did she have to go? As if bowing in reverence! The devil take her! What next! Well, she, Lyuba, simply did not want to go, and that was that!

This lecture was not a great event, and not at all because Brahova had given it—the presenter was irrelevant. In Lyuba's opinion, there was nothing important in the lecture, nothing that was truly worthy of giving her ovations of any kind.

"I won't go! I don't want to!" Lyuba decided, presumably for the last time. A minute later, however, something heavy and contradictory pounded at her thoughts: "Perhaps I should go? Perhaps they'll say . . ." Lyuba—weary, pale, her suffering visible on her face—continued pacing the room. She did not understand that her indecisiveness was a type of psychosis; she was ill, and the flow of blood through her brain was constricted . . . She continued pacing back and forth.

Oh! Someone was coming to her door! Probably to take her to the party! Well, what would she say? No, she would not go; she would not go, no matter what! *"Herein [Come in]!"*

With her permission, Korniyevych entered the room. "Have you had dinner yet?" he inquired. "Let's go! I came here directly from the restaurant when I saw that you weren't there. Let's go!"

His completely forthright and calm words about something so far removed from what she was debating revived Lyuba like a refreshing drink.

"Yes, let's go!" she responded in a voice that was unconsciously lively, and whose tone surprised even her. The outdoor air was bracing and rejuvenating.

Korniyevych was saying that on the way over he had dropped in to see some acquaintances whose children he tutored, and he had borrowed a new and very interesting volume of a Russian journal. If Lyuba wanted to, they could read it after dinner; in fact, it had to be read that evening, because he had to return it the next day.

"Oh, good!" Lyuba said. "What's in it?"

"There's a story by Slyeptsov, a few new verses by Nekrasov, and an excellent 'internal review.'"

"Oh, that's splendid! Slyeptsov writes very well."

"I knew that you like him too. We'll read it together."

"That's wonderful!" Lyuba kept saying.

In the restaurant, they found Kuzmenko seated at their customary table. The dinner was a cheerful one. Lyuba chattered and joked animatedly with Kuzmenko. Korniyevych made sure that she ate, and asked for his favourite wine—a wine with which he had treated Lyuba and Kuzmenko many times. Lyuba laughed and drank some of it. The dinner and the wine lifted her spirits.

"Well, Brahova really fired off some lecture!" Kuzmenko said quite unexpectedly.

"It was a woefully empty lecture," Korniyevych added. "I didn't expect anything like it. There was nothing in it."

"Well, you can't go so far as to say there was nothing in it," Lyuba objected.

"But he's right—there was nothing in it!" Kuzmenko said. "What did she say? The whole lecture amounted to no more than the tears shed by a cat—all of five pages in length, and nothing on any of them. I truly thought she'd have something new to say about the lungs and how they function. I even thought I'd use it in my doctoral dissertation one day. But, as it turned out, the mountain gave birth to a mouse! Well, the mob, of course, is just that—a mob, and so it applauded! I think that if Brahova had stuck her tongue out at them from the podium, they would have clapped their hands in the same way!"

"Now, really!" Lyuba said forcefully.

"No, really," Kuzmenko continued. "What was stated in that learned lecture? That the lungs are comprised of two sacks, that they start at the bronchial tubes and end in capillaries, and that human beings breathe with their lungs. Well, every fool already knows that a person breathes with his lungs, and not with his nose!"

"Well, let's allow the fact that the nose is involved as well," Korniyevych interjected.

"Yes, Slobodian Ukraine speaks the truth. Brahova didn't say that—but it would have been better if she had. It would have been more original!"

All three of them laughed so uproariously that the waiters and neighbouring Germans stared at them. Lyuba wanted to restrain herself, but simply could not. Finally, she stopped laughing and asked: "Nevertheless, what shall we do about the party that's being arranged for Brahova?"

"What about the party?" Kuzmenko repeated her question.

"Are you going?"

"What the devil for? What will they think of next? I'm not going, and I'd advise you not to go either."

"I'm not planning to. Dmytro Nazarovych and I are going to do some reading."

"Well, I'll come with you," Kuzmenko said, ending the conversation.

They went to Lyuba's place. Korniyevych picked up the volume; Lyuba sat down on the very edge of her bed and appeared to be deep in thought.

"You know what?" she said hesitantly to Korniyevych, "Perhaps we should go . . . to the party?"

"Don't even consider it!" Korniyevych said decisively. "I simply won't allow you to go. First of all, there's no reason to go, and secondly, you should show some consideration for yourself. In the last while, your studying and work in the laboratory have undermined your health terribly. You'll end up with a full-blown case of anaemia. You must conserve your strength and not waste it senselessly. We won't let you go anywhere. There, just lie down a bit, because you're ill. It will be good for you; your head will have a rest."

Korniyevych plumped up the pillow and stood over Lyuba. Then, holding her delicate hand in his strong one, he said once again: "Lie down, and I'll read to you."

Lyuba felt that she would not be able to resist that firm hand; laughing, she leaned against the pillow.

"There now, that's better," Korniyevych said, gazing into her eyes with a tender look, as if she were an obedient child.

"What about me, Korniyevych? May I put my head on a pillow? I also feel sick." Saying this, Kuzmenko took Pestsova's pillow and settled down on a couch at the other end of the room. "You can't see me, can you, my fellow countrywoman?" he asked Lyuba from there.

"Yes, I can, just a little bit! But God be with you, lie there."

"Thank you very much."

Seating himself at a table not far from Lyuba, Korniyevych began to read.

As she listened to him, Lyuba looked at his face, surprised that she did not fear him and was able to gaze freely at him. "His mouth is beautiful—so expressive—and his teeth are so white," she thought. "It's strange—he's blond, but his eyes are dark; that's not very common. He looks interesting today; his grey attire suits him very well . . . his appearance is so fresh and vibrant."

"Aren't you listening?" Korniyevych asked her, feeling her gaze upon him.

"I'm listening," Lyuba remonstrated, but with such a loving and bemused smile that Korniyevych, glancing up at her, stopped reading momentarily and ran his fingers through his hair in confusion.

"Hey, Korniyevych, read, if you're going to," Kuzmenko muttered from his far corner.

Korniyevych began reading clearly and distinctly. Lyuba listened more attentively now, looking less at the reader. The story was truly a fine one, and not very long; it was over before they realised it. They discussed it, praised it, and went on to read other things.

Later, Lyuba got up and treated her guests to tea. They conversed frankly, and in a different manner than previously—more like close friends.

It was quite late when Pestsova came home. "Ah! See where they are!" she shouted right off in a lively manner. "Why did you deceive me, Apollon Styepanych?"

"How did I deceive you?" Kuzmenko asked. "Attack some one else!"

"What do you mean? You said your usual 'uh-huh!' And so I thought you were coming; but you lied."

"Uh-huh!" Kuzmenko said distinctly.

"You're shameless," Pestsova said angrily. "You should have your hair yanked."

"Uh-huh," Kuzmenko said. He caught her by the arm and sat her down at the table.

Pestsova's angry tone became cajoling: "Just give me some tea, Kalynovska! I want to die! It was a madhouse there."

"Aha! Tell us, what really happened?" Lyuba inquired.

"Well, nothing special. Same as always. They tried speaking in 'speeches,' but it didn't work. They drank a lot of beer. That's it!" "Well then, there's nothing to talk about. Listen, I want to read you one more interesting piece," Korniyevych said, and began reading again. When he finished, he said: "That's enough! It's time for Lyubov Vasylivna to go to sleep."

"I beg you," Korniyevych urged Lyuba as he said good-bye, "be sensible. Don't talk late into the night; go to sleep as soon as possible. Don't forget that you're ill."

"No, I'm not. You've cured me," Lyuba replied, responding to the warm pressure of his hand as he shook hers.

XV

The time came when it was no longer possible to read stories or go for walks—final exams were approaching. It was such a critical time, that God forbid. Lyuba burned herself out completely. She studied with Pestsova for days and nights on end. From time to time, Kuzmenko or Korniyevych would run in, sit for a while, offer some help, and then the girls would be left alone again with their books.

Well, praise God, they successfully passed a few of their exams and could breathe a little more easily.

Kuzmenko dropped in to see them—he had regained his sense of humour and was cheerful once again. "Well, my fellow countrywoman," he said to Lyuba.,"you're cooling off today? And tomorrow you're going 'to forge' the books again? Oh, yes indeed, our Princess Biloselska chose the better way out; she spit on the exams and now she's on holidays, getting ready to leave for Paris."

"Why is she going to Paris?"

"What a thing to ask! Why go to Paris? You'd do better to ask how she landed here? She belongs to the category of 'cephalopods' [molluscs with tentacles attached to their heads]—do you know any like that? While I consider you to be a 'clear-headed' human being. That's the way it is."

"And what about me?" Pestsova inquired.

"And you should behave yourself! Yes, indeed! But Biloselska has it made, honest to God. Today, as I was walking past her window, the whole street was reverberating with the sound of the princess playing the piano. I stopped in, and there was Konstantyn Mykhaylovych listening to all the Schuberts and Chopins."

"Zahorovsky?" Pestsova asked.

"Yes, indeed! For the last month or two, I've noticed the stench of Biloselska's perfumes on him."

"Oh, Master Mykyta! What comical expressions you use—'the stench of perfumes.'" Lyuba laughed. "Has he given up searching for molluscs with Brahova?"

"Yes, he has. He's like Heine; he wants to experience love a hundred times over."

Well, they finally finished their last exam. Now they were free! Free! The wide world spread before their eyes. Where to now? How should they arrange their lives?

Everyone was preparing to leave, but in the interim, they were still in Zurich, getting their documents in order, and looking after one thing and the other.

While she was downtown, Lyuba ran into Rayisa at a photographer's studio. They exchanged greetings.

"How's everything? Are you leaving soon?" Lyuba asked.

"No, I'm not. I'm staying on as Stockmann's assistant."

"Really? So, that's how things are."

"Yes. Give my respects to my mother. Of course, I'll write and tell her all about it."

Not long after this conversation, a rumour spread like wildfire among the students: "Did you know that Brahova is marrying Stockmann?" "That can't be. Who told you?" "I'm telling you, it's true." "It can't be, perhaps it's just a rumour." "What do you mean a rumour? Stockmann's former assistant told me that the wedding is to take place in two months. And what's there to be surprised about? It will be convenient for both of them—Brahova will teach Stockmann more Russian, and then she'll cart him off to St. Petersburg; he'll write the medical exams there so he can establish his own practice, and they'll both work as doctors. What more could you want? And they'll have some practice, I tell you. Oh, yes they will! He's a competent doctor, and a foreign professor as well! It will be a St. Petersburg practice, not like the one he has in this indigent Zurich. And it will be good for both of them to develop their careers together."

But the young people were, nevertheless, preoccupied with the news, and even though she was not yet married to Stockmann, a nickname that Kuzmenko dreamed up for Rayisa began to circulate among them: "*Stockfrau!*"

Kost was caught off guard when he heard the news about Rayisa's impending marriage, but in reality, he was indifferent to it. In his thoughts, he was already in Paris.

"What? Is he going to Paris as well?" his acquaintances asked. "Why?"

Well, after all, how could he leave Europe without spending time in that hub of European thought and life? And Biloselska, having purchased an expensive, stylish, and elegant wardrobe, travelled to Paris with him on the same train.

Before his departure Kost came to bid Lyuba farewell. "Good-bye, Lyubov Vasylivna."

"Good-bye, Konstantyn Mykhaylovych."

Glancing at the open trunk and the piles of books, Kost inquired: "Are you also leaving?"

"Yes, I am," Lyuba replied.

"Where are you going? Back to Russia?"

"No, I plan to go to Vienna first. I want to spend six weeks or so completing a short, practical course in midwifery; I want to study at the clinic and see how things are done. It's said that midwifery is at a very high level there."

"But why do you need it?"

"It will stand me in good stead. When I apply for a position back home, I'll be able to carry on with both midwifery and my medical practice. And, as I'll be living in the provinces, in a village, it will come in handy."

"So you're going to live in the backwaters?"

"Yes, in the backwaters."

"What will you do there?"

"What do you mean?" Lyuba laughed. "I'll heal people. That's what I studied to do."

Kost paced the room. "Yes," he said. "Yes. We weren't fated to travel down the same road."

"I never even considered it. I was always aware of how divergent our paths were. *Kinderspiele [Children's games]* do not of themselves lead to a joint path in life."

"In any event," Kost stated, as he drew nearer to Lyuba, "believe me—I will always preserve your pure, beautiful image in my heart. Now I can see clearly that I'm not worthy of you. Your deep, integrated character . . ."

"What's this panegyric for?" Lyuba interrupted him impatiently.

"You don't believe me?"

Lyuba did not say anything; then, with a faint smile, she stated: "I believe you."

"Believe me, that the period of our—as you put it—*Kinderspiele*, that period of our . . . friendship will remain the most holy memory of my life."

Lyuba remained silent, her eyes lowered.

"Farewell . . . Lyuba!" Kost wanted to kiss her hand, but he did not dare to. Deeply agitated, he walked swiftly out of the house.

Lyuba did not move from where she was standing, nor did she watch Kost leave; she remained standing, deep in thought. After thinking about their former relationship, her thoughts turned to Kost himself, and she felt sorry for her friend, truly sorry for him. Would he ever find happiness at the crossroads?

Lyuba's final, pressing preparations broke into her heavy thoughts. There was so much to be done! And so many parties to attend, to say their farewells, as it were . . .

Lyuba was departing with her small group—Pestsova, Kuzmenko, and Korniyevych. Her friends were travelling with her as far as the turn-off to Vienna, where Lyuba was to part with them, as they were taking another route to Russia. Pestsova would travel to her native Russia—as Kuzmenko called it; Kuzmenko would go to Poltava, and Korniyevych—to Slobodian Ukraine. Everyone was dispersing.

It was a splendid morning when they set out. "Farewell, Zurich! Farewell, beautiful mountains! Farewell to you, our alma mater! And farewell to you, our university years!" En route, they sat together in an unassuming group surrounded by strangers.

"Well, my fellow countrywoman," Kuzmenko inquired, "when will we see you again?"

"I don't know," Lyuba replied.

"Just let Lyubov Vasylivna finish her studies in Vienna and come home, and then we'll visit her," Korniyevych said.

"Well, I don't know about anyone else, but if—as the saying goes—a mouse doesn't bite off my head, I'll definitely go to see how she's doing in her practice," Kuzmenko said. "It will be interesting, by God, very interesting! Here, show us how you're going to take someone's pulse. This is the kind of expression you have to assume." Kuzmenko put on such a serious, but comic, expression that everyone laughed.

"Oh, you're such a *skomorokh [jester]*," Pestsova cried out, slapping Kuzmenko on the back. Along with the reproach in the young woman's words, tenderness was reflected in her eyes—eyes that were constantly turning to gaze at "Mikita Styepanych." But what about Mykyta Stepanovych—did he not see those looks? Could he not guess what was so evident to all who were close to him? Who could tell—he always fended off the young woman with a joke, and he turned her tenderness into a joke as well.

In time, the banter of the travellers began to abate, and they said things more abruptly, with increasing tension and forced laughter. And now, there was no more laughter to be heard; they were approaching the station where Lyuba was to disembark and wait for the train that would take her to Vienna; the others would continue on without her.

"Will you write? Will you promise to write?" Korniyevych asked Lyuba. They were standing by a window. Lyuba, leaning against a pane, was trying to conceal her agitation.

"I will," she replied. And then, after a moment, she added: "You must also write . . ."

"There's no question about that—of course, I will!"

In the meantime, the train was whistling and breaking their hearts. It came to a stop.

"Well then, farewell!" Lyuba embraced and kissed Pestsova sincerely; then she broke away from her and, with tears in her eyes, whispered in a choked voice to Korniyevych: "Farewell!" Korniyevych pressed her cold fingers tightly and said: "Go in good health! Take care of yourself . . ."

With a mist clouding her eyes, Lyuba extended her hand to the silent Kuzmenko, barely uttering another: "Farewell!" Kuzmenko took her hand and tenderly pressed his soft, kind lips to it. Lyuba had not expected this; she was so agitated that she kissed him on the face. Kuzmenko kissed her hand once more. Wiping her eyes with her handkerchief, Lyuba descended the steps leading down from the train. She stood on the platform, looked up at her friends, and exchanged a few more broken words.

The train began to move; Korniyevych waved his hat; Kuzmenko also removed his hat, but he stood gloomily on the platform between the coaches. He did not want to see on which of her friends Lyuba's parting gaze would rest.

XVI

It is two weeks now since Lyuba arrived in Vienna, found a small apartment, and settled in. With her medical diploma from Zurich, it was easy for her to enrol in the midwifery course. And so she attended the clinic, studied, and noted carefully what was done there.

For someone with a sensitive heart, it was hard to work in this clinic, to observe cases of difficult childbirth, and to hear the wailing and heartrending cries born of human suffering. But Lyuba looked at all this anguish and listened to the screams with the thought that, one day, she would decrease the pain of women in labour, become a knowledgeable advisor to her unfortunate sisters, and, perhaps, even save some of them from death. She learned new skills, and the practical experience she gained was of far greater significance than what she had studied in books.

In Vienna, Lyuba was completely alone. When she strolled down the streets filled with a lively crowd, or sat in a theatre among rows of spectators, she felt herself isolated, alienated from both the troubles and the joys in this tumult. And she was alone intellectually. If she went to an art gallery, a museum, or a corner of the city that was new to her, she could share her observations, her impressions, only with herself.

Vienna, as a city—with the sharp contrast between its narrow, ancient streets dotted with churches and steeples, and its new wide streets, adorned with trees and buildings that were cheerfully whimsical but aesthetically pleasing in their architecture—appealed greatly to her. And the Danube river, that peaceful Danube, was magnificent. Standing near a bridge, she could watch it as it carried away its wide, deep, and calm waters. Yes, this was the Danube, whose name she had known since childhood from songs about a *kozak* watering his horse at its edge, while a maiden spread her hair on its quiet waters. She used to think: "Where is this Danube, and what is it like?" And now she could finally see it.

Returning from her walks to her tiny living quarters, Lyuba either studied or wrote letters. Those letters were all the comfort she had, because in them she could converse, at least for a while, with her soul.

Eventually Lyuba tired of going to the same restaurant, so she went to another one, just for variety. After her meal, she leafed through the newspapers—they were all either in German or French—and unobtrusively observed the other diners; all of them were strangers, and all of them were men. They looked at Lyuba with a degree of surprise and curiosity, but even the most brash ones did not dare to approach her; the gentlemen could see that the *junge Dame [young woman]* with the cropped hair was not the kind who would take kindly to their advances.

One time, Lyuba had just started eating, when two young gentlemen walked in—one was short and dark, while the other was tall and blond. They sat down by a table in the far corner, where Lyuba was sitting. They appeared to be Germans. Hearing them say a few words to the waiter in pure German, Lyuba did not pay any special attention to them. It did not matter to her whether they were handsome or not!

But then the two men began conversing. Lyuba stopped eating, and even though she felt uncomfortable that she was taking notice of them, her head involuntarily turned in the direction where the young gentlemen were sitting. What were they discussing, that Lyuba became so interested in their conversation? Actually, they were talking about some matters that concerned only them, and Lyuba could not understand exactly what was being said, because she caught only fragments of their conversation.

So why was she looking at her neighbours with such an animated expression on her face? Because Lyuba heard a language she had not heard for some time now, and which she had never expected to hear in this place. She quickly determined that the young gentlemen were talking, not in Russian, but in Ukrainian. And they were not just throwing in a few Ukrainian words here and there for a laugh—they were conducting their entire conversation in this language, and they were doing it easily and unaffectedly.

"What is this?" Lyuba pondered. A few of the words and expressions seemed a trifle strange or dialectal, but overall, the language was Ukrainian, and it touched her heart. And the young gentlemen who were employing this language—one that was incomprehensible to the Germans among whom they were sitting—were speaking with great confidence. They were unaware that their quiet, silent neighbour was listening intently to what they were saying.

"Give me that newspaper, Buchynsky," the dark man said to the blond one, after they had finished eating.

"Newspaper," Lyuba repeated in her thoughts. "Not 'gazette', but 'newspaper.'" Lyuba also picked up a "newspaper" but, occupied with observing the gentlemen, she read very little of it. They sat there for a while, and then, speaking with an impeccable German accent, paid their bill and left.

The next day, Lyuba eagerly sat down to have her meal in the same spot, but the young gentlemen did not show up. Lyuba was a little cross about that. The next time, however, she did see the blond one there, and even remembered his name. "It's Buchynsky," she recalled. Buchynsky was alone.

That day, Lyuba did not hear a single word from him—they only glanced at each other. "Well, the next time that I meet him, I'll speak to him! After all, there's nothing wrong with that!" Lyuba thought. And truly, the next time they met, she said: "Pass me the gazette, if you please." She had not dared to use the word "newspaper."

Now it was Mr. Buchynsky's turn to be astonished, no less than Lyuba had been earlier. And Lyuba, blushing all over, sat there reading. After a while they struck up a conversation and found out about each other—who they were, and what they were doing there.

Lyuba discovered that Buchynsky was a student in Vienna, and that he was a *Rusyn [Ukrainian]*from Halychyna [Western Ukraine]. "So that's what it is!" Lyuba thought, and this youth— or young gentleman, as she had named him in her thoughts— became even more interesting to her. They talked for a while and parted. But then they met again and strolled together through the city. Buchynsky, who had lived in Vienna for several years, knew the city very well. He kindly showed Lyuba around, taking her to places where she had not yet been and advising her where it was better to shop. They talked and conversed most enthusiastically.

Lyuba's studying was going well. Before long, she completed the brief midwifery course. Now she had another diploma—this time for a medical specialisation. The time came for Lyuba to leave Vienna. Buchynsky saw her off at the train station, and Lyuba thanked him for the assistance that he had so generously given her in a large, unfamiliar city.

XVII

In the small white parlour of Mariya Petrivna's cottage, the hostess was sitting with Kateryna Panteleymonivna. The latter had laid out a deck of cards and, at the request of Mariya Petrivna, was divining with the queen of hearts. No one could tell fortunes with cards like Madam Zahorovska.

"Well, what does it look like for her?" Mariya Petrivna inquired; she obviously had not asked that the cards be laid out for herself—for if she had, it would have been the queen of diamonds.

Kateryna Panteleymonivna sighed gently and peered at the cards—you couldn't say just anything at all without giving it some thought! "It's like this," she finally said, "nothing has come of it. As you can see, the path leads to the heart, over here—wishes are fulfilled . . . and here there's something relating to the king of diamonds. And over here, there's some red business. Hm . . . It's too bad, though, that the eight of spades got mixed up with the ten; there will be some kind of grief—but that's nothing . . ."

Mariya Petrivna peered at the mysterious cards and listened trustingly to the verdict of the fortune teller. "And why did that eight of spades have to get mixed up with the ten," she thought. "And what about the king? What kind of kings are those? Diamonds and spades!" Mariya Petrivna sighed.

"You're going to receive a letter," Madam Zahorovska continued her divination.

"What kind of a letter?"

"It might be one relating to a diamond."

"Perhaps! Who can tell!"

"When are you expecting her?"

"She wrote she'd be here on the tenth, but it's the fifteenth already."

"That's right—you can't guess what they're going to do," Madam Zahorovska said, as she shuffled the cards. "Take my Kost. He was supposed to come home, but now he's gone off to Paris. And why does he need to go to Paris? He's just like his father; he also used to take off—if not to Poltava, then to Kharkiv, or at least to Romen—as soon as he got hold of some money. He was always bored. Huh!" Madam Zahorovska angrily turned her head aside and stared out the window with her dark eyes.

They continued chatting. Mariya Petrivna once again picked up the stocking she was knitting for Lyuba, thinking: "Lyuba's probably worn out everything completely." She kept thinking about a lot of things, and then she suddenly realised that it was time to offer Kateryna Panteleymonivna some tea. "Why isn't Tetyana bringing in the samovar? She should be back from the river already," she wondered.

Mariya Petrivna was just on the verge of getting up to see what was happening, when Tetyana burst into the room, yelling excitedly: "Madam! The young mistress . . . Lyuba's come home!"

Mariya Petrivna started to shake, and the knitting dropped from her hands. Then she rose to her feet, but she did not know what to do first.

"Here she is! She's here! In the yard!" Tetyana said in an agitated voice. "I was coming from the river . . . and she was driving up."

In the yard, a Jewish carriage with a canvas top came to a stop by the veranda. Lyuba, the European wanderer, jumped out and rushed into the house. "Mother dear!" And she fell into her mother's trembling embrace.

Mariya Petrivna, tears running down her face, clung to her daughter, hugging and kissing her. She could hardly believe she had actually lived to know such happiness! Then she lookd intently at her Lyuba—she seemed to have grown and changed in some way. But no, it was Lyuba, her dear, beloved Lyuba.

A hubbub arose in the household. Everyone was running back and forth, carrying in Lyuba's luggage. Ulyana, the cook, ran in, and so did Tetyana's husband, who had completed his military service and was now living at Mariya Petrivna's. The neighbours who rented the smaller cottage in the yard also rushed out of their house; they heard that Mariya Petrivna's daughter had returned from abroad, and they wanted to see her, to see what she was like. And there she was—standing on the veranda, laughing with Tetyana.

Lyuba went back into the house and walked through all the rooms, observing everything. The rooms seemed to have become smaller and lower. But of course they hadn't—they had always been like this. Even the beams protruded, just as they always had. Lyuba looked around and turned to her mother: "Well, tell me, mother dearest, how are you?"

It seemed to her that her mother had aged perceptibly; she had become stooped and had more grey hair. But no, if you looked at her more closely—she was the same dear, kind mother! It even looked as if she was wearing the same cap she had worn the day that Lyuba was leaving home.

Lyuba ran through the living quarters at the rear: "How's everything in the yard, Tetyana? Is everything as it was? I'll go have a look."

"Go and look," Tetyana replied with a laugh, carrying the samovar into the next room.

After viewing the yard, Lyuba peered over the fence at the orchard. Then she went to the edge of the yard between the buildings, and there the same familiar landscape revealed itself to her. It spread expansively in the rays of the setting sun. There was the river, and there were the meadows, and over there—the distant, bluish pine forest. It seemed to her that the river had changed; there were more white sand banks in it. And over there, in the bend of the river, the willow had spread out even more. But still, there was no great change—it was the same landscape, the same familiar places.

Lyuba did not know why her heart was aching, as if grieving for something, as if some trouble were approaching. And then, a warm feeling once again flooded her heart—this corner of her native land was extending its embrace to her so warmly, so lovingly.

She returned to the house and sat down at the table that had been set, and at which her mother was already sitting with Kateryna Panteleymonivna. Her face shining brightly, she began saying something to her mother.

"Did you happen to see my Kost recently?" Madam Kateryna inquired.

"No, I saw him before I left Zurich. And then he went to Paris."

"Will he be home soon?"

"How am I to know?" Lyuba responded, laughing.

"Of course, he'll come; he'll come to see you," Matriya Petrivna comforted Kateryna Panteleymonivna.

Mariya Petrivna began to pour the tea and cried out: "Oh, my God! What have I done? I automatically put in the tea, you see, but I forgot to pour some water in the teapot, and it was right there on the samovar!"

Mariya Petrivna became flustered; Lyuba and Madam Zahorovska laughed, and Tetyana laughed heartily, as well.

"Listen, Lyubochka," Kateryna Panteleymonivna spoke up again, "is it true that the Brahov girl is marrying a German professor? Her mother's been bragging that her daughter sent her a letter about it."

"It's true, it's true!" Lyuba responded. "They're probably married already, because the marriage ceremony was supposed to be sometime now."

"God only knows what's going on," Zahorovska continued. "Why would she want to marry a German?"

"Well, who knows!" Lyuba replied with a laugh. "Maybe she took a liking to him!"

XVIII

It was in one of the villages that could be seen in the distance from the hill on which the Kalynovskys lived that Lyuba obtained a position as a *"feldsharytsya [a general medical practitioner]"* or, as the peasants said, a *"khvershalka"*. There was no hospital, but there was an opening for a medical practitioner for the whole district, along with a few of the nearby villages. Even without a hospital, there was more than enough work! You only needed the inclination to do it!

Kalynovska's elder daughter had come home with her children for a visit, so the older woman was not lonely—the house was full of children's chattering. And Lyuba was not too far away; she came quite often to visit her family—and then there was even more noise, and laughter, and pranks! The little ones would rush up to Lyuba, and she would pick them up in her arms; the older children also surrounded her, but they did not want to call her auntie. They all called her Lyuba, and that was that! But she did not mind—let them!

Lyuba would visit her family, exchange her books in the library, have a talk with Officer Bohdashevych about "higher" matters, and then she would once again descend "lower," back to her village. She had rented rooms—a small parlour and a bedroom—in the house of the previous general practitioner's widow, Hanna Markivna Malynchykha, and took her meals with her.

And so Lyuba began her medical practice. She looked after everyone who sought her help, but she did not always wait for the people to come to her—she made trips out into the district to see if anyone needed her assistance. The peasants began coming to see her and, as time went on, the number of their visits increased.

Lyuba had heard more than once that the peasants were "terribly distrustful" and "avoided the most sincere efforts of the best doctors who tried to assist them." But she quickly saw that it simply was not true—or that the truth had not been verified or investigated. Because, if you actually approached the peasants with advice and gave it to them frankly and capably, they were not at all distrustful; nor did they shun assistance.

The lords also heard the news about the new *khvershalka*. And, if you can imagine, the lords looked with even more "distrust" at the new woman doctor than the peasants. At the best of times, they simply shrugged their shoulders. But then, those who were nearest to the neighbouring villages began to call upon her, and it was possible to convince these distrustful people, to persuade them with her ability and courteous manner.

As the young lady started her medical career, the studies she had completed in the Viennese clinic proved helpful. She was often consulted when it was time—as old women say—to place a newborn soul on a pillow. And, of course, there were so many unfortunate women who were ailing with women's disorders, even if they were not having babies. She hoped fervently that she would have the power and the knowledge to help all of those who, at times, came to her with serious and long-neglected illnesses.

In her village the people knew Lyuba very well already, and she knew many of the householders, and still more of the housewives, by name. She often knew not only what ailed them, but how they lived.

You see, at a distance, peasant life seems so different and so simple in its composition, but when you take a good look at it— as if, let's say, you were putting a family or individual figures under a microscope—then it does not seem to be empty and monotonous at all; the various life forms appear rich and varied. If you have the desire to draw a little closer, you will find a wide field for observation and work among the people.

Lyuba did, in fact, bring her intellectual microscope to bear on the people in the district. Right now, let's take, for example, the nearest—and you might say, the most unimportant—neighbourhood. Was there not a variety of individuals in it? Were there not those who longed for spiritual balm?

Her landlady, the medical assistant's widow, was, after all, a former lady; but now, in her impoverished condition, she did not know what to do—continue thinking of herself as a lady, or become one of the peasants. When she looked at Lyuba and talked with her, she felt less ashamed that she no longer had any dresses and was reduced to wearing the simple skirt of a peasant.

Hrysha—her landlady's young son—was handsome, clever, and wanted to do everything, to know everything; but where could he go? What did he know? He could not go to visit the lord's children, because they would not accept him, but it was not seemly for him to associate with the children of peasants. The young boy was growing in isolation; he was so uneducated that he still had not learned to read, and there were no "means" to achieve this. Where was he to study? And so, whenever she had time, Lyuba, out of the goodness of her heart, began teaching him to read and write.

And then there was Melanka, the serving girl who worked for both Hanna Markivna and Lyuba; she was truly a most insignificant person, but her life was varied as well—she had served for townspeople in the neighbouring town, and then for lords, and finally, she'd had an affair. Yes, she had! With a corporal, a good-looking *moskal [Russian soldier]*. But the *moskal* had abandoned her and her little son and gone away. This was why Melanka wept so bitterly when Lyuba read her the poem "Kateryna" written on this very theme by Shevchenko, the great poet of the Ukrainian people. Others cried, as well, when they heard it, but not like Melanka.

Of course, Melanka's fate was not exactly like Kateryna's—Melanka did not drown herself; she remained alive for her little son, but her life was neither sweet, nor bright. It was dark and sad in Malanchykha's household, where Melanka served; it was only when that strange young lady, the doctor, settled in the house, that a bright ray of hope entered it.

The fate of Hryts, Melanka's son, was also not like that of Kateryna's Ivas; Hryts did not beg at the crossroads, nor did he act as a guide for beggars—but who can say if he was better off

than Ivas. Hryts grew up in misery—weak and sickly; when he
did feel a little better and went to play with the children in the
street, all he heard was the hurtful phrase: "Go away, you b . . ."
Knowing that he was illegitimate, everyone humiliated and picked
on him.

Lyuba began giving Hryts some medicines. His health improved,
and he no longer avoided his doctor. Why would he avoid her?
She would come home from town, bring some small buns with
her, call him into the house, feed him, and stroke his head. Both
boys would come to her—Hrysha and Hryts—and Lyuba taught
them the letters of the alphabet pasted on cardboard; they could
recognise them already. Or she would let them try to copy them
with a pencil—and the boys did not avoid this task either!

At other times, Lyuba would open a book with illustrations,
show them to the boys, and talk about them; and the eyes of the
boys would sparkle. Lively Hrysha caught on more quickly, but
Hryts, after thinking about it for a while, would also understand—
despite the fact that he sat so silently.

These were the kinds of different individuals that surrounded
Lyuba in the home in which she lived—but there were many more
beyond its confines!

And so Lyuba settled in, and she was not at all bored. At times,
however, she appeared to be sad and lost in thought as she walked
about in her rooms or strolled in the small orchard.

At this particular moment, she had returned from a walk along
the orchard path, and when she entered the house, she looked
serious and did not joke or laugh.

"Melanka," she called out. "You'll take a letter from me to Ivan.
He's going into town tomorrow because it's Friday, and he can
take my letter to the post office."

"Sure, fine!" Melanka said.

Lyuba paced the room and deliberated how to write a letter to
Korniyevych. He was really a strange one; he had written to her
regularly, but now, three weeks had gone by—no, a whole
month—and there had been no letter. What did it mean? He had
asked her to write, but now he had fallen silent. Why had he asked
her to write, even insisted that she do so? Well, he was enjoying
life. In his last letter he had written that he had many
acquaintances already, and that a very clever daughter of some

doctor had turned up; but, all the same, he could have replied to her letter. What kind of disdain was this on his part? It was quite unusual!

But the main point was that he himself had requested that she write to him. No, she would sit down immediately and tell him that she had not expected such conduct from him, and that if it was so difficult for him to reply to her letters—which he himself had pretended to desire—then, of course, it would be better to break off the correspondence altogether. She had thought that the letters would be a friendly, conversational exchange, but if he found it such an onerous duty to write them, she did not want to continue the correspondence; therefore, he shouldn't be surprised if she stopped writing to him.

With these thoughts strongly expressed on her face, Lyuba sat down resolutely to write her letter; she wrote for quite a while. The letter was finally sealed. Melanka quietly opened the door and said to Lyuba: "Miss! Give me the letter; I'll take it now, because they'll soon be going to sleep over there. Ivan will be leaving early tomorrow."

"You don't have to go. I won't be mailing any letter," Lyuba responded. And, after the door closed behind Melanka, she tore the letter she had written into shreds.

XIX

The next morning, Lyuba had just risen and had her breakfast when Melanka told her that a woman had come "with her foot." Lyuba already knew what such expressions meant and indicated that the patient could come in.

A young married woman limped into the room; one of her feet was bound in a rag. In answer to Lyuba's question as to what was wrong with her foot, the woman replied that she had pierced it some time ago in the river, and that something had happened to the sore. Her foot was swollen, and now she could not "step on it during the day, or fall asleep at night," because it was aching and paining her so badly. The woman slowly unbandaged her foot, and Lyuba saw a red swelling with a large yellow ulcer; the tip of the ulcer was pasted over with something and covered with a leaf.

"What have you pasted on it?" Lyuba asked in annoyance.

"It's dough. I've tried putting all sorts of thing on it, things that people told me about, but nothing helped. And so the people advised me to come to you."

"It hasn't helped that you let this sore go for so long, and that you kept putting things on it," Lyuba said, cleaning off the ulcer. "So, that's what it's like," she observed, as she got a better look at it. "I have to lance it, because the pus can ulcerate the bone, and then things will really be bad."

"Oh, my dearest dove, do whatever you have to do! I'm so sick and tired of it that God forbid!" But then the woman added shyly: "But maybe you could put something on it? Maybe you don't have to cut it open?"

"No, I can't. I have to lance it. Don't be afraid—it's nothing. And then I'll give you some medicine."

The woman had no choice; she had to agree to the treatment. Lyuba called Hryts; he liked to help her—that is, to bring her water and to hold whatever was needed. And so Lyuba, with her little assistant, began the operation. She cut open the sore, cleaned out the pus, then washed, soaked, and bandaged the leg—and it was all done. She did not feel any aversion, because what was there to feel any aversion about? If she had been able to dissect frogs, then this was nothing!

She led the woman out and told her she would come to see her; it was necessary to take good care of the wound, so that it would not turn into something worse. She was tidying up her room and her instruments, when the door creaked, and a dignified old woman, Maryna Shkuratykha—whom she had come to know already—entered the room. She placed her cane on the table and said: "I've come for you, my little dove. Come along, my dear birdie."

"What's wrong?"

"Ivanykha's in labour—the wife of Ivan who takes your letters for you. She's been suffering for two days now, the poor thing."

"Why didn't you come for me a long time ago?"

"Well, we thought we'd be able to do without you. Why trouble you unnecessarily? Because, after all, it's nothing unusual to give birth. But God only knows what's wrong—if it's because it's her first one, or what! No matter what the women do, nothing helps."

"Oh, I know only too well what the women are doing," Lyuba cried out, gathering up the things she needed.

"Well, I just said that I was going to get the young lady, because she would know what to do! Oh, it's so terrible for Ivanykha! I'm telling you . . ."

"Let's go, let's go!" Lyuba interrupted Shkuratykha's story, walking so quickly that the old woman could hardly keep pace with her.

Finally, Shkuratykha had to call out to Lyuba: "Wait up a minute, my little dove, my young lady—I'm too old to keep up with you."

They arrived at Ivanykha's house. Even from the porch, Lyuba could hear the heavy, distinctive groaning that she had become familiar with in the Vienna clinic. But when she entered the room, Lyuba saw a scene the likes of which she had never seen before.

Two old women standing near the bed were supporting a young woman holding on to a rod suspended over the bed near the ceiling. The hands of the young woman were numb, her head had fallen weakly to one side, and her groans tore through her teeth, filling the quiet room.

"What are you doing?" Lyuba shouted. "Let her down immediately. How can you torment a sick woman like that?'

The old women thought about it for a while, but they put the woman down. Shkuratykha supported what Lyuba said. "Come on, kinswoman," she said to one old woman. "You have to listen. She knows what she's doing."

Lyuba caught poor Ivanykha, whose face was deathly pale, in her arms. She had barely placed her on the bed, when the woman fainted.

"That's the way she keeps fainting and fainting," the old women said. "It doesn't look as if she'll live through this."

"Water!" Lyuba shouted. She sprinkled her patient's face and gave her some smelling salts, and the young woman regained consciousness. Then she examined the patient and set to work.

It was a very difficult case. Lyuba took charge, administered drugs, and told others what to do. But the groaning did not stop; it tore at your soul.

Lyuba was busy for a long time. Now, the screams chilled the blood in your veins. Lyuba's forehead was damp, and both her body and soul were tense; she mustered all her strength and skill in a final effort—well, praise God!

The patient fell silent, and the cry of an infant was heard in the house. But this was a welcome cry! The old women busied themselves preparing a bath. There was a general hubbub, a cheerful hum.

"Well, of course!" Shkutarykha went on and on. "I told you so! She knows what she's doing."

"Well, that's what they study for," other women agreed.

But Lyuba was still uneasy, and as she worked over the patient, she brought to bear all the training she had received at the Viennese clinic. Finally, there was nothing more to be feared. Now, she only had to give some instructions about how to care for the patient, or better yet, tell them that they should just leave her alone.

The woman who had given birth was lying very still. Pale and tired, she looked as if she had been taken down from a cross, but her head turned to Lyuba with a look seen only after the great suffering is over, and a tiny new being lies at your side—a being that is wrapped in swaddling clothes and has not yet been properly seen, but which is already inexpressibly dear to you. It's all so strange, and so lovely . . .

A bottle and a shot glass appeared out of thin air. The happy women begged Lyuba to have at least a token drink, but she refused. She felt hot—both from the heat in the room and the critical situation she had just handled. Moreover, she had bathed the baby herself, because she did not trust the old women to do it. Now she wanted to cool off her burning face, to wash it. It was hot! Lyuba walked out of the room and splashed her face with water that Shkutarykha poured for her by the door from a small dipper.

Refreshed, Lyuba stood on the threshold and dried herself with a towel. A dog leaped up from the earthen embankment abutting the house and tore off towards the gate. She heard Melanka's voice: "She's right over here!" Melanka walked into the yard and with her—oh, my God!—were Korniyevych and Kuzmenko!

Lyuba did not know what she was doing. She was both delighted and embarrassed—they had caught her completely unprepared in her everyday clothes, just as she was finishing her work. She quickly tugged at her rolled-up sleeves. Oh, my God! Her hands were all wet! But the young gentlemen did not pay any attention to this; they shook her wet hands, greeted her, and talked excitedly.

"Where did you come from? Lord!" Lyuba exclaimed.

"We're here, and that's that! And we came over here so we could see you sooner."

"I was at Kuzmenko's," Korniyevych explained. "We're neighbours—as you know—and then we kept on going. We'll spend some time with you, and then, tomorrow, we're off to Poltava; we both have business there. There's a chance I might get a position in that city, and Kuzmenko has to see to some of his father's matters. And that's all that matters!"

"But, my God, this is so unexpected! You didn't write to tell me! And here I was angry at you already."

"Why write? Isn't it better to see each other?"

"Well, of course, of course! Let's go to my place. I'm finished here."

"It's too bad we didn't arrive sooner; we would have seen you tending to you duties," Kuzmenko said.

"Yes, indeed! As if I would have let you!" Lyuba retorted, and she ran back into the house. After saying a few words and promising to drop in later, she returned to her guests.

The old women stood in the doorway and stared in amazement; Kuzmenko had already managed to crack a joke at Shkuratykha's expense.

Chatting excitedly, the three young people made their way to Lyuba's home. "Where are your horses?" Lyuba asked, as they approached her yard.

"We're staying not far from here, at the home of the district chief, and we came here on foot to pay you a visit."

Lyuba ran on ahead into her living quarters to check on things. Everything seemed to be in order; she just hastily picked up a skirt and the letter she had written to Korniyevych and then torn up.

"Please come in!" she called out. And, once again, there were greetings and the sound of excited voices.

Lyuba ran to the kitchen to ask Hanna Makarivna about dinner. The guests had to be offered something to eat; it was late already, and they were undoubtedly hungry. It was too bad she had not known they were coming, because they could have prepared something better for such welcome guests. Well, it did not matter—there was borshch, buckwheat groats and *varenyky [boiled dumplings]*. It would suffice.

Lyuba rushed back into the parlour where she busied herself setting the table.

"What are you doing?" Kuzmenko inquired. "Haven't you had dinner yet?"

"Oh, no! When could I have had any? I had to perform two operations today. That's how it is! Well, the first one was a trifling matter, but over there, where you found me, it was a complicated business."

"What was the problem?"

"Oh, what's the point of telling you! You're not specialists. But I did a manipulation today that would have done a surgeon proud!"

"But how did you dare to undertake it?" Korniyevych asked. "You don't have the right to perform any major procedures before the surgeon arrives."

"You don't say! By the time they'd send for a surgeon and by the time he'd be so gracious as to come to a village, to a simple peasant woman, then that woman would probably no longer be among the living. Furthermore, your surgeon may not have been able to do things properly. Oh, I'm so happy, so very happy."

"Ah, so that's why you're happy? And we thought it was because we had come to see you."

"Well, I'm also happy that you've come! Terribly happy!"

One glance at Lyuba, and you could see that she was speaking the truth.

"Well, let's eat!" she called out to them, as she served the borshch.

The young gentlemen seated themselves without ceremony; a lively conversation accompanied the informal meal. They talked so quickly that they kept interrupting one another. Kuzmenko was relating anecdotes about his practice, and Lyuba was weak with laughter. The conversation leapt into the past.

"Oh, please tell me what Pestsova is up to. Where is she?" Lyuba asked Kuzmenko.

"How would I know where she went after she returned to her native Russia?"

"What are you saying? Doesn't she write to you?"

"Of course, not! Why would she write to me?"

"Oh, you're lying! I'll never believe you as long as I live!"

"Imagine that! Why are you pestering me? Why don't you ask Korniyevych if he's conducting a correspondence with anyone?"

Lyuba was a bit nonplussed.

"And where's Zahorovsky, your childhood friend?" Kuzmenko inquired.

"In Europe," Lyuba replied with a smile "But he'll be here before long."

"Has he written to you?" Korniyevych asked.

"No," Lyuba replied. "I found out from his mother—she said she's expecting him home soon."

"Ah! Then it will be possible to renew an old friendship on old territory," Kuzmenko observed.

"It's possible, it's possible," Lyuba said jokingly. "I don't shun old friends—not like you."

The dinner was over. Korniyevych remembered that he had brought Lyuba a present. He walked over to the home of the district chief and brought back a few issues of the newspaper "Pravda," published in Halychyna.

"Oh, my," Lyuba said. "Where did you get these?"

"I subscribed to the paper," Korniyevych responded. "You wrote so much to me from Vienna about those 'nightingales' from Halychyna that when I was in Kharkiv I asked about their newspaper and subscribed to it."

"Just see how clever Slobodian Ukraine is—it managed to find it!" Kuzmenko said.

"I'm very, very pleased," Lyuba exclaimed, leafing through the papers.

"I'll get you the issues for an entire year—the annual, or whatever your gentlemen from Halychyna call it," Korniyevych offered.

"Why are they *my* gentlemen?" Lyuba asked.

"But can't that 'nightingale' Buchynsky—or whatever his name is—be called yours?"

"I'd like it if you warbled like that "nightingale." Lyuba retorted sharply. And then she became embarrassed, because what she said had not come out right. She started explaining that what she had meant to say referred to their command of Ukrainian.

"Teach me, teach me—I'll be very pleased. In principle, I have nothing against it!" Korniyevych said with a sincere smile.

"But I do!" Kuzmenko interrupted, "That's a literary affectation. I respect only the language of the people!" They began arguing.

"Be that as it may," Korniyevych interrupted, glancing at his watch, "it's time for us to go, Mykyta Stepanovych."

"Where?" Lyuba cried out.

"To Velychkovsky, your justice of the peace. His son was my friend in high school, and he's visiting his father now, so it would be awkward if we didn't visit him when we're here."

"There are young ladies there, as well," Lyuba remarked.

"So there are, so there are! But that doesn't matter; we won't be gone long. We'll stay for a bit, and then we'll come back here in the evening, because we leave tomorrow morning; we have to hurry to Poltava for an appointment."

"Well, be sure you come back! I'll be expecting you later," Lyuba admonished her guests, leading them out on the porch.

When Lyuba came back into her room, she caught a glimpse of herself in a mirror. "Oh, Lord! I'm so dishevelled, and so flushed!" Lyuba combed her hair and adjusted her clothes. She did not add anything pretty to her attire—why bother primping now, when they had already seen her as she was—but still, her coral beads were now arranged differently, and a ribbon was found somewhere . . . Well, a mirror, as they say, will always advise you what to do.

Lyuba, who usually just had some milk when she was alone, asked Melanka to have the samovar ready for the evening. Then, humming to herself, she took the issues of "Pravda" and went into the orchard. This orchard was small and rather neglected, but nevertheless, it was an orchard. There were tall hollyhocks beside the peonies, and wild poppies by the stile; there were also two lilac bushes with a small bench under them; a cherry sapling and an old pear tree stood near the path.

Lyuba sat down on the bench under the tall lilac bushes and flipped through the newspapers. Her heart was filled with such happiness! They'd come! She'd been certain that Kuzmenko would come, but she hadn't known what to think about Korniyevych. Who could tell . . . Even now, he was saying that he'd just stepped in on his way. Well, in fact, it wasn't on his way—it was a circuitous route. Why couldn't he be honest? Why was he always hiding something? But then, perhaps he didn't have anything to hide? There was never anything overly friendly in his letters and, in the last while, he'd fallen completely silent.

Well, in any event, he'd come! Was he happy? For some reason, she'd thought he'd be happier when they met . . . but, even now, he was still reserved, even though he saw how happy she was. And he'd brought those Velychkovskys into the picture. Why did he need them? Couldn't he have spent the entire time with her? And he'd come for just one day! What good is one day! They would see each other for such a short time, and there was so much to talk about!

Lyuba grew thoughtful, her glance fell on the newspapers, and she pondered: "He brought them . . . he subscribed to the paper. I'd like to know for certain why he subscribed to it—was it just to do me a favour and make me happy, or was it for himself, for his own satisfaction? It was for his own—because he says that he agrees with me in principle, that he thinks as I do. And he couldn't think any differently—it's logical to think this way, and he's very sensible. And the fact that he brought them here—it was done, of course, to please me. Well, so what? It's . . . it's very kind of him. I'll read them, and ask him to send me all the issues. And Kuzmenko's talking nonsense. 'It's artificial, literary; I recognise only the language of the people.'

"What a narrow concept of nationalism, what a constricting patriotism! To think in this way is to debase the concept of nationalism, condemning it, forever, to a primitive level! And, if you judge language in this way, then you must consider everything the same way. It means that there is no need to develop national talents—not in music or in anything. Let everything remain at its primitive-national level. Moreover, this means that there is no need to push back the frontiers of knowledge, that it is enough to have the world view of a simple person. This is sheer nonsense. With such a stultifying view of nationalism, everything would stay the same and grow stale.

No, you should take folk elements—not shun them—and, out of them, create a wider, more beautiful structure that will benefit the entire nation! Why separate the common people with an uncrossable line from the intelligentsia which has moved ahead? No, the best that this nationalism of Kuzmenko's can do is make you cry over your nation's sad fate, over the past. It's not tears that are needed, and not milling around in a single spot that is slipping out from under you; what matters is that you get the job done!"

Lyuba ran to look in on her patient. There was one thing that was troubling her—she was worried that there might be an inflammation, and she had to tell them once again not to give the patient too much to eat. The woman was delicate and in a precarious condition after such an extremely taxing birth, and eating too much could harm her. Lyuba took care of the matter and hurried home. Perhaps they had come already and were waiting for her? No, they had not come. What did this mean? Why didn't he . . . why didn't they come?

The sun had already set. Lyuba looked at her watch—it was almost nine o'clock. What were they doing? Becoming more and more troubled, Lyuba continued pacing anxiously through the orchard. "The Velychkovskys must be entertaining them very well—there's his friend, the young ladies, a piano, singing . . . Well, that's how it is! Let them enjoy themselves, the evening is long . . . But now it's almost ten o'clock, and they're still not here."

Thick shadows settled on the orchard, and only the path could be seen. The moon was rising. In the house, everyone was going to sleep; the lights would go out in a minute.

Lyuba walked along the path between the stile and the old pear tree, lost in thought: "Why did they bother coming, if we're to see each other for such a short time? They'll run in tomorrow, just to say good-bye. There's absolutely no reason to say good-bye, without having said hello in an appropriate manner. Of course, they're staying for supper there, for that festive 'uzhin [late supper]'; well, if that's the case, are they going to come to see me at dawn? That's really considerate!"

It was quarter to eleven! Well, of course, they wouldn't come now! Something bitter crept into Lyuba's heart—not just anger, but a deep hurt; it was seething within her, choking her . . .

Lyuba was standing on the path; a pale ray of moonlight caressed her lowered head; her hands were clasped nervously together, and her fingers cracked. "And I revealed such sincere feelings!" the girl recalled. Her hand went up to her eyes, eyes that were filling with tears . . .

"Lyubov Vasylivna! Is it you?" Lyuba suddenly heard Korniyevych's voice from the stile.

She jumped with a start and turned around. Her heart quivered. If the moon had been shining more brightly, and if a master painter had been standing opposite Lyuba, it might have been interesting for him to see both the recent sorrow and the new, joyous expectancy painted on her sensitive face.

"Is it you?" Lyuba repeated his question, and she moved down the path.

"Yes . . . Yes, I'm here!" said Korniyevych; he was already greeting her in the orchard.

"I thought you wouldn't come. It's so late."

"I couldn't tear myself away any sooner! They surrounded us there, both the hosts and the hostesses. Before everything was finished—the tea, and the singing! It was all I could do to get away as it was; I made some excuse and managed to break away."

"And Kuzmenko?"

"He stayed there. He said he'd come later . . . he's there with the young ladies. Let him!"

"Well, of course. Why not! If he thinks that it's more pleasant there, then let him! Let's go indoors."

"Why go indoors? It's so pleasant outside now. Let's sit down somewhere."

They seated themselves on the bench that Lyuba had been sitting on earlier. Her white blouse appeared still whiter in the moonlight, gentle hues washed over her tender face, her profile assumed a refined, picturesque look, and her hands, plucking at the edge of her dark clothing, were transparently pale.

"So you thought I wouldn't come at all?" Korniyevych asked.

"I did think that," Lyuba replied, lowering her head.

"What a strange inference! To travel all that distance just to sit at the Velychkovskys. It would seem then, that I came to see them?"

"I don't know. You said that you stopped in here because it was on your way."

"On my way, yes! But certainly not to visit your justice of the peace! I have to talk with you before I go to Poltava."

"With me?"

"With you. But first of all, I had to see you, to greet you," Korniyevych took Lyuba's hand and pressed it, as if for the first time. Lyuba did not protest; her heart was pounding, and her delicate hand with its long, slim fingers surrendered to Korniyevych. "I've missed you so much!" he said, holding her hands in his strong, warm ones. "And you? Have you missed me at least a little?"

"I missed you terribly!"

Korniyevych pressed the young woman's hand to his lips firmly and passionately. "You missed me, you missed me . . . my dearest!" he said.

Lyuba felt his gaze upon her, heard how his voice changed, felt his hot lips close to her . . . His passion touched her to the core, it swept into her breast . . . His *kozak* moustache, his burning lips, were touching the lower edge of her cheek. His powerful arm clasped her to his heart.

"My joy, I love you so much!" his lips whispered, breathing with fiery passion.

"Dearest," she replied, and her lips responded to his ardent kiss; her head bent in a swoon on the chest of her beloved *kozak*.

"My dearest! My sweetheart! I've waited so long for this happy moment! You're mine! Mine!" Korniyevych uttered, intoxicated with his good fortune, intoxicated with the kisses. His words burst out of him, as if they had a will of their own.

Lyuba regained her composure; Korniyevych was kissing every finger on her hand, and this seemed to indicate that he, too, was a little calmer now.

"Why then . . . why were you always so reserved, if . . . if you love me so much?" the girl asked.

"That's my nature! Or perhaps life made me that way. I don't know how to show tenderness—I'm not accustomed to it. I grew up without a mother—I have no recollection of her. I was raised by a severe father, who tried to appease my stepmother by showing me less kindness than he perhaps wanted to. Then I lived in a residence attached to a high school where the guiding pedagogical principle was not to unfold tenderness in a sensitive child's soul, but to suppress it, and so I knew no gentleness and did not learn how to be gentle myself. I did not experience any tender female companionship even after I matured. It was only in Zurich that I found such companionship for the first time. But you know what a motley crew that was! I first had to find my bearings in it. And I examined with interest those—as Kuzmenko called them—with 'tentacled heads' and the 'bright-headed' ones. And, as I looked around, I saw you."

"Oh . . . do you remember the first time that you explained something to me by the blackboard in the lecture hall? I'm ashamed of how foolish I was then."

These words gave Korniyevych an excuse to kiss her hand again. "Foolish!" he repeated in a reproachful tone. "Not at all! You entered the lecture hall and became flustered; then you sat down beside me, spread out your papers and listened so attentively—so wise, and so dear! It seemed to me that, in spite of myself, I loved you from that very moment. And as time went on, I loved you more and more. And the fact that I never said anything to you about my love, well, as I've told you, I never was good at saying such things. Moreover, I could see that you were not affectionate towards me . . . that I wasn't pleasing to you, or something like that!"

"I was a little afraid of you, that's all," Lyuba said, leaning towards him.

"Afraid? And at a time when I was ready to carry you around in my arms!" he said, embracing her closely. "I couldn't press my case when it seemed to me that there was another . . . but no, I don't want to talk about it. That time of jealous suffering was a very trying period for me. And later, I still wasn't sure about your feelings. The first time I was sure of them was when we were parting, and the train began moving away, and you were left with tears in your eyes, crying, it seemed to me . . . for me. From that moment on, I couldn't wait to see you again.

"Oh, during the period of our separation, I had ample opportunity to examine my love for you. As long as I could see you every day when we were in Zurich, I could endure it—I'd meet with you, talk for a while, see you; but when I was left alone—it seemed I'd lost half of my life. To put it simply and truthfully, I was even annoyed with myself at times—because really, I couldn't focus my attention on anything, as I should have. God knows why! My soul longed to be with you, and there was nothing I could do about it."

"Why didn't you write to me about it?"

"Hm . . . didn't write. Well, I didn't write. Instead, I set out for Poltava, I hurried to be with you, to tell you with my own lips, with my heart, that I can't live without you, that you have to be mine, at my side! We'll work together, and together we'll love everything you hold dear. To live together! Will you be mine? Do you desire this? My beloved, my fate, when will you be completely mine in the eyes of the world? Let them marry us, let them do whatever they wish to do, but let everyone know that you're mine, that no one else can have you, no one!"

Korniyevych sealed what he was saying with a kiss and embraces that were still more fervent, as if wanting to hide his beloved from the very moon itself. Lyuba's arms wound around the neck of her dearest one.

At such a moment, was it possible for Lyuba and Korniyevych to see that Kuzmenko had walked into the orchard and could see them? After glancing at them, he quietly turned aside and walked down the street . . . and the light echo from his footsteps was drowned out by the tender echoes of their kisses.

XX

Oh my, but there was a lot of tumult and trouble today in the home of Mariya Petrivna—after all, it was Lyuba's wedding that was being celebrated. Mariya Petrivna was beside herself, rushing about, trying hard to remain calm. She was pleased, but at the same time an anxious feeling was stirring in her heart—would things work out? It seems that an upstanding young man had turned up— at least he was not a German, or a good-for-nothing. But still, he had come out of nowhere and was taking her Lyuba away from her. Lyubochka said that he was a friend from Zurich, and that he himself was from Kharkhiv. "Yes indeed, as the saying goes: 'A daughter is of benefit to others!' You raise her, care for her, and then . . ." Korniyevych had not been able to endear himself fully to Mariya Petrivna; she could not rid herself of that slightly hostile feeling that it seems every mother has towards her son-in-law, to the husband of her beloved daughter.

"Mother dear, don't be afraid of him," Lyuba said on the day of the wedding, jokingly tapping the powerful shoulder of her bridegroom. "He isn't at all as terrible as he seems."

"But why should he be terrible, may God have mercy," Mariya Petrivna answered seriously, fidgeting at the table.

"Tetyana! Is my bridegroom handsome?" Lyuba asked on her wedding day.

"Oh, yes! He's so tall and stately."

"Tall! As if that's all that mattered—that he's tall. As if once someone is tall, he's handsome!"

"Well . . . he's also sturdy. Round-faced . . ."

"Really now! Just look at what beautiful eyes he has. You should know that!"

"Well, his eyes . . . As if I know what kind of eyes he has! You're the one who knows that!"

"And if you only knew how wise he is," Lyuba bragged jokingly.

"Well! No one would expect you to marry a fool!"

"Did you hear that, Dmytro Nazarovych?" Lyuba ran into the adjoining room. "Do you know how highly our Tetyana thinks of me? She says I wouldn't marry a fool! Ha-ha-ha!"

"I see," responded Korniyevych. "Are you telling me to accept this as a compliment as well—even though there isn't anything overly favourable in it?"

They both laughed so hard that the wreath on Lyuba's head quivered. Lyuba turned away from Dmytro and picked up her sister's little daughter in her arms. Oksana was her pet; she kissed her and played with her. Korniyevych also drew nearer to the little girl and tried kissing her soft face.

"Go away!" the child said crossly. "I don't like you!"

"Why not? Why don't you like me?"

"Because you're taking Lyuba away from us."

"No, I'm not taking her away. I don't need your Lyuba. It's she who is taking me away! Look!" Korniyevych placed Lyuba's hand on his shoulder.

"Go, go!" the little girl shouted. "Go away!"

"Oh, Dmytro Nazarovych, don't tease the child. Go away," Lyuba said. "Don't cry, my dearest, we'll chase him away."

"It's amazing how much she looks like you. It's almost as if she were your daughter, and not your sister's," Kormiyevych said, gazing tenderly at little Oksana, who was sitting on Lyuba's lap.

Oksana did not succeed in chasing Dmytro Nazarovych away.

The young couple returned from the wedding ceremony. It was crowded and noisy in the parlour. There was no music, and Mariya Petrivna did not invite as many guests as she could have, but there were still quite a few. What kind of a wedding would it have been without guests?

Among the many familiar faces in the group was Lyuba's aunt, who was asking the young couple which one of them had knelt first on the *rushnyk [embroidered linen ceremonial cloth]*—she wanted to know who would be the boss in the family! And

Bohdashevych was there, sporting a white corsage on his chest; because of his long-standing friendship with Lyuba, he had held the bridal wreath over her head during the wedding ceremony. And Petro Stepanovych was there with Vira Nykolayivna; he was gazing at Vira with such a tender, touching look. (That's how it still was, you see—nothing had changed; he always seemed to be courting her—but he never said anything definite. That was probably why Vira had already given her word to an wealthy elderly neighbour—after all, she could not wait forever.) Kuzmenko had also been invited to the wedding, but he had not come.

Madam Zaharovska was there with Kost. She had not waited in vain—her son had finally arrived. Kost appeared to have lost weight, and Paris had left its mark on his youthful face—it was pale and bore the stamp of weariness; his features were more sharply delineated, and his eyes were no longer fired by poetic passion. His eyes still gazed into the distance, but a pensive thoughtfulness was reflected in them . . .

Lyuba and Korniyevych extended a warm greeting to their friend from their Zurich days. There was no reason to shun him, was there? For Kost, however, this marriage had come as a surprise. Zaharovsky had returned home only a few days ago, and he had heard nothing during his sojourn in Europe about Lyuba's impending marriage.

He was looking in mild astonishment at the young couple— when had such an intimacy developed between them? But Kost could see that they were very much in love; they could not refrain from gazing passionately at each other, even in public; and just now, Korniyevych, for no good reason as far as Kost could see, had kissed Lyuba's hand twice, and the bride was laughing ever so happily, and she left her hand in his, even though she said: "Oh, Dmytro Nazarovych, stop it!" And the groom was stroking the little hand that now had a wedding ring on it with a gesture that seemed to imply that it really did belong to him.

That gesture grated unpleasantly on Kost's heart—it looked absurd and vulgar to him. What made Korniyevych think that Lyuba was rightfully his? Who was he, after all, this Korniyevych? Just an ordinary man with a cold nature and, as could be seen, very egotistical—not at all suited to Lyuba's tender, gentle nature.

Why was she marrying him? Why was she binding her fate to his? What could he give her in life? Sorrowfully, Kost speculated that Lyuba, poised on the threshold of the married happiness that she was envisioning with Korniyevych, might find, instead, the severe despotism of a heavy-handed, strong-willed husband. And yet she was clinging to him so eagerly, like a little dove.

How pretty she looked today. She had grown more attractive than she was in Zurich; she was no longer thin—she was blooming and had colour in her face. The colour was suspicious, but it made her look very beautiful! The French said that: *"chaque fiancée a beau succés [every bride is beautiful]."* Perhaps . . . However, not every bride was as beautiful, as alluring as Lyuba; the wreath of orange blossoms did not lie as attractively on every head. How soft the contours of her head, how gracious her movements, how brilliant her eyes! And her figure in the white dress . . . Where had she acquired such a splendid shape?

Kost's gaze became less indifferent than it had been; he kept turning to look at the bride—that is, at the young couple, for they were always together. The "owner" with the blond hair did not take a step away from his "property." An unpleasant feeling arose in Kost's breast and throbbed in his head; time and again, he drew his hand over his high forehead.

"Ah! Please, come in, please! Why didn't you come right after the church ceremony?" Lyuba greeted Madam Stockmann—her former friend, Rayisa—and exchanged kisses with her. This friend had not scorned her invitation—she had come to the wedding and brought her husband with her. Having come from St. Petersburg to breathe some of the southern Ukrainian air, they were visiting with Rayisa's mother, Madam Brahova.

Rayisa was dressed in the style of St. Petersburg in a fashionable, skilfully designed dress made of expensive fabric. She carried herself in a relaxed but self-important manner—even more so than before.

Herr Stockmann was the same as always, except he seemed to have grown a trifle stouter; but he had the same stiff bow, the same dry handshake. *"Ich gratuliere [I congratulate you],"* he said to Lyuba. *"Wünsche viel Glück und Wohlergehen [I wish you happiness and all the best]!"* he added to Korniyevych. The latter remained to converse with him, for who at Mariya Petrivna's could take care of such a guest while Lyuba was chatting with her friend? Even Mariya Petrivna's first son-in-law, a teacher from Poltava, kept his distance from *Herr* Stockmann.

"Ah! Konstantyn Mykhaylovych! What a surprise! Have you been in these parts long?" Rayisa called out amiably. "Tell me, where have you been, how are you?"

Seeing that Rayisa was quite caught up with Kost, Lyuba hurried away to mingle with her other guests.

"So he's the one, that German man?" Kateryna Panteleymonivna asked Lyuba, as she sat with a kinswoman who was also Mariya Petrivna's neighbour.

"He's the one," Lyuba replied with a smile. And, fearing that Madam Zahorovska might make her burst out laughing, she joined a younger group, where Bohdashevych was explaining something weighty to a neighbour's young daughter.

Herr Stockmann did not stay too long. Before the late supper was served, he said his farewells to the young couple and the hostess.

"Where are you going?" Lyuba asked.

"Lyubochka," Mariya Petrivna said. "Ask him to stay—however they say it in their language."

"No, don't bother," Rayisa interjected. "Let him go! There's no beer for him in our town, and he's bored wherever he goes. Let him get a good night's sleep—then perhaps he won't be so grumpy."

Herr Stockmann left, but *Frau* Stockmann remained. However, the young gentleman—her friend, Kost—who should have occupied himself with her, was not at all attentive—he just stared into space. Lyuba and Korniyevych, conversing animatedly, sat down with their friends. They recalled the past, various incidents from their life in Zurich, and their circle of university friends.

"Where's Biloselska?" Rayisa inquired. "It seems to me she stayed abroad, didn't she?"

"She's in Paris; she wanted to enrol in the conservatory to study singing," Kost responded. "Now it seems she's left Paris and gone elsewhere—to Milan, I think, or to take the waters somewhere."

The conversation ended.

"Well, how are you?" Lyuba asked Rayisa. "You haven't told me enough about your life in St. Petersburg."

"It's fine," Rayisa replied. "I have a medical practice; and I have a circle of acquaintances, mostly among the professors."

"Do you have consulting hours for patients?"

"Of course."

"Do you also have hours when the poor can visit you?"

"No, no! It's a lot of trouble, and there's no benefit from it."

"Well, maybe not for the doctors," Lyuba said, smiling, "but there certainly would be some benefit for the patients."

"Not all that much for the patients, either," Rayisa responded.

Supper was served. The guests, conversing noisily, sat down at the table. There were no fancy settings or excessive formalities; however, the young couple were, so to speak, seated ceremoniously in the place of honour. Lyuba was laughing—she felt happy and a little strange. The bride and groom were taken up with themselves, but others spoke to them and directed jokes at them.

During the supper Kost lost the last vestige of his good humour. He did not eat, or drink, or wait upon his neighbour—*Stockfrau*, he recalled Rayisa's former nickname—even though she was eagerly telling him about her life in St. Petersburg.

The conversation of the guests at the table was becoming livelier and louder. Someone stated that the wine was "bitter," and that the young couple should do their guests the favour of "sweetening" it; the guests should not have to imbibe a bitter drink. The husband of Lyuba's sister kept insisting, shouting that it was "bitter! bitter!"

Korniyevych hesitated, but finally he put his arms around Lyuba and kissed her right on the lips. After all, why not! In the first place, this was not the first time he had kissed her, and, secondly— he now had the right to kiss his princess in public. "Oh, now it's much 'sweeter,'" the guests said.

For Kost Zahorovsky, however, it was not sweeter; he was cut to the quick by this act, and he agreed wholeheartedly with Rayisa when she hissed through her teeth: "Such a stupid custom!" It seemed to him that Korniyevych had forced his kiss on Lyuba. And there may have been some truth in this. Lyuba blushed furiously and looked very embarrassed when Korniyevych complied with the request of the guests and family members. It was likely, however, that it was not a completely unwilling kiss that Korniyevych took, for his bride responded to it with at least the corners of her lips.

The supper ended, but the guests lingered on, because it was not polite to rise from the table and leave immediately. They once again spread into both rooms; it was hot in the house, and the door to the veranda was open. Lyuba, wanting to get a breath of fresh air, stepped onto the veranda.

"Where are you going?" Korniyevych asked, following her. "Do you want to catch a cold outdoors after being in such a warm house? You mustn't! Let's go back into the house!" And he put his arm around Lyuba to lead her back in.

"Let go of me, Dmytro Nazarovych," Lyuba said. "I'll go by myself. You must let go of me!"

"Let go of me, go away," Korniyevych teased her. "How much longer are you going to use the formal 'you' with me? When will you switch to the less formal 'you' in speaking to me? Well, kiss me one more time, just once, and then we'll go back in. Oh, Lyubochka, my darling wife."

Lyuba's arms wound themselves around Korniyevych's neck. One kiss became many kisses. After all, no one could see them.

But the bride was mistaken. Kost was pacing the yard, and he saw the entire scene. When Korniyevych and Lyuba disappeared indoors, he stepped into the veranda and fell into sorrowful thought—he had once stood here with Lyuba. But, it was not he who was fated to experience the happiness that Korniyevych now shared with the dear girl.

The words of a poet flashed involuntarily into his mind: "But happiness had been so close, so possible!"

The Nightingale's Song
(1889)

We were sitting in the orchard one marvellous spring evening. Spring was breathing gently—the way it does when its magical hand first opens the door to warmth, joy, and love. Nature had not yet unfolded all its wonders; it had just awakened and was only beginning its creative activity. A soft sigh lingered in the calm, light air filled with caresses. The force of life—new, young life— was omnipresent. The tender green of the young grass contrasted sharply, even in the evening light, with the damp, dark ground. The orchard stood motionless, covered, not so much with leaves, as with blossoms—the white and bright pink blossoms of hope, of tender, incorruptible beauty. The enchanting singing of the nightingale was coaxing the blossoms into bloom. Its song, blending with the blossoms and with the clear azure of the spring sky, echoed freedom and happiness!

"Do you hear the nightingale's song?" I asked my companion, who, deep in thought, was sitting next to me on an orchard bench under my wonderful chestnut tree, its branches spreading like a luxurious tent over the bench.

"Do you hear the nightingale's song?" I asked for the second time, breaking into the meditation of my neighbour, who had left my first question unanswered, probably thinking that I was not so much asking a question, as giving voice to my own delight.

This time my guest replied: "Yes, I do." However, in that phrase, in the tone of that reply, I heard something that sounded like discomfort. If it had been only sadness, I would not have paid any attention to it—the song of a nightingale has been known to evoke sorrow in one's soul. God only knows what a heart sometimes hears in that song, what memories it calls forth, but, every once in a while one feels a fleeting, piercing pain . . . Such a feeling is very familiar to older people.

But my guest was still quite a young man, and furthermore, he had a happy and outgoing disposition; therefore, the sorrowful tone of his reply and the still more sorrowful look on his face surprised me.

Probably sensing my surprise, my guest added: "I don't like the singing of the nightingale! I can't listen to it . . . I find it unbearable!"

"What kind of eccentricity is this?" I asked with a smile. "Have you succumbed to the numbing embrace of pessimism?" I laughed out loud, not considering it necessary to restrain myself in front of my guest, who was a good acquaintance of mine.

"No, it isn't pessimism," my guest replied. "It's just . . . It's been like this since . . . I really can't say why it is that the singing of a nightingale reminds me of a very distressing incident."

"An incident from your life?" I asked curiously. "But your life has always seemed so rosy to me!"

"No, it's not an incident from my life. But, then it could be said that it is from my life. It depends on how you look at it!"

"How can that be? It's from your life—and it isn't! It would be better if you told me all about it!"

My guest gestured apathetically and fell silent. I could see, however, that his soul was very agitated, and that it probably wanted to give voice—in an open-hearted conversation—to whatever it was that was weighing heavily upon it, in its very depths. It was not very difficult for me, therefore, with a few carefully considered questions, to bring the young speaker around to relating the incident that had ruined for him the wonderful, intoxicating singing of the nightingale.

"You see," he began, "it happened three years ago, just after I finished university. As you know, I graduated as a lawyer. I didn't have a position as yet, but I was highly motivated to get one. There I was—fresh out of school, with a head full of all kinds of laws, the laws of Rome, of *Rus [ancient name of Ukraine],* and of all the rest. I was ready to do something, engage in lawsuits, examine in detail the most complicated legal entanglements.

"Yes, I was ready! However, there was no position for me, and so in the interim I spent the summer in the village visiting my father, as if I were home on a school vacation. I passed the time in the bosom of nature, resting after my most recent bout of intensive studying. I went for walks and looked up a few friends. It was peaceful and quiet all around me—both in the home of my father, who is a priest, and in our village. And so I devoted myself completely to savouring life in this paradise.

"And then, in the midst of all this tranquillity, an incident occurred that disturbed the peace and confounded everyone. A crime was committed in our village—our lord, the landowner of our village, was unexpectedly murdered. How? Who? What? These questions were all that one heard among the villagers, especially among the village intelligentsia.

"To tell the truth, no one felt particularly sorry for the lord, because he hadn't earned the sympathy of anyone—not of the peasants, nor of anyone else. He was an old grouch, a man with views compatible with serfdom, and he had a cruel heart. There were rumours that he'd driven his children away to the far corners of the globe because they couldn't accept his ways, and that his severity had hurried his wife into the next world. God knows how much truth there was in all of this—all I'm saying is that the people didn't like him.

"Well, be that as it may, his death created a great stir in the district. After all, it was such an unusual event, such a heinous crime. A lord slain at night in his own home. This was an unusual occurrence, the kind that engaged the thoughts of everyone!

"Of course, this incident was of the greatest interest to me as a lawyer—and a freshly baked one at that! And what was more—I was intrigued by the mysteriousness of this crime. There was absolutely no clue as to *who* could have committed it! There could be no doubt that the lord had been slain by *someone*—his throat was cut in a peculiar manner—but no knife was found and, in addition to the pool of blood, there were signs of a struggle. But who had done it and why—this was not known!

"The lord, even though he was wealthy, was extremely miserly. He did not have many servants, and there were no family members living with him. And so, no one had heard or seen anything.

"The reason for the attack—what's referred to as the motive for the crime—was puzzling, because nothing had been stolen during the murder. Even though the lord had money, bills of exchange, and, as in any wealthy lord's home, some expensive artefacts, all of this remained untouched in desks and other hiding places. Who had wanted the death of the master of all this, and why? This was the question that intrigued everyone; it was baffling not only the investigator who had been sent there, but me as well. Yes, me! I even tried to assist him with his report.

"To tell the truth, the investigator did not seem to value my dependability and my desire to help him. At times, he listened indifferently—and even with a somewhat disdainful smile—to what I had to say, and later on, seeming to resent my interference in his investigation, he quite obviously began to keep himself aloof from me. This, of course, made me all the more eager to help and, to a degree, it became a question of honour to me.

"'Really,' I thought to myself, 'aren't I a lawyer like he is? Well, he has a position and has been working for a few years, but so what? I could be in his position, for I too have the knowledge to do the work! I haven't wasted all those years studying the same laws that he knows. And I, too, understand the seriousness of this matter very well.'

"This is what I was thinking, and I was both annoyed and very tempted to get involved in the affair. It gave me no peace; it was obsessing me.

"Whenever something was found not far from the diabolically mysterious study where the lord was slain—the mark of a nail on a picture frame, or another bloody spot—I was simply beside myself! I kept thinking: 'Why is it there? What does it mean?'

"Nonetheless, life went on in its usual routine—everything around me continued along its normal path as it always had, and even I did not occupy myself solely with the criminal matter. I went about here and there—some kind of diversion always turned up.

"One day, I went hunting. It was not the right time to go, because it was the off-season for hunting—it was the month of May—but, when you go out for a walk, you take along a rifle, because you can always shoot a magpie, or scare a hawk, or something.

"I was walking along in the forest, and my dog, Sniffer, was with me. (I named him Sniffer because his sense of smell was very good—he was a hunting dog.) We were walking along in the forest, and it was so pleasant—spring in all its beauty! The leaves—young, fresh, and healthy—created a pleasant shade; the grass underfoot was soft; in the trees, the birds were singing and calling animatedly and cheerfully to one another.

"I walked for quite a while in the forest. This time I did not shoot anything, but I was pleased with my walk. I just walked along, humming quietly to myself. When I came out of the forest, I was terribly thirsty! I had walked a fair distance, and it had turned out to be quite a warm day.

"I just happened to be approaching a dwelling, the home of a simple potash worker—we call them 'budnyks.' The man's name was Baydash. He was renting the land on a long-term basis, and had built himself a small peasant cottage. I knew old Baydash, as I sometimes had the occasion to go and see him about a hunting matter or the like. And so now I thought: 'I'll step in to the Baydash home and ask for a drink of water.'

"I was approaching the dwelling from the garden instead of through the gate, so I stepped over the fence and walked past the barn. Just as I was coming out from behind the barn, I bumped into the old man and his son. They were standing together next to the barn, huddled by a side wall, whispering about something.

"The grass was soft and springy, and I came up so quietly and unexpectedly that the Baydashes saw me only when I was very close to them. They both appeared to be startled, and the younger Baydash recoiled and shuddered. When I greeted them, he replied in a frightened voice.

"I did not pay much attention to this, and even asked laughingly: 'What's the matter? Did I scare you?'

"'Why would you scare us?' the older Baydash replied. 'Were we doing anything that would make us afraid of you? My son and I just came outdoors for a bit. Let's go, Andriy!'

"Having said this, the old man started walking to the stile. Andriy followed him.

"'I wanted to ask you for a drink of water,' I shouted after them.

"'Well, go ahead. The old woman is at home—she'll give you some water,' the old man replied nonchalantly.

"I went into the cottage, drank some water, and exchanged a few words with the old woman, just to be polite. She told me she was taking care of an infant in the house, while her daughter-in-law weeded the garden. I thanked her and left.

"The meadow that belonged to the Baydash family was right next to their cottage. My eyes were drawn to this meadow—it was so lovely at this time of the year. With its tall grass and sparkling flowers, it was a delight to behold!

"I came home. My father had just returned from the parish hayfield, which was being mown. Sitting down to have some tea with me and an old aunt who was his housekeeper, he began to talk about his hay. He was explaining what kind of grass it was— a particular variety had been sown on that field—and how he planned to manage it.

"Then I said to him: 'The Baydashes have wonderful grass in their meadow next to the forest. But I don't think they're planning to mow it just yet.'

"'Well,' my father said, 'their grass isn't a cultivated variety, and so it's too early to mow it. When the time comes, they'll mow it. They have enough time to do it. However, it's true that this year it will be more difficult for them to do everything that has to be done, because their older son is gone.'

"'He's gone?' I asked. 'Where is he?'

"'Why, he's in jail.'

"'What do you mean, in jail? Why?' I asked in surprise.

"'He was packed off to jail by the deceased lord!" Father began relating what had happened. 'To tell the truth, God only knows why he had to go to jail. The lord caught him in the winter with a cartload of wood that had been cut in his forest, and so he took him to court. And Baydash was sentenced to a few months in jail for the theft. God only knows why it happened! The man had to abandon his family—a wife and a small child—and the whole household is in disarray. And the man himself is ruined—once he's been in jail, it's all over for him! And just stop to consider for what the man's life is being destroyed—for a miserable cartload of wood!

"'All the Baydashes complained bitterly about the lord and cursed him fiercely. Well, may God have mercy on his soul—he's atoned for everything now. What a way to die—a sudden death at the hands of a murderer, without time to repent for one's sins!'

"My father continued talking, shaking his head, but I felt something begin to seethe in my chest; blood rushed so rapidly to my head, that I felt hot! The Baydashes . . . the lord . . . It seemed that a chain of circumstances tied the lord to that family, to the Baydash son who had been sent to jail by the lord, to the unhappiness of the entire family.

At first, all of this was a jumble of unconnected thoughts; but then those fragmented conjectures began to group themselves into a meaningful whole. I began to think: 'Isn't it possible that revenge—the seeking of revenge—led the Baydashes to take the life of their enemy, the enemy of the entire family? It was not without reason that they had cursed him so fiercely!'

"At that point, a thought entered my head—the recollection of something that, up to now, I had not paid any attention to. I don't know why it was, but just when my father was relating the story about the Baydashes and the unfortunate incident with the wood, I recalled very clearly the moment when I unexpectedly came upon old man Baydash and his younger son. I recalled how the two of them seemed to be plotting something, and how confused they became when I suddenly appeared before them.

"Now, it even seemed strange to me that I had not paid any attention to this—how I had not noticed that it was not a simple family conversation, and that they were hiding, plotting something, conspiring. Of course, the Baydash men would need to hold such secret exchanges furtively, so that even the rest of the family did not hear them. Of course! The investigation was ongoing . . . the investigator returned today . . . they knew about this, they heard about it . . . How could they not have clandestine conversations!

"I didn't say anything to my father about my terrible conjecture—I didn't say anything at all! I only asked once again about that other trial, when the Baydash son had been put in jail, and other things like that. My father answered, without any idea as to why I needed to know all this. Then, exhausted by the day he'd put in, he went to bed early, while I . . . I could not go to sleep, even though I too was quite tired from my walk. I kept pacing from corner to corner, like a windlass that winds up and then unwinds, and I kept thinking, ruminating over what I knew. I would sit down for a while, and even lie down and put my hot face against a pillow, but then I would jump to my feet again and begin pacing the room.

"Within a few hours, it was clear and indisputable to me that *the Baydashes had murdered our lord*. It was the face of the young Baydash—when I stumbled upon their furtive conversation—that stood out most clearly in my mind . . . his trembling shoulders, his panic-stricken appearance . . .

"I could not remain at home any longer. I grabbed my cap and dashed out of the house. My dog, Sniffer, glanced at me uncertainly as if he were surprised, but nevertheless he followed me. Oh! I remember everything!

"I arrived at the district office where the investigator was staying. He was sitting and writing, probably something to do with the case, because he had conducted some additional investigations at the lord's manor that morning. The evidence he had gathered was insignificant, but he still had to put his notes in order.

"I sat down by the investigator and told him that it was thus and so. At first he had a wry look on his face, then he bit his lip and started to listen attentively to what I was saying. 'Ah!' I thought to myself. 'So you're listening now? But wasn't it I who found the trail? Formerly, you looked at me as at a puppy that scampers about underfoot and gets in the way. Oh! We also know a thing or two! Of course, knowing how to connect and combine even the smallest minutiae is a great skill—haven't more than a few notable crimes been solved by focusing on small details? It's true they were small, insignificant to the average person, but for those who are perceptive, they're the key to the mystery.'

"I spoke confidently, and the strength of my convictions gradually convinced the investigator. It's true that a couple of times he called me by the name of the famous French detective, Lecocq, but in the end we took a couple of witnesses and went through the forest to the dwelling of the Baydash family.

"It was night; and, my God, what a beautiful night it was! The moon was so bright that you could see a needle on the ground! Bathed in a silvery light, the trees at the edge of the forest were clearly visible. And the full-throated singing of the nightingales echoed far and wide. It was quiet all around, you see, and the grove was dreaming, but their trilling and warbling resounded in the thicket! Oh, Lord God! They were singing so charmingly, like the nightingale was singing just now; but the singing was stronger, and louder . . . there must have been a great many of them.

"Well, we were walking along the edge of the forest, and Sniffer was scampering about at my feet. We arrived at the Baydash cottage. They were sleeping, of course, and the doors were locked. We began to knock. The people in the house woke up, and someone glanced out of the window. However, even though a commotion could be heard in the house, no one came to the door. It was only after a little while that the door was opened.

"A lamp was lit, and the task at hand was begun. We instigated a search. I looked at the members of the Baydash family. The younger son, pale as a sheet, was standing with his head bowed. The father, standing next to him by the hearth, his head lowered to his chest, seemed to be petrified. A young married woman, the wife of the older son who was in jail—that made her the daughter-in-law—was fussing with an infant; she was trying to pacify him, but she herself was terrified.

" And the old woman was sitting on the floor—do you know what the floor is like in a peasant's cottage? She was sitting on the floor, completely dishevelled, because she had been startled out of her sleep. Tightly clasping her hands together, she was following us with her eyes. I remember that I thought to myself then: 'How can the eyes of an old woman gleam like that?'

"Well, we began our search. I don't know what was transpiring within me then! I felt a hunter's fervour in my chest, probably similar to what a dog feels when he finds a bird which has fallen into the bushes after being shot down, but which can still get away if it isn't found immediately. My dog was very good at such searches. I was so agitated I could hardly breathe!

"Together with the investigator, I crawled and searched through every nook and cranny; I examined all the clothing, rummaged in the trunks; I looked in every corner—even when it was quite obvious that there was nothing there! But, then, if you're a Lecocq, you must scrutinise everything, pay attention to everything!

"So, we combed through everything—the house, the storage room, and the attic. We looked in the stable—it was empty at the time. There was absolutely nothing suspicious anywhere! The investigator became very angry, and he began muttering quietly to me in an accusatory tone: 'The devil knows what you've raised a fuss about! You've dragged me and these other people here because of some whim of yours! We'll spend the entire night crawling around here like fools. The devil knows what all this is about!'

"Well, I—you know the saying—put my tail between my legs and shrugged; my forehead was damp with perspiration, and I really didn't know what to say or do, because I could see only too well that there was nothing here! What the devil—could it be that my deductions were worthless? Perhaps they were wrong! God only knows! There are times when mistakes can be made.

"I felt foolish. I felt foolish before the investigator and before myself. Some Lecocq I'd turned out to be! I sighed heavily, but what could be done? If it was a mistake, then it was a mistake—nothing could be done!

"We returned to the cottage from the stable and began gathering our papers in preparation for returning home.

"Frustrated, I sat down on the bench to rest. I was just sitting there, and Sniffer was close by, standing on his hind legs and resting his paws on the bench. As I glanced around the room, my eye fell on the kneading-trough standing uncovered next to me—they were probably going to do some baking early in the morning, because the dough had risen already. But when I looked more closely, I was struck by the fact that the dough seemed to be depressed in the middle—and that the depression was ragged and uneven . . . I tugged the investigator by the hem of his coat, and told him this as I pointed at the trough.

"We rushed to the trough—and saw that something had been hastily stuck in it. We pulled it out—it was a shirt. We stretched it out, examined it—and found dried blood on the sleeves and bosom.

"And so, all the evidence we needed was in that kneading-trough!

"We walked away, taking our quarry with us.

"After this, it was smooth sailing all the way. The boots of the younger Baydash matched the footprints found in the lord's orchard and near his window, and herdsmen—who spent the nights with their horses at the edge of the forest—were located, and they said that they'd seen him returning home very late on the very night the lord had been slain. In a word, it was smooth sailing.

"'You're a great fellow!' the investigator said to me. 'A true Lecocq!'

"I just looked at him in triumph, as if to say: 'What did I tell you? But what did you think?'

"Everyone began talking about the investigation once again. Everyone was asking me about this matter, about the solving of the crime—such a terrible crime, such a daring crime and, most importantly, such a mysterious crime. And I gave them—because I was in a position to do so—the most interesting information, because after all, it was I, I who had solved it!

"Some time went by. One morning, probably about eight o'clock, I decided to go for a swim. The stream—a rather small stream that flowed beyond the village—was quite far from our home, and I had to pass through most of the village to get there. I set out from home and, as always, my dog was at my side. I was just walking along, without paying much attention to anything in particular. As I passed by the district office, I saw a group of people gathered near it, and there was a wagon there as well.

"As soon as I saw the people, I immediately surmised what was happening. Andriy Baydash, who up to now had been locked up in the district office, was being transferred to a prison.

"It was the last moment before his departure. Andriy should have been seated on the wagon already. His family had come to say their farewells. I looked at them—and my heart turned cold.

"Andriy was standing there, and it looked as if he had grown dark, like a cloud. He was quietly saying a few words to his father, probably: 'Farewell, father!' I did not hear exactly what he said. The old man did not say anything—he could not utter a word. His lips were twisted in mute grief, and only tears, silent tears, rolled down his old, gaunt face to his long grey beard. I could clearly see those large tears rolling down his cheeks.

"'Come on now, come on! It's time to go!' Some official—probably the county policeman—shouted, as he walked out to the porch from the building.

"At this point, a woman broke her way through to Andriy. I had not noticed her at first, because she'd been standing stooped over the fence. But now she tore herself away from the fence and threw herself at Andriy. I realised that it was his mother. She embraced the young man, wound her arms tightly around his neck, and began to wail.

"Oh, my God, my God! What a lament that was! It was an inhuman, unearthly shrieking.

"It was no wonder—they were taking her last son away from her. One had been taken away because of a cartload of wood, and the other because of revenge. And she did not expect to see this one at home ever again. He was being sent to Siberia for two years, and she was old already . . .

"She was wailing: 'Oh, my dear Andriy, oh, my da-a-a-rling little dove! You're my own dearest little child!'

"When I heard this wailing—I don't know what happened to me! Something beyond my power tore me away from where I was standing and carried me far, far away, so that I would not hear that shrieking and wailing!

"I found myself beyond the village, and I walked as if I were in a fog, giving no thought to where I was going.

"I ended up in the forest, in one of its densest spots. I can't describe what was going on in my soul at that time. But my anguish must have been quite evident, for even Sniffer sensed it. He came up to me, placed his muzzle on my knees, and looked up at me ever so sorrowfully. I shoved him away, even though, if truth be told, I had no right to do this. Was not Sniffer a truly worthy companion for me? What had urged me on to do the investigation? And now, all because of me, those unfortunate people were weeping.

"Had I felt sorry for the murdered man? I didn't know him; I'd only heard about him, heard that he'd decided to ruin an entire family because of a load of firewood from his forest. Did I feel sorry for him? No! I hadn't even thought about his life on that cursed night when I'd gone—and taken others with me—to conduct an investigation. At that time, I'd only thought about the fact that I would solve a *mysterious* crime! So there you have it— it was the canine fervour for 'the kill' that had urged me on and led me to the kneading trough!

"I collapsed on the grass and sat there, grievously reproaching myself. I attempted to console myself with the thought that, after all, Andriy Baydash had committed a crime. But another thought immediately surfaced in my mind: 'Whose sin was the most heinous—the old lord's, Andriy's or . . . mine?'

"Of course, it was this last question that caused me the most profound anguish. My ears were ringing with the unearthly lamenting of the old mother; my eyes were brimming with the voiceless tears of the silent father. I was wringing my hands so hard that my knuckles were cracking.

"And all around me, everything was so joyous, so beautiful! This idyllic spot in the grove was full of life, of earthly delights. The sun peeked through the branches at my little clearing, and its rays were also dancing, farther away, on a little lake. Close by, a little bee was buzzing busily over a freshly opened forest flower. And the warbling of a nightingale permeated the air. Somewhere, quite close by in the thickets, a nightingale was singing joyfully, exultantly, and its singing reminded me of *that* night—even though its song was different now.

"Then, in the nocturnal singing, in the grove flooded with moonlight, there was something mysterious, some kind of grief and oppressiveness; but now, on this bright, fresh, sunny morning, the nightingale's song rang with joy, with pure happiness, with freedom. But it was tearing my soul apart. I rose to my feet and fled from the grove, so that I would not hear that singing.

"And there you have the whole story—the one you wanted to hear."

My guest sighed and fell silent. I also remained silent. Silence descended all around us. But then, in a remote corner of the darkened orchard, the nightingale sang out once again, and its brilliant singing resonated in that silence, prevailing over everything else.

"Let's go into the house! It's turning cool, and you'll catch a cold. Come!"

It was my guest who whispered this in a husky voice. I silently did as my guest desired. I rose from the bench and set out for the house, even though I knew that it was not his concern for me that was driving my guest from the orchard—it was the nightingale's song.

Help!
(1897)

"It's so beautiful! Lord, how beautifully they're singing! It's as if we were in paradise!"

This is what the more serious young married women were whispering to each other in church. And as they softly recited their prayers, they kept glancing at the cantor's corner—the source of the clear and moving chanting.

It was the girls who were singing: Orysya Yaroshenko and Tetyana Bilyk, who had been singing for a good three years, and a few younger ones who followed their lead. Although these two older girls had left school a few years ago, the teacher, Mykolay Semenovych, encouraged them to come and sing in the church on feast days, because they were the best singers in the village.

This was especially true of Orysya Yaroshenko, who sang with the voice of an angel. Her mother, Yavdokha Yaroshenko, listened with unabashed delight. Her blissful smile never faded as she crossed herself and bowed her head in prayer. After all, she was the mother. It brought such pleasure to her maternal heart! Her soul rejoiced!

"We sing to You, we praise You, O Lord, and we pray to You, O God of ours!" Orysya intoned vigorously and passionately, oblivious to the people around her.

She always looked straight ahead. Directly in front of her was the icon of the Resurrection. The Lord, having risen from His grave, appeared to be soaring into heaven; and heaven was incredibly bright and blue, with the light of the Lord penetrating it. Wisps of incense wafted under the icon, and the figure of the Lord rose from them as if from behind heavenly clouds.

It was a cold day, the wintry Feast of St. Nicholas, and Orysya was bundled up in a warm, white cloak. But her head was not covered; it was only tied around with a narrowly folded scarf that left the top of her head almost completely bare. Her braid was also left free. She was thin, or rather, slender, and young—she had turned seventeen on the Feast of St. Mary the Protectress—and quite attractive. Her delicate face was like an open flower, and her eyebrows, as the saying goes, were finely strung, like beads.

It is quite understandable, therefore, that Orysya would catch the eye of some people! Take Panko Sakhnenko; he was always admiring her and smiling. He even smoothed his moustache with his hand to hide an affectionate smile, but it was no use. As they say, you can't keep the cat in the bag!

Now the parishioners were coming out of church, and as they advanced down the street, the older people moved along in one line, and the younger ones in another. The young lads pretended not to be walking with the girls, but the dark beauties knew that the talk in the boys' cluster was about them, and nothing else. It was true—the laughter and the conversation centred entirely on the girls.

"We no longer need cantors in our church." Omelko laughed. "The girls can manage quite nicely, ha-ha-ha!"

"Perhaps one of them will even become a priest, and we'll drive her around in a sieve! Did you hear that Tetyana?" Petro shouted.

"I hope you get as many sores as there are holes in a sieve," Tetyana tossed at them, giggling.

The boys continued laughing and joking, not at all offended by her remark.

"Well, holy and pious ones, see that you come to Solovyikha's place tonight; we'll bring the musicians," Panko said gently, and he leaned towards Orysya as he walked by the girls.

Orysya did not say anything; she did not even look at him, but Panko discerned something in her appearance and her laughter that told him she would be there. He walked swiftly past the girls and set out for his home, which was quite far off to the right. Orysya, continuing her conversation with Tetyana, arrived home first; her mother, Yavdokha, followed soon after.

Her father, who was not feeling well, had stayed at home; he had suffered aches and pains since Sunday, when he had gone to town to sell some oats. He asked that dinner be served as quickly as possible, and soon they were all sitting at the table: the parents,

Orysya, two younger teenage girls, and three little boys—quite a large family! They discussed this and that; but what kind of conversation can there be with so many children? This one wanted more cornmeal mush, that one wanted some bread, and still another had to be chastised for fooling around.

After dinner, the second eldest daughter, Sanka, and the two younger boys went to the skating rink, but the father told the eldest boy, Semenko, to read from the Holy Book. He should be reading, because he was a pupil already; and, after all, the book had been purchased especially for him.

Well, it truly was a momentous occasion! Yavdokha even burned some incense. You see, the potters now make special little pots with perforated covers for this purpose; all you have to do is throw in some coals, add a little bit of incense, put the cover back on, and the incense burns quite nicely.

Semenko read at the head of the table. At first the father leaned on his hand and listened; then he lay down on a pillow on the floor and fell asleep. Yavdokha took some hemp to the priest's wife, who was going to card it. To whom was Semenko supposed to read? He cut short his laborious sounding out of the words and ran off to the skating rink as well.

As Orysya picked up the Holy Book to put it back on the shelf, she took a good look at it. Even though she had gone to school for a while, she was not able to read this book; she had never attempted anything like it. Her schooling had been cut short, too short, because her mother needed help at home.

The reading Orysya had done in school was different somehow; it was not at all like this. She took down from the shelf her old primer that Semenko was now using. The words in it were slightly different than those in the Holy Book.

Orysya grew thoughtful. She began to recall a few things the teacher had said about why this was so, but then she sighed deeply. She couldn't remember now, and even back then, it hadn't made much sense. If only she'd been able to stay in school just a little longer . . .

The door creaked open, and Tetyana glanced into the house.

"Are you alone?" she asked, as she walked in and began to take off her outer garments.

She had just come in from the frost, and a fresh breeze came in with her and wafted through the house.

"I've come," she continued, "to restring my necklace. Maybe you have a finer needle. Is your mother at home?"

The girls sat down, began stringing the beads, and carried on with their conversation.

"There are going to be two violins tonight," Tetyana went on, "because Kalenyk has come back."

Orysya's face lit up. Everyone knew that no one could play like Kalenyk. Oh, how he played! Orysya could hear both the sound of the violin and the clatter of heels and . . . just as sometimes in her dreams, she saw Panko, his smiling face . . . He was bending over, laughing, and tugging at her sleeve . . .

Tetyana was saying something, and Orysya smiled joyfully— but not at her . . .

II

One certainly could tell where the young people were gathered that evening. It was not easy to hear the violin, but the drum could be heard from far off! The girls rushed to Solovyikha's house. The children ran there too, and they crowded around the house and kept peeking into the porch and through the windows until they were chased home.

The house was filled with noise and dancing. The tables were laden with food and drink. After all, if it's pot luck—then let's have a feast! And if there's music—then let's dance!

Yes indeed, there was Orysya—flitting about like a butterfly. There was no stopping her! She was dancing opposite Tetyana with such teeny, tiny steps that, when she spun around, her necklace jingled. Her ribbons streamed behind her, and her face was flaming; her eyes were sparkling—she could no longer keep them lowered to the floor. They darted around the room and flashed a brilliant smile at Panko! Then she moved backwards with her arms outstretched, and her girlish figure swayed ever so lithely, while her heels made tapping sounds—tap, tap!

There was bedlam in the house—some couples were leaving the dance, others were joining in. Only the musicians did not rest; they played vigorously, without stopping.

Inflamed and flushed, Orysya ran out of the house. She felt hot, boiling-hot, and wanted to cool off outdoors. It was dark outside, with only the odd star sparkling in the sky; but the air was exhilarating, and it rushed in a cool stream into her overheated breast.

"Oh!" Orysya shrieked.

Someone was tugging at the cloak that was flung carelessly over her shoulders.

"Are you hot? Silly! You'll freeze to death like that! "

Oh! It was his voice, Panko's . . . It was he.

"You silly little thing! Silly!" he said. "At least if you'd dress properly!" He adjusted the cloak on her back, all the while drawing her closer and closer . . .

"Let me go! Go away!" Orysya cried, resisting him.

"Why would I let you go! You see, you can't escape, and I won't let you if I don't want to!" Panko said. "Anyway, what reason is there to escape? And where to?" He was breathing heavily as he spoke, and his flushed face bent ever nearer.

There was no escape! She felt faint . . . Had she really kissed him? Oh! Her head dropped weakly on his chest and, all the while, he was hugging and kissing her!

"Orysya! Orysya, where are you?" Tetyana was calling from the porch.

Orysya fluttered off to the house like a startled bird. At the last moment, Panko tried to stop her by grabbing her hand, but she snatched it away from his burning touch. Someone might see!

III

"You're going to marry him, yes you will! I can see that!" Tetyana said to Orysya in the springtime, as she dug alongside her in the lord's garden.

Orysya remained silent.

Tetyana chattered on: "Why, even Solovyikha said that Panko is sending matchmakers. Who would he send them to, if not to you?"

"Why me? There's no shortage of girls!" Orysya retorted, and she continued digging diligently.

"It's true there are lots of girls. There are also many young men in the district, but I know you'll marry Panko. You might even marry him this spring if he sends his matchmakers."

"Oh, who'd send matchmakers now, in the springtime! There's no money or anything else."

Orysya had barely finished saying this when a cry resounded in the garden: "Girls! Girls!"

"What is it? Why is Zinka running like mad?" the girls wondered.

They stopped digging and watched as a flushed, chubby girl ran swiftly across the garden towards the female work brigade.

"Girls!" Zinka said, trying to catch her breath after her frantic run. "Over there! They've come . . . for girls . . . from the Andronivska farm. They're calling us to work . . . to weed . . . in the beet fields . . . and so on . . . for the whole summer! Oh, Lord, I'm exhausted!"

There was noise and confusion. The girls, dropping their hoes and gathering into a group, peppered her with questions and deliberated.

"Hey, come on now! Come on! Why have you stopped working?" the lord's housekeeper shouted. "Is this how you work? I take my eyes off you for a minute, and you declare a holiday? You stand around doing nothing?"

The girls reluctantly began to dig again. They did not say anything to the housekeeper about what had caused them to leave their work—why should they?

As they continued digging, however, they did not stop talking among themselves. After all, was this not an exciting matter?

Before long, they were given a break for lunch. That was when the talking began in earnest.

But it was not only here; there was talk everywhere, even on the other side of the village. The girls conferred, the mothers conferred—should they go to work in the beet fields, or should they not? It was said good money could be earned there. The year before, the girls from the village of Petrivka had gone to Yakhnivka. Well, the Andronivska farm was farther away, but what did that matter? If only the wages were good. As it was, what was there to live on? How could you buy anything at all—even what you really needed?

IV

It was suppertime in the Yaroshenko home. But not all the family was eating. The father and the children were at the table, but the mother was sitting apart on a bench, deep in thought, with her hands resting on her knees. Orysya was standing by the bake oven, leaning on her hand and looking intently at the flickering, dying embers that had been raked out on the hearth.

"Sit down and have your supper, Orysya," her mother called out. "Why are you standing there? What's there to worry about?"

"I'm not worrying!" Orysya replied. Frowning, she abruptly stepped up to the table and silently picked up her spoon.

"What in the world should we do?" the mother reflected out loud, remaining where she was, off to one side. "Should Orysya go to the beet fields, or shouldn't she? What do you think, old man?"

"What's it to me? the father responded. "It doesn't matter to me. Do as you see fit! It's your business . . ."

"There's a man for you—honest to God! After all, you are the father! You should help me decide what and how things should be done."

"What kind of advice am I supposed to give? It's for you to decide whether or not it pays."

"Well, if it didn't pay, people wouldn't go!" Yavdokha retorted.

"It's no big deal to go, but what does one bring back?" the father observed. "What if they cheat the workers?"

"But why should they cheat? After all, there's an agreement; even an official document is signed. How could they do such a thing? The pay is guaranteed!" the mother argued.

"Well, if it's guaranteed, then it's guaranteed," the father responded curtly.

"There's only one problem—she's still young, and it's far away."

"Yes, she is young. Why should she be going off somewhere to work? She's kind of sickly, as well."

"Well, and just what will she accomplish sitting at home?" the mother was annoyed again. "What will she earn here? She certainly could use a penny or two. In the fall, matchmakers may come, and what will she bring to her marriage? What does she have in her hope chest? How will we put on a wedding? Do we have so much as an extra penny?"

"Good Lord! I've already told you to do whatever you think is best! I'm not getting involved in this!"

The father, crossing himself, moved away from the table.

"Is Tetyana going?" the mother asked Orysya.

"Yes, she is," the girl replied as she went out into the porch.

"Where are you going?" Yavdokha asked.

"I'll go fetch some water. The children splashed around and used it all up."

Orysya took the pail and went to fetch some water. She thought that maybe . . . But no, she did not meet Panko anywhere.

She did, however, meet him on the street later that evening. He had not been around for two days, but now he was here.

The girls were singing, some more loudly than ever, but Orysya did not feel like singing—her throat felt constricted.

"So, are you going to the beet fields?" Panko asked, sitting down on the logs beside her and stealthily putting his arm around her waist in the spring dusk. "Are you going?"

"I'm going," Orysya replied quietly.

"And how are things going to work out?"

"What things?"

"Well, everything . . . I wanted to send the matchmakers. Will it have to wait until autumn? That's what it looks like. It's true it's more convenient in the fall; now, it's hard to know how father will . . . it's not the time for it. There's not much money now."

"Well, that's just it! Money!" the girl interrupted impatiently. "It's all because of money."

Panko fell silent. His arm dropped from the girl's waist. Then he embraced her again, but this time around the shoulders, and said: "But it's so long to wait! Not to see each other for the whole summer. You won't forget about me there, will you?" he asked, smiling and pressing his moustache against her cheek. "You won't stop thinking about me? You won't renounce me?"

"No," Orysya said softly.

A star rolled across the pale sky, and Orysya shuddered. It seemed to her that something had brushed against her heart. She felt a cold wave of fear wash over her.

V

After two weeks at the Andronivska farm, the girls became accustomed to the work, to the people, and to the sheds in which they had to live. They gradually became accustomed to everything.

But all the same, it was, one must admit, a faraway place, not like their own villages. The people here were unknown quantities. Something strange was happening in these villages in matters of faith. There were so many villagers who did not attend church, who did not pray in front of icons. They were even throwing the icons out of their homes! Lord! It was all very frightening. Why were they doing that? What made them do that? What were they thinking of?

"They've gone mad!" some of the villagers said.

But those Khlysts, or whatever they were called, argued their point of view. Orysya thought a lot about one of the village girls, Kharytyna, who often worked in the beet fields alongside her. She was tall, pale, scrawny, and not that young anymore. When she looked at you with those dark eyes of hers, it felt as if she were gazing right into your soul, and you felt so sad.

She had already borne witness to Orysya several times. Yesterday, she had even said that she had not married, and never would, because marriage was a sin. After all, do people live only to satisfy and debauch their bodies? Our Lord suffered, endured so much torment, and are we to indulge ourselves like animals and propagate sin as our legacy? It was an abomination, a sin!

"But that's not so," Orysya shyly responded. "What kind of sin is it? After all, people enter into an honourable marriage, they stand before the altar in wedding wreaths . . ."

"Marriage! Wedding wreaths! It's more than a sin!" Kharytyna shouted. "It's worse. They've contrived a deception, and now they're rejoicing in it—and they're deceiving both themselves and others. When a woman sneaks about furtively with someone, she's called a prostitute, a whore. But if a priest leads her around the tetrapod before the altar and, instead of a young girl's wreath, the periwinkle wreath—that shameful cover of marriage—is placed on her head in church, then she may indulge in lewd behaviour with public approval? She can then participate as much as she wants to in that abomination, and she can guide as many children as she desires into the same kind of sin and dissolute behaviour? Did our Lord get married? Did He have children? No! Instead of accepting the marriage wreath, He accepted the cross. Instead of children, He had only brother apprentices and faithful sisters."

Orysya remained silent. What could she say to Kharytyna? She didn't know anything.

Kharytyna, seeing that Orysya was silent and deep in thought, gazed ever more intently into her eyes.

One Saturday evening Kharytyna said: "Come, Orysya, let's go join our people. We're having a gathering this evening."

It seemed to Orysya that her heart turned cold; however, in the evening she went with Kharytyna. She was trembling, but she went.

The house was full of people, and a light was burning. Holy Books were being read at the table, and heated discussions were being held.

It was frightening to watch these people; they seized each other by the arms, and their eyes blazed. Then they sang a prayer, or a song—a "psalm," as they called it. It sounded something like those sung in church; but no, it was not the same. For some reason, your heart trembled from this singing. People were gravely beating themselves on their chests with their fists, and they were singing loudly, with emotion—as if a groan were spreading through the house.

Then, a woman—quite young yet—really did groan. She fell to the ground, clasped her hands to her breast, and lamented loudly: "O Lord, my only Saviour! You're patient. You're merciful. Have pity on me, a sinner. Forgive me. Give me the strength to live according to the truth!"

The young woman was weeping, repenting, and everyone was quietly praying with their hands folded.

"Nazar, Nazar has come!" Everyone in the house began to buzz. "Nazar Smaliy has come!"

Orysya turned around to have a look. In the middle of the room, an elderly man was pushing his way through the crowd. He was emaciated, hollow-eyed, and his feet were wrapped in cloths oozing with blood and pus.

Whispering in fragments, Kharytyna told Orysya that this man had suffered greatly during the winter at the hands of his fellow villagers. He had been beaten in the district office; everywhere he went, he had been beaten. He had been dragged by his feet through the steppes, with his head scraping the frozen ploughed fields. He had been forced to walk barefoot over the frost, and that was when he had frozen his feet, and the sores were still putrefying. Despite all this, they had not been able to break him. He had not repudiated his way of thinking; he had not betrayed the true Lord; he had not renounced his beliefs.

Orysya observed the old man silently. He was crushed with grief, and he appeared to have a fearful, pleading look on his face, but all the same, he had come! He fell to his knees and, in a broken voice, began to sing a psalm, straight from his heart and his aching soul:

"Oh, our most beloved Saviour,
It was for us that You suffered on this earth!"

The people in the room immediately joined in: "Our righteous Lord, teach us to be worthy of Your great sacrifice!"

Orysya did not even know when she began to sing with them in that beautiful, young voice of hers. Kharytyna glanced at her, grabbed her quickly by the arm, and led her into the very midst of the brethren.

VI

The girls returned home just before the Feast of St. Mary the Protectress. Orysya walked into the house early in the evening. Her father was not at home; he was threshing at his brother's place. But her mother was fussing by the cradle with the youngest boy. When she glanced up, she almost dropped the child.

"Oh, dear mother of mine! Orysya has returned! So how are you? Did everyone come back?"

As Orysya stepped into the house she glanced up at the icon corner, and a shadow fell across her face. Then, after standing still for a short while, she silently put down her bundle, went to her mother, embraced her, and kissed her hand.

"Well, how are you? How was it?" her mother asked. And then she interrupted herself. "Take off your cloak, my child. Do you want to eat?"

The door creaked as it opened time and again, and various kinfolk and neighbours rushed in, asking about everything and chatting among themselves. All the children also came home. A fire was set in the stove, and Yavdokha began to prepare supper. She was so happy now, so very happy, Lord! She talked and talked . . . and kept glancing at Orysya. There seemed to be something different about her: she seemed thinner, paler, so much so that her eyes appeared bigger, very big indeed. Even a neighbour began to question Orysya: "Why have you lost so much weight?"

"That's right, that's what I think, too," her mother picked up on the question. "Perhaps you're not well, my child?"

"No, I'm fine!" Orysya replied softly.

"Listen, what do you expect from her?" a kinswoman of Yavdokha's spoke up. "The poor thing is tired from the trip, and she's exhausted from the summer's work. Do you suppose it was easy there? You'd do better to give her something to eat as soon as possible!"

"Of course, right away!" Yavdokha bustled about. "It's already on the table, Orysya. There's also fresh bread; I just baked it today—have some!"

But Orysya pulled out a piece of cloth from the bosom of her blouse, took out her money, and gave it to her mother: "Here you are, mother, put it away—for the taxes or something."

"What a thing to say!" her mother said joyously, as she counted the money. "Why should it be for the taxes? Your father will sell our young bull to cover them; we've been keeping him for the market. But this money is yours! I'll put it away in the trunk. Maybe it will come in handy for you."

"Of course it will come in handy!" the young women chimed in merrily. "You might be receiving matchmakers soon!"

"I swear to God, my dear kinswoman," the eldest among them said to Yavdokha. "I was washing clothes in the pond yesterday, and old lady Sakhnenko told me that their Panko will send matchmakers to your house just as soon as the girls come home. And she herself wants this, because she really needs a daughter-in-law: 'I'm not feeling all that well anymore,' she said."

The old kinswoman kept on talking. Orysya's heart fainted when the old woman mentioned Panko and the matchmakers, and she gripped the table where she was standing . . .

VII

The next day, Yavdokha tied a new, dark wine kerchief edged with a delicate design on her head. It was an important holiday, the Feast Day of St. Mary the Protectress, and she was going to church.

"Aren't you dressing yet?" she ask her daughter. "The bell is ringing already. Aren't you going to church?"

"No . . ." Orysya responded quietly.

"Why not?"

"Just . . . because . . . I'm not feeling too well."

Her mother glanced at her. She truly did look quite pale and sickly. The poor girl had really wasted away on that farm. Or perhaps she'd been hexed by someone . . . or put under an evil spell! In any event, old lady Kalynykha should be called in. But maybe it would pass without that. The girl hadn't slept enough yet; she hadn't had enough rest.

The mother left for church, and Orysya remained behind. She sat in deep thought for a while, then she sighed and went outdoors. She found it stifling in that house. Outside, Orysya's younger sisters amused her for a while. They chattered away and pointed things out to her.

"Look, the carnations are still blooming."

"And here's the dahlia our godmother gave us in the spring."

Everyone had something to say.

Yavdokha came home from church, and she was very happy. May God forgive her, but she had enjoyed watching Panko Sakhnenko today. He kept staring around the church—he'd look at the deacons' corner, glance here and there, walk out of church, and come back in again! Well, she knew only too well what he was looking for—and she found it so amusing! And old lady Sakhnenko had asked about Orysya, and the two women who expected to be in-laws exchanged a few words . . . Others had inquired about her as well, for everyone knew the girls had returned.

"Everyone was asking about you," Orysya's mother said to her kindly. "The people missed your singing; they said: 'No one can sing in church for us like your Orysya.'"

Orysya only nodded her head silently. After dinner, instead of lying down to rest, her mother opened the hope chest and started going through it, rearranging the bundles of cloth and the *rushnyky [embroidered linen ceremonial cloths]*.

"What are you doing, mother?" Orysya asked. She watched her mother intently out of the corner of her eye.

"I'm just rearranging things a bit," her mother said seriously. Orysya's heart thumped, but she did not dare to say anything.

Towards evening, just as Orysya was crossing the threshold with pails in hand—she was on her way to fetch some water—some people carrying ceremonial bread came through the gate. She glanced at them and stood dumbstruck for a moment; then, with superhuman strength, she dashed back into the porch, dropped the pails helter-skelter, and raced off into the orchard.

But the matchmakers interpreted her actions in their own way: "Oh, what a clever girl! She didn't want to cross our path with empty pails. Well, it's a good thing that she turned back. What a fine girl!"

The old folks welcomed the guests. They talked about this and that, and the matchmakers saw that things would go just fine. Anyone with experience in these matters can tell from the very first word how things will work out. There was no need to engage in long conversations, but they had to talk—for the sake of tradition.

Panko, trailing the matchmakers, wandered about in the yard and peeped into the windows. He walked through the porch and out into the orchard. Oh, my Lord! He had thought Orysya was in the house, but here she was, standing by the stile! She caught sight of Panko, caught hold of the fence and, like a wounded bird, slumped down on a stump beside it.

"Greetings, Orysya dearest!" Panko shouted happily.

"Greetings," Orysya responded softly, and her heart fluttered so wildly that it threatened to leap out of her breast.

"Well, how are you? You've lost weight! But that's nothing. You'll get better! I've really missed you! I thought you'd never come back! But here you are . . . my little swallow has flown home!"

Orysya blushed, and a joyous smile involuntarily urged itself to her lips. Twisting her apron in her hands, she got up the nerve to glance at Panko. He was the same, only even more handsome! Either his eyes had grown brighter, or his moustache had grown darker. And his smile!

"Orysya, Orysya darling! Where are you?" her mother called in a dignified manner. "Oh! Here she is! And you've come here as well, my boy? Well, if the wind has sent you to us, then you may as well come into the house. There's no point wandering in the lanes. Just go to the house now—and you too."

Yavdokha touched Orysya on the shoulder, ever so tenderly. The mother was well aware that Orysya liked Panko. All three entered the house. The older folks joked and went through the usual ritual. Panko stood there, mashing his cap in his hands. Then he glanced at Orysya and, appearing to grow happier, he smilingly said something in response to the matchmakers.

But Orysya stood by the bake oven as if in a dream . . . Where was she? What was happening here? What was happening to her?

Her mother took the *rushnyky* and a kerchief out of the chest and gave them to her to present to Panko and the matchmakers. Panko took the kerchief from Orysya and began tying it on himself; then he smiled and said to her: "Well, come on, help me!"

Without realising what she was doing, Orysya, her hands trembling, helped him tie the kerchief. Panko gazed at her tenderly and joyfully. He was so handsome, so good, so dear!

"There, now we've been bound," the matchmakers said. "So now the matter is settled. Thank the good mistress, bridegroom, for having instructed her daughter to get up early and embroider *rushnyky* . . ."

Bridegroom! Panko was now a bridegroom. The bride staggered and fell against the bake oven; but the matchmakers, walking out of the house, thought that, in keeping with the time-honoured tradition, she was modestly averting her eyes and ritually picking at the lime facade of the oven.

She had bound him! She was a bride!

VIII

Two days went by. At dawn, Orysya woke from a terrible dream. She rose from bed and, just as she was, in her night-gown, she kneeled on the bench with clasped hands. Once again she'd had that horrible, terrible dream. "O Lord, O Saviour! What has happened? How could it have happened? What will happen now?"

Had she ruined herself completely? Completely? Already? What, oh what, was to be done? The girl pressed her hands to her face, and hot tears poured down her cheeks.

Morning came, and her mother told her to do this and that, but Orysya walked around as if she did not have the strength to do anything, as if she were dreaming, or not quite herself.

"What have I done? What has happened?"

A dreadful thought stirred somewhere within her, and then, like a cold stone, it weighed down upon her soul. Orysya walked and talked, but she had no idea what she was doing, why she was doing it, or what would happen next. It was as if she had drowned, as if a wave were sweeping her along . . .

The days kept passing by. It was Friday already, and the wedding was on Sunday. Mother had already gone into town and bought everything; and she had taken Orysya with her to buy kerchiefs and presents for everyone, even the priest!

On Saturday evening, Orysya found herself sitting behind the table. The girls were singing and weaving the wedding wreaths out of periwinkle, but Orysya was not crying as young brides-to-be are supposed to. No, she could not cry. She sat as if she had been struck by lightning. It would be a sin to cry now. She was a sinner, beyond redemption. She had betrayed her Saviour; she had betrayed the Lord! For what had she betrayed Him? For her sinful love of a young man, Panko. Was she to live with him as others live together? Was she to bear children? How many souls would descend from her into the same sin, into perdition?

Orysya wrung her hands, but nothing could help her now! The wedding wreath, the last wreath of her girlhood, was being prepared for her head.

On Sunday, the clamour in Yaroshenko's yard and house began very early in the morning. There were the sounds of cooking and baking, and of wagons and horses being readied to drive the young couple to church. There were all kinds of matters to attend to. Everyone had his or her own task to do. Both the old and the young came to watch the bride being dressed for the marriage ceremony.

The bridesmaids had come very early. Orysya's heart filled with grief when she looked at their happy faces, especially at Tetyana's.

She was her true friend, but even she could not save Orysya, nor could she help her in any way.

More and more people gathered in the yard. The sound of music could be heard. The bridegroom was coming with his best man! And, oh, he was so handsome! His black hair was shining under a grey Persian lamb hat, his face was ruddy, and he was such a vigorous and vibrant young man.

He strode into the house, glanced at Orysya, and gave her a hint of a smile. She looked at him as well, but very piercingly, fearfully, as if she were looking at an enemy. They were seated together on the wedding dais. The bridesmaids were singing, and a heavy tear rolled down Orysya's cheek.

"Don't cry. Why are you crying?" Panko was speaking softly. He wanted to cheer her up with a smile and took hold of her hand under the table. Orysya removed her hand. For just a moment, she had blushed, but now she was once again as white as the wall. Only her eyes flashed with fear, with despair, like those of a cornered animal.

"Come on, let's go! It's time to leave!" the best man shouted. "The priest told us not to be late!"

Everyone began bustling about.

The young couple was led out from behind the table. Her father and mother, holding icons and holy bread in their hands, were sitting on the bench under the icons. When Orysya came up to her mother, she fell to her knees and could not rise to her feet again. Panko had to help her up. She fell down once again, buried her face in her mother's hands, and began to weep.

Orysya's heart cried out: "Mummy, my dearest mummy, my dearest dove! Save me, save me!"

But that cry did not reach her lips, for Orysya knew her mother would not save her.

Her mother was also crying. She was shedding tears over her child, but not out of sadness. She would not listen, she would not understand the deep grief of her child . . .

"Come on, quickly! Let's go. Honest-to-God! How long is this going to go on?" the best man shouted again.

They began to move out of the house, and Orysya was led away. There was no way out, no turning back. Nothing more could be done.

The church was filled with people. There were three couples that were to be joined in marriage that day. Panko and Orysya were at the head of the line.

Since she had returned, Orysya had not been in church. Oh, my God! She had come here, into this—as people called it—God's home, for the purpose of betraying her Lord and Saviour! There He was, over there; His image was painted on the iconostasis, in the place of honour. What a stern face! His eyes appeared to be looking at her, and His hand was outstretched, not as if He were offering a blessing, but as if He were cursing her! Orysya looked at the icon in terror. Why had they painted Him as being so severe, when it was they who were sending innocent souls to perdition?

Orysya's head was swirling; her ears were buzzing. She heard nothing of what was being said, of what was being sung around her. Now their hands were being bound; she could no longer distinguish her hand from that of the one to whom she was being wed forever, to the eternal damnation and ruination of her body and her soul.

Orysya walked out of church as if she were drunk. She was lifted up into the wagon, and they set out for home.

The musicians played, and the young women greeted them with raucous singing:

"The cranberry is shredded, it's shredded,
And our Orysya is wedded, is wedded!"

Once again Orysya was behind the table. Everywhere around her there were people eating and drinking; there was noise, laughter, and singing. And the talk! Such ribald talk! Even Panko lowered his head at times, embarrassed by some of the things that were being said. The young women were already talking about the married woman's head-dress, and they were bringing it to her.

"What?" she thought in a panic. "Right now? They would remove her young girl's wreath right now and give it to him— her husband?"

The horses were harnessed, and people began to say it was time to take the bride to the bridegroom's dwelling. Everyone was moving in, drawing nearer . . .

A last rush of strength, born of despair, filled Orysya's heart. Her hot eyes darted about like those of a trapped weasel. An idea flashed into her mind like a streak of lightning. But no! That thought had occurred to her more than once. Only now, in this last moment, it no longer seemed impossible, but the only way . . .

Yes, there was still time, there was still a moment in which to save herself from this shame, from this betrayal of her Lord.

"My Saviour, save me, help me! You will forgive me, for You know why I'm doing this!"

"Where is the bride? Where is Orysya?" the young women asked those who were supposed to take her to the bridegroom's home.

"Why, she was right here. She was standing right here!"

"She ran into the cellar!" Orysya's little sister said.

The trapdoor to the cellar was open. During all the commotion, Orysya had jumped in. Oh, how she hurried!

"Oh, my Lord! Why won't the sash come undone? There are so many knots! Ah! There . . . it's undone. Where can it be fastened? Ah, yes! Right here, on the ladder."

Her hands were tangled in her ribbons, but the noose encircled her neck . . .

"My Saviour! Forgive me! Accept my innocent soul! It is not to blame!"

"Orysya! Orysya!" someone was shouting right by the ladder.

"Who is calling? Mother? No, it's Christ! There's a light shining in bright broad beams, in golden sparks. It is His kingdom that is shining; it is His wreath! I'm coming to You, I'm coming to You, my Saviour, my World! Oh, where's the light? Where is the road to Him? It's dark! Dark! So dark!"

Orysya was silent, numb. But her mother was screaming and weeping over her: "Help! Help her, my good people! Save her! My child has hanged herself!"

But no one saved Orysya.

No one!

The White Cat
(1901)

Master Mykola is writing his "major *oeuvre[work]*." Master Mykola is such a young scholar that he does not have a separate study, but only a small anteroom off the bedroom that looks like a sitting room, and it is in this room that his desk stands. And the appearance of that desk is such, that if you glanced at it, you would immediately be able to tell that the master of the house is writing his "major *oeuvre.*"

On the table, and above it, there are heaps of books, all those reference books—those "sources"—some big, and some small, some closed, some opened, and some marked with bookmarks; there are many scraps of paper, some with neat writing on them, while others are all scratched out; and then there is a large number of small cards on which entire excerpts have been copied. There are also all the tools required for writing—pens, pencils—in a state of great disarray.

Master Mykola, however, does not want anyone to tidy up his desk; indeed, he would have preferred if no one even dusted it, if no one attempted to bring about that infamous tidiness which is so dear to people who look after the desk of a person who is involved in writing, but which Master Mykola resented, because that tidying up disrupted the train of thought that tied him both to his "sources" and to the writing in which he was engaged.

It was not only Master Mykola's desk, but also his life, that had reached that chronic state when a young scholar is said to be "writing his 'major *oeuvre* for his degree'." Master Mykola could not enjoy his former pleasures, and he seldom saw even his closest friends. And as for the theatre—there was no point in even talking about it! He could not become engrossed in reading the newest novel serialised in his favourite journal; he could not sit in a chair and "*far niente [do nothing]*" while indulging himself delectably, and to his heart's content, in dreaming his poetic dreams. Master Mykola was rarely even permitted to go for a walk, despite the fact that he liked to stroll down Khreshchatyk, Kyiv's main thoroughfare, or other streets.

But who was it who could allow or disallow Master Mykola to do certain things when he was twenty-three years old, was no longer a child, and was his own master? Well, that was the rub—he was his own master, and he was not, for Master Mykola was married. Yes, notwithstanding the fact that he was only twenty-three years old, Master Mykola was married. Now do you understand?

Master Mykola was not quite finished university. Master Mykola did not have a "position" yet; he would be given a position at the university only after he had fulfilled the requirement of writing up his findings and completing that "major *oeuvre* for his degree." It was only then that he would be able to create some kind of a position for himself. And he really needed it, for he had crossed over from a bachelor's free and easy existence to a married man's life, and had, so to speak, responsibilities vis-à-vis his family; there were no children as yet, but that family norm was looming threateningly before him!

Despite her youthful years, his wife knew how to speak very curtly and pointedly about his responsibilities vis-à-vis this principle. Her arguments resounded so decisively, that Master Mykola rarely uttered so much as a word of disagreement; he listened silently, and only sighed heavily when his wife finished speaking. But sighs, even if they are heavy, are not words, and this meant that the lady got the final word.

So it was, that this morning, when the young couple was conversing over their morning tea, the final words of Mykola's lady were as follows: "I'm pleading with you, Mykola, don't waste your time before dinner today like you did yesterday with Savchenko! You jabbered away the entire morning!"

"But I can't chase a friend out of the house, can I?" Master Mykola responded.

"There are certain times," the lady said, tapping the new sugar bowl, "when even a friend has to be chased out. Indeed, it's your obligation to do so now."

A pained grimace crossed Master Mykola's face; however, the scraping of his chair, as he pushed it away from the table, made it impossible to hear if he uttered anything in reply.

He walked into the little anteroom, and this is where we can see him now, sitting behind his desk. Throughout the entire room, it is immediately possible to see the unmistakable stamp of a woman's hand; you know—doilies, mats, knickknacks, and small artefacts fashioned by a woman—all those things by which a woman makes her statement: "I live here; I am the one who has adorned the dreary ugliness of a bachelor's desolate abode."

But let us return to the work of Master Mykola. In a manner of speaking, his "major *oeuvre*" was already finished. At least that was what Master Mykola thought, and he had even said this yesterday to his friend, Savchenko; because the entire work, as he had stated, was already composed in his head—the theme had been thought through a long time ago, the entire outline was prepared, all the necessary laboratory research had been completed, and all that was left to be done was to put all this down on paper. This, of course, was a trifling matter—simply a mechanical task; all one had to do was to devote oneself to it for a period of time. And so, Master Mykola was slowly committing his work to paper.

My dear reader, do you, perhaps, want to know exactly what it was that Master Mykola was writing—the theme of his scholarly research? Oh, don't even ask! Master Mykola was a medical student, and you and I are not too familiar with such things, with his area of study. Of course, we are not to blame for this, but still, a fact is a fact. Well, the work was entitled: "Regarding the histological formations of mainly homogeneous matter in scars."

Well, what did I tell you? However, to put the matter more simply, this is what it was about: while doing his preliminary research for his work, Master Mykola slashed dogs—well, not to death—but he made deep slashes in them and, when the wounds began to heal—or, as medical people say, when scar tissue began to form—Master Mykola took particles of flesh from the scar and placed them under a microscope to observe how new elements are created in the scars, and how the cells of homogeneous matter are formed from them.

Yes, indeed. But all of this, no matter how well researched it was, and how well thought out it was in his head, had to be committed to wretched paper. And an exposition—even though it is not a poem written in rhyme—is, nevertheless, an exposition and, as such, it requires talent.

But often there were distractions so vexing that they put the author completely out of sorts! Just like now, for example—God only knows what had occasioned the disappearance of two cards on which were drawn the homogeneous cells as they appeared under a microscope. Yesterday, Master Mykola had placed them right here, a little to one side, in a spot that was most visible, because they were needed next, but now it seemed that some devil had taken off with them!

"It's that damned tidying up," Master Mykola thought. "That putting things 'in order' on my desk. I don't know how many times I've begged and pleaded: 'For the love of God, don't touch my desk or my papers!' But no, they had to go and tidy things up! And now one has to search!"

The drawings were finally found; they were under a hefty histological text. Now one could get down to work and begin to write. A pen was picked up, but for some reason it wrote terribly, and it was necessary to try another one. This one appeared to be somewhat better. Now, where was it that the author had stopped last time? The sentence was unfinished, and Master Mykola had absolutely no recollection of how he had intended to complete it.

This was very vexing! Oh, the devil take it! After all, was this a translation? Strike out the unfinished sentence—may it go to the devil—and write it differently. Differently! Yes, but how, exactly?

Master Mykola was lost in thought. His eyes were wandering over the desk, and completely unrelated, irrelevant thoughts were passing through his mind. Why had it occurred to his wife Manya to give him, as a birthday gift, a little cardboard basket trimmed with embroidery, intended for visiting cards? What kind of visits? Two dusty cards were lying there like orphans. How loathsome those cards had become!

Well, it was necessary to write! How was it to go? The thoughtful gaze of the author lifted itself upwards to the walls, and there, over the table, hung some paintings and photographs.

What a wonderful physiognomy Darwin had! It was terribly wise! Yes, his was a phenomenal intellect. What vigour and creative power filled his thoughts. And what colossal gains his work had bequeathed to humanity—in everything, in absolutely everything. Darwin's theory of evolution had paved new roads in history, in economic studies, in philosophy, everywhere . . .

"Listen, Mykola," his wife's voice broke into his thoughts. "I'm going out, to Vira's. She's inviting us to go half-and-half on a theatre box for a Ukrainian operetta, and I have to tell her as soon as possible not to buy the tickets, because we won't be able to go—you're far too busy."

"It would be so interesting! I haven't been to any this year."

"There are many things that are interesting! But now is not the time for theatres. If you start to go to theatres in addition to everything else, then your work will not proceed quickly. Besides, what's so interesting about it? Haven't you had enough of that Ukrainian drivel? It's time to put a stop to such nonsense!"

As she said this, Mykola's wife approached the window. Pulling apart the curtains, she once again addressed her husband, without turning around to face him: "What do you think? Should I put on a summer coat or a fall one?"

"Put on your summer one; it's probably quite warm outside, just as it was yesterday. Look how bright it is, and how pleasant! Listen, I'll accompany you to Volodymyr Street; then you'll go on alone to Vira's, and I'll return home. I have to buy some tobacco."

The young lady quickly turned away from the window; while Master Mykola was still speaking, her eyes became rounder and angrier, and she finally interrupted what he was saying: "What are you thinking of? I beg you, rid yourself of these whims! He's going to go to Volodymyr Street! This means abandoning the writing and wasting the entire morning."

"But it's only a walk of two blocks!"

"Oh, I know those walks! All that's needed is for you to move from where you're sitting, and all will be lost—you'll waste the entire morning! There's no need for it! I'll buy you some tobacco myself. You know, I wouldn't go anywhere either; I'd rather stay at home. But I'm going on a matter of *business*. And *your business* is to stay at home."

Master Mykola leaned his head on his hand and glanced at the lady. How crossly she was saying all this! How coolly and indifferently she was treating him, as if he were her yoked ox! And how severe her face was; her eyes, normally a cornflower blue, were now leaden in colour, and her lips were pouting with angry disdain. It was dreadful how everything had changed! In such a short time there had been a terrible change. Why did she comb her hair that way? It did not suit her at all; it gave her face a sheep-like appearance.

The lady was standing and buttoning up her gloves. It was possible to get a good view of her figure, and Master Mykola thought: "What fool was it who coined the expression 'an interesting condition'? Well, perhaps it really is 'interesting.' When a woman is in that interesting condition, everything that was attractive in her face and figure is lost, spoiled. It really is quite strange that nature has not devised some other way for human beings to make their appearance on this earth. Why was it necessary for the more beautiful half of humanity to become so unattractive, and for such a long time, at that?"

In the meantime, the lady had finished putting on her gloves. "Well, I'm off!" she said. "How much tobacco shall I buy you?"

"Buy a quarter of a pound, for now," Mykola replied rather sadly.

"Good bye!" the lady said, kissing her husband on the temple. "Lock the door behind me, and be sure to behave yourself. Don't even consider scribbling silly verses. And take my advice—if the wonderful Savchenko or someone like him shows up again, send Martha to tell them you're not in."

"Oh, leave me alone!" the gentleman replied to all this, angrily slamming the door behind the lady. His disagreeable thoughts did not go away when he went back to his little room.

"How disgusting this has all become, how extremely revolting!" he thought. "And how is it that she doesn't understand that she destroys whatever enthusiasm I have for my work with all of that. So she's gone off by herself—'on business,' she says—but, she'll get a walk out of it. But don't I also need to get outdoors for a walk? Do I have to sit here without any fresh air, choking on my own ptomainic gases? How wonderful!

"No, it seems that for women, everything—even the little bit they know from their studies—is somehow disassociated from life.

My wife, after all, is not an ignoramus like Martha, her cook; she knows about hygiene; she's heard about fresh air and oxygen, but all that knowledge lies in her head as if it were in a separate storage bin, because when it comes to applying it in real life, she forgets all about it! She's closed up the windows, and I'm to sit here in the fumes, the gases from the kitchen, and the miasma from the bedroom!" Master Mykola jerked at a pane in the window and opened it up all the way.

After walking around the room, the gentleman seated himself at his desk. He had made a few corrections in his "sources" and written a quarter of a page, when a completely extraneous obstacle turned up.

The door squeaked, and a white cat sidled into the room. Coming to a stop by the gentleman's feet, she began to meow. The gentleman continued writing and, without even looking at her, shoved her aside with his foot. But the cat did not go away, and rubbing herself continually against the gentleman's leg, began to caterwaul.

"Get out, you damn thing!" the gentleman shouted, looking at her with loathing. He hated this cat; he really felt a deep hatred in his heart for this creature.

You might well ask why he felt this hatred. Ah! Why? There was a reason for it, a most compelling reason. This cat was to blame for the fact that Master Mykola had been deprived of his liberty through marriage at the age of twenty-three, that he bore a heavy burden on his shoulders, and that on this beautiful day in the early fall he had to sit, chained to his desk, and tend to his urgent work without the slightest enthusiasm or desire to do so.

It was all because of her, this damned white-faced, tawny-eared cat! She was the reason why there was no turning back now, why there was only a heavy, sorrowful remorse.

Was this not so?

It was a fact that he had been acquainted with Manya—that is, with Miss Marusya—a petite blond with a fair complexion; well, it was also a fact that he had casually courted her. So what? It was not only seemly to court a young lady casually—it was almost considered to be the duty of every young man who was acquainted with her. But such casual courting does not lead inevitably to marriage! Why should it? There are decisive people who, after even the most serious courting, are able to step back. But Master Mykola did not have a decisive nature, and because of that, his fate was decided by the white cat with the reddish splotches.

It happened like this. Someone abandoned a kitten in the yard, and Miss Marusya adopted it and took it under her loving care. This gesture seemed very charming, as it suggested a tender, sensitive soul. The white kitten with the tawny spots was still small and, at the time, it actually seemed quite pretty. Moreover, like all little kittens, it was lively and gentle. It quickly grew accustomed to Miss Marusya, jumped up on her lap, tumbled about in her arms, and grabbed at her little fingers or at the kerchief around her neck.

At times, when it wanted to be petted, it nestled quietly, gently, and with half-closed eyes, against the young lady's breast, and revelled in the caresses bestowed upon it. And the young lady would remark: "Look how pretty she is, Master Mykola. See what a white neck she has, and what a tawny tail! Go ahead! Pet her!"

It was a moment like this that was the downfall of Mykola. It was a Sunday. They had returned from an afternoon performance of a Ukrainian operetta, and the young lady had invited him to her home for dinner.

The entire time, the young lady sang excerpts from the show, while exclaiming loudly: "Lord, how beautifully they perform! And those songs! It was paradise, simply paradise! You, my dear poet, have revealed a new life to me!"

After dinner, he sat with Miss Marusya on the couch—her aunt was somewhere in the other rooms. The young lady was holding the kitten in her arms and petting her. "Just look, Master Mykola, how sweetly she's looking at you, as if she were begging you to pet her!"

They began to pet the cat together. Master Mykola's hand kept touching the hand of Miss Marusya, and the white hands of the young lady kept touching the hands of Master Mykola. It so happened—God only knows how it had happened—that as Master Mykola bent down towards the kitten, he kissed the hand of Miss Manya . . . and then . . .

Well, you know what this led to. Master Mykola is married; Master Mykola is labouring over his urgent work, because he has responsibilities to his family. And so, since he did not have a decisive nature, was not Master Mykola justified in considering the white cat to be the guilty one in all of this?

"Get away, damn you! I wish you'd drop dead!" he shouted at her. But the cat continued to stand beside him and, sticking out her little red tongue, she continued caterwauling and gazing upwards, right into his face.

Master Mykola involuntarily took a better look at her. How ugly she'd become! She was big and fat, and the tawny patches had spread so widely that one reddish streak now covered half her face over her right eye. Even Marusya no longer considered her to be either pretty or sweet. Not at all! At times, when the cat did something bad, she gave her a really good smack!

All the same, however, the cat stayed in their home in order to carry infectious bacteria into the house, to give them her own micrococci when she licked their plates, to bother Master Mykola—yes, to annoy him specifically—because, of course, she no longer ever sat in the young lady's arms; instead, she came crawling to him. Just look. Now she was scratching his clothing and raising herself on her hind legs in order to clamber up into his arms.

"Oh, you ugly beast! Why are you scratching? You're old and fat, and you've become too heavy to sit on my knees. Are you recalling the past? Get away, damn you! Drop dead!"

Master Mykola grabbed the cat around the middle and hurled her through the open door into the other room. After this, Master Mykola was able to write without any interference. But thoughts did not come easily into his head, the writing was somewhat laborious, and he was getting his "who's" and "whom's" all confused . . . In a word, he could not write!

"Manya just doesn't understand," the author thought, "that there are times when one simply cannot write; she doesn't understand, but she gets after me, all the same. And why is this work so urgent? At least if she were interested in my work—but she hasn't the slightest interest in it! She's totally indifferent to what I'm writing—it wouldn't matter what kind of drivel I wrote, as long as I kept on writing!

"And that's strange, for when she was still single, she was enchanted by my verses—at that time, I was enthralled by poetry—and she was interested in my work. Indeed, she asked me more than once to show her something with the microscope. I even remember her saying that the cells of the homogeneous matter were very lovely.

"But now? Now she says, 'Put away your disgusting stuff.' This is how she refers to the harmless slides I've prepared for the microscope. 'You know,' she says, 'that all this is repugnant to me now in my condition, but you're spreading all this doggy stuff on all the tables!' And then she goes on, 'I've had enough of all this Ukrainian drivel as well!' Huh?

"So, her attitude towards all this 'doggy stuff' has completely turned around? She used to say: 'Poor little doggies! Why are you slashing them?'

"But now, when I told her that it might be necessary to make a few more cuts on the dogs, she said, 'So what? You've more than enough dogs in the laboratory, so go ahead and slash away at them.' 'But three of them have already died because they're so weak.' 'Well, so what? Can't you find more vile creatures like that?' There it was—the kindness of her heart revealed!"

The cat once again interrupted Master Mykola's thoughts. Having roamed through the other empty rooms, she returned to the little antechamber and, straightening out her reddish tail and caterwauling disgustingly, she once more approached Master Mykola.

"Oh, just you wait, you damn beast! You won't be turning my stomach any more!" Master Mykola exclaimed out loud. He leaped to his feet, grabbed the cat by the tail and, paying no attention to her heartbreaking yowls, flung her through the open pane way beyond the window. He did not feel the least bit sorry for the cat— the former darling little pet. On the contrary, Master Mykola looked on with a delighted grin as she thudded to the ground. The cat rose to her feet, shook herself angrily, and ran off into the distance. Master Mykola was left by the window, looking out through the open pane.

How wonderfully fresh the air was, how gorgeous it was outdoors. Two students strolled down the street. How poignantly those young men in their uniforms reminded Master Mykola of his own unfettered student days! How recent it all was! How interesting it had been! Especially in the early autumn, after the holidays . . .

You'd arrive in the city after resting up at home, and you'd feel so healthy and full of vigour. It was so pleasant to find yourself once again among your friends in the big city, after stagnating in a provincial backwater. You'd walk around, find out about the others. It did not matter if classes had started already or not. You either visited your friends or acquaintances, or just roamed about in the streets. For some reason it was always so pleasant in Kyiv at that time—in the early autumn. It was so warm, so bright, and the air was so fresh, transparent, and wonderful—just as it was now!

Master Mykola leaned against the open window, fell deep into thought, and did not notice when his wife rounded the corner. She was walking past their house, yelling from the street at Mykola in the window: "So, you're home, are you? Are you writing, or aren't you?"

Mykola jumped in surprise and went to open the door. The lady walked in with a gloomy, angry expression on her face.

"This is beyond all comprehension!" she started saying as she tore off her gloves. "One has to sit over you with a cudgel in one's hand. No one is bothering you, and you still aren't doing anything. I was thinking to myself: 'Oh, he's probably working so hard!' But he's standing by the window, gazing stupidly outside. Aren't you ashamed of yourself? Have you no shame at all? You know very well how imperative it is that you finish writing your stupid 'major *oeuvre*' as soon as possible. Indeed, you should stop to consider that you don't have the right to be lazy, because you are a person who has responsibilities to his family! But no! You either roam around the city, or sit and talk nonsense with your Savchenko, or simply stand gaping at an open window!"

Closing the window with a clatter, the lady turned to her young husband with more recriminations. "What did you see that was so interesting out there—when you were looking out at the street? Were you ogling the girls or the young ladies passing by, or what?"

His wife continued reproaching him, and Master Mykola sat silently with lowered eyes. No, actually he did look up once to peer closely at her. She seemed to him to be very similar to the odious cat: her hair was dishevelled and sticking out all around her swollen, reddened face, just like the reddish ears of the cat; her eyes were festering with anger and showering rapacious sparks; and she scratched him with her words, just as the cat had scratched him with her claws. "Why are you silent? Why don't you say something? What are you thinking about?"

Oh! What Master Mykola had been thinking just a few seconds ago you already know; but I do not know how to tell you what he was thinking right now . . . More than likely, the following thought was stirring way down deep in the soul of Master Mykola, the young husband: "What a pity it isn't possible to grab all odious cats by the tail and hurl them out the window!"

Artichokes
(1903)

Do you know what artichokes are? What they really look like? Try putting this question to a few of your acquaintances, my provincial friend, and you'll discover something interesting—not one of them will admit that he doesn't know what an artichoke is, and that he's never seen one in his life. Why won't he admit it? Well, who knows! But he won't. His brow furrowed, his face serious and strained, he'll begin to mumble something indistinctly, as if he indeed has eaten this vegetable.

Why do things like this happen? Well, it seems to me that it's because the person who has never seen an artichoke is certain of one thing—artichokes are an aristocratic delicacy. So, how can you admit that you don't have the foggiest notion what they are, when even Madgie—do you remember Hohol's [Gogol's] story about the little dog that lived in an upper-class home?—mentions this food as being served in her aristocratic household.

So, listen to what happened once, in an equally sophisticated home, because of these artichokes.

First of all, however, you have to know what kind of a household this was, and what kind of lords lived in it. The manor was in a village, but it was aristocratic to the core; and it was very attractive until fortune—that Lady who rules over us all—played a cruel joke on its owners, the Svoyskys. It was a joke that looked like it would bring about the ruination of their entire property.

The father of Lady Svoyska had mortgaged the property in an agrarian bank, and the husband of the lady had improved on this situation by remortgaging it at the nobiliary bank. It's true that after this transaction the manor of the Svoysky family was truly greatly ennobled—the lord covered it with a new iron roof and topped it with very cunning chimneys, while the lady bought new quilts and, for the new fireplace in the living room, an ingenious bronze clock surmounted with medieval knights and the genius of time. This genius, however, did not seem to shower too many blessings upon the Svoysky residence, for it became still more run down.

The manor—not to mention the barns!—peeled in a most ignoble fashion. The brick pillars of the gate began to crumble, and the entire manor yard appeared to be veiled in a cobweb of decline. Even weeds were beginning to grow in places where it was not at all fitting for them to put in an appearance—they grew especially vigorously in the spot where the greenhouse had formerly stood. In a word, when those who had known this residence in former times drove past it now, they always said: "Uh-oh, look at that!"

Of course it would have been possible to put everything back into order again—if only there were the money for it. Yes indeed, if only there were the money! The point was, however, that there was no money.

In the Svoysky family, however, there still remained capital of a special kind and, in their scheme of things, it was very significant capital—their beautiful daughter, Lady Olimpiya. Even though this kind of business venture requires the investment of capital, things often turn out quite unexpectedly. Sometimes it is possible to swing an extremely profitable financial return—even for the entire family—if a well-heeled buyer can be fortuitously found for the kind of lips and Grecian nose (as her mother referred to it) that graced the patrician face of Lady Olimpiya Arkadiyivna. Such beauty could be looked upon as nothing less than a capital reserve.

And this was how the entire family considered it. If rich suitors did not come to court Lady Olimpiya, everyone attributed it solely to the fact that there was an absolute dearth of such suitors. "Where are there rich suitors nowadays?" the mother asked rhetorically. "God knows, none of the present suitors amount to anything!" And it was true—they were all either petty lordlings, or, even if they were lords from good families, they were scarcely able to maintain themselves on their "ennobled" estates.

Thus it was that the Lady Olimpiya was fated to be born with such exquisite comeliness in such sorry times.

And then, quite unexpectedly—and in quite close proximity to the Svoysky family—a certain bourgeois who could truthfully be called a rich suitor made his appearance. He was the son of a wealthy trader, and hailed from the province of Moscow. His father had endowed him with some capital and, with this capital, he had bought, at an auction, an estate that had belonged to Yevhraf Petrovych, an uncle of Lady Svoyska.

Poor Yevhraf Petrovych! What splendid banquets he had formerly hosted, what a splendid equipage he had maintained! But now he was reduced to living off the kindness of a son-in-law, and his place in the manor was taken over by Khomutovnykov. Yes, the name of the new owner was precisely this—Stepan Kuzmych Khomutovnykov. Upon hearing the name of their new neighbour for the first time, Lady Svoyska recoiled in horror: "What? Khomutovnykov?"

In the meantime, the new master began setting things aright in his newly acquired property. He was still a young bachelor, but he led a staid and orderly life. It is true he was not the type "to set the world on fire"—and this was why his father had not kept him in his business—but, nevertheless, he was able to manage his property quite well, especially since he had a grey-haired peasant assistant at his side. This peasant advised him not only when it was the best time to harvest and sell his crops, but also when to buy up the crops of others. There was enough capital to do this, and the necessary business ties were nicely in place.

The young Khomutovnykov lived quietly and did not establish overly friendly relationships with the lords who were his neighbours. Moreover, if the truth be told, his appearance was such that he was not entirely suited to gracing aristocratic drawing rooms. Even though he was a robust young man—"a husky lad with a ruddy complexion"—it was precisely his plebeian ruddiness, his tousled hair, his stoutness and homeliness, and the staidness of his conversation that made him ill-suited for the drawing room! It seemed that Khomutovnykov realised his own unsuitability and, in the words of the nobility, "knew his place." On the rare occasion when he had to appear in society, he behaved modestly, almost bashfully.

It was said that when Khomutovnykov first arrived to buy wheat from Lord Hrafovych, the latter—taking in Khomutovnykov's appearance and listening to his "yes, sir, that's exactly right, sir," "no, sir, that's not the right price, sir,"—took him to be a steward from the estate. It was only when the young man took out a few thousand banknotes from his bulging wallet and slowly traced his name—Stepan Khomutovnykov—under the agreement, that Hrafovych invited him to sit down and even extended a hand to him in farewell. Up to then, he had not even considered asking him to sit down in his study, let alone inviting him into the drawing room!

And so it was this dealer, Stepan Khomutovnykov, who presented himself, in the eyes of the Svoysky family, as the illusive wealthy buyer whom they had long hoped for with respect to their great treasure—the beautiful Olimpiya. Was this actually possible? What would their deceased granny, Aleksandra Lvivna Myloradova, have said if she had lived to see this day? Indeed, what would their aunt, Olha Nykolayivna Duduliy, say even now, when she got wind of the fact that Olimpiya—the dear little Limpochka—was betrothed to Khomutovnykov?

Betrothed? Dear God, she was not betrothed as yet! Her word had not been given, and nothing definite had been said! It was all rather vague. It was true that Khomutovnykov seemed to be deliberating the matter—one could say that he appeared to be wooing the lady—but he had not yet proposed to her. Indeed, he had been in their home only three times thus far—when he paid his first visit, during the holidays, and one other time.

It was also true that Lord Khutorenko, a neighbouring petty lord who was his mentor, was speaking on his behalf. It was he who had introduced Khomutovnykov into the Svoysky manor, and who had stated rather clearly that Khomutovnykov had every intention of becoming betrothed, but was concerned as to how his proposal would be received.

Upon hearing what Khutorenko had to say, Lord Svoysky did not reply decisively, saying that this was a serious matter that had to be carefully considered. All the same, he once again brought his conversation with Khutorenko around to Khomutovnykov, inquiring more precisely about his financial status—in whose name had the estate been purchased, had the entire bank loan been paid off, and so on.

It turned out that everything was in order, indeed, in very good order. Nevertheless, it was still necessary to consider the matter, "to mull it over with the family." This was what Lord Svoysky had said in reply to Lord Khutorenko, when the latter stated that on Sunday he and Khomutovnykov would pay him another visit to receive a definite reply.

And so, a couple of days prior to the visit, the Svoysky family assembled in the living room and discussed the matter. They thought about it most diligently! The lord pondered it with great care, the lady deliberated it seriously, and the young lady contemplated it sorrowfully. If only this Khomutovnykov did not have such a disgusting name! Now, it could have been Petrov, Andreyev, Antonov, or even Baranov *[a ram]*, or Kozlov *[a goat]*—but no, it had to be Khomutovnykov! Khomutovnykov, Khomutovnykov—no matter how you said it, it was still repugnant, vile!

"Khomutovnykov!" Lady Svoyska said out loud to her husband, as she sat in an armchair smoking a cigarette. "It's all too evident that his family prospered by dealing in *khomuty [horse collars]*."

"Well, it can't be helped!" Lord Svoysky replied, pacing the room. "But just look at how much money they made!"

"Money! Of course! What would such an illustrious descendant be worth if he didn't have money? No one would permit him to so much as cross the threshold!"

"So, there's nothing more to be said!" the lord continued. "Besides, what thresholds are we talking about? It's generally accepted—it's the spirit of the times—that the nobility, thanks to many factors, has weakened and can no longer remain within the rigid confines of its position. More and more, it has to make way for the element . . . the element of the future, the so-called aristocracy of the *nouveaux riches [newly rich]*."

"Aristocracy! It's simply riffraff, but it comes with a wallet!"

"That's just it—with a wallet! This is why it's called the aristocracy of the *nouveaux riches*. That's exactly the point. And now, returning to Khomutovnykov. Granted, he's from the merchant class, but what more could one want—he has bought an estate here, become one of our neighbours, and he's the same kind of a manor lord as any other!"

"Manor lord! So does this mean that our Hawrylo is also a manor lord simply because he bought some land?"

"There's no point in discussing Hawrylo. He's a fool—a peasant, a lout, who will always remain a stupid peasant."

"He's not that big a fool if, after working as a steward for you, he was able to purchase land right out from under your nose!"

"It seems to me that he did the same thing to you, as well!" the lord corrected her. "You also could have seen what was going on. You're a true lady of the manor, and you were well aware of the financial position of the estate while your father was still alive; the estate is yours!"

"Yes, it's mine!" the lady said bitterly, and she fell silent.

"Moreover," the lord picked up the conversation again, "there's absolutely no need to talk about whether Khomutovnykov is or isn't a lord. We should be considering only one thing—is it possible for Olimpiya to marry him, such as he is? Is he a suitable match for her?"

"That's exactly it—a suitable match for her! Let Limpochka decide this for herself! I won't assume such a responsibility!"

"One thing can be said with certainty—she would have security for the rest of her life," the lord stated calmly.

"It's true that she would be secure . . ." the lady began to say.

"And this is the main consideration," he interrupted her.

"It's the main one, to be sure, and if it weren't for this, then there would be nothing at all to discuss. But there is still another consideration—our position in society. I don't know if this position won't be ruined forever if Limpochka marries Khomutovnykov! Let her decide for herself if she can imagine herself in refined society with such a husband, even if he were to be accepted into it!"

"With such a husband!" the lord repeated. "He'll be a husband like any other husband! I don't know what can be expected of Khomutovnykov. It's true he's a simple man, and not very . . . refined, but I don't see anything so terribly dreadful in that!"

"Oh, for the love of God! Leave me alone!" the lady cried out. "It's Khomutovnykov himself who is dreadful! He's just a scarecrow, a blockhead, and nothing more! He's impossible! He doesn't know how to enter a room, or how to seat himself properly—not to mention the fact that he has no idea as to what he should say. He just blushes and perspires; it always seems to me that he reeks of a horse collar!"

Having said this, and accompanied it with a demonstrative gesture of her hand, the lady realised that she might have gone too far and been too vivid in her censure. Lady Olimpiya who, with her head lowered in thought, was sitting a trifle apart on a small sofa, suddenly raised her head in displeasure, as if her Grecian nose could truly detect the odour of a horse collar. She even took a deep breath, and a pained expression appeared on her face. It was quite possible that she might say something rash at a moment such as this!

"Of course, I'm not saying anything!" the lady said, lowering her voice. "We aren't in a position to expect too much when our financial matters are in such a sorry state!"

Oh, these financial matters! Lady Olimpiya hated—she truly hated—the expression "our financial matters" or "our circumstances." These words truly jarred her nerves! If ever you thought about spending the winter in a big city, or taking a trip to St. Petersburg, or just buying a new winter outfit, these hateful words—"our circumstances"—immediately entered the conversation. My God! Given this situation, one would be ready to marry the devil, let alone Khomutovnykov! Just so as not to hear those loathsome words! Lady Olimpiya stared straight ahead, unhappily, but decisively.

In the meantime, her mother had finished what she had to say about the matter, and now she turned to Olimpiya: "What do you think, my dear Limpochka? Do you think, perhaps, that . . . you might be able to agree to this?"

"What am I to think!" the daughter replied ambiguously, in a grim tone of voice. Did this mean that she was not the one who had to think about this, or that there was nothing to think about when there was no other way out . . . in these pleasant "circumstances"?

"How much land does Khomutovnykov have anyway?" the lady asked her husband after a pause.

"Quite a lot!" he replied. "In addition to the estate of Yevhraf Petrovych, he's bought up the land of the peasants who have gone off to Siberia."

"So that's how it is!" the lady said, and her full face seemed to grow smoother, her eyebrows rose in pleasant surprise, and something resembling a smile appeared on her face.

"Limpochka!" she addressed her daughter again. "Do you remember the home of Yevhraf Petrovych? You used to go there when auntie was still alive."

"I seem to remember it a bit," the young lady replied, still speaking quite curtly.

"It's a very attractive manor! Truly a nobleman's abode!"

"It's a wonderful manor!" the father picked up on the conversation. "Of course, it's a trifle neglected, but if it were put in order . . . Khomutovnykov doesn't care about it; he lives in the small house, but if he were to begin fixing up the manor . . . Of course, it would be necessary to replaster it and put on a new roof."

"I think it would also be necessary to put down new parquet floors," the lady interjected, "and to renovate the interior completely."

"Khomutovnykov said that he was about to begin refurbishing the entire building. He also said he would be buying new furniture," Olimpiya spoke up.

"He told you this?" the lady inquired explicitly. "How did this happen? Was there a conversation of some kind? Did he tell you anything about his intentions? Was he hinting at something?"

"No, he didn't say anything! It just came up in the course of a conversation," the young lady replied, and she walked out of the living room to the veranda.

"I'm sure," the lord added, "that Khomutovnykov won't have the nerve to propose himself. It's evident that he's delegated this matter to Khutorenko. So, on Sunday, when they come here . . ."

"What do you mean, on Sunday? For dinner, perhaps?"

"Of course, for dinner! At least, when Khutorenko told me that they'd be coming on Sunday, I invited them to dinner. There's nothing wrong with that, is there? It isn't as if we were currying his favour!"

"Of course not! As yet, there's no suggestion of anything," the lady agreed. "Khomutovnykov, after all, is an acquaintance of ours, and so it's all quite normal. But if this is what's happening, we'll have to think carefully about the dinner . . ."

"What's there to think about? Besides, it's still three days away!"

"What do you mean, three days? It's Friday tomorrow. I wanted to get a few things from town anyway, and so now we can buy whatever is necessary, and prepare it . . ."

"Well, that's your department!" the lord said, and he reached for a newspaper.

"Although, to tell the truth," the lady continued, thinking out loud, "there's not much point in fussing for such guests—a lot they know! I'm sure they probably can't even appreciate a proper dinner!"

"All the better for us! It's less of a bother," the lord said, spreading out the paper.

"Well, there's still the same amount of bother. For I can't serve them a dish of rye flour and water, or their peasant cabbage soup, or buckwheat groats. Some thought has to be given to the matter, if only to preserve the honour of our home."

"Do as you wish, it's your business!" the lord said, decisively screening himself from view with the newspaper.

"I think," the lady continued deliberating out loud, "that *pyrizhky [turnovers]* filled with calves' brains can be prepared to accompany the soup—our Arseniy makes them superbly. Or, perhaps a *pyrih [large meat pie]* should be prepared; it's all the rage among Muscovites. Well? What do you think?"

"Oh, for heaven's sake, I don't know! It's all the same to me!" the lord responded in annoyance, rustling the paper impatiently.

"No," the lady said to herself, "a *pyrih* isn't suitable—it isn't as if this were some special occasion. There's no reason for it! It would be better to have the *pyrizhky*. Well, of course, the bouillon will be delicious, fully flavoured. A fish can be prepared for the next course, and whatever else goes with fish. I think that, prior to the Sabbath, there should be fish in town. For the meat course, we'll have some kind of fowl. But what about the vegetables? What kind of vegetables? Oh, that's right, I have some artichokes! Do you hear? Dementiy brought me some from Hrafovych when he stopped by to visit us for old time's sake!"

The lord looked up from his newspaper, but he stared at her with bewildered eyes until she repeated everything.

"So, then we'll have artichokes?"

"Uh-huh . . . sure," the lord said indifferently, and he turned to his newspaper once again.

"Wonderful! Except that this is such an exotic dish that it's unlikely that they'll know what it is. Perhaps they've never seen artichokes in their life. Well, it doesn't matter. I certainly can't serve something like steamed turnips as a vegetable!" the lady concluded with a smile. Then she continued thinking about what kind of sweets to serve. Finally, stating: "Yes! We'll have crème for dessert," she rose to her feet and, her corpulent body swaying slightly, floated grandly out of the room.

On the veranda, she lit a cigarette and approached Limpochka. The young lady was leaning against a pillar and gazing straight ahead, but somewhat less severely than previously.

"What are you thinking about so deeply?" the mother asked, as she exhaled a stream of smoke.

"Nothing in particular!" the young lady replied lightly, and a smile crossed her face.

The lady also smiled almost imperceptibly as she placed the cigarette to her lips and gazed sideways at her daughter with half-closed eyes. As she did so, she noticed something and asked abruptly: "What's happened to your brooch? Where's the dove? Did it break off, or what?"

"It broke off," the young lady responded casually, "but it doesn't matter! For some reason the dove didn't appeal to me. It's better like this—with just the branch."

"That's fine, that's fine! You'll soon have another dove, a golden dove, and then you'll have a brooch far better than this one!" the mother said with a short, delighted giggle, and she inhaled the smoke from her cigarette deeply and luxuriously.

Sunday came. Lady Olympiya attired herself in a very attractive, light grey dress that was deceptively simple in style. The faintly lilac shade of the dress was especially well-suited to Limpochka's tenderly pale face, and the oblique cut flattered her slender, supple figure. A delicate white eyelet trim on the front revealed her neck just the slightest bit and was accented under her slim throat with a golden pin—the branch without the dove. Her light brown hair was pleasingly arranged. At the back it was simply curled, but in front, wavy tendrils, tumbling whimsically over her delicate forehead, harmonised delightfully with her fine, dark eyebrows.

Lady Svoyska declared that Limpochka was very, very alluring. As she gazed upon her, she even wondered in her own mind how Limpochka, with her refined beauty, could have appealed to that one . . . the one with the grey paws! Could he comprehend how beautiful she was? She gazed with delight at her daughter—and felt a pang of bitter sorrow! My God, she was so lovely—and she was to be delivered up to Khomutovnykov! Oh, it was enough to deluge her heart with blood.

Last year, at the prince's birthday, everyone had gazed in astonishment at Limpochka. The prince himself—and he certainly was knowledgeable about such matters!—had uttered endless compliments about Limpochka, about the artistic slant of her eyes, the exceptionally fine outline of her mouth, her gracefulness—and everything!

Yes, there had been plenty of compliments, but a year had gone by already—an entire year—and still there was nothing! Except for that . . . Kuzmych! Alas! Kuzmych, Kuzmych! I wouldn't set eyes on you, and you wouldn't set eyes on Limpochka—just as you can't ever see your own ears—if it weren't for those damned circumstances!

"Nevertheless, why aren't they coming? It's certainly high time!" the lord interrupted her thoughts, tapping his watch.

"It really is time for them to be here already!" the lady agreed, and she became uneasy. "Perhaps they've changed their minds?"

"No, why would they change their minds? They'll come! They probably went to church, and by the time they got home . . ."

"Ah, yes, that's true. He was likely raised with great piety. . . by his dear father!"

"Of course!"

"Come to think of it, how will his dear father react to all this? Do you think he might be opposed to the marriage of his dear son? Could it be that he'll tell him to find a bride with money?"

"What a thing to say! Just let them try to find a bride with money among us nobles!"

"That's true. And even if there were one, would she marry Khomutovnykov if she did have money? It's a great enough honour for him if someone from a good, noble-born family agrees to marry him. Even so, it's difficult to take this step—oh, it's ever so difficult! Dear me, I simply don't know what to do! Just think what people in high society will say!"

"They're coming!" the lord cried out, as he stepped up to the window. The lady also rose to her feet and looked out. "Oho!" the master noted. "Today, there's a big change! He's come with his finest carriage—with four horses harnessed to it!"

An involuntary smile brightened the young lady's face. "What of it!" she said affably, as if she were encouraging him to say more.

"What's this?" the lord suddenly shouted. "There's a lady with him!"

"A lady?" the hostess inquired anxiously.

"Yes, a lady! I don't know . . . It's somebody under a veil."

"Oh, my God!"

Truly, in the covered carriage another figure wrapped in a blue veil was seated next to the male one.

"Ah! It's not them!" the lord said when the carriage drove into the yard and drew near the porch. "How could I have not recognised the equipage? It's the Naskys!"

"The Naskys? Oh my dear God! They couldn't have come at a worse time; they simply couldn't have! It's as if they'd done it on purpose! What a disaster!"

"Well, what's wrong? Exactly how are they going to hinder us?"

"What do you mean, in what way? It goes without saying that it's a great hindrance, a truly terrible hindrance! It's simply a disaster, a disaster!"

But there was no time to faint, for it was necessary to go and greet the guests.

A few moments later, loud exclamations could be heard. Then the guests and the hosts entered the living room and, with everyone talking at the same time, they settled in not far from the table. Lady Naska, seating herself on a couch, was telling the hostess that she had been planning to come and see her for such a long time, but she just had not been able to actually do so. And then she inquired about everyone's health, how they all were, and how Lady Olimpiya was doing.

It was at this moment that Lady Olimpiya walked in. Lady Naska greeted her and, after stealthily and intently eyeing her from head to foot, told her that she was most unkind because she did not seem to want to visit her—Lady Naska's—daughters, who sent her their regards and were awaiting her visit. Lady Svoyska and Olimpiya excused themselves at great length and tried to explain why they had not visited the Naskys for quite some time.

In the meantime, the gentlemen were discussing their own matters. The host was asking Lord Nasky about his equipage and about his trip to the county office regarding the distribution of payments.

After some time, however, the conversations merged and turned to a topic that was a burning issue to all of them—tobacco. It could not have been otherwise! This year, even though the selling price of tobacco was extremely low, and even though it did not pay to bother with it, tobacco once again did not cease to be of great interest to the citizenry.

Yes, indeed, the plebeian tobacco plant that was grown in these parts, and was so sorely required by peasants, was a lively topic of reflections and conversations, and was addressed even in the living rooms of the nobility! And the lips of the lords themselves—and even those of the ladies—time and again pronounced such unseemly Ukrainian words as *potert' [tobacco remains]*, *papusha [roll of tobacco leaves]*, and *makhorka [strong tobacco of bad quality]*. And all of this was said without any translating!

For those of you who are interested in the history of our Ukrainian language in higher circles—where they don't "speak" it—it is necessary to add that other Ukrainian words were also used without translation, words such as *perezymok [something kept over the winter]*, *zbirka [harvesting]*, *pasynkuvat' [to tear off side shoots of plants]*, and *odvolohnuty [to become damp again]*.

They attempted, it is true, to ennoble these Ukrainian words by giving them a Russian twist and saying *zborka*, *pasinkuvat'*, and *otvolognut'*. However, some words such as, for example, *papusha* it was simply impossible to ennoble! It was, however, one of the terms that had to be used, so what could one do! When something is of such great import to someone, then the terminology simply has to be accepted! At least, such was the case with tobacco.

So Lady Svoyska was making her point that the price of tobacco was lowered by the *zborka* of the tobacco that traders bought up from the lesser lords, and even from the peasants—the peasants had also begun to sow tobacco, and they sold it very cheaply, agreeing to a very low payment because, of course, "their work doesn't cost them anything!" Yes, indeed, just when Lady Svoyska was making this point, and Lady Naska was assuring everyone that it did not matter to her if, by springtime, all her tobacco deteriorated into *potert'*, she still would not sell it now at such a low price—it was exactly at this point in the conversation that a rumble or, more accurately, a clatter of wheels was heard in the yard.

It was Khutorenko and Khomutovnykov who had now arrived. They had not driven up in an equipage, or with four horses, but with a pair of farm horses harnessed to a farm buggy.

"Who is it?" Lady Naska inquired, straining to see through the window from where she was sitting.

"I can't quite see from here!" Lady Svoyska replied, although her heart jumped, and hot blood flooded her face.

"Lord Khutorenko and Lord Khomutovnykov!" the servant announced loudly.

A few moments later, an awkward hubbub arose in the living room—and a still more awkward confusion. The introductions and seating of the new guests were handled in a rather embarrassed manner . . . with some discomfiture . . . The conversation proceeded somewhat sluggishly . . . ponderously . . . well, to put it simply, so ponderously, that the hostess was forced to fan her face a few times with her handkerchief because she felt so flushed. The host tried to help her along, but as for the guests—it was as if they had made up their minds to be difficult.

Lord Nasky, never overly talkative—he always just sat with his half-blind eyes half-closed and agreed with his wife—had now completely stopped talking, because for some reason his wife had also fallen mysteriously silent. From the look in her eye, it seemed that she absolutely, but absolutely, did not see either Khomutovnykov or Khutorenko, despite the fact that Khutorenko was sitting quite close to her.

For his part, Khutorenko—either exhausted from his trip or annoyed to find other guests were present—was gloomy, and only grumbled something in reply from time to time. Some guest he was! Dressed in a coarse, canvas jacket, his hair cut in the strangest fashion, and his moustache long and unkempt—he looked like a peasant bumpkin from the village! Well, that was Khutorenko—he was an old man. God be with him!

But Khomutovnykov? My God, Khomutovnykov! Never before had he presented himself as such an oaf! His clothing, it is true, was acceptable—made of good woollen cloth, and not too badly tailored—but why had he put on that wretched, bright purple tie with yellow polka dots? And his hair? Oh, dear God! Had he actually greased it down with olive oil to make it so shiny? And the way in which his hair was parted! Oh, dear Mother of God!

He had sat down, without thinking, right next to Olimpiya! And he was completely silent; he simply gazed around in greasy confusion and wordlessly kneaded his red hands . . . Well, God be with him, it was better that he remain silent; otherwise he might blurt out something in his peasant argot.

The hostess was close to fainting. She saw, even without looking, the serpentine smile—which supposedly was being restrained!—that lurked on the venomous lips of Lady Naska.

However, regardless of how much you may feel like fainting, when you're the hostess of a drawing room you must lead the conversation. And so, mustering her courage, the hostess led it. She stated that it couldn't be fifteen *versts [kilometres]* from the village of Ivanivka to the village of Petrivka, but only ten, at the most. Then, she observed that it was closer if you went by way of the village of Terevenya, because the road was much better, and the dam could be avoided . . . because the road over the dam was very bad just now, very bad indeed! Everyone tried to avoid it. Even the lumber for the new church in Ivanivka was being delivered in a roundabout way. It would be a lovely church! They wanted to build a church in Terevenya as well—the count was promising to help, and the peasants too, of course—and Petro Nykolayevych had convinced them to come to an agreement. And it was high time, too! The hamlets had grown into such a large village, but there was no church!

Oh, what could she say next? Everyone knows about those scintillating conversations in French salons. But there, more than likely, the guests do not dare to sit like bumps on a log! Just let one of those French women try to get a conversation going with guests like these! She would certainly have a job and a half on her hands!

Well then! Our hostess, because of a dearth of material and assistance, was finally forced to utter the hope that the roads might improve because it seemed that the rains were tapering off, and good weather must be on its way . . .

Then, quite unexpectedly, Olimpiya came to her rescue.

In a private conversation with Khomutovnykov, she had managed to wring a few words out of him. Then she had inquired if there was an orchard in his manor yard, and if he was planning to plant a new orchard. She then proceeded to inform him that she had her personal orchard where she planted grafted plants, and that she was quite successful at doing this.

And, after telling him all this, she invited him to come and have a look at her orchard.

Khomutovnykov eagerly rose to his feet, saying that he would be delighted to "learn a bit." Olimpiya flashed him a tiny animated smile, protesting that she did not consider herself to be such a wise gardener that someone could learn from her. However, they both walked out of the room.

Following this fortuitous example, the host invited his guests to take a stroll as well, and to have a look at his binder—the very latest model—that he had bought at a farm exhibition.

All the gentlemen went to see the binder that was the very latest model.

The older ladies were left alone. The hostess breathed more easily, but not for long. Lady Naska immediately began to question her about how often Khomutovnykov visited them.

The hostess paused for a moment, thinking: "Well, it's beginning!" And then she started to say something.

"You know," Lady Naska continued, "he tried to ingratiate himself with the Hetmanskys, but he wasn't received there—they simply refused to see him. Their servant sent him packing, saying that the lord and lady were not receiving anyone. Understand this as you will . . ."

The hostess squirmed. "My God," she thought, "did this really happen? What will they say when they find out . . ."

"But how could it be otherwise!" Lady Naska was making her point, "Khomutovnykov is a trader, a social climber!"

"It's said that his father is a prominent merchant," Lady Svoyska attempted to interject.

"A merchant!" The guest uttered disdainfully. "He's just a beggar; he trades in leather and goods made of leather— somewhere out in the boondocks."

"That may be. Nevertheless, the young Khomutovnykov behaves very properly, and there are no rumours about him. He's a simple man, and he lives quietly and modestly . . ."

"I should think so! All he'd need to do was to create a ruckus! He has no choice but to sit quietly in his burrow!"

Even though the hostess was defending Khomutovnykov, she did feel it necessary to comment: "Well, I really don't know him all that well. It's Khutorenko who acquainted us with him . . . Khutorenko is on good terms with him; he's introduced him to some of the neighbours, and he brings him along when he comes to visit us. Because of Khutorenko, I didn't consider it possible to turn Khomutovnykov away from our home, or to refuse to become acquainted. You see, my husband served with Khutorenko in the same regiment, and it seems to me that they're old school chums as well . . ."

"But tell me, why has Khutorenko chosen to live here? I don't think he's from our district, is he?"

"No, not from ours. His married sister lives here, and he's renting a piece of land from the count."

"A lot?"

"No, I believe it's a *hundred desyatyny [270 acres].*"

"Is that all?"

The hostess changed the topic of conversation to farming and the leasing of land in general. However, after everyone returned to the house, she no longer could find within herself the imperturbability that—albeit with extraordinary effort—she had found earlier, and now, she felt that the same flicker of indifferent arrogance was crossing her lips that was scarcely noticeably snaking its way around the mouth and uplifted chin of Lady Naska.

It was rather late already, but the Naskys were making no move to leave. It was becoming obvious that they would have to be invited to stay to dinner. Well, what could be done! It did not make any difference now! And the dinner was elegant—there were even artichokes. The very best people could be invited to such a dinner!

The hostess left the room for a few minutes. Not long after she had returned and seated herself once again in the living room, a servant announced that dinner was served.

"Oh, we've really overstayed!" Lady Naska said in feigned confusion. "We left shortly after breakfast, and I thought we'd visit you and return home in time for dinner! Our daughters are probably waiting for us."

Of course, the rules of hospitality obligated the hostess to invite the guests to remain for dinner. Lady Naska also must have considered it her duty to be polite and remain, rather than flee from a dinner once it was being served.

Everyone moved into the dining room.

Dishes, knives, and forks clinked and tinkled, and there was the usual bustle that accompanies the beginning of a formal dinner. The men exchanged niceties as they had their first drink, and the women chattered.

Before long, however, Khutorenko once again fell silent in the men's group. Now that he was sitting at the table, he noticed that the Naskys were seated in places of greater honour than he and Khomutovnykov, and he also had the overall impression that there was something untoward in the behaviour of the hosts, especially that of the hostess. They did not ply him with food, nor did they evince any special attentiveness towards him. It was almost as if, instead of being an expected guest—and a matchmaker at that!— he was a landless peasant whom they hardly knew, and who had come along by chance for dinner. And the old lord was devoting himself to conversing with Nasky. Well, really now, what could they be thinking of? They had been told quite clearly about this day, so why were they indulging in some kind of aristocratic caprices?

In the meantime, the dinner was moving along in a well-organised manner. The *pyrizhky* were superb, and the bouillon was excellent. The hostess was gratified. During all this time, the lady guest, who was sitting next to her, had noticed from the appetisers, the *pyrizhky*, and everything else—there are tiny, almost imperceptible signs that permit ladies to discern such very important matters—that the fine dinner, even though it was a Sunday dinner, had not happened by chance, but had been especially prepared, as the saying goes, for very special guests. Yes indeed! And there was Khomutovnykov, still almost completely silent, but seated next to the young lady. Ah-hah! So, that's what was going on!

They ate the fish, and it, too, was garnished with a sauce that Lady Naska recognised as very special. As for its taste—well, the fish was prepared to perfection! But oh my dear Lord, she remembered that when the lady's father was still alive, fish even better than this one were prepared in this household—there used to be ever such huge trout, and sturgeon ordered from abroad, and even sterlets! Why, if the truth be told, it was because of one such marinated sturgeon that her dear deceased father had crossed over into the other world. Certainly, it had not been prepared like a mere perch!

And then, the hostess's greatest moment of triumph arrived—the artichokes were served. As the lady guest helped herself to the artichokes, her face assumed a nonchalant expression, but the hostess was not fooled by it. She immediately grasped the significance of this pose, and it made her feel even more triumphant; at the same time, of course, the expression on her face was even more nonchalant than that of her guest.

The artichokes, lightly covered with a sauce, were artfully arranged on a platter, and their attractiveness and novelty drew everyone's eyes. When Khutorenko's turn came—that is, when the servant brought him the platter with the strange vegetable—he glanced askance at it and, for some time, did not know what to do.

"Please, help yourself!" the host urged him.

Khutorenko transferred some of the vegetable to his plate, but then he once again gazed at it, pursing his lips self-importantly. His simple but expressive face appeared to be saying: "What the devil is this?"

The host noticed this expression and smiled wickedly as he watched him. The hostess also took note of Khutorenko's indecision and asked him, with a smile: "Perhaps you don't like it?"

"Oh, what a diabolical hag she is!" Khutorenko thought. "She's prepared the devil knows what, and now she has the nerve to ask me about it! Well, it doesn't matter! Do you think I'm afraid of you?"

"What is this?" he asked the hostess loudly.

"Guess!" the hostess replied, smiling mysteriously.

Khutorenko, glancing sideways at a piece of sliced artichoke on Khomutovnykov's plate, observed that it had some stuffing in it.

He had once had the occasion to eat stuffed little pumpkins, and it seemed to him that what was being served must also be tiny pumpkins, especially since he recalled that when they had strolled through the orchard before dinner to have a look at the mill, he had seen an entire shed all overgrown with very curious little pumpkins which the host had said could be eaten.

Therefore, Khutorenko, very authoritatively, asked the hostess now: "They're probably little pumpkins, right?"

"Little pumpkins, little pumpkins!" the hostess replied laughingly, and then she stated once more: "Yes, you've guessed it—they're little pumpkins!"

Suddenly a cloud crossed Khutorenko's face. When he glanced at the hostess once again, she appeared to be restraining herself from laughing, but her full shoulders were shaking so violently with stifled laughter that her face had turned a deep red.

"She's growing livid!" Khutorenko thought and, breathing heavily, he shoved away his plate with the incised artichoke.

"What's the matter, don't you want to taste it?" the hostess inquired.

"Thank you!" Khutorenko replied expressively.

"What about you, Stepan Kuzmych, will you have more of the little pumpkins?" the hostess turned to Khomutovnykov with a smile.

"Thank you very much," Khomutovnykov said in some confusion and, without thinking, placed more artichokes on his plate.

The next course was served. When it was Khutorenko's turn, the servant brought him the roast duckling stuffed with apples. Khutorenko, however, pushed aside the platter and said to the servant: "No, I won't have any!"

"Why, won't you have any?" the host asked him with a cajoling tone in his voice.

"Thank you!" Khutorenko once again replied curtly. This response, however, did not seem overly strange, as another guest, Lord Nasky, also refused the roasted meat. And indeed, they all had had enough of everything.

Lord Nasky, however, did have a crème after this, while Lord Khutorenko pushed aside the platter with the crème saying: "Sweets are completely superfluous!"

At the conclusion of the meal, the hostess murmured the customary words: "Please forgive me if everything wasn't just so!" And then they all rose from the table.

After everyone had finished thanking the hostess as they moved away from the table, Khutorenko came up to her in the dining room and said: "My respects!"

The hostess extended her hand to him, responding with the standard: "Forgive me." But she looked at him in surprise, thinking: "Doesn't he know the proper way of thanking someone after a meal? Why come out with 'my respects'?"

"He's a strange old man," she said to Lady Naska, justifying Khutorenko's behaviour to her guest after his broad back had passed by them into the adjoining room.

Khutorenko walked through the living room without stopping and went directly into the yard, where he told Khomutovnykov's coachman to harness the horses. "And do it quickly," he shouted the final words. Returning to the house and finding the entire company, except for the hostess, in the living room, he did not sit down, but paced the room with his hands behind his back.

The buggy drove up.

"Well, let's go!" Khutorenko touched Khomutovnykov on the shoulder.

"What?" the latter asked. "We're leaving? We're going home?"

"Of course, we're going home! Where else?"

The hosts were stunned.

"What's this? What's wrong? Where are you going?" There was a flurry of cries.

"My respects!" Khutorenko said again, addressing the hostess.

The hostess, forgetting about everything else, sprang abruptly to her feet. "But what is all this? Where are you rushing off to? We'll have tea in a moment."

"Thank you! You've treated us enough already! It's quite enough!" Khutorenko refused.

"Really, this is so . . ." the hostess said sincerely to Khomutovnykov when he came up to say his farewells. "You're in such a hurry! Do stay a while! We'll have tea!"

"Well, it's fine with me, but that one over there . . ." and he pointed his huge finger in the direction where Khutorenko was waiting.

"It's time, it's time to go home!" Khutorenko stated decisively. "Thank the hosts, Stepan Kuzmych, for their kindness—and for their respect—and let's be on our way!"

They both moved to the exit. The host caught up with them in the middle of the living room and said softly to Khutorenko:

"What is this? Where are you running off to? How are things going to be?"

"It would seem to me that you should understand why there's no reason for us to remain here any longer," Khutorenko replied abruptly.

The host glanced obliquely at the Naskys who were sitting with their backs to them and thought: "It really is most unfortunate that things turned out this way." He decided to accompany his guests to the buggy to come to some understanding as to when they could expect to see them again. Just at that moment, however, bad luck brought Nasky to the porch; he wanted to have a smoke in the open air. Well, the host couldn't very well run after Khomutovnykov with Lord Nasky looking on; moreover, the lord engaged him in a conversation.

In the living room, the talk among the ladies was following its own course. But the thoughts of the hostess were far away—she was sitting in an almost unconscious state.

Lady Olimpiya, standing silently at the window, was gazing in the direction where Khomutovnykov's blond curls were disappearing beyond the gate. She had absolutely no idea why Khutorenko and Khomutovnykov had departed so abruptly, but she had noticed that Khutorenko appeared to be angry, and she felt a foreboding in her heart. She had turned pale and appeared to have wilted.

"What a fine-looking young woman your Olimpiya is!" Lady Naska was saying to her hostess at this moment. "She has a wonderful figure!"

But this compliment did not cheer up the hostess. She replied: "You're very kind." In her thoughts, however, she was saying metaphorically: "If I could, I'd slaughter these Naskys. It's almost as if they did it on purpose to annoy us! Of course, Khutorenko must have lost all hope of outsitting them, and so he left."

And Lady Naska—it really did seem that she had come purposely to annoy them—did not stay long after Khutorenko departed. She called her husband, and they drove away without waiting for tea.

After all the cordial farewells and kisses, accompanied by all the appropriate words—"Take care now not to forget about us!"—had been exchanged, and the Nasky carriage was rolling out of the yard, Lady Svoyska muttered angrily: "What the devil brought you here, you damned woman! Now the matter will have to be put off to another time! How soon can we expect to see those other two again?"

In the meantime, Khutorenko and Khomutovnykov were already out on the main road. At first, Khutorenko sat in furious silence, and then, when they had driven out of the village, he began speaking: "Yes, our great Ukrainian poet, Kotlyarevsky, said it all: *'A horse should get together with a horse, and an ox with an ox!'*"

"What do you mean?" Khomutovnykov asked.

"Just what I said! There was absolutely no reason for us to intrude there today. It's not for us—with our coarse mugs, as it were, and our peasant rank—to go wooing in such a noble home. Oh, the fiendish aristocratic trash! They'll soon be sold, along with their souls, for their debts, but they're still stupidly arrogant, and they still put on airs. 'You see, we are great lords, and lesser people shouldn't hasten to join us!' May you all drop dead, you cursed lords."

Khomutovnykov just shrugged his shoulders, but Khutorenko raged on: "Others in similar circumstances would welcome us with open arms, but they, you see, are capricious and picky! And it's all because of that ridiculous mother. She, of course, can't forget that she's descended from a grand family, that she's a marshal's daughter, and that her father lived in St. Petersburg and handed senators their galoshes! She just can't forget all of that! Well, go on and stay there in all your arrogance, and keep on searching for some grand lord to marry your penniless daughter. May the devil take your father!"

"But why are you so angry?" Khomutovnykov asked.

"Because I'm also of the nobility!" Khutorenko thundered, tapping himself on the chest. "And let them not think any differently—I won't permit them to make a fool of me, and I won't put myself up to ridicule! And when I bring someone else with me, then the honour or the disrespect that are shown him affect me as well."

"But what is it that has happened?"

Khutorenko did not reply immediately; he just snorted furiously. Then he spoke more calmly: "They've ridiculed you and sent you away with nothing!"

"What are you saying?"

"That you're a fool, that's what!"

"Why call me names?" Khomutovnykov spoke gently.

"Because," Khutorenko flared up again, "you don't have any sense in your head if you don't understand this. *They served you a pumpkin!* Didn't you eat it during the dinner?"

"What?"

"I'm saying, didn't they serve you a pumpkin during the dinner?" Khutorenko shouted still more loudly. "You heard what the hostess said: 'Guess what it is.' Of course, for a wise man that's enough, but for a fool—well, you can spit in his face, and he still won't get it. And you went on to say: 'I thank you most humbly!' and took another serving, and all the while the hostess was choking with laughter!"

"What was so funny about it?"

"Fool!"

Khomutovnykov did not understand why this word had been addressed to him, and so he just shrugged his shoulders. Then he inquired, in a guilty tone of voice: "Wasn't it proper to take a second helping? She was entreating me to do so."

Khutorenko once again snorted in anger: "I'm telling you, you fool, that you were being served a pumpkin—or a *tykva [gourd]* as we call it. This means that the suitor, instead of receiving *rushnyky [embroidered linen ceremonial cloths]*, is told in a delicate fashion that he's a fool, and that he's to go away empty-handed. And that's why we have the saying: 'he was served a pumpkin'—in other words, he was refused as a suitor."

"But what kind of pumpkins were they? They were really very tiny."

"It's all the same! If you were a peasant, they might have served you one as big as the block of wood on your neck, but the lords do it in a lordly fashion!"

"That's really something!"

"Oh, yes indeed! I noticed right from the beginning that the old lady was very different today, as if she were turning up her nose, and it became more pronounced as time went by; and then, the pumpkins made everything absolutely clear! And that's how it really is—she knew we were coming to dinner, because I told her old man that we would come on Sunday to make a proposal of marriage, and he said: 'We'll have dinner waiting for you and, in the meantime, we'll discuss it at home.' And I even said: 'Take care now, discuss it, but be sure to come to a firm decision, so that you don't dishonour us.' And they certainly did discuss it and prepare for us!"

"It's a sad state of affairs! It's a lost cause now! It's too bad; it's really too bad!"

"Why is it so bad? Is there a lack of young ladies? They'll marry you willingly—with all their heart! It's understood that there's no point in crawling into the mansions of grand lords—you have to keep in mind that a gander isn't a proper match for a hog! Come on, there, my good man, go faster!" Khutorenko yelled at the coachman. "Why are you straining your ears?"

Indeed, the coachman was either deeply engrossed in the conversation, or had simply nodded off. His head was tilted to one side, and he was completely neglecting the horses, which were going along at their own speed. Now, he picked up the reins, snapped his whip at the horses, and the buggy, bouncing along swiftly, clattered down the road.

"Why in the devil are you in such a hurry?" Khutorenko once again shouted. "Don't you have any sense of proportion? Do you want to shake the bones out of our bodies, or what?"

"The lord is really in a foul mood today," the coachman thought. "It's impossible to please him!"

The buggy rolled along more slowly—farther and farther away from the Svoysky estate.

Two weeks went by. The Svoysky family was still expecting Khutorenko to come with Khomutovnykov; but the two men did not show up. After waiting for them in vain the first Sunday, Lord Svoysky drove off on the next one to see Khutorenko, but he did not find him at home. Then he went to Khomutovnykov's home, thinking: "After all, we're acquainted, so there's nothing untoward about returning a visit." However, Khomutovnykov was not at home. The servants told him that the young lord had gone visiting.

"Where to?"

"God knows!"

"Perhaps he's gone to our place?" Svoysky thought. "Perhaps I missed him on the road, because I took a short cut."

He rushed home, but Khomutovnykov was not there.

On the third week after the dinner there was a market in the little town. Lord Svoysky wanted to trade his horses—he did this quite often—and, at the same time, he hoped to see either

Khomutovnykov or Khutorenko there. The older lady and the younger one were also convinced of this, and they impatiently awaited the return of the master.

The lord returned rather early with the same horses—obviously, he had not traded them. He stalked angrily into the manor and, greatly agitated, began to pace the living room.

"What's wrong with you? Why are you so upset?" his lady inquired.

"I have good reason to be upset!" the lord replied.

"What is it? Didn't you have any luck with the horses?"

"Oh, who cares about the horses! If only it were the horses that were our misfortune! It's all over as far as Khomutovnykov is concerned!"

"What? Did you see him?"

"I saw Khutorenko."

"Well, what of it?"

"Well, I found out that you've ruined our chances forever!"

"Me? How's that? In what way?"

"Yes, you! With your foolishness, your stupid aristocratic caprices, and your delectable artichokes!"

"My God, what are you saying?"

"Just this—that all because of the artichokes, a terrible misunderstanding has taken place. Khutorenko understood that you had served him a pumpkin, and, of course, he was offended, and that's why he rushed away so quickly, and the whole affair ended, and they went away without once looking back."

"My God! How can that be? How could he think that?"

"What else was he to think? He says that you even explained it to him—you were making jokes with your 'little pumpkins'."

"Oh, my God! It was all just a joke—nothing else even occurred to me."

"But it should have occurred to you! That very day, after the dinner, I told you that such jokes were dangerous. Do you remember?"

"But how was I to keep in mind some kind of peasant superstitions! I know very little about all that . . . although I did hear something like that once!"

"Ah! But it doesn't hurt to know about different traditions, and to remember about them, and not to spit in peoples' faces!"

"But who was spitting?"

"Of course, mother," Lady Olimpiya interjected angrily. "Of course, you . . . you were laughing right at them."

"Oh, my God! Why don't you, at least, be quiet!" the mother responded. "Why are you both attacking me? If there was a misunderstanding, then it's easy to fix it! As soon as I see Khutorenko, I'll explain everything to him myself! Better yet, I'll write a letter to him right now, explaining everything!"

But the lord stopped her and stated tragically: "Calm yourself; it's too late to explain the matter."

"Why?"

"Because. Khomutovnykov is getting married."

"What do you mean, married?"

"Just that. He's getting married—like everyone gets married. He's already betrothed."

Olimpiya turned pale and sat as if she had turned to stone.

The lady exclaimed insanely: "To whom is he betrothed?"

"To Nasky's daughter!" the lord replied gloomily.

"The Nasky's?" The lady's eyes almost leapt out of their sockets in anger. Then, dropping heavily into her armchair once more, she spoke as if she were stunned: "What baseness! My God, what vileness! What treachery!"

"What kind of treachery are you talking about? Lady Naska wasn't foolish, and that's all there is to it!"

"But how can it be? When she was here, she went on and on about how Khomutovnykov should not be received in our home because he's a 'petty merchant' and God knows what else. And after all this—she's betrothed her daughter to him?"

"She's got a good head!" Lord Svoysky cruelly continued making his point. "She turned you against Khomutovnykov, provoked your most noble honour, you listened to everything she had to say, turned your nose up at the two of them, and she plucked Khomutovnykov right out from under that nose of yours! I've found out everything about this matter—Moshko told me all about it when I was waiting at his place. He says that right after they were at our place, Lady Naska sent her husband to visit Khomutovnykov . . ."

"What? He went to visit Khomutovnykov first?"

"Well, she thought up some excuse or other, as if she had some wheat to sell, or something. Suffice it to say that Lord Nasky was

at Khomutovnykov's place, and invited him to come to see them—
as if on a business deal. And then the Naskys began working on
him—they really went to work on him, insinuating themselves into
his good graces—and they caught him in their net. It doesn't take
much to catch a fool like that!"

"My God, how vile people are, how base!" the lady kept
repeating. "Which one is he marrying?"

"Who the devil knows which one?" the lord retorted angrily.
"It's either Sonka or Olka! The middle one, Moshko said."

"That means it's Sonka! Oh, she's a b. . ."

At this point, a word escaped from the lady's lips, a word not
at all suited to a salon, but used very widely in those parts, not
only by peasants, but also by the nobility—of course, only when
conversing in an intimate group. Moreover, as you have seen, the
lady was very deeply stricken and, in such cases, a person no
longer chooses words very carefully; the words just fly out from
someplace all by themselves.

"But then, who knows!" the lady was trying to calm herself.
"Perhaps Sonka appealed to him more—really, to Khomutovnykov
and the likes of him, a *herhepa [a big, awkward person]* like
Sonka may have more appeal."

"Well, she may or may not be a *herhepa*, but she certainly will
be a lady, a manor lady."

"Yes, of course" the lady sighed.

"Yes! It's all over! And just think what ended it. It's all because
of such a trifling thing, such a distasteful thing—those fiendish
artichokes!"

"But perhaps," the lady began anew, "perhaps Moshko has made
it all up? Perhaps it's not all settled yet? Perhaps if we were to
see Khomutovnykov . . ."

"Well, there's no reason to see him. It's a done deal. I heard it
from Moshko, and Jews never talk without knowing what they're
saying. Lady Naska has already sold all her tobacco—I was told
this by the tobacco dealer—because it's understood, of course, that
money is needed for the wedding."

"What? She sold her tobacco?" the lady once again exclaimed
wrathfully. "Why, she said that at these prices she wouldn't sell
it before spring."

"Well, she said a lot of things! She flapped her tongue, but now
she needs money for the wedding, and so she sold it."

"Oh, the baseness, the baseness of people!"

"Yes! It's a done deal. Soon Lady Naska will send us an invitation: 'On the occasion of the marriage of my daughter—whatever the devil she's called—to Stepan Kuzmych Khomutovnykov, I humbly beg you to attend with your family.' Moshko said the wedding would take place this month."

A heavy silence descended on the living room. After some time, the lady began speaking again: "It wouldn't be so vexing if . . . But that's how it is! I'd simply spit at such suitors as Khomutovnykov, and I wouldn't think about such trash, such beggars, if it weren't for our circumstances . . ."

Olympiya could not listen to any more of this. Once again it was those "circumstances!" She abruptly rose to her feet and, walking out of the house, made her way to her orchard, ever farther and farther away, in order not to hear anything and not to see anyone!

But even there, in the bosom of calm, soothing nature, Limpochka did not find either any peace or any relief from the heavy grief that filled her heart. Indeed, everything that she came across in her walk through the flower beds and the orchard increasingly aggravated the painful wound in her heart—it was here that she had strolled on that Sunday with Khomutovnykov when he had come to ask for her hand in marriage. When they were alone, he did not feel himself so constrained, and he talked more; it's true that he threw in some dreadful dialectical words, but he spoke more enthusiastically, and quite pleasantly.

Here was the bush with the big red roses that so greatly appealed to him. She had picked one flower and given it to him. He was so delighted that, in his delight, he himself turned just as *ponceau [vivid red]* as the blossom and, thanking her for the flower, extended his hand to her. His hand was damp and repulsive—the young lady had to wipe the palm of her hand surreptitiously—but Khomutovnykov began to say that if she planted this rosebush by herself, then he would plant his entire manor yard with these bushes, and his entire orchard! You could only smile pleasantly at such candour.

And here was the bench—it was here that they had sat down to rest for a minute, because it was very warm outdoors.

Khomutovnykov had become still bolder; he no longer feared her at all and, as unassumingly as before, he sat down quite close to her, so that when he bent over and talked to her, she could smell the scent of his pomade—oh, what an acrid, overpowering scent it had, probably "Northern Rose," or "The Tsar's Jasmine." As he leaned towards her, Khomutovnykov asked her how she would advise him to furnish his manor, and what kind of silk should be used to cover the furniture.

Then the conversation had turned to the fact that Khomutovnykov wanted to buy "a team of four dapple grey horses" from Hrafovych. Olimpiya advised him that it would be better to buy black ones instead. Khomutovnykov had leapt from the bench and, beaming radiantly, said with a beautific smile: "It shall be as you say! I'll travel to Romni to look for black horses at the market."

And now it was Sonka Naska who would be sitting on silk furniture and driving those horses. And what about her, what about Olimpiya?

Angry tears burst in scalding drops from Limpochka's eyes. My God! Why was she fated to remain unhappy forever?

It was all because of her mother—because of her damned artichokes!

Returning to the salon, Olimpiya lashed out at her mother: "You, you're the one who has brought misfortune down upon me!" And tears streamed once again from the eyes of the beautiful young lady.

Wait for the New Laws, Old Woman
(1906)

Occasionally, an old woman called Granny Maryna sells me butter. One market day I heard her voice in the kitchen, where she was carrying on an animated conversation with my cook. I caught only her last few words: "Dear me, what a misfortune!"

I entered the room, and we exchanged greetings.

"Will you take some butter?" Granny Maryna asked.

"Yes, I will." We removed the cabbage leaves in which the butter was wrapped, transferred the butter to a dish, and completed the transaction.

It was late autumn already and rather cool outside—there was a hint of frost in the air—and Granny Maryna agreed to stay a while to warm up.

The old woman sat, drank some tea, and once again began alluding to something that seemed to be concerning her greatly.

I came right out and asked her: "What's wrong? Has something happened?"

"Oh, dear lady, it's best not to talk about it!" And Granny Maryna gestured despairingly. Nonetheless, she could not refrain from talking about it and, before long, was telling me everything in great detail.

"This trouble of mine—it's all because of my old man," Granny Maryna began her story. "You see, he signed over the house to me—and the land that goes with it. He realised it was the right thing to do! After all, when I married him, he was a widower with three children. I worked hard all my life, I didn't wrong any of the children, and I cared for them as if they were my own. Well, the boy settled in the Don River area—he's married there and has his own business. And the daughters I married off here. Well, the two of us are old now, and we don't need all that much—but you still worry about what you'd do if something should happen.

"Of course, no one knows how many years the Lord has given us, but it's a fact that my old man is a lot older than I am! Well, God forbid, but if something should happen to him, then I'd be left alone in a house that doesn't belong to me, and then what would I do? If that should happen, the relatives—his brothers— would chase me out of it. And now that my strength is spent, where am I to go in my old age? Where am I to find shelter?

"And so, you see, I began telling him this, and he went ahead and signed the house over to me—that is, both the house and the yard. He did everything the way it should be done. We went to the district office, and my old man had them write down everything on a piece of paper, just as it should be, and then he gave me the paper.

"I hid the paper in the trunk—I looked after it as I look after my own eyes—and I felt a lot better. Whenever I thought of it, I'd look through the things in the trunk, and I'd see the paper, lying right there. And so that's where I kept it, at the bottom of the trunk.

"But I noticed my old man was gloomy, and he was giving me strange looks. That didn't really bother me. After all, sometimes people just feel out of sorts. Then I happened to go to the trunk— I probably needed some thread—and when I felt around for the paper—it was gone! The paper was gone! Oh, it was terrible! I felt all over—here and there; I ransacked the trunk and rummaged through everything—it wasn't there!

"So I asked my old man: 'Where's the paper?'

"And he says: 'I don't know. I gave it to you, so take care of it!'

"'But I did take care of it! I hid it away and locked it up. What else could I have done? And there's no one else in the house! Is it you?' I asked. 'Did you take it?'

"'Leave me alone!' he muttered—and walked away.

"Well, I searched everywhere and rushed about here and there, and then I sat and wondered where he could have put that paper! Because this was his doing; I could tell by looking in his eyes! But I couldn't find it. Where could he have hidden it? As the saying goes, I combed every mousehole, but I couldn't find it!

"Then, one day I went into the garden and there, behind the little shed, I saw something white. I rushed over—it was my paper! Yes, it was my paper, but it was all torn and ruined. I tried smoothing out the scraps and putting them together, but it was no use. It was hopeless."

It was at this point that I interrupted Granny Maryna's story. "But perhaps it wasn't your paper?"

"Oh no, my dear! It was mine! It was mine! I know what it looks like. It doesn't matter that I can't read—I recognised it right away. The stamp was the same, and everything! I recognised it from the way it looked. But, as I said, it was ruined. With a paper like that, you couldn't expect to get anywhere! How could you? It was embarrassing to show it to someone. Nevertheless, I showed the scraps to my godson—he goes to school—and he said it was my paper. But he added, of course, that it was worthless now! Oh, I could see that myself! So, I went to my old man and asked him what this meant. What kind of conscience did he have—to give me a paper and then do something so cruel.

"'Get away from me,' he kept repeating. 'I don't know anything! You should have taken care of it. I gave it to you—so you should have looked after it!'

"O merciful God! Hadn't I looked after it? Hadn't I taken care of it? But is it possible to guard against a thief in your own home? Well, even if I didn't look after it, give me another paper anyway, because this one is ruined! But he said: 'Oh, no! That will never happen. I was stupid once, but I won't be stupid again!'

"Well, what in the world was I to do? I cried—that's all I could do. But people told me: 'Go to the district head and ask him to make you a copy, because it should be recorded when, and how, and what kind of a paper it was—you'll get another one just like it.'

"And so I set out for the district office. And my godson's father, Andriy Shamrayenko, went with me. You see, he had his own reason for going. Oh, something terrible happened to him, as well. His nephew quarrelled with him on the hayfield and tipped his haystack into some water! Not a big haystack, mind you, only three bundles or so—they'd been left there temporarily—but still, it amounts to a tidy sum of money, and then there's the work that's gone into it; and it really made him angry that it was done on purpose.

"So, he thought, since I'm taking a loss, then so should he. And no one knows how the nephew did it—if he dragged the haystack with a cattle rope, or what—but the haystack is no longer on the riverbank; it's lying in the water. It's not very deep there, you know; it's just a little inlet all overgrown at the edges with reed-grass, but it's still water, and the hay is all wet! How can one ever forgive such meanness? So, this Shamrayenko decided to sue him, because there were witnesses. Some shepherds saw the nephew doing it.

"And so the two of us set out together: I—to do something about my troubles, and he—to take care of his problem. When we got to town there was a small feast day celebration. Well, that was good. We knew we'd get some help, because both the secretary and the village chief would be in the office; they're always there after a church service. And we were right; we got to the office, looked in, and saw both of them sitting there. The secretary was reading a newspaper, and the chief was peering at it as well. They were reading out loud.

"We walked in and bowed, as you're supposed to, but they didn't seem to notice us; they were so busy reading that neither one even nodded his head. We stood there for quite a while . . . Then my godson's father stepped forward and told them about his problem, that it had happened thus and so.

"'That's a frivolous complaint,' they said. 'There's nothing in it that can be judged!'

"'Why can't it be judged?' he asked.

"And they told him: 'It just can't be!' Then they turned to me and asked: 'And why have you come here, old woman?'

"I scurried to the table; I wanted to tell them everything in detail—exactly how things happened—and I showed them the scrap of paper that was the biggest and the cleanest; and it had the stamp on it too. But it was no use! As soon as they heard that it was about a destroyed paper, the secretary burst out laughing: 'The old man sure came up with a sly trick!' and he roared with laughter. And so did the chief.

"Then the secretary said: 'Don't apply for any copies and judgements, old woman, because nothing will come of it!'

"'What do you mean, nothing will come of it?'

"'Just that,' he replied. 'It's hard enough to take care of things that are important, not foolish matters like yours; it's a very difficult time now . . . to pass judgements on anyone.'

"'Why's that,' I asked.

"'Because the old laws are gone, and the new ones haven't been brought in.'

"That's when I got mad. 'What is this?' I asked. 'Are we to sit in the rain until the sun breaks through? Where are those new laws? When will they be brought in? And in the meantime, are we just supposed to sit and suffer?'

"This was when my godson's father joined in and added his bit, saying that it wasn't right to leave people stranded on the ice this way when they have really pressing matters.

"And that's when they jumped on us! 'May the devil take it, what kind of pressing matters are these? It's all just nonsense! Is some old haystack or some stupid paper such an important matter? Do you have any idea what kinds of matters are afoot now? Far more important than yours, you can be sure! Do you think only nephews and husbands do things that are bad? There's confusion and disorder in the entire Russian empire, despite its huge size. And not only in the Russian empire, but in the entire world. Take the Swede, now—he's been split! And you just sit at home and don't know anything.'

"'What Swede are you talking about? Why was he split?' my godson's father asked.

"'What Swede? The same one who was at the Battle of Poltava. Did you ever hear about it?'

"'Why, yes, I might have heard something . . .' he answered. 'And you say he's been split, or something?'

"'He's been split in two. You see, there was one kingdom, Sweden that is, and now it's been split in two: one part, about as big as a province one could say, has separated; it says it doesn't want to stay with the rest! So now it's going to be by itself, just like that. This means that the Swede has been split in two. That's the way it is! That's what's happening in the world, and the same kind of thing is going on in our own country, and yet people keep crawling to us the devil knows with what and what for! With haystacks and torn papers of some kind! It's enough to make chickens laugh!'

"'Well,' I said, 'some people might laugh, but others might cry. What if I have to live out my days as a beggar, among strangers! But there's no judgement or law to be had!'

"'So what kind of laws are you talking about?' the chief shouted. 'Where are you going to find that law? We're telling you clearly that the old laws are finished, and the new ones haven't been brought in yet. When they're brought in, then you can put forward your claim!'

"'But when will they be brought in, those new laws?'

"'Who knows? That's not up to us. Wiser people will find the means to do it in an orderly fashion. Wait a while!'

"I turned around and walked away. So tell me, dear lady, am I supposed to sit and wait for the new laws? Why is he telling me about that Swede who was split? Maybe it means nothing to that Swede that he was split, but now that my piece of paper is torn, it's as if my heart has been split!"

"Well, my dear Maryna, you'll just have to wait for the new laws."

"But, dear lady, will they come soon?"

"Well, perhaps it won't be too long now . . . Things appear to be moving in that direction."

"Oh, if only the Merciful Lord would make it so!"

That's what Granny Maryna said, and she crossed herself as she said it. Then she rose to her feet, bid her farewells, took her dish with the cabbage leaves . . . and shuffled off to await "the new laws."

Oh, how long will Granny Maryna have to wait before she— and we, along with her—finally get the new laws?

One and A Half Herrings
(1908)

God has given us Sunday. And so the village teacher, Oleksandra Andriyivna or, as we are going to call her, Madam Oleksandra, could have her breakfast—or rather, she could drink her tea—at leisure. Sitting at a table covered with a white tablecloth, she was drinking her tea unhurriedly and conversing with a friend.

Yes indeed, because it was Sunday, a guest—Andriy Semenovych Lozovaty—had come to see her. Andriy was Madam Oleksandra's friend—and how could he not be a friend? They taught in the same school! He had already had some tea at home and had just dropped by to inquire about something pertaining to the school; but the lady teacher, allowing herself to be somewhat tardy today as it was a holiday, was only now drinking her tea, and, of course, she had invited her guest to sit down as well.

They were sitting and discussing some school matters. That's the way teachers are! You would think that by now all of this would have become as distasteful to them as bitter horseradish. But no, whenever they get together, they immediately begin talking about their work—about "groups," and "texts," and all the rest of it.

Perhaps you would like to know what they—these friends—are like, and it will not take long to tell you. Madam Oleksandra is rather short, middle-aged, and a trifle plump. You would not call her beautiful, and she has a snub nose, but she is quite attractive, especially if you consider her rich blond hair. Madam Oleksandra, however, does not flaunt her hair—she combs it down smoothly, braids it tightly, and fixes it rigidly on the back of her head; she does not let it hang loosely in whimsical curls and bangs like some of the younger teachers who sometimes are reproached for being "flippant" because of their unruly hair.

Madam Oleksandra was dressed for the holiday, but her attire was simple—a dark grey skirt, and a jacket of the same plain material. A shawl she had knitted herself was draped over her shoulders.

Her friend, Andriy Semenovych, dressed in clothing that was somewhat worn, did not look like a dandy in comparison to Madam Oleksandra; however, he did have an appearance that was quite a bit more pretentious, and there was something vaguely bachelor-like about him. Having noted his loosely hanging thick hair, his wide and startlingly red belt buckle, and the two strange ornaments hanging on his watch fob, everyone would say—this teacher is not married. I'm not saying that a married man can't have such hair and such a buckle—not at all!—but nevertheless, one look at Andriy Semenovych, and you would definitely say that he was a bachelor. Perhaps it was something about his figure or his look—it is hard to say—but it was evident that Andriy Semenovych was not yet, so to speak, harnessed in the yoke.

And, indeed, Andriy Semenovych was not married.

The lady teacher, on the contrary, was not only married—she was already widowed. And she had a little daughter, Katrusya, who was playing in another part of the room.

They were having their tea, you see, not in the parlour, but in the smaller room that served both as the lady teacher's bedroom and dining room.

Not far from the bed, which was attractively made up and adorned with several pillows, Katrusya, the little four-year old daughter, was busily feeding a dark grey spotted kitten a dish of milk. This was probably a special day for the kitten, as well.

Either Katrusya or the kitten had spilled the milk—it was not clear how it had happened—and now a puddle was spreading alongside the dish. Neither Katrusya nor the kitten paid any attention to this—the kitten was lapping up the milk in a charming manner with its little pink tongue, and Katrusya, inadvertently spreading the milk with the hem of her dress, was gazing into the kitten's eyes and taking great delight in its appetite.

But the child was not satisfied with being the only one to enjoy the kitten—her mother also had to see it.

"Look, mummy, look!" the little girl shouted. "Look how the kitten is eating!"

"I see, I see," Madam Oleksandra replied, without turning around.

But it was not possible to conclude the matter just like that. Katrusya ran up to her mother and, tugging at her skirt, led her to the kitten.

It was then that Madam Oleksandra saw the spilled milk. She also noticed that Katrusya's apron and the hem of her freshly laundered little dress were spotted with milk.

"Oh, just look at you, Katrusya! What have you done? I just changed you into clean clothes, and here you've gone and crawled into the milk. Shame on you, you naughty little girl!"

Her mother was reproaching her, but the severe words must have been uttered in a voice that was not very frightening, because the little girl did not pay the slightest attention to these reproaches and crouched down over the kitten once again.

At this moment, someone rattled the doorknob and inquired in a fresh, happy voice: "May I come in?"

"Ah! Miss Oksana!" Madam Oleksandra called out delightedly, as she quickly wiped the hem of Katrusya's dress. "Of course you may! Come in, come in!"

An attractive, round-faced young lady entered the room. Her head was draped lightly in a delicate white shawl that did not conceal her fluffy blond hair, and had been thrown on only for the sake of covering her head.

The young lady entered the room, greeted the gentleman teacher, and extended her hand to him as to an acquaintance. She exchanged kisses with Madam Oleksandra, and then she hugged Katrusya, kissing her several times and greeting her with all sorts of nonsensical prattle.

Madam Oleksandra, watching all this with a smile, interjected: "Perhaps you, as her godmother, might change your godchild's clothes. She's spilled milk all over herself! She won't stay clean for so much as an hour. She's ever so naughty!"

"Now, now! You and your pedagogical severity! That's quite enough!" the young lady laughed. "Come here, Katrusya, I've brought you something!"

"As I've said before, you're spoiling her! And she just loves it!" the mother said happily.

"But this is a treat I brought back from the city . . . Take it, Katrusya!"

The kitten was forgotten, and the little girl, snuggling in the young lady's arms, unwrapped a pretty box of dainties.

Madam Oleksandra bustled about as she poured the young guest some tea, and Miss Oksana glanced out from behind Katrusya's head at Andriy Semenovych with a little smile half hidden in the corners of her pink lips and bright eyes. Even though Andriy Semenovych was not looking at the young lady, he appeared to be conscious of her gaze; he smoothed his hair with his hand and looked very intently through the window, notwithstanding the fact that the street outside was completely empty.

"How is it that you're dressed so lightly?" Madam Oleksandra asked the young woman, as she looked at her thin blouse and the gauzy shawl that was now lowered to her shoulders. "You've come here just like this?"

"Of course! It isn't far, is it?" the young woman replied. "And furthermore, it's so warm outside—it's truly *babyne lito [grandmother's summer: Indian summer]*."

"Yes indeed, it's a splendid autumn," the hostess agreed.

After talking about this and that, Miss Oksana lowered Katrusya from her lap and, kissing her resoundingly a few times, said: "Well, run along now and play, because there's some business I have to discuss with your mother."

"Business?" the lady teacher asked in surprise. "Miss Oksana—and business? Well now!" She was speaking jokingly; however, after a moment, she became serious and inquired: "What kind of business?"

"It's like this," the young lady began, sitting up straight and tugging at the ends of her shawl. "Actually, my daddy sent me over to tell you . . ."

"Your daddy?" the lady teacher repeated, as if she were somewhat concerned.

"Yes. You see, this pertains to you, and to the school in general." The young lady cast a glance at Andriy Semenovych. "Daddy, as the trustee of the school, wants you to know that . . ."

"What it is?" Madam Oleksandra asked. She was now becoming quite concerned.

"Don't be alarmed!" Miss Oksana smiled soothingly at her. "Here's what it is—a new inspector will be coming to visit you in a few days."

"An inspector? Why?" the lady teacher exclaimed, truly alarmed now.

"Well, you see," the young lady explained, "he's known us since the time we lived in the city. He was a teacher then. He even taught me at one point. Well, during our recent trip to the city, he met up with daddy and came to visit us a few times in our hotel. He told us he'd been appointed to our district as an inspector. He also said that he was planning to travel here to have a look at our school, and that he'd come to visit us. Well, and so daddy sent me . . . Of course, I was going to come and see you anyway, now that we've come back, but all the same, daddy did say that I should inform you. Daddy wants you to know; it goes without saying that you should know."

"Yes, of course!" the lady teacher said, as she nervously adjusted the shawl on her shoulders. "It couldn't be otherwise! Of course, we should know!" As she said this, she glanced at Andriy Semenovych; but he, with an even more indifferent look on his face than before, was gazing idly and gloomily in another direction.

The lady teacher did not conceal her concern: "Thank you for telling us," she said to Miss Oksana. "It goes without saying that we should know . . . everything has to prepared, both in the classroom and elsewhere . . . indeed, in the entire school . . . so that everything is in order."

"He's so exacting," the young lady added. "I was afraid of him when I was in his class."

"You say he's exacting?" the lady teacher asked.

"Yes, very exacting! He's somewhat irrational, and it's difficult to please him." the young lady said.

"Well, he won't eat us," the gentleman teacher stated.

"'He won't eat us'!" the lady teacher mimicked him in annoyance. "Of course he won't eat us! But then again, he could eat us if he wanted to!"

"God won't hand us over—so the pig won't eat us!" the gentleman teacher persisted.

Miss Oksana glanced at him with a smile, but, for some reason, Madam Oleksandra became incensed: "I really don't like people saying things like that!" she cried out. "Why bluster? It's frightening, it really is, so there's no point in bluffing!"

"No one's bluffing, but there's also no point in fainting with fear," Andriy Semenovych said in the same tone of voice, and he bravely met the amused look of the young lady.

"Well, well! We'll see whose heart will be the first to fall to his heels!" the lady teacher responded.

"Ha-ha-ha!" Miss Oksana laughed out loud. Then, rising to her feet, she said: "Well, I'm going now; I have a lot of things to take care of after my trip."

"And just when will your terrible Lucifer, or, I should say, your friend, arrive?" Andriy Semenovych inquired.

Madam Oleksandra flashed him an irate look, but Miss Oksana, blushing slightly, replied with the same smile: "I don't know. I don't know either the day, or the hour. Be prepared to receive the guest at any time; do not extinguish the lamp of learning and discipline—maintain it diligently!"

"It also would be in order to remember to be polite!" the lady teacher added emphatically.

Oksana giggled, exchanged kisses with Madam Oleksandra and, nuzzling Katrusya's face and neck, she bounced her up and down. Then, extending her hand to the gentleman teacher and bowing in a mockingly formal manner, she moved towards the door.

"Perhaps you could walk the young lady home, Andriy Semenovych, to protect her from the dogs," the lady teacher said.

"Oh no, there's no need for that!" Miss Oksana stopped her. "I want to follow the example that Andriy Semenovych has set—he's not at all afraid of Lucifer, so there's no reason for me to fear some dog called Lucy! Farewell!"

Oksana's white shawl swept past the window, and she disappeared from view.

"Well, you're a fine one!" the lady teacher attacked Andriy Semenovych. "What do you mean by talking to people like that?"

"Like what?" the gentleman teacher growled irately.

"You know very well, like what. With a growl! Why snarl at the young lady? 'Your friend, Lucifer . . .! The pig won't eat us up!' Is it proper to talk like that? After all, she is a young lady, the daughter of a lord, and her father is the trustee of the school. One could show her some respect!"

"Oh, the devil take them!" Andriy Semenovych muttered.

"What was that for? Why say that? One would think you're a bandit of some kind, a truly wicked man. But you're not! You just like to show off and say the devil knows what to people! I know you assume this manner only when you're speaking to Miss Oksana—but, you know you're dying of love for her."

"Me? Dying for her?" Master Andriy was enraged.

"Of course!' Madam Oleksandra was seething with anger. "You're in love with her! You love her, you love her—I've known this for a long time!"

"Leave me alone!" Andriy Semenovych retorted, and he rushed furiously to the door.

"Wait! Where are you going?" the lady teacher stopped him. "We have to give some thought to a few things—the hows and the whats! What are you doing in arithmetic right now? What kind of problems are you working on?"

Andriy Semenovych came back and sat down again. But we won't tell you about the rest of the discussion, for there are probably many people who would find it boring to hear about arithmetic problems.

The conversation of the pedagogues was interrupted by Tetyana, the janitor's wife. She entered the room and asked in a strident voice: "Madam, I'm making soup for dinner. What about the groats?"

Startled, the lady teacher looked up and exclaimed: "Please don't shout! Just ask nicely: 'What about the goats?' Well, take them into the shed immediately; don't leave them out in the open! Do it this very minute!"

Tetyana stared in silent astonishment at the teacher; she could not understand what had come over her.

II

During the next few days Madam Oleksandra worried constantly about the expected arrival of the inspector. God only knew when he would come, but it was necessary to have everything in the classroom ready. After all it was she, Madam Oleksandra, who was the principal of the school—the more senior teacher, as it were—and, therefore, she would be asked more questions.

She had become the principal because her husband had formerly been in that position—and she had been his assistant. After her husband died, the lord of the village, who was the trustee of the school and the father of young Miss Oksana, saw to it that Madam Oleksandra was promoted from the position of assistant to principal, and she had been sent another teacher—Andriy Semenovych—as an assistant, because it truly would have been too difficult for one person to run the school.

The school was large, and the pupils were divided into three groups. It was located in a spacious, new building—not in an old hovel, as is often the case.

***

If you are interested, we can go and see what is happening in the school—lessons are being conducted there even as we speak.

Over here, Madam Oleksandra is energetically instructing a group of young boys. She's relating something from the Holy Scriptures, because even though the priest has an obligation to teach in the school, ever since the old priest died, he has to serve two parishes, and he has no time to teach the pupils; he only drops in for a moment from time to time.

The lady teacher has once again narrated the proverb, or rather, the parable, about the sower of the wheat, and now she's asking the pupils questions about it—because, for some reason, this is the parable that is most often referred to during classroom visitations. The boys are a trifle confused about what happened to the seeds on the different plots of land. She has to explain it very carefully, so that it will sink into their heads!

After the lesson from the New Testament is concluded, a Russian language lesson is begun. The proper text is opened.

Madam Oleksandra tells them what's in it, then she questions them on what she has said, so that they will know how to retell intelligibly what is in the book—as if they were saying it in their own words. The boys conduct themselves freely, and it is evident that they do not fear the teacher; they even ask her questions when they get stuck.

Fine! Now it is time to write. They work diligently; the odd one even bites the tip of his tongue because he's trying so hard. It doesn't go too badly. The dictation comes out as it should have, without too many errors; it is only the "soft sign" that has either disappeared, or appeared where it should not be at all; and there is still a problem with one or two of the vowel sounds. All the usage rules about where the "soft sign" and the vowels should be placed have to be reviewed again, because, after all, this is the senior group of pupils.

They still have to do some arithmetic problems. She is certain that the inspector will ask them to solve some problems, because this is what inspectors like to do. Madam Oleksandra picks up the arithmetic text, written in Russian, and begins giving them a problem: "Someone bought 768 pencils . . ."

"Oh, my goodness!" Kuzma Tkhorenko, a boy with curly hair, shouts out in Ukrainian. "That's a lot of pencils! Why does he need so many pencils? Oh, if only we had that many!"

Any other time, the teacher would have discussed this comment, but now she stops the pupil: "Now, now, Kuzma, don't get off the topic, please. We have to do our work. The inspector may come at any time, and you have to understand the problems and know how to solve them quickly. Now, keep on writing everything down."

The pupils copy everything and, in a relatively short time, they figure out how much the pencils cost, and how many there are per pupil. Then they go on to figure out other purchases. One problem, involving the division of an inheritance, really causes them a lot of grief before they finally get things right.

Finally, one of the younger pupils, who lisps a bit, says: "Well, that 'thomeone' ith a weal bother! When he buyth thomething or beginth to diwide it, he geth thingth tho muddled up that it can't be thwaightened out again!"

"It's a good thing this "someone" is dead already," another pupil adds, because they had just been given a problem that began with the words: "Someone died and divided his wealth like this . . ."

The senior students begin to make fun of the junior ones: "You're a fool, if you think that this 'someone' really died! You'll have another problem about him soon enough!"

And this is how they study and prepare for the visit.

"Well, that's enough," the teacher finally says. "You may go now; but watch out, don't forget anything, and remember everything you've been told!"

"We won't forget! We won't forget!" the boys shout happily, as they rush about, preparing to leave.

***

Exhausted and worried, Madam Oleksandra returned home. She did not even want to eat when Tetyana brought her the borshch. And it seemed to her that Katrusya was bothering her more than she usually did.

She had hardly finished having her dinner, when Andriy Semenovych walked in. He appeared pale and worried.

"Here's a note for you," he said, handing Madam Oleksandra a small piece of paper. "A serving girl brought it for you from your daughter's beautiful godmother. It says that the guest from the city has arrived."

"What guest?" Madam Oleksandra inquired.

"What do you mean, what guest? The inspector . . ."

"The inspector?" the lady teacher repeated anxiously.

"Yes, the inspector. Go on and read it; perhaps she's written something about him."

"You're right!" the lady teacher exclaimed, quickly skimming the note. "He's arrived, and he's at their place! Oksana has written that he'll be at the school tomorrow. Oh, my God! What's to be done?" She began rushing about the room. "Where's that serving girl? Is she still here?"

"No, she's gone; she left as soon as she handed me the note."

"Oh, my God! Why did you send her away before telling me?" the lady teacher was irate.

"But she said that she was told just to hand over the note. She said she couldn't wait . . . probably because of the guest. What is it that you wanted to do?"

"I might have written something to Oksana. Well, what are we to do now?"

"What are we to do? Well, we should send someone to tell Father Mykola," Andriy Semenovych advised. "He ought to know as well."

"Yes, yes! Of course he ought to know! We have to send someone immediately. But whom will we send? Matviy had to go to the district office for some reason, and Tetyana is busy in the kitchen. Unless, perhaps, you might go?"

"I suppose I can," Andriy Semenovych agreed willingly. "I should ask him a few things—he knows much more about all of this. . . ."

"Yes indeed! Go! Or no, wait a moment! Let's go together! We'll discuss everything together," Madam Oleksandra said, rushing about the house; then she called out to the kitchen: "Tetyana, come here! Or, take Katrusya to the kitchen with you. I have to leave the house for some time. It's a very urgent matter!"

Buttoning up her coat as she walked, the lady teacher left the house with Andriy Semenovych. They hurried down the street to see Father Mykola.

III

The next day it seemed as if the air in the school had heated up. It actually was quite warm, for the weather was exceptionally fine for an autumn day—the sun was hot, almost scorchingly hot, and its bright rays filled the air.

It was bright, calm, and pleasant. Everyone who was not waiting for the inspector, or who did not have some other worry of some kind, looked out the window at such a wonderful day and rejoiced.

Yes, indeed, everyone—but not our school teachers!

They felt very nervous, but they had to pretend that nothing unusal was happening, that they were not expecting anything evil to befall them.

They were in their classrooms, aware that their guest might arrive at any moment. It was already past eleven. Father Mykola had also come to the school. He was sitting with the senior students, conducting a lesson on the New Testament as if this was not at all out of the ordinary. And why should he not be teaching it! After all, he was the religious teacher in the school, and he was just fulfilling his obligation.

And so, Father Mykola was telling the pupils about the Sermon on the Mount. He was speaking calmly and deliberately, as always, but a keen eye would have discerned that Father Mykola was not at ease. The way he kept adjusting the sleeve of his dark wine cassock made it quite evident that he was anxious.

As for the lady teacher, there was no need to have a keen eye to see that she was very anxious, indeed. She was walking up and down among the benches, picking up texts and putting them down again, straightening something here and over there, whispering something, and looking out into the street through the window. Suddenly, quite perturbed, she stalked angrily out of the classroom into the porch and picked up a broom that Matviy, the janitor, had left there. "Oh Lord, there's no hope for that man," she thought.

Then she darted into Andriy Semenovych's classroom. Everything seemed fine, and there seemed to be no reason for concern. Andriy Semenovych, nicely combed and presentable, was reading with the boys. He was not wearing his red buckle.

Madam Oleksandra went up to him, said something rapidly and quietly, and then instructed the pupils how to rise to their feet when the authorities walked in, and what they should say when they greeted them. She also said that they should calm their fears, because they were more likely to say something foolish when they were nervous, and she told them that they should reply calmly, sensibly, and in an orderly manner.

Then she whispered softly to the gentleman teacher once again: "Please, Andriy Smenovych, don't say some of the things that you like to come out with at times! I beg you! Because it will all come down on my head. Be polite!"

"As if I don't know that! Why are you telling me how to behave?" Andriy Semenovych snapped at her.

"Well, that's fine, that's fine!" the lady teacher waved her hands apologetically, so as not to irritate him further. And she returned to her classroom.

She had scarcely entered the room, when Father Mykola rose to his feet. "He's coming!" he said, as he glanced outside.

Madam Oleksandra flung herself headlong to the window. It was true! Walking up to the porch with Pokrovsky, the lord and the trustee of the school, was *he*, the inspector, a tall, thin man in a uniform; alongside him trudged a neighbouring landowner—a diminutive, short lordling; God only knew where he had appeared from, and why he was tagging along! He had probably come to visit Lord Pokrovsky and, on impulse, had come to the school with the other two.

Father Mykola and the lady teacher stepped forward to meet them, coming to a stop on the threshold of the classroom. The children also hastily slid out of their desks and stood up.

The authorities entered. Lord Pokrovsky introduced the priest and the principal—the lady teacher.

The inspector sternly and politely nodded his head to the lady teacher, and then walked up to Father Mykola to receive a blessing. This immediately set the proper, dignified tone.

Observing that a lesson was being conducted on the New Testament, the inspector said: "Please continue, Father—we'll listen."

They seated themselves. That is, the inspector and the school trustee sat down, while Madam Oleksandra and the landowner stood close to the wall. The landowner whispered something softly to her, but she could not hear him. She shook her head to discourage him from trying to engage her in any more conversation, because the inspector had already sent a reproving glance in her direction. Moving slightly away from him, she touched her collar to check if it had slipped to one side. Then she stood as if she were in church, respectfully, and without moving.

The look on the inspector's face became less severe. Then he began listening attentively to the lesson; he did not look at the lady teacher again.

Father Mykola finished his narration about the Sermon on the Mount and asked the inspector and the trustee if they wished to ask the pupils some questions.

The inspector, who was approaching the first row, was already thinking about questioning the pupils.

"So, do they know their prayers?" the inspector inquired.

"Of course they know them! Special attention is paid to this!" Father Mykola replied, nervously adjusting his sleeve.

And truly, the boys knew the two prayers that the inspector asked about—"The Prayer before Studies," and "O Heavenly Father,"—very well. The inspector asked them about the Ten Commandments—the boys knew them as well.

"Good!" the inspector said. "And now tell me this, my boy, how many sons did Noah, the ancestor of mankind, have?"

Semen Lemishchenko, a short and stout boy, rose to his feet—for the inspector had pointed at him—and said that Noah had three sons, and that they were called Sym *[Shem]*, Kham *[Ham]*, and Akhvet *[Japhet]*.

"Akhvet!" the inspector repeated, turning to the trustee with a look that was neither a smile, nor a reproach.

The school trustee smiled ingratiatingly, as if he were asking that Semen Lemishchenko be forgiven: "You see, Anton Ivanovych, this is the local pronunciation! It's very difficult to change it."

"Yes, that is true," the inspector agreed, "Pronunciation is a difficult matter; nevertheless, one must strive to overcome it. But they know everything very well. Now, you, the blond boy, tell me, what kind of dream did Yakov *[Jacob]* have?"

The blond-haired boy, Yakiv Prykhodko, knew the dream about the ladder and the angels, and Yukhym Chupriy did a truly marvellous job of narrating the incident about Yosef *[Joseph]* and his brothers.

The replies of the boys to questions about the New Testament were no worse. They only did not know that the Holy Day of the Saviour was called the Transfiguration. The parable about the sower, however, was narrated superbly—and the inspector was delighted.

"Your pupils know everything very well! You deserve high honours for this, Father!" he said to Father Mykola.

"We try, to the best of our ability, to strengthen them in the teachings of the faith," the priest replied with a bow, "for this knowledge is the foundation of everything!"

"Of course, of course," the inspector agreed, "it is the foundation of everything."

Then the inspector added: "And now, permit me to ask them a few questions in the other subjects." He turned to the lady teacher. He asked her what texts she used, and how much had been covered. Then he asked the pupils to read aloud, and to retell what they had read in their own words. The first and second pupils succeeded very well at this task.

It seemed that it was not so difficult to breathe in the classroom any more. Everyone was beginning to feel slightly more at ease. Something resembling a smile appeared on Madam Oleksandra's face—or, at least, the frown that had hovered over her eyebrows all morning had now vanished.

They moved on to arithmetic.

"Are the pupils secure in their knowledge of the multiplication table?" the inspector inquired.

"Oh, yes indeed!" the lady teacher said confidently. "They've known it for quite some time now."

Almost as soon as she said it, the lady teacher felt in her heart that she should not have added the last sentence, but it was too late. As the saying goes: a word is not like a sparrow—once it flies out, you can't catch it by the tail!

But the boys really did know the table for the "tens," and even for the "sixes" and the "sevens."

"Good!" the inspector said, after questioning three of the pupils. "Now, something from the oral problems. How far have they progressed in the arithmetic text?"

The lady teacher told him they had completed the first section of the text and also knew the first rules of division.

"So . . ." the inspector said. "So as not to waste any time, we'll move on to division."

"You, the boy with the keen eyes," the inspector pointed at Kuzma Tkhorenko, "you probably know everything very well! Solve this problem. 'Ten herrings cost 60 *kopiyky [cents]*, and someone bought one and a half herrings. How much did he pay?'"

Kuzma looked at the inspector and said: "That can't be."

"What? What are you saying? What can't be?" the inspector asked.

"What you've just said," Kuzma persisted.

"Why can't it be?" the inspector asked sharply.

"Because," the boy stubbornly replied, "no one will sell half a herring—you can either buy one, or a pair of them, but no one will cut a herring in half, because he'll spoil it. It just can't be," the pupil stated once again—and he even shook his head.

The lady teacher's heart skipped a beat, and everyone felt that something untoward had occurred in the classroom. The landowner stifled a giggle, but this made matters even worse. The dark face of the inspector grew still darker; at first he bit his lip, and then he totally ignored the boy and turned sharply to the lady teacher, saying: "How are your pupils replying? What manner of responding is this?"

"They . . . please forgive them, your excell . . ."

"I'm asking you, what kind of replies are these?" the inspector shouted more loudly, flashing an angry look at Madam Oleksandra. "What kind of guidance are you giving them?"

"I . . ." the lady teacher began saying something. It seems, however, that the inspector had not asked the question to hear the teacher's reply. In a thundering voice, he replied to it himself: "It's the kind of guidance that leads to the gallows! Young boys lose their respect for their elders, they lose all understanding of politeness and obedience; they lose all sense of their obligations. You're undermining the basic foundation of a good, proper upbringing; you're destroying young souls; you're leading them to perdition, to the gallows—as I've said. Is it likely that such an arrogant boy," he pointed at Kuzma Tkhorenko, "will understand his civic duties? Will he respect the property of others? I ask you— will he hold anything sacred?"

Madam Oleksandra could not venture an opinion as to whether anything would be held sacred by Kuzma Tkhorenko, or if he would respect the property of others. For one thing, something was squeezing her throat so tightly that she could not make a sound, and, for another—the inspector did not wait for her reply.

He thundered on still more loudly: "No, he will not respect the property of others! He will not have any understanding of his obligations, and there is only one road that lies ahead of him— the road that leads to a violent death!"

Having made this statement, the inspector seemed to change his tone; but what he said next, even though it was stated in a calmer voice, was much more frightening to Madam Oleksandra: "It is not permitted to teach in this manner, my good lady. Such teachers are not maintained in service."

After this remark, nothing more was said to the teacher. The inspector turned to the school trustee. "Well, let us proceed to the next classroom."

Lord Pokrovsky led the inspector to see Andriy Semenovych. The lady teacher did not know if she should go, or remain where she was. Lord Pokrovsky gestured to her with his hand that she should stay. Swaying, she made her way to the desk and leaned against it. But she did not find any relief there.

"What have you done?" Father Mykola started in on her. "What is it that you've done? Oh, my God, my Lord! Everything was coming along so well, it was all so exceptionally successful, and then—just like that—everything was lost in a minute, a second. Why would you cause such a tumult! What have you done? What have you done?"

"But did I do anything?" the lady teacher came out of her trance, and tears almost burst from her eyes. "And did anything so out of the ordinary happen? What kind of tumult? There was nothing out of the ordinary! The boy said that half a herring can't be bought—and it's true, and it shows that the boy *is thinking*, that he's accustomed to replying consciously, and that he isn't talking like a *parrot*. What's wrong with that?"

"What? Don't you understand that the boy made him look like a fool?"

"Not at all!" the lady teacher shouted.

"Ah! If you don't understand, then there's no point in talking to you!" Father Mykola was also shouting. "But you ought to understand that you have caused much trouble, not only for yourself, but for me as well! You have spoiled all my chances for advancement! Do you understand this? You've harmed me as well!"

"How have I harmed you?" the lady teacher responded angrily now. "By teaching them everything you should have, so that they knew it all very well, and could give the correct answers?"

"I don't want to talk to you," Father Mykola flung at her and stalked wrathfully out of the classroom. He had noticed that the inspector was already departing from the school.

A few moments later, the lady teacher also rushed out.

The pupils watched them go without understanding what was happening.

When she came home, the lady teacher collapsed on her pillows and wept freely. Her shoulders were heaving. Then she raised herself, but she did not know what she should do next; she sat on the bed as if she had turned to stone.

Suddenly, Andriy Semenovych dashed in. He looked all dishevelled once again, and his face was distorted and grim.

"Yes!" he shouted at once. "You're sitting and resting! You have good reason to do so! You've destroyed the school, you've destroyed everybody!"

"Whom have I destroyed?" the lady teacher asked heatedly.

"Whom? Everyone!" Andriy Semenovych screamed. "Father Mykola told me everything after they all left."

"Why did they leave so quickly?" the lady teacher inquired hesitantly.

"The devil knows why! But why should they stay, when that man—the inspector—was so enraged that he couldn't even ask anything; he could only find fault with everything!"

"What happened in your room?" the lady teacher asked in a hollow voice.

At first, Andriy Semenovych could only pace the room with his fists clenched, but then he stopped and began to recount what had happened: "He came in like a snake. I introduced myself, but he didn't extend so much as a finger. His look was exactly like that of Lucifer—it cut to the quick! Well, that's fine, I thought to myself, perhaps that's his manner.

"And then he began. He immediately went on the attack: 'Why,' he asked, 'is the air so heavy in this classroom?' What was I to tell him? Viktor Pavlovych explained something to him. And then that fool, that visiting lordling—the devil knows what his name is—began to make some silly jokes.

"Well, after this, the inspector began asking questions. He told the pupils to read from the class reader. So they read. Then he asked Ivan Khandra to retell in his own words what he'd read, and the boy did it correctly—he even knew what the difficult words were, because I'd really stressed them.

"Then the inspector glanced at the wall, at the maps, and asked: 'Do your pupils know anything about geography?' I indicated those in the second group. So he immediately pointed to Africa on the map and asked Hrytsko Chmil: 'What is this?' 'Africa,' the boy replied. Well, what the devil more did the man need to know? Nevertheless, he continued: 'And what is it—this Africa?' Chmil replied: 'A country of sorts.' And that one looked daggers at me: 'How are you teaching them? He ought to have replied: a part of the world, and not a country of sorts. What kind of free thinking is this?'

"And then he let loose with a lot of fiendish nonsense that wasn't worth listening to! And, with that, he left, without asking a single other thing—after being there only a minute.

"I thought to myself: 'Has he gone mad, or what?' I simply couldn't understand what was going on, why he'd become so upset over nothing! But then Father Mykola came to me after they left, and told me that it had all begun in your classroom—because everything had gone fine at the outset! The devil only knows what happened! Now, I wouldn't be at all surprised if my neck were on the line as well. Well, I owe you a great big thank you!"

At this point the lady teacher boiled over. "Why are you attacking me?" she shouted, holding back her tears. "Why are you blaming me? Even without your accusations, it's all so distressing that I would like to shut myself off from the world! Because of me, because of me! How am I to blame? And if anyone will be chased out, it will be I—before anyone else! So, they'll fire you! What a tragedy! You're single, and you'd have only half the grief that I'll have. If they fire me, where will I go with my child?"

Once again, Madam Oleksandra could no longer hold back her tears. They gushed from her eyes—and her handkerchief was already soaked . . .

Andriy Semenovych ran out of the room. In the doorway, he almost knocked over Tetyana who, holding Katrusya by the hand, was walking into the room. Tetyana just exclaimed: "Holy God, what's happened to them?" Then, leading Katrusya up to her mother, she said: "Let the child be with you now, for all the gentlemen have gone away. And the priest has left already. Why are you crying? What happened? I overheard a bit of what the priest was telling Andriy, that it was all because of some kind of herring. What kind of a herring was it? How did it get into the classroom?"

"Oh, leave me alone!" the lady teacher wailed wrathfully.

"How strange!" Tetyana said, as she walked out of the room and went to the pantry to fetch a pumpkin and make some gruel.

IV

A month went by. The golden autumn that had flaunted its beauty when the unfortunate incident happened in the school, had vanished. Now it was late autumn, wretched and stingy with its colours, and melancholy trees dropped their pitiful remaining leaves; it was an autumn with a gloomy, low sky that shed cold, drizzling rains, and severe winds that could bring snow at any moment.

The streets in our village of Budushchi were very muddy. If you wanted to walk on drier land, you had to go by way of the gardens. When the pupils—especially those from out of the way corners and hamlets—came to school, their boots were so muddy that it was painful to look at them.

Nevertheless, they did come. The work in the school was progressing as it should. Both the gentleman teacher and the lady teacher had stopped worrying too much about the incident with the inspector, because they had not heard about any distressing consequences. At times, however, Madam Oleksandra experienced such anxiety and grief that it felt as if cats were clawing at her heart.

And, to make matters even worse, Miss Oksana had gone away again. She had left very soon after that incident, so soon, that it had not been possible to have a proper conversation with her. The lady teacher did not feel at ease visiting the young lady's parents; moreover, the young lady's father, the school trustee, having run into her in a shop one day, had waxed eloquently, and at great length, about the "tumultuous incident" in the school. Well, God be with them, why go and visit them? She might have gone to see the priest's wife, but the latter was angry with her as well; Father Mykola had told her everything that had happened.

Of course, if you have absolutely no one to visit, life can become very boring; therefore, the lady teacher sometimes called on an acquaintance by the name of Hanna Stepanivna, who lived at the opposite end of Budushchi.

This lady was no longer young—she had already married off her elder daughters. She lived in a little manor that had some land attached to it—she rented out the land—and owned a fairly large orchard that also had been rented out for more than a year. The lady also knitted things to sell—woollen kerchiefs and socks— and, at times, she embroidered shirts for train conductors and other gentlemen. And so, by doing a bit of this and a bit of that, Hanna Stepanivna managed to make ends meet.

It seems that this lady did not go anywhere, except, perhaps, to church, and sometimes to the market on a market day. Despite this, however, she knew absolutely everything that was going on.

"So, my poor dear, you aren't going to be teaching here any more, are you? Where are you going to go?"

The lady teacher blanched and nearly fainted. "What do you mean, I won't be teaching? I haven't heard anything!"

"Really? That's strange!" Hanna Stepanivna said. "People are talking about it as if it were a done deed. They say that another teacher has been assigned to your position, and that he'll be here shortly."

The lady teacher's heart turned cold. "Who is saying this? How? What?"

It took a little prying, but eventually Hanna Stepanivna told her that Klymentykha—a kinswoman of the priest's wife, and the one who baked the bread for the Host—had heard it in the priest's house. And people were saying that a document about this matter was on its way from the inspector. And it was all because, supposedly, when the inspector was here he was very dissatisfied with the school.

So this was how it was all coming out and being settled! Oh, how terrible all this was! And it really did have an aura of truth about it. They would chase her away? Perhaps the document had already arrived? Well, it couldn't be helped! After all, did it take long to get rid of someone? In the village of Pereshchepen, the teacher had been released in an instant. He had still been teaching at the beginning of the week, but by Sunday he was gone. He simply was told that it was necessary "to clean the lodgings immediately!"

Madam Oleksandra sat completely wilted, more dead than alive.

"You should plead your case with Miss Oksana," Hanna Stepanivna advised her.

"She's not here; she went to the city again and hasn't returned yet."

"What's with you, my dear? On what planet do you live, that you don't know anything!" Hanna Stepanivna exclaimed. "I live at the opposite end of town, but I know that she came back yesterday. And you live so close to her—and you don't know anything. It's really very strange!"

"Perhaps . . . but I really didn't know," the lady teacher said. And then she thought: "What she said about *that matter* must be true, because Oksana used to come to see me as soon as she returned, but this time she hasn't come." Overwhelmed by her sad thoughts, she added out loud: "But what can Miss Oksana do to help me?"

"What do you mean, what? Let her put in a good word to her betrothed, and it will all blow over! Or did you also not know that Oksana is marrying your inspector?"

"Oksana? Marrying the inspector? What are you saying!"

"Yes, indeed! She is. Why are you so surprised? Why shouldn't she? Praise God, she's the right age! And she's not the only one in the family—there are still Katya and Maruska. And there certainly is no surplus of suitors in these parts. Well, it's true that the groom is a trifle old for her, but where are young ones to be found nowadays? In any event, she's marrying this one—why be picky? He has a good job in the civil service, his pay isn't too bad, and he'll have a pension. And her father's estate is not that large, and there are two sons as well.

"It's a sure thing," Hanna Stepanivana continued. "I knew some time ago that the young lady was planning to get married, because her mother hired a seamstress from the town to sew shirts and pillow cases, and Leyzer has been called in to examine the fur coats.

"I just didn't know who the young lady was marrying, but then I heard them say it was the inspector. He's coming tomorrow— not to the school this time, but to ask formally for the young lady's hand in marriage."

"Who? The inspector?"

"Yes, of course. They got to know each other very well at her aunt's home in the city. Yesterday, Oksana came home alone; but Mordko—when he came to buy geese from me—told me that tomorrow horses were being sent to the station again—this time to fetch the suitor. So that's that! You'd better hurry, sweetheart, and beg Oksana to help you right now. After all, she is your child's godmother, so let her do what she can, before it's too late."

The lady teacher, not wishing to stay much longer, got up to leave. Hanna Stepanivna, however, detained her for a moment, to tell her fortune. And it turned out just as might be expected—an older king, and next to him, a diamond that indicated a marriage. There were quite a few of those bad cards—spades—but in the end, the heart was calmed with good cards.

"Run along now; don't waste any time!" Hanna Stepanivna concluded. "And if the opportunity arises, please get a sample of

Oksana's shirt pattern; perhaps it's a new style of some kind—since they're sewing it just now—and I'll save it for my Olya."

"Fine, fine!" the lady teacher murmured, as she exchanged farewell kisses. Upset and worried, she set out for home.

V

Miss Oksana's room was in the attic. It was quite cold there in the autumn, but young ladies sometimes like to find a nook somewhat removed from their mother and father—they like to feel a trifle more independent!

When Madam Oleksandra ran over to see Miss Oksana the next morning, she went in through the west entrance and found the young lady in her room getting dressed—she was combing her attractive blond hair. As the lady teacher walked in, Oksana noticed her obvious agitation.

"What's wrong?" she inquired.

Tears, mixed with passionate words, were the answer to this question.

"I'm as good as dead now," Madam Oleksandra concluded. "Where, tell me, where am I to go with a child—and just when winter is approaching? I don't have any relatives who can help me, I don't have anyone. . . . Oksana, my dearest dove, save me! If you don't save me, I'll perish along with Katrusya! At least take pity on her. For what sin are we to perish? Save me, my dearest!"

"How can I save you?" Oksana replied. "Perhaps father can give you some advice."

"No, it's you, you!" the lady teacher said. "You have only to say a word, when the inspector comes . . . and you'll have your way."

"So you already know that he's coming?" Oksana smiled.

"Yes, I do know. I was told . . . People, you know, are saying that you . . . that you're marrying him."

"People say a lot of things!" the young lady, still smiling, responded blushingly.

"You will talk to him, won't you? You'll intercede with him for me?"

"Well, fine, I'll talk to him. I'll ask him."

Madam Oleksandra rushed up to kiss Oksana once more.

After this conversation, the lady teacher returned home with high hopes. She dreamed all night about a king of spades with a cudgel in his hand and a queen of diamonds with a flower.

The next day Oksana came to the lady teacher's classroom. Taking her to one side, she whispered: "Well, don't worry any more! You'll remain in your position. The inspector has arrived; I've talked to him, and he gave me his word that nothing will happen to you!"

The lady teacher kissed her. Then Oksana added: "But, you know, the document really was going to be sent. It seems that your position had already been designated for someone else."

"There, you see! This means that what the people were saying was true."

The lady teacher wanted to ask Oksana more about it—what and how, but . . . "I'll do it another time," she thought. Instead, she asked: "The inspector won't be coming to the school, will he?"

"I don't know . . . he won't be coming soon, but later, he might!" Oksana said with a smile. "Because he's going to be at our place for quite some time."

"Oh! Did you hear that, boys!" the lady teacher turned to her pupils. "The inspector has come once again, and he might come to the school. So you better act properly and not say anything that you shouldn't! Especially you, Kuzma. You'd better behave and hold your tongue! Well, do you think that you'll know now what to say when you're asked how much one and a half herrings cost?"

"I knew the answer then," Kuzma Tkhorenko called out. "Nine *kopiyky*. But I still think that no one will sell half a herring! However, since that foolish gentleman got so upset with you about it, I won't say it again."

The lady teacher turned cold.

But Oksana laughed and said: "He's not foolish; he's just severe. But he's grown kinder now!" She kissed the lady teacher and quickly ran out.

The lady teacher caught up to her on the porch, embraced her closely, and said emotionally: "Thank you, my little dove! You've saved us!" Then, she could not hold back her curiosity any longer, "When will the wedding be, my dear Oksana? Will it be now, before Advent, or after Christmas?"

"I don't know. Perhaps now," Oksana said, and she ran off.

The lady teacher followed her with joyful eyes. She returned to the classroom, feeling as if someone had placed her on top of a hundred horses.

"Just think," she thought, "if it weren't for the wedding, they would have thrown me and my child out of the school. And why? Because of such an inconsequential thing—because of one and a half herrings!"

When Madam Oleksandra went home a short time later to feed Katrusya some gruel, the gentleman teacher walked in to see her.

"Ah," the lady teacher greeted him. "Do you want to find out about Oksana? Did you see that she was here? Oh, what good news she brought me!"

"Well, it must be really something! You're as radiant as the rising sun."

"Of course I'm radiant! And I'm not trying to hide it! Did you know that our Oksana is getting married? The wedding is going to be quite soon. She told me herself."

Andriy Semenovych, who was standing near the table, reeled in disbelief. His fingers, holding a cigarette, began to tremble. He said softly: "Ah! so that's it!"

"And do you know whom Oksana is marrying?" the lady teacher asked. "You would never guess!"

"I don't know. Who is it?" Andriy asked quickly.

"She's marrying our inspector!" Madam Oleksandra announced triumphantly.

Her guest was stunned. "The inspector?" he finally gasped.

"Yes indeed, yes indeed, he's the one! Well, now you and Father Mykola can stop worrying that, because of me, something terrible will happen to the school! Now, nothing will happen to anyone! Now, Africa can be either 'a part of the world,' or 'a country of sorts;' and let it even be stated that 'a herring can't be cut in half'—nothing matters anymore! Do you hear, Katrusya? Your godmother is going to marry the inspector!"

With these words, Madam Oleksandra began kissing her daughter ecstatically, while the bemused child looked at her in astonishment.

Andriy Semeovych continued holding the cigarette in his hand, but he did not light it . . .

Nataliya Kobrynska

1855-1920

Biographical Sketch

Nataliya Kobrynska was born in 1855 (1851 in some sources) in Western Ukraine—a part of the Austro-Hungarian Empire. Both her paternal grandfather and her father were priests who participated actively in the development of Ukrainian literature, the former through his involvement in Ukrainian theatre, and the latter by translating and writing poetry and plays. On her mother's side, Nataliya's younger cousin, Sofiya Okunevska-Morachevska—who studied in Zurich Switzerland and, in 1894, became the first female physician in Austro-Hungary—wrote under the pseudonym of Yarena.

In her era, women in the Austro-Hungarian Empire were barred from completing more than an elementary level of education; therefore, Nataliya was educated at home. She learned German, French, Polish, and Russian from her father, and immersed herself in world literature by reading books her brothers brought home from institutions of higher learning.

At the age of twenty, Nataliya married her intellectual soul-mate, a young seminarian, Theofil Kobrynsky. A talented musician and avid folklorist, he actively supported his young wife's feminist and literary aspirations. The couple decided to forego raising a family, formally identified themselves as feminists, and dedicated their lives to ameliorating the position of women in society. Unfortunately, Kobrynsky died a few years after they were married, and Nataliya, left without any means of support, had to return to her parents' home.

After her husband's death, Kobrynska travelled to Vienna with her father, an elected member of the Austrian Parliament. While there, she made the acquaintance of Ukrainian activists who recognised her literary talent and put her in contact with Ivan Franko, Ukraine's leading man of letters. She also travelled to Switzerland, where she met Olena Pchilka's brother, Mykhaylo Drahomanov, the famous Ukrainian scholar, historian, and political publicist who encouraged her to devote herself to the task of raising the social and political consciousness of Ukrainian women.

Under Ivan Franko's mentorship, she became deeply involved in organising a women's movement. In her articles and speeches she discussed the deplorable social and economic status of women within the Austro-Hungarian and Russian empires, and encouraged women to attain equality with men.

In the absence of opportunities for formal education for women, Kobrynska firmly believed that literature was the most effective vehicle for convincing women of the need for change. With this goal in mind, she formed a women's association in 1884, which, through an active program of cultural and educational enlightenment, fostered reading circles and promoted an informed discussion of women's rights.

A leading theoretician of feminist thought, her approach to real-life issues, conceptualized within a socialist framework, was pragmatic, and attempted to reconcile radical and conservative points of view. Her concerns cut across what she saw as the artificial and divisive boundaries of social class. In her view, it was only by banding together into secular women's organizations that all women could improve their lot in life.

While actively developing, refining, and propagating these views, Kobrynska continued writing. In her first work, *The Spirit of the Times*, which appeared in 1884, she recognized both the inevitability of change and the upheaval it caused in human lives. In 1887, together with Olena Pchilka, she edited and published *Pershy vinok (The First Garland),* a groundbreaking almanac of writings by women authors, poets, and publicists from both Eastern and Western Ukraine. It was one of the first such collections in Europe to be produced by women.

In 1890, she headed a delegation of women from Western Ukraine that petitioned the Minister of Education to allow women to enroll in university studies, a move viewed by some of her opponents as an attack on the sanctity of the family. A year later, she organised a women's conference that called for the establishment of high schools for girls. Between 1893-1896, she published three issues of a women's almanac called *Nasha dolya (Our Fate).*

At this time, Kobrynska tried to establish village day care centres and communal kitchens, urging women from the intelligentsia to convince peasant women of the desirability and possibility of social change. Unfortunately, her ideas, including her advocacy of universal suffrage, were ahead of her time, and her efforts were not always appreciated, even by the women she wished to help. Alienated from much of society because of her strongly held views, she spent the last years of her life in her native village, where she died in 1920. In keeping with her wishes, her final statement to the world was inscribed on her tombstone: "My heart no longer aches."

Kobrynska is acclaimed as a talented writer and a pioneer in the women's movement in Ukraine. Her short stories, written primarily about events that transpired within her family and circle of friends, present a poignantly accurate picture of the social conditions of her day and their devastating effect on women.

The Spirit of the Times
(1883)

It was a misty winter day. Heavy grey clouds hung low above the horizon, enveloping everything in a dark and gloomy haze. White layers of snow piled up into thick mounds, blanketing the frozen mud.

Instead of settling down for her afternoon nap, Lady Shuminska picked up a sock she was knitting and seated herself by a window. There was nothing to disturb her peaceful mood. She knew exactly what, where, and how things were being done in the household. She knew that the maids were washing dishes in the kitchen, and the young serving men were cleaning the stables and attending to the cattle. Besides, servants do not require strict supervision in the winter. Spring, autumn, and summer—these are the seasons when everyone has to work long and hard.

At sixty, she was no longer a young woman, and her eyes were failing her. She pulled a pair of horn-rimmed eyeglasses out of her pocket, positioned them on her nose, tossed a ball of yarn into a corner, readied her knitting needles, and began to ply them swiftly. The yarn looped itself into stitches that irrevocably followed one another, like the days, months, and years of a person's life. Just how many moments of pain and pleasure, of sorrow and joy, these days had brought with them—it was impossible to remember!

Her repetitive work lulled her into a reflective mood. Days and events from long ago began to come alive, to assume the colour and vitality of those bygone times, to radiate with their former clarity. Lady Shuminska's thoughts flew into the distant past, somewhere into the moments of her youngest childhood years— years that were emerging from her dim memory as if everything had occurred only recently, as recently as yesterday.

As her needles clicked away, she recalled the time when she was just a little child learning the art of knitting from her older sister.

How clumsily her fingers had snarled things up then, fumbling with the needles and stretching the yarn held in place by her instructor. Memories from her distant past shimmered and floated by like dreamy visions. They clung for a moment to the stem of a flower, babbled in the obscure language of a child, moved on to pivotal moments and events, and then returned once again to indistinct minutiae, illuminating along the way what was most significant and important in her life.

If someone had been observing her, they would have known, from the fleeting spasms on her pensive face, that her thoughts had taken a giant leap. And truly, she was reliving the most important moment in a woman's life—the moment she stands beneath the bridal wreath.

She had been scarcely sixteen years old at the time. Her future husband, who had already completed his studies at the seminary, was the son of a priest from the same diocese as her father. She did not know him, and saw him for the first time when he accompanied his father to their parish feast day. The two of them spent the entire day together. After the mass, at which his father had been a co-celebrant, he stayed for dinner and on into the evening.

She had not known that she would be his choice, but she had nothing against it. All those who were dearest to her felt it was a perfectly suitable match, and she herself had no reason to think otherwise. It would have served no purpose to delay the marriage, so they married, as God intended, and had time enough after the wedding to get to know one another.

A deep crease furrowed her forehead. The yarn continued unwinding itself uniformly from the ball and looping itself into stitches, but her thoughts ranged ever farther and farther afield. With the first stirrings of motherhood, she was gripped with shame and terror. She was embarrassed in front of everyone, even herself, and almost came to despise her husband.

When her mother told her that her condition would bring her honour, and that a woman's worth was measured by the number of her children, she was not able to see it this way and was hurt by her mother's lack of sympathy. It was not until quite a few years later—after she had become accustomed to these things—

that she accepted her mother's ideas and concurred wholeheartedly with her views.

Initially, her maternal horizons were clouded because she gave birth only to daughters.

Traditionally, it was accepted that a son brings more honour to a mother than a daughter; however, she was still young, so she did not lose hope that God would bless her with a son. When her wish was finally fulfilled, her joy was boundless. She gave birth to three sons in all, and even though she loved her little daughters dearly, she would have preferred to see them transformed into boys, not so much for her own satisfaction, as for their own good.

"A boy is more fortunate than a girl," she stated quietly.

She compared herself to her husband, her mother to her father, and women friends to their husbands, and something like an invisible worm gnawed at her heart. All the same, she was cheered by the thought that God would help her find good husbands for her daughters, and fine, upstanding sons-in-law for herself.

Only rarely does a mother rear all the children to whom she has given the gift of life, and Lady Shuminska's fate was no different. Of eight children that she bore, she was left with only two sons and two daughters. The other four, without having known this world, had flown away to the land of eternal rest.

Life and death had visited her children in turn, bringing her pain and sorrow, happiness and joy. Even though she grieved deeply over her dead children, so much hope is attached to every life, that her heartache lessened as she gazed upon those who remained. She thought about their futures, about herself, and about how, one day, she would be surrounded by a garland of children and grandchildren. And, positioned at the hub of this family circle— her every word heard, her every whim fulfilled—she would rejoice in their happiness, devotion, and respect. She would take pride in her motherhood and find blessedness in it. Even if she were to close her eyes forever, these children that she had brought forth to serve God would venerate their dear mother and, candles in hand, would lead her to the altar of the Almighty.

The future of her children constituted her whole world. It was her single thought, her single hope. This future, about which she so often thought, was not a puzzle to her. On the contrary, she envisioned everything clearly, just as all her plans were clearly and carefully thought out. Her sons would become priests, her daughters—the wives of priests, and all of them would live in affluence.

She worked incessantly to realise her dream, managing everything herself to ensure that as much wealth as possible was acquired for her children. As for other matters, she placed her faith in the beneficence of God. Throughout the entire mass, her eyes did not stray from the thick Polish prayer book she had inherited from her grandmother, and no one prayed more sincerely or kneeled in such an exemplary manner. She made donations to the church on behalf of all her children: an altar cloth, a cushion for the kneeling stool, tassels for the candles.

On behalf of her eldest son, whom she hoped God would guide according to her wishes, she embroidered a wide, red gusset for the priest's vestments. In a clerical family, a mother's greatest hope rests upon her eldest son. God forbid that her eldest should stray from the path for which he was destined. He had to have a sure way of earning a livelihood, for who would look after his poor mother and younger siblings in the event of a misfortune? Even though her husband was young and healthy, the almost daily spectre of death filled her mind with images of poverty and the disintegration of her family if its head should die.

In the midst of these sad thoughts, happier and more pleasant ones occasionally emerged. Often, as she sat at her work, neatly laying down one stitch after another, one thread after another, her thoughts grew rosier and brighter as she saw the smooth red leaves and flowers appear under her fingers. She saw herself in church, with her young daughter-in-law beside her, and her son in these vestments, at his first mass. She imagined him singing, facing the congregation, exciting the fervour of the people. How proudly she and her husband would walk out of the church! And the householders and their wives would block their path, kiss their hands, and congratulate them for having lived to see such happiness.

"You will be a priest," she would say to the little boy playing at her feet.

"I will be a priest," the child would respond seriously, and she would give him a heartfelt kiss.

Even now, after so many years, a smile rose to her lips when she recalled how her beloved son, when he was just a toddler, had given his nanny a piece of twine and told her to save it to bind the sack of *kalachi [braided circular ceremonial bread]* he would give her when he became a priest.

The years passed by quickly. Before Lady Shuminska knew it, the children had all grown up. The sons were sent to school, the younger daughter was studying with a governess, and the older one was leaving her childhood years behind and becoming a young woman. And such a pretty one! She was as shapely and supple as a freshly blooming spring flower. And her eyes! Oh, what beautiful eyes she had! Blue as the sky, and serene and soulful, like the evening star.

Lady Shuminska sighed deeply, and the knitting needles jerked spasmodically in her hands. Because of this child, she had come to know the greatest joy and respect, but also the greatest sorrow and grief. By the time this daughter was sixteen, she—like her mother before her—already had a number of suitors. But her mother was reluctant to part with her daughter so soon; she wanted to have her at her side for at least two more years. Recalling the onerous duties that had descended upon her after her marriage, she often stated that a woman is fortunate only as long as she stays with her mother.

In all too short a time, however, Lady Shuminska regretted heeding her own sage counsel. Suitors appeared, stayed a while, and vanished. When her daughter was eighteen, not a single one remained, and it was only when she turned nineteen that two appeared at the same time. But here again, things did not work out as the mother wished. Both of them were seminarians, but their backgrounds were markedly different.

The first suitor came from a proper priest's family. The parents were pleased he was paying court to their daughter, and she herself had nothing against him. All that mattered was that she not appear too eager, in the eyes of the people, to latch on to a suitor. The whole affair was to be decided and settled in a few weeks, after the parish feast day.

But then, something happened to upset all their plans. On the day of the feast, the girl met the one who would later become her husband and, after that, she would not hear of anyone else. He was a good and polite young man. But in the eyes of Lady Shuminska, he had two major faults—he was the son of a peasant, and he would not complete his studies for another two years. Even though Lady Shuminska did not belong to those who considered people of inferior rank to be not quite human, the youth did lose some status in her eyes because of his origins.

This feeling would not have been as painful—indeed, she would not have experienced it at all—if it were as common among priests' families, as in lords' families, to have only a few witnesses present at the wedding ceremony. But a wedding is a proud occasion in a priest's family, and it was distressing to think that, instead of a priest and his wife, a father in a sheepskin coat and a mother in a peasant head-dress would be blessing their daughter, who would have to kiss their hands. Once the wedding was over, it did not really matter who her in-laws were. She would be living with her husband—not with them—and her husband would be a priest; therefore, she would not lose rank.

But this day—this one day! She discussed the matter with her daughter. When she attempted to present—in the greatest detail— her concerns about the young man's origins, her daughter first paled, then reddened, but resolutely refused to change her mind. She was not going to ruin her future and her entire life for the sake of one day.

If only they could marry now. But there would have to be a two-year waiting period, and Lady Shuminska was against such a delay. She had heard long ago that it was not a good idea to put off such matters; two years is a long time! God knows what could happen, how many rumours might be started. The wedding could be called off, and the young lady would be left cooling her heels. She was twenty years old, and it was no longer a joking matter— her situation was beginning to take on the distinctively dangerous odour of spinsterhood!

Lady Shuminska began to regret that she had not married off her daughter at sixteen, that she had departed from age-old traditions. The earlier a girl got married, the better. Oh, the older people knew best! They had the experience! If her daughter had two children by now—like her mother had at her age—her head would not be filled with romantic notions, and her parents would have some peace of mind, knowing they had managed to give at least one of their children a secure future.

All the same, Lady Shuminska was luckiest with this child. The two years flew by like a minute, and she saw her daughter joyful and happy at the side of the one she loved. Oh, how few mothers—how very, very few—experience such joy!

When one is spiritually content, there is a tendency to forget all that one has endured—until new disappointments inflame old wounds. That year, things went well for Lady Shuminska—her daughter married, her son graduated. Everything fell into place. The money spent on the daughter's wedding would be compensated for by the decrease in their son's expenses when he entered the seminary.

Then, suddenly, a new problem arose—the eldest son declared he had no intention of becoming a priest! The son who had given his nanny a piece of twine to tie the sacks of *kalachi*, the son on whose behalf she had donated priestly vestments, the son who was descended from a long line of priests—this son did not wish to become a priest! It was beyond all comprehension!

"What's wrong with you, my son?" the mother asked. "Why are you renouncing your station in life? Can there be a better position than that of a priest?"

"Well, my dearest mother, it may well be that there is no better position, but I don't feel drawn to it."

"What do you mean, you don't feel drawn? What does it mean—not to be drawn to it?"

"It simply means that I don't have a calling for it."

"But until quite recently you thought of nothing else! What's brought about this sudden change?"

"It's true that I thought of nothing else, but what am I to do if my ideas have changed? It's the Spirit of the Times. I greatly respect that station in life, but I can see that it would be too stifling for me. My ideas would be hemmed in by rigid boundaries, whereas I require wide open spaces and the freedom to acquire knowledge, learning."

"Wide open spaces, learning! It's the Spirit of the Times!" Lady Shuminska repeated, staring at her son in bewilderment. "It's the Spirit of the Times!"

What was this Spirit of the Times? Something indistinct, but huge and powerful, flashed before her eyes. It was taking away and shattering her peace of mind. It was causing the old order to fall, and this disintegration was estranging those who, until now, had been so closely and amiably conjoined.

Even in her dreams, she felt the force of an inexorable change. She saw an invisible hand move dishes from the pantry into the room and back again. She saw everything slide from the attic into the cellar. Beds and tables moved of their own accord; chairs stacked themselves into a single pyramid; pictures stepped out of their frames; and even the coiled springs in the old clock snapped and flew out, while the little wheels and the tiny links of the chain unwound in all directions.

"It's the Spirit of the Times! Huh!" As if she did not know enough about it. Was this not what had given her daughter the courage to admit she was in love and say she would marry only for love?

What a scandal it had created when she attended parties and balls with a daughter who always had her "dear one" in tow! How the people had whispered amongst themselves that the mother "permitted" such a romance! "A romance"—this was a terrible accusation for a girl with a good, moral upbringing. Even now, it overwhelmed Lady Shuminska with shame. A girl who was properly brought up did not fall in love before her wedding, and it was a mother's duty to see to it that a young lady did not "act rashly" in this respect. If someone had told her, as she sat over her little one's cradle, that this daughter would have a romance one day, she probably would not have tolerated such a remark, but the time came when she had no choice. She had to listen to the jibes and patiently endure the malicious comments.

"Let them!" she thought to herself. "How wise they all are. They whisper about others, but if it happened to them, they would have to be quiet and remain silent just like me."

But these thoughts did not bring her consolation. Helpless anger filled her heart. She was most hurt and offended that her husband, the natural ally of a wife, did not, in his male wisdom, advise her in her distressing situation. Instead, he acted as if he neither saw nor heard what was happening around him. When she told him what the people were saying because of the behaviour of their daughter, he became so distraught that she had to calm him down and, eventually, conceal everything from him.

The needles were moving faster and faster. The knitting was growing in her hands, and the yarn was continually looping itself into new stitches.

"This is how life flows onward," Lady Shuminska thought. "It rushes on to the end and, like these dropped stitches, it leaves behind dreams, hopes, and those dearest to your heart." How many sacrifices had she made? Oh, Lord, how bitter is the fate of a human being! The longer one lives, the more sorrows and losses are woven into one's life. But of all the losses in this world, none can wound you like the loss of a loved one.

On the forehead of the woman deeply engrossed in thought, a few wrinkles appeared and settled into deep folds. She sighed soulfully and attempted to chase away her gloomy thoughts, but it was all in vain. Feelings from long ago, which supposedly had abated and died in her heart, reverberated with lacerating overtones and pierced her soul profoundly. A heavy helplessness enveloped her body, and her withered hands fell weakly to her knees.

The poor mother could never think calmly about the cruel death that had taken away the most favoured of her daughters in the prime of her life. The death of her parents and of her little children, painful as they were, had seemed, nevertheless, natural. But the death that had mown down her eldest, married daughter in the prime of her life—in her thirtieth year—was so horrible, so devastating, that she could neither forget nor rationalise it. The heartrending images of her daughter's loving marriage, the despair of the husband, and the anguishing moment when they brought her the little orphan—her daughter's only child—for her to raise, came alive before her eyes as vividly as if it all had happened yesterday. For a long moment, only the sobbing of a disconsolate mother could be heard.

Eventually, she raised her head and picked up the knitting that had fallen from her hands. At first, the needles moved slowly and lethargically in her fingers, but the same tranquillity that had swept a wave of sad memories over her, now made it recede. The pain that had made the old woman's breast heave began to subside. Her agitated mind calmed down—like the muddied waters of a pool when the black sediment gradually settles in fine particles at the bottom, and the quivering, clear surface can once again reflect the nearest objects: a broken stump, clusters of reeds, a blue or yellow flower.

In Lady Shuminska's trembling soul, thousands of lines and convolutions began to trace themselves into the contours of the object that always occupied her mind—her home, her whole world. She saw nothing beyond it except for what she could see from her windows, and her thoughts did not extend beyond its walls. It fixed the limits of her entire life, and she desired only what fell within its confines.

This home, so outwardly calm, defined her happiness and satisfied her completely. If only it were not for the Spirit of the Times—that demon which corrupted and destroyed everything dear to her. It insinuated itself in varying shapes through the cracks in the walls, stared out at her from every corner, and disrupted the old order; it was the agent of the disintegration that had crept into her home, and it spun the magic circles of its boundless will, indifferent to a woman's bitter tears and lamentations.

Everything that this Spirit desired—regardless of how much it went against her will—came to pass. All of her children—her sons, her daughters, her grandchildren—had gone down paths different from those she had envisioned and desired. It had shattered the fondest and most treasured hopes of her heart.

The sons had risen up against the father, and the daughters against the mother. If the son who had first called the terrible demon by its name had chosen the path of his parents—would he not have been much happier than he was now? He would long ago have become a priest, been married, and had his own child. But what did he have now? He had become a "professor," as village teachers were called and, more than likely, would remain uncertified and an old bachelor the rest of his life. And, in the interim, the family had suffered so much trouble and unrest.

Even though she herself was crushed and broken in spirit, she had to ignore her own grief and attempt to reconcile the father and son who were so stubbornly antagonistic towards each other. The older man had fallen ill from all the dissension, and the son finally gave in and entered the seminary. He enrolled, however, in that ill-starred philosophy department and, after all that, he had still renounced the idea of becoming a priest.

This same invisible and powerful force took possession of Olya, their younger daughter. Like her brother, she had become disillusioned with the priestly station in life. A few seminarians had courted her, but not one of them had appealed to her. Her wish was to marry a layman, thereby securing a position that probably seemed preferable and more convenient to her, only because she had no experience of it. Lady Shuminska would have been satisfied if Olya had fallen in love like her sister, but even that did not seem likely.

Everyone thought she would change once she was married. But far from it! Even though she had a good husband, beautiful children, and a good parish, she was always out of sorts and discontented. She was under the sway of some wilful, wayward chimera that led her to defy quiet, dignified, and composed women. Her wild imagination poisoned her whole life, including what should have been the trouble-free and happy days of her girlhood in the home of her parents.

Slowly, imperceptibly, because of petty matters that seemed unimportant, but which had dire consequences, an implacable misunderstanding developed between the mother and daughter. Every "innovation" introduced by the daughter, every chair that was not positioned just so, every new rule of etiquette, and every new book irritated and angered the mother to the nth degree.

It was the books—the books that appeared heaven knows from where and were always in her daughter's hands—that infuriated her the most. Lady Shuminska could never forgive herself, or remember without a feeling of shame, the one time when, overcome with rage, she had torn a brand new book from her daughter's hand and ripped it into tiny pieces. At the time, she had been so wretched and so close to despair, that she had not known what she was doing. She sensed that something alien wafted from those books, that they were the emissaries and tools of the demon that was her enemy, and that from them flowed the current that was eroding the shore of her peaceful harbour.

Lady Shuminska's fingers moved swiftly. The shiny needles flashed in the tiny stitches, while her thoughts unravelled along with the yarn that was unwinding from its ball.

When their younger son graduated and told his parents he was going into law, they did not argue with him.

"Let him be what he wants to be," they said—as long as he did not complain about them later. There is nothing worse than when children complain that their parents have ruined their future.

It was with a heavy heart that the mother saw her son off to the university. Until then, he had been a child, and even though he had not lived at home, he had still been under the watchful eye of his parents. Now, all alone, without any protection, he would be thrown into the whirlpool of a large city, into that abyss of boundless immorality. Oh! How many good young men—the children of upright parents—had fallen prey to the big city! Once again, the life of one of their children was being engulfed by the fog of a vast void where all warnings—and even the voice—of a mother are lost.

It was with fear and trepidation that the mother followed every word and movement of her son when he brought his friends home for the holidays. Not a single word of their uninhibited conversations slipped by unnoticed, and the more she heard, the more her heart bled. She caught unfinished words and phrases which spoke only too clearly about the life of the young people, the life she feared so greatly. In addition, her ears resounded with sentences and slogans that issued from their lips, but which were completely incomprehensible to her: "The people, equality, freedom, the French Revolution, the exploitation of the peasants, the year of 1848!"

The less she understood of what they were saying, the more frightened she became. But she was most alarmed by what they had to say about God, their questioning of the truth of His existence and protection. She also noticed that her son no longer prayed, and that he behaved like a pagan in church, without piety and Christian humility.

"Oh, God," she often said to herself. "From whence is Your grace to flow if people no longer believe in You? Oh, you young ones think you're so wise, so very wise! But you're only incurring

God's wrath and calling down punishment onto others! You say there is no God! Then from where did everything appear in this world—the trees, the birds, the animals? Who created all of this, if not God?"

Whenever a storm erupted in her soul, and her heart, touched by pain, shuddered, she sent invisible messengers—her prayers—to God. And she could sense God's angel, that she had called forth, draw near and bring her peace. The power of her prayer had never been needed more.

To turn aside the just wrath of God from her son, she picked up her prayer book and recited a prayer prescribed for sadness and suffering. However, instead of laying her sorrow to rest, the words exacerbated it. It was a hymn to God, one that praised His mightiness, His power, and His boundless kindness beyond all understanding, and it ended with the pleas of the lowliest servant:

"May Your thunder strike only those
To whom You have given life,
But who do not know You.
This is my humble, daily prayer
With which I, Your faithful servant, praise You."

The words of the hymn were transformed into flaming arrows before her eyes, and cold sweat broke out on her forehead. For ever so many years, she had prayed for vengeance against those who did not believe, and now this vengeance was slowly drawing nearer to her. It was hanging like a black cloud over her own nest, threatening it with its thunder . . . It seemed to her that the storm was already close by, that she could hear its dull clatter in the air, that the first lightning bolts were already splitting the horizon.

One day, her husband happened to read in the newspapers: "Today's young people are given to fanciful dreams, and they strive to effect changes in society, but all of this is really just a fantasy and a poisoning of their young minds. No one can change the age-old order of things; it changes by itself, through industry and invention. Those who think that societal relationships can be changed like one's clothing—like making an outfit for a ball out of a soldier's uniform, or a long peasant coat out of a short jacket—do not know that they will only succeed in calling down a bloody catastrophe on themselves. They will not attain anything, either for themselves or for society as a whole, and they will become the victims of their fleeting error, tools in the hands of people who are rushing after honours for themselves."

She did not understand very much of what her husband had read, but she felt in her heart that it must be tied in some way to what she heard coming from the lips of her son and his friends. Something very, very evil could come of this. Obviously, God had forsaken those who did not respect Him and were going astray without the illumination of His wisdom and mercy. The earth would shake with the noise of battle, with the din of heavy blows. Some would be killed on the spot, while others would hang in the air, and only ravens would caw hoarsely over their corpses. Still others would rot in the bottomless pits of dungeons hermetically sealed by iron gates.

Why should we not sit quietly and praise God, the Ruler over all of us? Who was it that was calling down the wrath of the All Highest, if not "that one," the Spirit of the Times, the one that nothing could appease or lay to rest? Oh, God! Why have You permitted the Devil to acquire the power to spread the disease of evil everywhere?

The knitting was almost finished, but the fingers and the thoughts of the old woman did not stop working. The Spirit of the Times, in its most threatening pose, was standing before her on the charred ruins of all her plans and hopes. It had not left her the slightest comfort or spared a single child. It had even cast its eye upon her young granddaughter—her dead daughter's only child—who was still so young, so naive with respect to the world.

Alas, how bitter it was, how difficult to lose one's last hope! She had clung to the belief that she might be able to protect at least this one tender shoot. But then, just a few months ago, she had discovered that the cursed Spirit of the Times had already infected her granddaughter with its contagious touch.

She had been sitting, just as she was sitting now, picking over seeds for her vegetable garden, when her granddaughter approached her.

"It's a good thing you've come," she said to the girl. "You can help me pick over the seeds."

The young girl began to help her grandmother, but her fingers were trembling, and her face was paler that usual.

"What's wrong, my child?" her grandmother asked worriedly. "Are you ill, perhaps?"

The young girl shook her head, but two tears fell on a packet of seeds. Upset, her grandmother peppered her with questions, which only made the girl cry even harder. Finally, she replied, with great difficulty, that she wanted to continue studying.

"Why, don't you think you've learned enough?" her grandmother asked in astonishment. "Didn't you have a governess?"

"It's true," the young girl whispered, "but I . . . I . . . want to earn my own livelihood—I want to be a teacher!"

The old woman felt as if someone had plunged a knife into her heart. The basket tipped, seeds of all sizes rolled over the ground, and a stream of bitter words tore from her lips. "The daughter of my daughter—a teacher! Oh, you ungrateful child! Are you so poor that you have to work to support yourself? Are we not capable of providing you with a dowry? After all, you also have a father. Doesn't he care about you?"

The young girl, pressing her hands to her lips to stifle her bitter sobs, walked quietly out the door. And, curling up in the darkest corner of the adjoining room, she wept for a long, long time . . .

It would be difficult to describe how painful those tears were to Lady Shuminska. She saw that the discord between herself and those to whom she had given life was growing ever greater and encompassing ever wider circles. They were all breaking away from her and forming other, separate groupings.

Oh! How different this scene was from the one she had planned for herself when they were still little ones at her feet. What a contrast there was between reality and what she had envisioned—how she, encircled by her children, would be the highest authority for them, and how this new generation, obedient and respectful of her experience, would carry out her every word. She knew that they did love and respect her even now, but this love was not the kind she had dreamt about. This respect was more *pro forma* than the outcome of real relationships.

Was she not similar to the brooding hen that unwittingly hatched little ducklings? The poor little hen denied herself so many pleasures for so long. She sat as if chained to one spot, rising from the nest only to appease her hunger. She hoped that later, surrounded by her brood, she could lead them out into the wide world, teach them to peck with their little beaks, call them to the bounty she had found, and gather them together under her protective wings.

The moment finally arrived when her young ones broke out of their confining shells and began moving about freely. Contented and happy, she led them to the edge of the stream. At first, the young creatures approached the unknown element hesitantly and fearfully; however, as soon as they dipped their beaks into it, they grew bolder. Instead of stretching their necks out to it from the bank, they plunged right into the water.

In vain did the hen run along the bank and call out to them in a heartrending voice. Her young ones did not look back at her, nor did they heed her call. They were being carried off by a restless wave that dipped, crested, and vanished. In some spots, the wave sparkled with a luminous light, while in others, it appeared like a mysterious shadow; and it carried them ever farther and farther away, rocking them, caressing them, winking at them, luring them, and gently whispering:

"Du liebes Kind, komm, geh' mit mir,
Gar schöne Spiele spiel' ich mit dir!
Manch' bunte Blume wächst an dem Strand,
Meine Mutter hat manch gülden Gewand!"

["Come, dearest child, come away with me,
The most wonderful games I'll play with thee!
On the shore—rainbows of flowers for thee unfold,
My mother will clothe thee in garments of gold!"]

Only a few stitches were left on the knitting needles. The yarn became taut. Lady Shuminska tied the last stitch, and the yarn was broken.

Everything in this world comes to an end.

The Judge

(1884)

The judge was feeling irritated as he made his way home from the office—an unpleasant court case had set his nerves on edge.

"Is the mistress in?" he asked the maid when he arrived.

"There's no one at home, if you please, sir. The mistress and the young lady went to visit the counsellor's wife, the young gentleman is off somewhere, and the mistress told me that I could go to my sister's, because she thought the master would go directly to the clubhouse."

"Run along, then, if you've been given permission. But light a fire in the fireplace before you leave; it's a bit chilly in here."

The maid lit the fire, threw on some firewood, took another look around the room, and put on her kerchief. A moment later, the judge was left all alone in the house.

The fire quickly engulfed the small logs; it crackled and scattered showers of embers.

The judge packed his pipe, opened the fireguard, and became mesmerized by the blazing flames. It was gradually becoming warmer in the house; the heat from the fire spread through the room, enveloped his shoulders, suffused his cheeks, and permeated his entire body. He forgot his advanced years and grey hair; more recent impressions gradually faded, obscured by memories that lay hidden in the depths of his soul.

It seemed to him that he was still a child, running after his mother and clinging to her clothing. His father, who had travelled to town, had not yet come home; the child knew his father would bring him a treat, and so he was impatiently awaiting his arrival and imagining with great delight the wooden horse or the sugar candy flute that would be his.

The bluish flames dissolved into green fields and meadows. Field insects were buzzing in the tall grass, and mowers' scythes flashed in the distance. Flushed with fatigue and contentment, he chased after butterflies, picked brightly coloured flowers, and bounded after leaping grasshoppers.

The only sorrow in his young life came when summer passed, and old Granny Winter seized everything in her grasp, blowing cold air everywhere. Even then, however, things were not all that bad. Winter was when St. Nicholas came; he could go sledding; and he loved to go on sleigh rides—to listen to the crunching of the snow under the horses' hooves and the tinkling of the bells, a sound that carried far and wide over the white fields.

He had a good life under the loving care of his parents. Winters and summers came and went, bringing with them joys that were ever fresh; and even though there were times when tears rolled down his face, they dried quickly, vanished without a trace, and left no lingering grief in his little heart.

At the end of one such frolicsome summer, he was driven to town and enrolled in school. It was very sad to be left alone among strangers in someone else's house. At first, the schoolwork caught his interest, but later, it became increasingly difficult. The lessons were long, very long; at times, as he sat and studied, he had to force his eyes to stay open in an effort not to fall asleep.

"Dear Lord!" he thought. Why had he been brought here? Why was he being told to study? He would be so happy to go home, to return to his father and mother, to leave the cursed school and never lay eyes on it again. If only he could have been sure that no one would be angry with him if he did, because he became very frightened whenever anyone became angry with him.

"Will the holidays ever come?" he agonised. "For when they do come, there will once again be green meadows, happy times, and freedom."

The poor little child counted the days and the hours; he counted them even though summer was still a long way off. It seemed to him that he was no longer a single being; it was as if there were two of him—one who skipped and raced through the village, and another who, with books under his arm, trudged past stone walls as he wound his way through the streets of the town.

Over time, however, a person becomes accustomed to everything. Emulation replaced compulsion, and school was transformed into an arena of progress and achievements. His efforts were rewarded. No one ever had better report cards than he did, and no one could look forward to a more brilliant future. As he grew out of childhood and became a youth, his spirit unfolded its white wings ever more widely.

Life at university freed him from the confining shell of a high school existence. The winds of change swept him away. He was driven by new feelings and needs; his ideas clarified, strengthened, and took on new directions. His associations with others were no longer determined solely by personal feelings and the need for friendly support; now they grew out of broader spheres of interest that encompassed shared views and striving towards a common goal.

He sighed, as only those who are old sigh when they recall bygone days. He tamped the tobacco in his pipe and added a few fresh logs to the fire.

Thousands of red-hot sparks flashed and scattered upwards. A long, spacious hall, illuminated with bright gaslight, gradually came into view. Centred amidst all the gold frames and large mirrors, and overshadowing all of them, stood a serious portrait—without any dazzling adornments—of a famous national genius. The room resounded with the loud hum of voices raised in conversation, the tinkle of glasses, and the scurrying of servants. At one table, a young man with a swarthy but pale face rose to his feet. Casting a fervid eye over those who were present, he indicated to them that he wished to speak.

The old judge rubbed his forehead with his hand. Much water had flowed under the bridge since that moment, but the scene remained so vivid in his memory that he could still recall fragmented phrases from the speaker's address.

"Gentlemen and friends," the speaker had said, pointing at the portrait. "There are many of us here, and we have all assembled because of one man—the man, now dead, whose penetrating eyes are looking out at us from that painting—and because of our desire to commemorate his service to our native land. We all share the same idea, we all desire exactly the same thing, for we are the sons of one land, the branches of a single tree; we are the architects of the future, committed to the common good. How unwise, how narrow-minded is the man who does not know that only the good of all can bring happiness to an individual! How evil is he who wants to lead a carefree existence at the expense of others! 'To live and to make it possible for others to live'—this is what our motto should be!

"But all work, like all structures, will be lasting only if it is established on solid ground and a strong foundation; and the foundation, the basis of the common good, of the common interests of the people, is national pride! It is only on this foundation that the culture and civilisation of all mankind can unfold in a healthy and beneficial manner! Every nation should fight for its independence! Therefore, so long as ignorance and darkness stand in our way, let us fight, my brothers, to the very last drop of our blood, for our hapless native land!"

The speaker finished his address. Everyone was deeply moved; many shook his hand; some exchanged kisses with him. Only his closest friend did not draw near him or speak to him; he was afraid to move from his place, to look at him, to utter a word; tears were welling up in his eyes, and he felt his words would stick in his throat.

Everything the speaker had expressed so ably in his address was now seething in his young friend's soul and embedding itself in his heart. Everything that he was unable to put into words— everything that pained him, that made his chest ache with mute grief—his friend had expressed emphatically and passionately, clearly and confidently.

Both of them were students in the faculty of law, and there was only a small difference in their ages and in the level of the courses they were taking. But this difference was reason enough to make the older student like a mentor to the younger one. He drew his younger colleague into a group of young people in which he occupied a position of respect because of his views and oratorical skills—the same views and skills that had immediately won him the affection and the respect of his new friend.

Young, fiery, and talented, they became almost inseparable. They read widely, engaged in heated discussions, and created the most elegant models of civic equality, order, and responsibility—the responsibility for which life was preparing them, and which they were to assume in the future.

In their studies, they saw more than a means of earning a living. They believed that if the good intentions of sincere people are to exert a rejuvenating and benevolent influence on the masses, then such intentions must be equally noble in their idealistic conceptions, their underlying principles, and their execution. That which is good must be just as absolute in practice as it is in theory. Where there was no balance between theory and practice, they saw no moral justice, no strong conviction about what was right and what was wrong. Does not a deed, most righteous in itself, but not bound tightly with strong threads to the soul and the entire life of a person—except for the degree to which it is occasioned by external circumstances, as in the times of serfdom—become a mockery? This lack of harmony between thoughts and deeds leads to the lies and bad faith that charaterise both public and private relations, and it deeply incensed the enthusiastic young students.

The judge gazed fixedly at the flaring bluish flames, lowered his head to his chest and, with trembling lips, whispered:

"Oh, all mankind is perishing
For lack of passion and spirit . . .
Give me broad wings,
O time of youthfulness!
I will soar above the torpid masses
To holy paradise
Where a sacred fire
Blazes wondrously in souls . . ."

Oh! Where had it all disappeared—the courage and daring, the originality and capacity for sacrifice, and even—yes—even integrity?

It is a terrible moment when one's soul unwinds the entire roll of one's memory in an instant and pours the bitter deeds of a lifetime into a single drop of time . . .

From days long gone, the supple figure of a young woman with golden hair and clear blue eyes emerged. He had been still young then, at the very height of his powers. The comely girl ruled his feelings, became his happiness, his delight, everything that he found most dear in life—in a word, his love. His heart, brimming with feeling, sought relief; flooded with new impressions and trembling with joy and longing, it could not contain itself and poured out its secret to the friend.

"I love her madly, passionately, with all my soul! There is no world, no life without her! Believe me, my friend, it is not worth living without love!" he once said in an agitated voice.

His friend did not reply; he simply stood before him, placed his hand on his shoulders, and looked him square in the face. His lips trembled slightly, changed their shape, and turned up in the corners. He burst out laughing.

"Why are you laughing?" our young hero almost hissed through clenched teeth.

"My friend," his comrade replied. "Don't be angry, but you're telling me something that I've known for some time, perhaps sooner than you yourself became aware of it. This does not point to a great perceptivity on my part, because it always seems to those who are in love that no one knows their secret, while, in truth, the whole world is already talking about it. But I'm happy that you have started this conversation, because I was waiting for this moment."

"Why is that, if I may ask?" he queried as before, but without anger this time.

"One can say much about this. There is no doubt that your ideal—your young woman—can capture the heart of a young man, but have you stopped to think what you are doing? Have you considered all the consequences? Imagine the life that either one of us would lead if his wife did not bring any money at all with her into his home. Imagine a miserable life where every crumb of bread is eaten, where only the most careful budgeting makes it possible to eke out a bare existence. Why did one study? Why did one nurture dreams and ideas in one's breast? Was it just to bury oneself within four walls? Which one of us would now be able to live if he had to depend on a few hundred guldens? Our origins may be humble, but we have acquired higher cultural needs. There can be no question that a great patriotic duty lies ahead of us; we have a fatherland that requires money—and where are we to get it?"

"But I love her!"

"There is love, but there is also the strength of one's will. The roots of an inappropriate love should be severed immediately; that kind of love should be choked as soon as it appears, because, with time, it becomes more difficult to do so, and the struggle becomes harder," the friend added seriously.

Not even a despairing look into a dark, bottomless abyss, nor a snake crawling out from under a bush, nor a slimy worm crawling over his body could have evoked more revulsion and fear than the words that were apparently spoken out of concern for his welfare: "The strength of one's will, patriotism, cultural needs" resounded in his head as in a hollow dome. Such beautiful, brilliant words—but they were rotten to the core! What kind of culture is it if it lowers the dignity of a man? Surely the strength of one's will—a characteristic of the soul developed with such great effort by mankind—and patriotism—the highest understanding of the common good—are not meant to contribute to the demoralisation of a person! Is one to renounce, under the banner of culture, the most noble impulses of one's nature?

Not to be dependent on a few guldens meant not to be a slave to money. Yet who is more of a slave than the one who, for the sake of paltry monetary gain, renounces those things that no money can ever buy?

What a contradiction! Was it actually possible that something so despicable, so unhealthy, could develop in a decent social system?

And this abomination was being touted by his friend—the ideal man whom he revered so greatly!

Life continued flowing along its course and brought with it a rupture—one taut string at a time—in their friendship. Everything changed and was transformed. Their souls grew apart, their hearts cooled; committed to the same cause, they differed in their specific approaches.

The sincere young man could not understand how his friend could devote himself to a political government that constrained the freedom of his convictions and, what was even more puzzling, how he could choose for his life's companion a foreign woman, one from the opposing camp. How could he have married a Polish woman? How could that man, that preacher of equality and freedom who had encompassed all of life with his far-ranging thoughts, change his way of thinking so radically? How could he be satisfied with such a lowly government career, and how could he marry a Polish woman? There were two possible answers: either this man had become disillusioned, or he did not consider a woman to be capable of feelings that a man takes such great pride in; he did not acknowledge that she, too, should be conscious of, and concerned for, the aspirations of her native land.

No matter how hard the young man tried to excuse these things, no matter how he tried to colour them to make it seem that his friend wanted to demonstrate how a *Rusyn [Ukrainian]* should comport himself in a position like his—this friend stopped being an ideal man in his eyes.

No matter how convincing his friend's words—that his marriage to a Polish woman was proof that in such a situation a *Rusyn* did not have to cease being a *Rusyn*—for him, this friend no longer was an honest man.

No matter that, with each passing day the authority and stature of his friend grew in the eyes of the people—for him, this friend no longer was a man of integrity.

Night was descending swiftly upon the earth, and stillness, its faithful companion, accompanied it, smoothly and imperceptibly. The rumbling of carriages and peoples' voices were heard less frequently on the street. His wife and children—who must have been enjoying themselves very nicely—had not yet returned home. There was nothing to prevent him from continuing to think about days long gone by. The flames from the fireplace flickered on his slumped, reclining figure and diffused themselves dimly in the corners.

He glanced around. A struggle was being waged in his soul; a wave of turbulent feelings rose and ebbed, while dreams of youth and hope flitted before his soul, like shadows. Oh, why had they gone by so swiftly, changed, and been frustrated? Why had they not erased their traces from his memory as they flew by, instead of remaining there, as painful, badly healed wounds, heartbreaking recollections?

Accustomed to reckoning time on a daily basis, he could not recall how many years had gone by—yes indeed, how many years ago was it?—since he joined the court. But it did not make any difference. He had been young, very young, and he had extended his hand to his beloved who, blinded by her love, looked forward with a trusting heart to a comfortable future, unaware of the cloudy days and misfortunes that lay ahead, lurking silently on the road of life.

The first tiny clouds passed by unnoticed on the horizon of their conjugal journey. However, even though they were tiny, light, and transparent, they did not disappear; instead, chancing upon others, they turned darker, spread out, and gazed downwards with an ever more gloomy eye.

It was the debts he had incurred—both as a student, and during the first years of his court internship when he did not bring in any money—that hung over them like dark clouds, dampening their joy and eroding their contentment. If he had had a certain sum of money at his disposal then, and if he had been able to settle the debts in time, his happiness would not now have been clouded over. As it was, however, his debts continued to grow, and the longer they lasted, the more difficult it was to consider repaying them.

Time went by. His family grew, and the most pressing expenses competed for his attention. At one time he had been repulsed by miserliness, but now, more than one coin, flung out for a trifling pleasure, or lent to a friend without any hope of ever being repaid, multiplied tenfold, found itself in the company of new debts, and weighed heavily upon him.

A few more logs crackled cheerfully in the fireplace and roared up the wide chimney, but the deep furrow on the judge's forehead did not vanish; instead, it grew deeper and descended over his sorrowful, extinguished eyes. He saw how people in similar straits managed; he saw what methods they chose, while remaining resolute in their convictions and the fulfilment of their duties. Why could he not do likewise? Quite often, there were matters before the court from which, with only a slight bit of dexterity, more than one gold thread could be unravelled to stand him in good stead and free him from his very difficult situation.

Once, it was simply a matter of placing a sheet of paper among some documents and letting it lie there unobtrusively; in exchange, he would have received a banknote of a high denomination. All that he needed, as the judge in the case, was a kinder heart; but he rejected the proposition indignantly, for he found bribery abhorrent. He could not divest himself of his youthful dreams; he could not tolerate the idea of taking advantage of someone who was poorer and weaker; on the contrary, he used all the pertinent statutes, the full power of the law, to defend them. He explained, instructed, and assisted the illiterate and the ignorant to the best of his ability.

His own problems, however, were not solved by his noble stance; on the contrary, they became even more entangled, and he could not come up with a solution. He wracked his brain, thrashed about helplessly, and agonised in vain. Even though the methods suggested to him were opportune and convenient, he could not reconcile them with his conscience. Some very critical moments arose. The borrowed money made its claims on more money, the interest on it was growing, and all the while, life was making its own demands for an appropriate level of existence . . .

During one such depressing moment, a few rolls of bills left by a rich gentleman on the desk in his office could have rid him of his worries to a large extent. This money had the power to untangle a complicated court case in which it was impossible to get at the truth, but the judge, realising why the gentleman had left the bills in his office, did not hesitate. He hurried after him and returned them.

Who, in defending the poor and the weak, has not ended up in a confrontation with the powerful and the mighty?

Rumours began to circulate that the judge was an evil, mean, and unscrupulous man . . . A few individuals spoke highly of him, but the majority spoke against him. An inescapable evil hovered over his head. His life began to pale, to lose its brilliance. It was mutilated, torn, and trampled by melancholy deliberations in which disillusionment, with broad strokes, was delineating a solution in dark and muted colours.

The children were growing up and, with every passing day, they demanded more care and incurred more expenses which, given their domestic situation, it was almost impossible to satisfy. His wife wept and worried, and her health began to fail. She was a mother, and this was what dictated her responsibilities and shaped her ideas. The noble righteousness of her husband did not guarantee her children's future.

At home, his indifference to money strained family relationships; at work, his patriotic dreams caused him problems and posed impediments to his promotion; among the people, his high moral principles earned him their anger and ill-will.

His wife was a mother, and she strove to earn her children's love and gratitude. Children are grateful to their parents when the latter are able to secure them the proper conditions in life. The purity of their father's character would not provide them with a livelihood, and what were they worth without that? What was a person worth if he was badly clothed, poorly fed, and inadequately housed?

And poverty inevitably elicited the contempt of others. What must children think about parents who are the cause of their suffering, who place their own virtue above the well-being of their offspring, who cast them into a situation which sooner or later will dig an abyss of moral collapse beneath them.

The boys had to be sent away to receive a higher education. The judge tried to negotiate a transfer to a larger city, but he was told not to meddle in politics. The daughters were growing into young ladies without dowries, and the poor mother's heart ached at the thought that they would never experience a fate better than hers, that they would agonise and tremble over every *kreytsar [penny]*. What good did it do that she never stopped to rest, that she worked and pushed herself mercilessly? She could do nothing more than decrease the amount that she spent on the needs of daily living.

It was painful to look at her. Formerly an attractive young woman, she was all shrivelled now, like a dry reed, with a sunken face and eyes that were worn out from crying. She was withered and faded before her time. The state of her health alarmed her husband, and he called in a doctor. His diagnosis was a terrible blow to the family. The sick woman was forbidden to do any housework, and she was prescribed a treatment that involved huge expenditures.

What must have been happening in her husband's heart as he heard this? Had she not entrusted her fate and happiness to him? How had he fulfilled her trust? Had she found happiness with him? Who had given life to those small, weak little beings, and why? To have them thrown, helpless, into the dirty waves of the world's sorrow?

Is not a woman told: "Follow your master in good faith, love him, and obey him!" And how is her master to repay her? If no one has the right to ask, then let one's conscience reply. "I do not tolerate superiority over others, I do not tolerate taking advantage of people and doing them harm—this is my guiding thought, this is what inspires me, for it has arisen out of my spiritual needs. But what about her? Does she have to follow me, even though what I believe in goes far beyond her range of thoughts, concepts, and activities?"

Self-sacrifice is not inherent in human nature. A man does not sacrifice himself willingly—it happens only when he can no longer accept the circumstances in which he is forced to live; in short, he sacrifices himself because the situation in which he is living becomes intolerable. The desire for a change is, at times, so strong, that other considerations become insignificant in comparison to it; he gives up everything else to attain what seems most desirable. He lets it go, for what he is leaving behind is no longer of any value to him—it is old clothing that he has to doff.

But did he have the right, because of his convictions—because of the bright star that shone in his breast and illuminated the dark recesses of his soul—to deprive his life's companion of peace and comfort, and to deny his children the light of education and security in life? Oh! Why do the duties of a citizen stand to injure one's own family, an institution that is the very basis of civic order? Oh, no! It could no longer be like this!

Do not the duties of a husband and father lie in a man's heart where they have been placed by nature's law? Could he watch his wife wither and waste away? Could he stand by and let the mother of his children perish?

His pipe went out for the third time; he reached for the tobacco, refilled it, and struck a match on the red-hot doors of the fireguard. The match burst into flames and peered into his face.

He half-closed his eyes, flung the burning sliver to the floor, and brought his foot down on it forcefully, as if he wanted to forget everything, to choke everything within himself. But the turbulent wave of his thoughts did not ebb.

This was a time of a more animated national awakening; a time when the dejected and oppressed were momentarily allowed to participate actively in civic affairs—to stir and to observe—so that, for another few years, they would once again be content to fold their arms and patiently await their salvation. All who were alive, whose hearts still beat warmly in their breasts, hastened to find at least one more fighter for their country, and encouraged the most capable among them to assume leadership positions.

In the ranks of the leaders, he had always stood among those who were in the fore, but now he felt himself to be powerless. He saw the surprised and oblique glances all around him, but could he pay any attention to all that? He had no time. There was an important matter before the court. Oh, yes! A very important matter!

The issue at hand was about some land that belonged to four orphaned children. A shrewd Jew had made a convenient agreement with their guardian about purchasing this land. All that remained was to have the court agree to the terms. The court agreed. The land went up for public sale. The matter was concluded, and the land was purchased by the one who found it most convenient to buy it. The children received a quarter of what the land was worth, but the judge was able to send his wife to a health spa, and his older son to school.

Cold sweat covered his forehead. His thoughts—which chased and persecuted him like black clouds—had exhausted him. His days were filled with sorrow and worry, but they were better than his nights—these were merciless. Everything that was pushed out of his mind during the day rose up before him at night, tormented him, gnawed at him, and devoured his soul.

His long-forgotten friend suddenly appeared before him; he sauntered about and flitted in and out of sight. "You see," he said, standing in a triumphant pose before him. "You held me in contempt! Oh, you impractical idealist! You should have looked more closely at life and got to know it in its ordinary, everyday forms. You should have understood that theories, be they the very best, ought not to take complete control of a man's soul."

The old judge raised his head and leaned back against the wall, but the apparition did not disappear. The formerly handsome young man with the fiery eyes now walked around with a well-rounded paunch, looked cunningly at him, and smiled.

"Look at me," his former friend said. "I, too, once soared to the clouds in my thoughts, but my practical mind won out. Respect the authorities, regardless of what they are like. Respect money, and good fortune will be yours. To foresee the chance happenings in life, to maintain control over oneself, to overcome impulses—this is what marks the mind of a man. I threw myself with enthusiasm into the task of serving my country, but everyone knows what they can expect from me, and what they can't—so at least they are not misled. I stifled only ideas that were too chimerical for everyday life, for what good would have come from them? Tell me, are you a better man now than I am? Was it worth suffering so much when, in the end, you were not able to avoid that which had to happen? Your suffering is punishment for your intransigence."

Long, sleepless nights were taking their toll on his body; a fever raged within him, drying his lips. There were times when he uttered fragmented words and waved his arms about.

"Vanish, damned apparition! What is it that you want from me? I don't know you, and I don't want to know you. You're not a man—you're an animal, a lowly animal. You never had anything genuine, higher, or worthy of respect within you!"

But the apparition did not disappear; it grew and expanded until it split into two huge arches; then it unfolded and stretched out in two wide roads positioned in opposing directions. He was standing hand in hand with the person dearest to him but, from the very first steps of their joint life and responsibilities, unforeseen obstacles emerged, worked their evil, threatened his most precious dreams, and undermined his understanding and fulfilment of his self-imposed rights and duties.

And, with every step, the roads grew farther apart. He was pulling his companion in the direction where the achievements of mankind for the common good proudly displayed themselves, where one man helps another, where great temples of harmony and goodness flourished.

Why did the hand which he was holding slowly slip out of his and pull away from him? As he walked along in one direction, she remained on the other road and, surrounded by her children, reached out her hand to him and begged him not to abandon her. He had come back to her, but the other road became littered with debris and overgrown with weeds.

Everything changed. Some dark, revolting outlines—misshapen figures and faces—were being transformed into terrible monsters that flew in a maddened circle and appeared to be overcome with lacerating laughter. The obligations of a husband, a father, threateningly armed, stood opposed to the duties of a citizen, a member of the general public. The clattering of arms, the wheezing of gasping chests, the noise and the crashing, the roaring of water, and the rumbling of thunder fused into a clamour that ruptured and killed all thoughts.

In one corner, a black, tightly packed mass of people whirled in a fiendish dance. From out of the crowd, more distinct figures emerged. Lords and ladies were walking over the heads of peasants; his friend, in a uniform with a gold collar, extended his hand to the guardian of the orphans' land and, behind them, like a bloodsucker, wound a long, satin coat.

They all tried to appropriate the most room for themselves in the crowd, without caring that others were choking, as they shoved one another with curses on their lips. They rose ever higher and higher; the crowd parted and then came together again, until, finally, those who were on top fell under the feet of the very ones they had just trampled. They were crushed mercilessly; blood flowed copiously and poured into gory swamps.

Four young orphans grabbed him and, screaming piteously, dragged him into the bloody mire: "You wronged us for the sake of your children! You wronged another family for the sake of your own!"

It grew darker by the moment, and a cold desert wind began to blow. Clouds of fog rose from the earth, and a single question flooded the air: "Must it be blood—only blood that will wash away the sins of one generation and baptise the next one?"

The shadows drifted away. There remained only reality, life. And what had life made of him? The years of his youth, the paradisiacal visions adorned with flowers and replete with live-giving dew, had come to rest in an obscure, deserted cemetery—a nebulous mist on the grave of a beguiling delusion. In the middle of the cold light stood pale grief. Once a righteous opponent of all injustice, he now bowed his head low before it. Having once stood boldly under the banner of his ideas, he had renounced them because they brought him into conflict with the circumstances of his era; the protector of the poor now lived by the injustice done to them.

Grief squeezed his heart, for he realised that, even if his youthful years were returned to him—with his noble aspirations and his love for everything great and beautiful—if he had to traverse the same pathways in life, he would have lived as he had lived, and become what he was now . . .

He laughed so hard that the pipe fell from his lips. From the fire that had long since gone out in the fireplace there remained only a small pile of grey ashes.

Yanova
(1885)

I

In our renowned Pokuttya, there is a small town called Pistyn. It is situated on a mountainous plain, and if you leap across a few streams, you can reach the forest without clambering up the mountainside. A cobblestone road edged with trees runs through the middle of the town and, on either side of it, there is a mixture of peasant cottages and wooden houses with flower beds. The business section—a tightly knit conglomeration of Jewish houses and stores—is off to one side of this road, and you can pass right through the town without ever seeing it.

In Pistyn, an old church that stands on the steep bank of a mountain stream is worthy of attention. Local folklore has it that the church was built in another location, and that it moved to this spot of its own accord.

Another interesting building is the hydropathic spa, which has almost crumbled to pieces now—so much so, that it is scary to go there, for fear that some part of it will tumble down on your head or collapse under your feet. When this establishment was flourishing, some people were in the habit of spending their summers in Pistyn. This is why a couple of families from Lviv, a few single men, and several people from the surrounding area still go there.

More than one of these Pistyn guests would probably recall a tall, pale old woman, stooped with age, dressed in a patched but cleanly laundered shirt, a skirt of the same vintage, and a faded, sky-blue kerchief knotted at the back of her neck. She hailed from a family of townsfolk in Kosiv. At one time, her parents had been not too badly off. They owned both a house and some land, but her father had squandered everything, her mother had died from the worry of it all, and the children had been forced to scatter and lead vagrants' lives; so, as a small child, she made her way to

Kolomiya, where she worked as a servant in a lord's home until she married.

Her name was Yustyna, but she was called Yanova after her husband. Actually, he was just a common Ivan, but because he wore a top coat and was a cobbler by trade, he changed his Ukrainian name to the Polish "Yan"; he also wanted to switch to the Latin rite and nursed this idea to the end of his days—a common ailment of our working classes. In the lower levels of society, the esoteric conceptions of the intelligentsia are transformed into concrete national-religious practices.

Ivan was born in Pistyn, where his father and, later, he himself, stitched ordinary boots. On one of his frequent trips to Kolomiya, he met Yustyna, and when he married her, he brought her back to his patrimony. They did not have any land, just an old cottage and a garden plot.

As long as Ivan worked at his job, things were so-so, but when he fell ill with a prolonged, serious illness that eventually laid him in his grave, poor Yustyna lived through very difficult times. She had several children, but they died, and she was left with only one son. He did not want to carry on his father's trade, so he drifted from one place to another, served his term in the army, got married, and ended up as a railroad worker in Burshtyn.

Yustyna did not go to live with her son; she stayed in Pistyn because she did not want to sell her cottage. She feared her daughter-in-law. Moreover, thinking that only God knew how things would go for her son, she decided that having a corner of his own in the world might stand him in good stead one day.

This is how the old woman lived, and perhaps she's still living there now, happy that she at least has a place to call her own. But walls do not feed you and, with every passing day, it became more difficult for her to earn a living. As the saying goes—old age does not make for happiness.

She began to go from house to house among the Pistyn intelligentsia, looking for work. In one house she would sweep the floor; in another she would wash the dishes; and in a third she would tend some baking in the oven. In the winter she plucked and tore feathers, and so the days and the years passed by.

She was induced to go to the homes of the intelligentsia by a small failing of hers, a carry-over from her serving days—she had an unusual fondness for coffee. As she could not afford to buy coffee, she was prepared to work a whole day just for the chance of having some. Coffee put Yanova in a very good mood and made her very talkative. She liked to narrate events from her life—a life that was prosaic and devoid of extraordinary happenings, but which, because of that, was actually typical of the lives of countless similarly humble and ordinary people.

I wrote down one of her narrations, which I am bringing to the kind attention of the reader. It seems to me that, beyond the readily obvious comic elements of this sketch, there is a deeper significance in it that merits consideration by individuals of a reflective bent, namely this—how poor, simple people can be grievously affected by the progress and inventions of our civilisation, and how they console themselves at such difficult times.

II

I hadn't visited my son since he got married. And I was so anxious to lay my eyes on him again and to see how he got along with his wife that he was all I could think about.

"I could die," I thought, "and never see how my son and his wife are getting along in the world."

But, as the saying goes: the soul would gladly soar to heaven, but its sins weigh it down. And even though I'd have been happy to go and see them, the distance was so great, that when I thought about it, shivers raced up and down my spine. If I could have travelled by wagon, I wouldn't have been afraid. Nowadays, however, everyone travels on that thing called a train—and I fear it as I fear a madman.

I nursed the idea for a long time, but I couldn't decide what to do; one day I'd be going, and the next day I'd be staying at home. Maybe I'd never have gone at all if I hadn't dreamed about my son one night, and it was such a lovely and pleasant dream that I forgot my fears and decided to go.

"I'll go, come what may," I said to myself. From that moment, I didn't waste a single *kreytsar [penny]*. I earned as much as I could and saved it all up. And I kept asking people about the train. They told me you had to have a ticket and be on time.

"Well," I thought, "I just might be able to do that!"

I finally saved up a few *levy [gold coins]* so that I could pay for the trip and still manage a present or two for my son and his wife. On the way, I wanted to stop in at Stanislav to visit my daughter-in-law's mother and get her advice about what to buy the children. Obviously, in a town like Stanislav, it's possible to buy something better.

Around the time of the Feast of the Transfiguration, I set out on my journey. I travelled to Kolomiya with a man from Pistyn who was taking some cherries to market. We left during the night and arrived in Kolomiya along with the dawn. The man drove straight to the market; I got off, thanked him—he didn't want any payment for taking me—took my small bundle, and went directly to that place that's called a station. I know all the roads in that town quite well, so I didn't have to ask for directions from anyone.

When I got to the station, there were already two wagons there, and people were milling around. "Maybe I got here too late?" I thought.

"Have I come too late?" I asked an elegantly dressed man.

"Where are you going?"

"To Stanislav."

"Oh, in that case, you've a bit of a wait yet."

I went inside to settle down somewhere and get out of people's way. You see, I thought I'd find a place to stand, put my bundle down beside me, and wait until something happened; all I had to do was find out from someone where to buy the ticket and where to sit when it was time to go. But there was no one to ask. Whenever a train arrived, a young gentleman or a lady would jump out, dash about this way and that, and then go into the inner room; or some Jew with a lot of baggage would come along, and then he'd take off somewhere or other.

Then I heard a railroad man shouting: "The ticket office is open, the ticket office is open!" The young gentlemen and a group of Jews ran out and crowded around a window. I watched them and saw they were buying tickets.

"I'd better go there as well," I thought.

So off I went. All around me, all kinds of trunks were being carried or lugged around on little wheels, and one man was doing nothing but pasting cards on them.

"Am I supposed to buy a ticket now?" I asked him.

"Where are you going?"

"To Stanislav."

"Well then, go ahead and buy one; but this is an express train, and it seems to me that ladies like you don't travel on express trains."

"What's an express train?" I asked. "I've never heard of express trains."

But before I could finish what I was saying, the young gentleman who was selling the tickets shut the wicket, and everyone disappeared, as if they'd been swept away. I only heard something hoot and whistle.

"Oh, my poor little head! The train has gone!" I shrieked, flinging out my hands in despair.

The trainmen burst out laughing.

"My good people," I said. "Don't laugh; tell me, will the train go to Stanislav again today, or won't it?"

"It will, it will," they replied. "That was the express that just left; your train is still coming."

"Well, thank God that mine is coming, and may the devil take the express!"

After another hour or two, more people began to arrive. They kept coming and coming, until there were so many of them—Jews, and gentlemen, and peasants, and soldiers—that the room was overflowing. A Jewish woman ended up standing next to me.

"Where are you going?" I asked her.

"To Stanislav."

"I'm going there too!" I said, and I couldn't have been happier—even if she'd been my own mother. "Have you gone there before, or is this your first time?" I asked.

"Oh, my! I probably have fewer trips ahead of me than behind me!" the Jewess replied.

"Well then, I'll stick with you because I don't know where to go or what to do. If you'd at least tell me when to buy a ticket."

"Sure, fine," said the Jewish woman. "Stay close beside me. When I begin to move forward, you move as well."

"Do we have to wait long yet?"

"No, not long; maybe half an hour."

In about half an hour, or maybe a bit more, a man began to shout again: "The ticket office is open, the ticket office is open!"

The Jewish woman began to edge forward, and I followed her; but, oh my God, there were so many people shoving and trying to get ahead of one another! Somehow or other, the Jewish woman managed to shove her way through, but I kept being pushed aside.

I saw that people were placing money on a counter and taking tickets. So I took out my money as well—I'd found out from others that you had to pay two *levy* and twenty *kreytsary* to go from Kolomiya to Stanislav. I got as close as I could to the window, took out my money, and put it down on the counter. But the young gentleman didn't even blink; he gave out the rest of the tickets, banged the window shut, and even put a board across it.

I began yelling in alarm: "Please, sir, what about my ticket?"

He raised the window and asked: "Where are you going?"

"To Stanislav, if you please, sir."

He pulled out a ticket and said: "That will be two *levy* and twenty *kreytsary.*"

The world turned dark before my eyes. "I've paid you already," I told him.

But he shouted at the top of his lungs: "Either you pay, old woman, or I'll have the police haul you away!"

I stood there dumbfounded. "What should I do?" I started to think, but there was no time for thinking—I either had to pay him again or go back home! I took out the handkerchief that I'd wrapped my money in, but my hands were shaking so badly that I could hardly untie it while holding on to the ill-fated ticket he'd given me.

Oh, woe is me! What a terrible disaster! I was so overcome with worry that I didn't hear the train arrive; if it hadn't been for my Jewish woman, I would have been left behind. I wanted to travel with her, but the man who was telling people where to sit wouldn't hear of it; he packed me off in one direction, and the Jewess in another.

I sat down and shook as if I had the ague. For one thing, I was afraid to travel on this thing, and for another, I couldn't get over the loss of my money!

"Lord Jesus Christ!" I thought. "Couldn't this disaster happen to someone else instead of to someone like me, who is already so poor? Do people have nothing better to do than pounce on my little bit of money? There's truth in that old saying: the poor get taken twice. It was hard enough for me to pay once for the ticket, let alone a second time. Now I don't have any money to buy the children presents. Well, it can't be helped—they'll have to forgive me. I was happy, and an evil eye got jealous."

The people around me were talking and laughing, but I didn't feel like joining in. I sat and thought my own thoughts. And that thing—that train—kept spewing steam and racing along like a madman.

Suddenly, I glanced up and saw that I was in Stanislav already. I hadn't realised that so much time had gone by! "That's how it is," I thought. "A person sits and worries, but time keeps on flying."

The man who had told us where to sit came and opened the door—clearly, it was time to get off. Others were getting off, so I got off as well. Everyone was going through a little gate that had a bell next to it, so I followed them. A man in a wool coat was standing there, collecting tickets.

"Your ticket!" he said to me.

I gave him my ticket and started walking away. I looked around, and no one said anything, so I thought everything was fine.

"I suppose I should go to town," I said to myself. I was walking along, and the road stretched on and on, and for some reason it looked different than when I'd travelled on it to my son's wedding.

"Well, now," I thought. "Can it be that I'm walking down a different street? Maybe Stanislav burned down, and they've built another town?" I was curious to know what had happened.

It was Sunday, early morning, and people were on their way to church. A man carrying *kalachi [braided circular ceremonial bread]* tied in a kerchief was going somewhere, probably to a service for someone who'd died.

I walked up to him and said: "Glory to Jesus Christ!"

"Glory forever!"

"Tell me, my good man, am I on the right road to town?"

"You'll soon be right out of the town."

I thought he was poking fun at me. "What's happened that Stanislav has become so small?" I asked him.

And he just stared at me. "What Stanislav are you talking about? This is Otyniya!"

Oh, my heavens! Dear God! Save me! My legs were trembling and swaying, and I felt that I might have to sit down—right in the middle of the road.

The man also looked confused, and he didn't budge a step in either direction.

"I thought I was in Stanislav," I told him.

"No, this is Otyniya," he said.

"But I paid for a ticket to get all the way to Stanislav."

"But this is Otyniya; you can ask anyone!"

"My good man! Give me some advice, and I'll be grateful to you forever, for as long as I live."

"What advice can I give you?" he asked

And so I began to tell him what a disastrous trip I'd had: how I'd had to wait in Kolomiya, how I'd paid twice for my ticket, and how I now seemed to have arrived in Otyniya and not in Stanislav.

He scratched his head. "Well, you know," he said, "maybe I can give you some advice."

"May God and the Holy Mother speak through you!" I said.

"There's a lord who lives nearby, just down this road—I can show you where—and if he can't give you any advice, then no one can. Lords, of course, know how to deal with things like this—but peasants like us don't have a clue."

I didn't know what to say to him at that point. I just asked him to take me to that lord.

It wasn't too far away—just a few steps. He showed me where to enter, I thanked him once again, and we parted. I walked up a ways, and there, on a porch that was all overgrown with hops, a military man was sitting on a bench by the wall. I didn't know if he was the lord or not, and if I should say something or not. Finally, he started to talk. And, from what he said, I understood that he too, had come to see the lord and was waiting for him.

"Can I go in to see him?" I asked.

"He's still sleeping; wait a while."

After some time, a servant came out, and we asked if the lord was up. "No, not yet," she said.

Well, it's fine to wait if you have the time, but if you have pressing matters, even an hour seems forever.

"I'll go in to see him," I said.

"Well, let's hope you don't get a knock on the head," the military man laughed.

I went into the porch and slowly pushed open the door into the main room. Just then, someone shouted: "Who's there?"

I looked in and saw that the lord was still in bed. I shut the door as quickly as I could and turned back.

"See," laughed the military man. "What did I tell you?"

We kept on waiting, talking about this and that and, little by little, I told the military man why I'd come to see the lord and what kind of advice I needed.

"If I'd known that," he said, "I'd have advised you long ago. I'm a military man. I served in the Dragoons for twenty years, and during that time I learned a lot in my wanderings. As far as the train is concerned, this is what you have to do: if something happens, you have to report it to the supervisor. Did you report it?'

"No, I didn't report anything."

"Then go and report it! Neither the lord, nor the minister, nor anyone else in the world, will give you any better advice. Just go and report it to the supervisor—there's no point in waiting and wasting your time. That's what the supervisor is there for—to keep things in order. You'll wait here for a long time yet," he added, nodding his head at the door.

Perhaps the military man was telling the truth. Why should I wait any longer? If, indeed, there was a supervisor, then he probably could give me the best advice.

"So you're saying I should go?" I asked the military man again.

"Yes, go, and don't be afraid! I'll answer for it if I'm not telling you the truth."

I took him at his word and left. When I got to the station, I asked for the supervisor, like the military man said. And I told him how things stood—that I wanted to go to Stanislav, but the man in the wool coat had taken my ticket.

The supervisor flew into a rage! "Why did you give him the ticket, you stupid old woman?"

I was sure that all was lost, but then I heard him send for the men who take the tickets. They finally came—the one in the wool coat, and two others as well.

"Which one of you took this old woman's ticket?"

They all spoke at the same time: "Not me, not me, if you please, Mr. Supervisor."

"May God punish you," I said to the one who took the ticket. "Weren't you the one who stood at the gate and took my ticket?"

"Get lost, old woman!" he said. "What are you saying? I didn't see you, and I didn't see your ticket!"

"Come on, give it back to her," the supervisor muttered, and then he turned around and left. But the men started laughing and making fun of me.

"Oh, my poor little head!" I grieved. "What am I to do? I barely made my way to these foreign parts—and now all is lost!"

It was almost noon already, and I was feeling hungry, because I'd had nothing in my mouth since Kolomiya. I figured I'd get to Stanislav in no time at all, but instead I'd got into real trouble. I wandered around the buildings until I got tired and felt like sleeping.

I put my little bundle under my head and began to drowse, but I was afraid to fall sound asleep for fear someone might steal what little I had. And those men kept walking around, hooting with laughter. The trains were coming and going, but I couldn't budge without a ticket.

"Holy Mother," I thought. "Who dreamt up such a thing as a train? It goes quickly, that's true enough, but of what use is that to a poor person? They'll just rob you—and then laugh at you to boot. I'd rather go begging for bread with a cane than travel on that cursed train!"

But once you're on your way, you have to manage somehow; otherwise, you may as well lie down and die. "I'll go to see the supervisor once again," I thought, "and I'll ask once and for all: 'Is it like this—or like that?'"

Suddenly a piece of paper that looked like a ticket flew out of the window where I was sitting. I leaped to my feet, grabbed it, and peered at it— yes, it was a ticket! And the man in the wool coat was standing in the window, along with his friends, and they were roaring with laughter—as if they were devils in hell.

Well, I was furious! No, I won't forgive you for this, come what may! I went to the supervisor, showed him my ticket, and said: "If you please, sir, the man in the wool coat said he didn't have my ticket, but he's just thrown it at me from the window—after so many trains have gone!"

"There, there," the supervisor said, "your train will come!"

And it really did come. When it started to grow dark, the train came, and they told me to get on it. That's how I got to Stanislav. By the time I got off, and by the time I found my in-law's home, I was so weak that I was dizzy. When my in-law laid eyes on me, she crossed herself.

"Oh my dear little in-law!" she exclaimed. "Where have you come from at this late hour?"

"Don't even ask," I replied. "Give me something to eat, because I can hardly stand."

My in-law rushed around and scrambled some eggs. I regained some of my strength, and when I began telling her about my misadventures, she didn't know what to say or do. Finally, she made up a bed for me. I said my prayers and thanked the Lord God for seeing to it that I'd finally arrived safely. Then I slept so soundly that I didn't wake up until the sun was way up high in the sky.

I stayed with my in-law for two days. I didn't buy any gifts—because I had no money. On the third day, my in-law went with me to the station. She had an acquaintance there, and he saw to everything—bought my ticket for me, and told me when it was time to board. I was given a place by the window, so in Burshtyn my son saw me right away and took me home.

My children made me stay with them for a long time. On rainy days, we'd sit around, and I'd begin to recall my travels.

My son said: "You know, mother, if I reported that official, he'd have to return your money to you."

But I didn't want to do that. God is more just than people; one day He'll summon that man to face His judgement.

The Elector
(1889)

Dedicated to Ivan Franko

Yakym Machuk was ploughing the field for the spring seeding.
Suddenly, there was a crrr-ack!—and the plough-scraper snapped.
Enraged, Yakym began invoking all the devils! He would have
finished ploughing the field by evening, but now, this mishap made
it doubtful if he could. There really was no point in being angry—
it was just a waste of time; he had to go home and look for
something that could serve as a scraper.

He left his driver in the field with the oxen and set out down
the paths to the village. His wife was not at home. The house was
locked, but no matter—he did not really have to get into it. He
walked over to the woodshed, found a suitably curved piece of
wood, hewed it, and fashioned a scraper. He was about to leave
when he heard someone calling him

"Yakym! Hey there, Yakym!"

Yakym looked up to see who it was—and saw Vasyl, his
kinsman and neighbour.

"Are you home already?" Yakym asked, for he knew that Vasyl
had gone into town quite early. "Did you manage to get everything
done?"

"Oh sure, I managed, all right!" Vasyl said. "God forbid that
anyone should have to go to trial. It's the fourth day, and there's
still no end in sight. But aren't you out in the fields?" he inquired
of his neighbour.

"The devil broke my scraper, so I had to come all the way home.
In the time it's taken, I could have gone around the field a few
times with the plough. And I don't know where my woman's gone
off to. Is she at your place?"

"No, she's not. Oh yes! I almost forgot. The assistant bailiff was
here, and because your wife wasn't at home, he asked me to tell
you that on Tuesday you're supposed to go to the community
meeting room for the election."

"What election?" Yakym asked.

"Who knows!" his neighbour said. "The commissary is supposed to arrive, and there's going to be an election of some kind."

"Phooey! The devil take it!" Yakym spit in disgust. "There's so much work to be done right now that a man doesn't know what to tackle first, but their heads are full of nonsense, and so you have to go and waste your time!"

"What does it matter to the lords?" Vasyl said. "They don't have anything to do, so they dream up all sorts of schemes. But a Godfearing peasant has so much work to do these days that, as you've so rightly said, he doesn't know what to turn to first."

"Oh, they deliberate and deliberate. If only there was some benefit from it all," Yakym grumbled.

"Well, maybe the lords do get something out of it," the neighbour observed, "but all we seem to get is higher taxes."

"And if the taxes don't go up, then the corvée does," Yakym added.

"Oh, that corvée, that corvée," Vasyl seized on his kinsman's words. "It's getting impossible to put up with it. My son lost two days—days that can't be repaid, even with gold!"

"You think that I don't have the same problem?" Yakym said. "I had to spend a whole day hauling stones with my oxen!"

There was no time to continue the conversation—the day was slipping away—and so the neighbours parted. Yakym once again hurried down the paths to the field where he had left his young driver with the oxen. The boy, spotting him from afar, harnessed the oxen and readied the plough. Yakym, without saying a word, set to work. The soil was damp, the ploughshare had to be lowered deep into the ground, and the oxen plodded laboriously.

"Gee! Haw! Gee! Whoa!" the driver called out in a thin voice, urging on first one ox, then the other, with a short whip stuck in a cherrywood handle. Yakym added calls of his own: "Come on, my little oxen, come on, together now! Hey you, grey one, to the right! Together, my little ones! Hey, my little oxen, hey!" Their voices carried into the distance and disappeared in the vast expanse of earth and sky.

The plough moved with difficulty; the oxen strained their necks and plodded forward slowly. It was as if the men and the oxen were united in a single force, a single power, that was opposing another force and power that resided in the ground, and which they were able to overcome only a bit at a time as they carved out one furrow after the other.

They grew tired. It was time to give both themselves and the cattle a rest. Unharnessing the oxen, they threw them some feed—weeds that had been saved for the ploughing. Yakym untied a bag, pulled out salt and garlic, broke off a chunk of bread for himself, and gave the rest to the driver. After the oxen finished eating, they had to be watered. The water was quite far away, way out in the field. Even though water as clear as a tear shimmered in the nearby marshes, the cattle would not drink it.

"Go water the oxen," Yakym said to the boy; then, he sat down on the boundary and began to eat.

The sun was shining—the green winter wheat and the freshly ploughed fields seemed to be absorbing its warm rays. The broad, clear surface of the large marsh shone amid the green grass and the tall, tough bulrushes.

Some delicate swamp plants screened the stagnant water with their spreading leaves, as if they feared that the sun might drink up all the water from which they drew their sustenance. Swift little flycatchers flitted high and low over the surface of the water, darted sideways, and zoomed after their prey.

Yakym gazed straight ahead. Every year, the ploughed field was covered only sparsely with the seeded crop, but weeds jutted out all over it. Large clumps of quack grass and scutch grass stayed on friendly terms so that through their friendship they could claim more land.

"That damned grass!" Yakym growled. "That damned grass! I have to make sure during the harrowing that not a single rootlet is left!"

One clump of quack grass seemed to rise and lift itself upwards. What was it? It wasn't a mole, was it? Yes, it was a mole. Loose soil was being scattered in small, soft lumps.

"Goddamn . . ." Yakym swore. He jumped up with the scraper to dig out the saboteur. But the mole hid itself—diving into the ground and vanishing, as if it had never been there.

Yakym sat down in his former spot and watched closely to see if the mole would show itself again. At his feet, a worm crawled out of the ground and laboriously inched its way forward, dragging a half-rotten stem behind it. A little farther off, an ant was struggling with a bread crumb—a tiny portion of Yakym's food. It was turning its head first in one direction, and then in the other; whenever it dropped the crumb, it picked it up again, and so it went, on and on. A bee droned plaintively, as if it were humming a quiet, sorrowful dirge.

On the boundary, overgrown with various grasses, tiny primroses peeked out, a red lungwort flaunted its bright petals, and some curly clover covered the ground. The sweet scent of the clover attracted the bee; it groped at the flower's curly head with its little feelers and stuck its tongue deep into the slender tubules.

The mole once again threw up some soil. But this time Yakym did not get up, nor did he grab the scraper lying beside him. His head was besieged with swarming thoughts; everything that he had heard and seen today became all jumbled, and one thought trailed after another, as if someone were pulling them with a rope.

Take the mole that was digging up his field—it was working, toiling. And the worm that was creeping beneath his foot, and the bird, and the ant—all were striving to live. Obviously, this was the law—that if something wants to live, it has to work. Why then, was this not so among people? One fellow works, toils, while the next one only amuses himself in this world! The peasant has to feed everybody—if he didn't work to produce bread, then people wouldn't have anything to eat.

Oh, it was hard work! You have to dig about in the earth like a worm. You have to plough, harrow, sow the grain, and then hope that the plants will grow, and the kernels ripen. And afterwards, you have to harvest and thresh it! Life is easy for lords, but you, the peasant, have to work so they can live. The lords hoodwink you and pretend to call you to some meeting, and then they tell you to pay for your own backbreaking labour and impose taxes to take away what you have earned.

The fresh, black earth was being scattered into new little piles. The mole did not cease its labours, but Yakym had forgotten about it. He was gazing far into the distance, above the fields and the marshes. A large crane with outstretched wings and a long branch in its sturdy beak fluttered over his head and disappeared slowly into the horizon, while from beyond the hill, the small figure of the driver, walking alongside the big, horned grey oxen, was slowly coming into view.

On Sunday, Yakym heard that the priest had summoned all the village elders, and that what he had said to them about the election was really worth listening to. The old priest had so much to say, that he had bounced up and down as he gave them instructions regarding the election.

The people could not stop talking about what the old man had said—it was enough to make your ears buzz!

"You so and so's," the priest had said. "You don't care about your rights, and then you say that a peasant has it hard in this world. You wish that things were different, but then you just hopelessly scratch the back of your head! You complain about the lords, but when the election comes, you elect a lord, a Pole, as your representative. You've already forgotten about serfdom, when a peasant had to work like an ox for the lord, when he had nothing of his own because everything belonged to the lord, when he had to pay a tithe, was beaten, and wallowed—worse that any dog—on the lord's threshold!"

The priest's son, Master Nykoltsya, had also been there. He was studying at some institute or university, but had come home for a while. This young man had even outdone his father.

"You're the native people here! The Poles arrived later, but despite this, they rule over you, and they're taking everything into their own hands. There is no Ukrainian justice, no Ukrainian language. In the school—it's Polish, in the courtroom—it's Polish; Ukrainians do not have access to anything, and all the talk in the country is focused on Polish matters, as if Ukrainians didn't exist. And Ukrainians abet them in all of this with their indifference and their lack of knowledge about their rights! If Ukrainians stuck together, then the Poles would soon see—as Shevchenko, our great Ukrainian poet said—that 'in one's own house, there is justice, and power, and liberty!'"

These words were carried throughout the village. They were spread, of course, by word of mouth, from one person to another—and, before long, the whole village was buzzing with the same talk.

Yakym might have forgotten about the election, but after he heard what the propertied men were talking about, he really wanted to go to the meeting on Tuesday—the day on which the electors were being called together.

On Tuesday, a group of men had already gathered when Yakym arrived at the village office. Some were standing in the yard, while others were walking in and out of the building. They talked about this and that, mostly about farming matters, and about the tavern keeper who was causing great misery in the village.

The older men, who had been at many an election in their day, were worried that they would have to wait for a long time for the commissary to come from the city. One time when the people had gathered like this, they had waited until well into the night, and finally had gone home without ever seeing him. The people were probably aware of this, and that was why they were gathering so slowly. Even the priest had not arrived. The people often had to wait for him, but when it came to matters of this kind, he was usually very prompt.

"Here comes the priest now," one of the men said.

It really was the priest—shrivelled and old, wearing a small black hat. The people were able to recognise him from afar.

"Glory to Jesus Christ," the priest said in a voice that was fairly loud—considering his advanced years—as he approached the citizens.

The men bowed to the priest and lined up to kiss his hand.

"Isn't the commissary here yet?" the old man asked, winking slyly with one eye, as if he felt that he was among friends and was waiting, along with them, for someone who was an outsider.

"Who knows—we may have to wait for a good while longer," the men who were standing close by replied.

The priest, followed by the older and more important property owners, walked into the office; the younger men stayed outside.

"Well, my propertied gentlemen, what have you decided?" the priest asked, seating himself behind the table.

The men frowned. It was so quiet you could hear a pin drop.

To tell the truth, they had not held counsel of any kind, and so they had nothing to say to the priest. All eyes turned, therefore, to the church elder, who had been the leader in the village for a long time.

He was an old man, approaching ninety, and had been the church elder for about forty years. At one time, he had been a "plenipotentiary" and had settled more than one matter in the village when no one else had known what to do.

Now, when everyone turned to look at him, he saw that he would have to say something.

But he was in no hurry, as if he were waiting to see if there might be someone else who could take his place. He liked to hold back a bit, using as an excuse his advanced years and the fact that he should be thinking about the next life, not about the one on this earth.

He had all the Holy Scriptures at his fingertips and liked to quote from them when he spoke. And now, after waiting for a while, he cleared his throat and began his address with words from the Holy Scriptures: "'I am a good shepherd and I lay down my life for my sheep'—and so we, too, have been waiting for our shepherd."

The faces of the men brightened—the words of the church elder seemed to them to be their very own.

"It's true," one of the men, also elderly, nodded in agreement. "It's true that sheep don't do well without a good shepherd," he said, translating what was written in the Holy Scriptures into his own words, for no one in the entire village could speak in the manner of the church elder.

The priest's eyes flashed contentedly and joyfully. At that moment, however, his glance fell on a man sitting in a corner, whose gloomy appearance was not in keeping with the cheerful faces of the others. The priest ran his eyes over the entire gathering, and his look rested on almost every individual face, as if he were searching for more gloomy faces which, by their very appearance, would argue against the words of the church elder.

"Well, my propertied gentlemen," he finally began, "you know that you are to elect electors, that is, the people who will then elect our member of parliament. Elect whomever you want to. I'll go along with your choices, but elect people who are solid, who know they're Ukrainians, and who will vote for one of our own to be a member of parliament. So, elect suitable people who fear neither the lord, nor the village chief, and who will not sell their conscience for a few niggardly *kreytsars [copper coins]!*"

All eyes turned involuntarily to the man in the corner.

Everyone could guess that these words were being addressed to the village chief because, in the last election, he had sided with the county chief, and from that time on, things had not gone well between him and the priest. The people began stirring; they knew that the priest did not want them to elect the village chief as an elector, and this was what was causing all the problems and complications. The priest was the priest, but the village chief was the village chief; you needed a priest, but you also needed a chief. The chief was a proud man, and very severe. Hearing the words that were directed at him, he turned red with anger.

"We'll see what happens!" he said loudly, and his usually even voice trembled slightly.

The priest, pretending that he had not heard this remark, walked out of the building.

Now the citizens were sharply divided into two camps—some upheld the chief, while others supported the priest. There were also those who wanted to elect both the priest and the chief, so that—as the saying goes—the wolf would be fed, but the goat would be whole.

In the meantime, another matter was unfolding outside. The village was very large, and it could send up to four electors. This meant that, in addition to the priest and the village chief, two more electors were required.

The lead in this matter was taken by Ivan Rybak. Even though he was not that old yet, in terms of experience and wisdom he may well have rivalled the church elder; he was not as knowledgeable about the Holy Scriptures but, to make up for it, he knew more about what was happening in the world. He was literate, bought books, subscribed to Ukrainian newspapers, and knew how to behave in all sorts of situations—what to say and how to say it. He had already been an elector a few times, and so now it was taken for granted that he would be elected—even though the chief did not like him and called him "the priest's sidekick" because, at the elections, he always took the side of the priest.

Before the community could reach consensus about what to do, the commissary arrived, and then there was no more time for any talk. The commissary was in a hurry—as if he were being hounded by a hundred devils—and almost flew into the building. He was followed by the priest and all the elders, except for Ivan and the church elder—they stayed outside among the people.

The assistant bailiff, red-faced and alarmed, ran out a few times, calling the people to come indoors. But the problem of the fourth elector was still not resolved—the people could not decide who it should be. They were saying that perhaps it could be this man, or that one, but things just were not working out, because it was difficult to come right out and say that this man was better, and that one was worse.

Ivan realised that the matter would not be concluded soon; therefore, without saying anything, he pulled out a box of matches from the pouch on his leather belt and began rubbing away the red heads. Everyone caught on to what would happen next, and they all agreed to it as they watched Ivan's hands. He left only one match with a head on it, and then he moved out among the men. Even though no one said anything, everyone knew that if he pulled out a match without a head, then that was that, but if he pulled out the one with a head—he would be an elector. Ivan moved from one man to another, and everyone pulled out a match.

Finally, Yakym also pulled out a match—and his was the one with a head on it.

He stared around in astonishment, and it seemed to him that he saw reflected, in all the faces, the same astonishment that had overcome him. Some of them, it is true, began to mutter that it would have been better to have a free vote instead of pulling matches. This deeply offended Yakym, and he started asking to be excused, saying that he was still young, that he wouldn't know what to do, and it would be better if they selected someone else.

The bailiff once again ran out of the building in great consternation—the commissary was in a hurry. Yakym was still protesting, but time had run out, and the church elder almost ordered him to accept the fact that he had pulled out the match with the head.

"It's the luck of the draw, my good fellow," he said. "You were fated to be an elector, and you can't resign."

"If that's how it is, that's how it is," the rest agreed. "If that's how it's turned out, then so be it!"

And saying this, the men entered the building. The commissary was rushing about, fuming that they were doing everything so slowly.

Finally, the voting began. They started with the priest. He voted for the church elder, Ivan Rybak, and the first two men who happened to catch his eye.

Then the church elder was called up. He excused himself, saying that this task was not for him, that he should be thinking about other tasks now.

The commissary was losing all patience. "This isn't the place for such talk! Just tell us who you're voting for, that's all."

If one of the elder's own people had spoken to him in this manner, he would have earned a severe tongue lashing, but when it came to the lords, that was a different matter. So, without saying anything more, the church elder voted for the priest, Ivan, one of the men that the priest had voted for, and Yakym.

When the chief was called forward, he stood up, frowned, and after a moment, said that he was voting for Ivan, Yakym, one of his neighbours, and himself. The people exchanged glances. It was not fitting to vote for yourself; obviously, he really wanted to be elected. So, when another propertied man was called up to cast his vote, he voted for the priest, Ivan, Yakym, and the chief.

It all went very smoothly after this—everyone voted for the same men, and only the odd person threw in someone else's name. Yakym could hardly breathe; at first, he had tried to get out of being an elector, but now, he watched everyone's lips anxiously, and he muttered about those who did not mention his name.

When the voting was concluded, the commissary read out the names of those who had been elected, Yakym rejoiced when he heard his name among them; he never would have thought that an event such as this could bring him such happiness.

The commissary departed immediately; he still had to hold an election in another village. The people began to disperse.

"So how is it going to be, Yakym?" the priest inquired, as he walked away. "The community has shown that it can stick together; so now, all of us have to stick together and not throw our vote away into the mud."

Upon hearing these words, Yakym became even more excited; he was one of the younger men, and the priest had never before stopped to talk to him.

Proud and happy, Yakym found himself back in his own yard almost before he realised it. His wife, Yakymykha, was calling the chickens to come and get their supper. She was standing in front of the house, throwing them handfuls of grain siftings from her apron. Yakym could hear her voice from afar.

"You sure stayed there long enough!" she said when she saw her husband at the gate. "I thought that maybe the devil had run off with you, or the plague had got you."

"So what?" Yakym murmured smiling.

"What do you mean, so what? Doesn't it mean anything to waste a whole day?" his wife replied indignantly.

Having said this, she hurried indoors, because she knew Yakym could not always be talked to like this. And when Yakym walked in right after her, she became anxious that she might have said too much. She watched him furtively as he took off his hat and coat, and was surprised to see that he was still in a good mood.

"Do you know what, wife?" he said, as if he had not heard what she had been prattling on about a moment ago. "Do you know what? I've been elected an elector!"

"An elector?" Yakymykha repeated, still more amazed. "What does it mean—to be an elector?"

"It means to be like the chief and like Ivan, who were elected to be electors three years ago, you know?"

"No I don't," his wife replied. "What is it—a chief, or a bailiff?"

"Oho! She wants to be the wife of a bailiff!" her husband roared with laughter.

"So, who elected you?"

"Well, just try talking to her—once a fool, always a fool! Who else but the community, of course!"

She just shrugged her shoulders; she did not understand to what position her husband had been elected, but she knew it must be something important. The whole community had elected her husband, so she no longer was angry about the wasted day.

"Maybe one day they'll elect him as the bailiff; it's really nice to be the bailiff's wife in a village," she thought.

The following day Yakym's joy began to ebb, and troublesome questions reared their heads.

"What's going to happen now? What am I to do now?" he asked himself involuntarily, and uneasy thoughts began to stir in his mind. Now, he truly began to regret that he had agreed to being elected. He had no idea who to vote for, or what to endorse. So would it not have been better to stay at home, do his work, and not go to any meetings?

The more he thought about it, the more worrisome his thoughts became. He was still thinking that it might be possible to resign and avoid the whole problem.

But when he started telling his wife about his doubts, she drove them right out of his head.

"The community has elected you, so it's no good resigning. You'll do whatever the others do. 'The thread always follows the needle.'"

"You're right, wife. I should go and talk it over with either the priest or the chief; I'll do whatever they do."

But before Yakym could sort out in his own head where he should go first, Ivan came to see him.

"And here I was, worrying for nothing," Yakym thought. "Everything is working out all by itself."

As it turned out, Yakym went to see the priest first, because Ivan stopped by to take him to the priest's home for a briefing.

At the time that Ivan came for him, Yakym had been making a rake for his wife, because the garden was dug and ready to be raked. Yakymykha was annoyed that her husband had not finished his work—it was not worth being even the bailiff's wife if her work had to suffer, and the entire farm was to go to ruin!

"A man can get used to roaming around without doing anything—it does happen. Not so long ago, he wasted a whole day, and now he's gone off again, and he hasn't finished making the rake. If only I had something to rake the garden with. Should I go and borrow a rake from the neighbour? It's quite far to the priest's home, and they may stay there quite a while, and in the meantime the garden will dry out. Maybe it would have been better if he'd resigned from whatever it was he's been elected to, but I, fool that I am, told him not to. If only I knew what it was he's been elected as, and for what?"

Quite unexpectedly, a happy thought crossed her mind. She decided to visit Ivan's wife, Ivanykha, to ask her about everything and find out what was happening. She had heard that Ivanykha's husband had already been an elector—the same kind that Yakym was now—so she would know what it was all about and could tell her if it was a good thing that her husband had been elected.

As soon as Yakymykha got the idea, she acted on it. She put on her new sheepskin coat, tied a large, shawl-like kerchief on her head, locked the door, and went on her way.

Ivanykha was a proud woman who came from an important family. Yakymykha was happy to have the occasion to become more closely acquainted with this woman, for she had been just a child when Ivanykha got married.

"Well, a bear must have died in the forest if you've come to see me! I should get some ashes and sprinkle your footprints," Ivanykha began speaking in proverbs as Yakymykha drew near.

Yakymykha kissed Ivanykha's hand, while the latter kissed her on the head.

"Please be seated," Ivanykha said, clearing off the bench. "Tell me, what's new in the village?"

"There's nothing new; everything's just as it always is."

"Then tell me, what are you doing that's good?"

"What am I doing? Whatever's easier!" Yakymykha replied jokingly.

"Well, what's the easiest thing to do? Sleep?" Ivanykha asked in the same jocular vein.

The women laughed.

"O God, let us of laughter have our fill, and spare us both from becoming ill," Ivanykha observed. "Oh, may God protect us from being sick like Maksym Ivanyshyn's wife—she was sick for half a year, and yesterday, she died. Some other woman will now ride roughshod over the little ones, and then she'll complain that she had to work hard for someone else's children. God forbid that children be left as orphans!"

"Your husband isn't at home?" Yakymykha finally asked, making it appear as if she were just making small talk.

"Oh no, no—he's not at home! He went off to see the priest. And wasn't your man supposed to go with him?"

"He was supposed to finish making me a rake today, because I don't have anything to rake the garden with, and instead, he just up and went someplace."

Ivanykha shook her head. "Do you think it's any different here? He was planning to plant the potatoes today, but then the cantor's helper came and insisted that he had to go and see the priest."

Yakymykha was very pleased that she had turned the conversation in the direction she had wanted it to go. And, little by little, she began to ask Ivanykha what Yakym had been elected as, and what it was for.

"You've been involved in this before, Ivanykha, so you know all about it; all I know is that my husband is being dragged away from his work."

"It's true. How could you know, my dear Yakymykha? I wouldn't know either if my husband weren't always being elected to everything."

"That's why I said to myself: 'Go and ask Ivanykha—she's lived through it, and she'll know all about it.'"

"At first, Yakymykha," Ivanykha said, "I thought my husband had been elected to gather taxes, so I quarrelled with him because I was afraid of people's curses. But then I found out that the tsar was calling together a council of some kind. Ivan said that when this council assembled in the city, there were more lords and priests gathered there than you'd ever see at a market or even on a church holiday when indulgences are granted. And there were hordes of Jews as well!"

"Was the tsar there too?" Yakymykha inquired.

"I don't know, but I don't think so; he probably had to be someplace else. But Ivan told me that the lords were treating the peasants as if they were their kinsfolk. Our priest walked arm in arm with Ivan and kept referring to him as 'my kinsman, Ivan.' And when the chief did something wrong, the priest turned to Ivan and said: 'If only everyone were like you, Ivan, then we wouldn't be as poor as we are now.'"

Ivanykha continued talking for a long time about how the lords and the tavern keepers kept following Ivan around in droves, so much so that he had beaten them off with a stick. And he'd really let one tavern keeper have it.

Yakymykha's head was spinning from everything Ivanykha had told her, and even though things were not much clearer, she still thought she had found out a great deal.

In the meantime, Yakym and Ivan were at the briefing in the priest's home. Everything that Yakym had previously heard from others, he now heard with his own ears.

"What power Ukrainians would have if they just stuck together! If only the peasants knew their rights and understood the tsar's laws!"

When the son spoke, it was as if he were reading from a book—how many Ukrainians there were under Polish rule, how many under the Russian tsar! And flames flashed from his eyes when he reckoned that, among the several dozen men who were elected to parliament, there were only a few Ukrainians.

"And it's all because the people aren't enlightened. They're so unenlightened that there probably isn't another nation as ignorant as ours in the entire world, and it's because of this that our people suffer as they do. This is why our people are so poor and are treated so badly."

Yakym seemed to be awakening from a long sleep. He knew that the peasants were ignorant and uneducated, but now he felt terrified when he found out that they were completely stupid, and that it was this that accounted for all the world's problems. He found it even stranger when Ivan started saying that the people were unenlightened, that they did not know who was their enemy and who was their friend, and who was leading them on the right path, or the wrong one.

Yakym was now prepared to do everything that they wanted, if only not to have all this evil weighing on his ignorant peasant conscience.

In the end, he was told that he was to vote for a man from Lviv—an educated man and a good Ukrainian—who would know when to speak up for Ukrainians, and what to say on their behalf.

But when they told him his name and surname, Yakym's tongue could not get around it; he could not pronounce it properly. Ivan, however, promised that he could teach him how to say it, because he had voted for this man once before—all that Yakym had to do was to stick closely to Ivan at all times.

"Well, what did the priest say?" Yakymykha asked Yakym when he returned home.

"You'd want to know everything! We're going to be electing our own member of parliament, a certain lord from Lviv. Do you know what a member of parliament is?"

"What's he needed for, this member of parliament?" Yakymykha inquired.

"What's he needed for! To stand up for the people, to make demands on behalf of his people. Outsiders have ruled over us and taken advantage of us long enough! We need our own man now!"

"But you said he's a lord of some kind!"

"It doesn't matter that he's a lord if he's a good Ukrainian."

"Do you mean to say that a lord can be Ukrainian?" Yakymykha asked with great interest.

"What a thing to say! If he couldn't be, he wouldn't be."

Yakymykha shrugged her shoulders. Yakym had not succeeded in explaining it to her, and he barely understood it himself. But at least his mind could not be compared to that of a woman!

Yakym was waiting for the day when he would be called to the city to cast his vote, and he kept repeating the name and the surname of the lord, so that he would not forget it and be a laughingstock!

A couple of days before he was supposed to go to the city, the chief and the sequestrator came to see him. Yakym was surprised. He had paid his taxes, and he had not borrowed money from anyone! What could they possibly want from him?

The chief seemed to read Yakym's mind, and he immediately said: "What do you think, Yakym? Why have we come to see you?"

"Well, I'll wait to hear what you have to say to me," Yakym replied. "Please, be so kind as to come in."

Yakymykha, seeing the guests, rushed into the house. She wiped off the benches and asked them to be seated. The guests sat down. Yakymykha stood quietly by the oven and, leaning her chin on her hand, waited to see what would happen next. The sequestrator made himself comfortable on the bench and began rolling a cigarette.

"Well, have you really not guessed why we've come?" the chief addressed Yakym.

Yakym, perhaps, did have some idea already, but why should he say anything—let those who had come to see him tell him about it themselves.

"Well, did you visit the priest with Ivan not so long ago?"

Yakym felt ill at ease, but he did not deny it, as it seemed that the chief knew about it.

"And did you talk about a lot of important things?" the chief asked diplomatically.

"Well, yes, we talked about a lot of things—both important and not so important . . ." Yakym replied, trying to squirm out of saying more.

"And who did he tell you to vote for?" the sequestrator asked directly, not mincing his words.

Yakym once again felt ill at ease. He became confused and did not want to answer straightforwardly, even though he saw that there was no way out. They knew that he had been there, and more than likely they also knew what had been said.

"For some lord from Lviv," he stated firmly, after pausing for a moment.

The sequestrator laughed and gestured disparagingly with his hand. "Do you know him?" he asked, looking directly at Yakym.

"How am I to know him?" Yakym now replied more boldly. "But the priest told us to elect this lord because he'll stand up for his people."

The sequestrator burst out laughing again. This laughter made Yakym shiver, and he regretted having blurted out the truth so quickly.

The sequestrator laughed as he said: "The priest told you! The priest told you! It may well be that I can tell you something a whole lot better than the priest if only you would listen to me! But he didn't tell you to elect the lord from Kivkovets, right?"

"Well, as I understand it, he isn't Ukrainian—or is he?"

"Oh, yes, I can see that the priest has 'prepared' you very well, yes indeed!"

"It doesn't matter if he's prepared me or not," Yakym said irately. "It's true that one of your own is better than an outsider!"

The chief gave Yakym a long, piercing look, It became very quiet in the house . . . The look confused Yakym, even though he did not know why it should.

"They're both cut from the same cloth!" the chief said slowly, without taking his eyes off Yakym. "They're both cut from the same cloth . . . do you understand Yakym? A lord from Lviv and a lord from Kivkovets—tell me yourself, aren't they one and the same? A lord is a lord, and a peasant is a peasant! A peasant will never be better off under a lord's rule. All of them pull for their own kind—the lords are at the top, and the lord's justice prevails. The lords and the priests know their business, and the peasants know theirs. If someone thinks that I'd let myself be converted, even if I saw some benefit for the peasant—he'd be wrong. No, I'm not one of those, let the priest say what he wants to about me."

"Do you believe the priest?" the sequestrator started in again, in his reedy, wheezing voice. "Isn't it enough that they extort money from the people and take them for all they're worth? And now they're confusing them, as well? Don't the people know that your priest once took a man's last sheep for conducting a funeral? They skin the hides off the peasants, and yet they set themselves up as their guardians, as if they cared about them!"

"We all know this," the chief interrupted him respectfully, "there's no point in talking about it. Oh, we know—if you don't pay him, he won't take a step out of his home, even though in church he talks about God's mercy and human kindness. But we also know what lords are like! The blood on our bodies is still drying. We still remember their cudgels and whips; and when the mandators and hetmans were all gone, the land-stewards, game wardens, and forest rangers remained!

"Once, my neighbour's boy was almost killed in the manor yard because he was grazing cattle on the riverbank, even though these banks used to be ours, communally owned. But is this happening only here? The lords, with their sticky fingers, have taken over our forests, meadows, and pastures everywhere! There's no use expecting anything—either from the priests or the lords. We should obey the will of our most illustrious monarch and wait for him to make things better; it is only he who can make things better for us, and I'm saying that there's no use expecting anything—either from the priests or the lords! Everyone does what profits him most. Let the peasant do likewise!"

Upon hearing these words, the sequestrator reached into his pocket. The chief cut short what he was saying and glanced around the house. From his words and his look, it was clear that he wanted to say more, but was restraining himself.

"Let the peasant do likewise," the chief repeated in a dignified manner, glancing around the house once again.

"I'd say more," he added with a cough, "but there are too may of us here . . ."

"Woman, leave the house!" Yakym said.

Yakymykha walked out, but she stopped just outside the door and listened intently.

The chief was talking again: "This is why we've come—the sequestrator will give you some money, you'll vote for the lord from Kivkovets, and that will be the end of the matter. And I'm telling you, Yakym, and I'll swear on a stack of Bibles," at this point the chief thumped himself so forcefully on the chest that something inside him crunched, "that all those shenanigans won't bring any more benefit to the peasants, and that's for sure, believe me!"

The sequestrator took out a ten-spot and put it on the table. The banknote was brand new, and its fresh blue colour grabbed the eyes.

"Put it away, put it away; keep it for yourself," Yakym said, turning his eyes away from the alluring piece of paper.

"Oh ho-ho," the sequestrator hooted, like an owl at night, as he caught the rather uncertain tone in Yakym's voice. "Why indulge in pretences here, my gentleman elector? I'm telling you—take the money and keep quiet about it, and everything will be just fine! Don't throw away money that falls into your hands. I'm telling you—take it, and vote for the lord from Kivkovets, and don't say anything to anyone. Something is better than nothing! The chief was right when he said that the peasant won't be any better off with a lords' council . . . Are you afraid of the priest, or what?"

Yakym knew that the chief had always said you shouldn't be afraid of the priest; moreover, he himself had bragged that he wasn't afraid of him, so now he was embarrassed by the sequestrator's words. He stated rather loudly that he wasn't afraid of the priest, that the priest had his own mind, but he—Yakym—also had his own mind, and that the priest's business had to do with the altar, and not with him. The sequestrator picked up the banknote from the table and tried shoving it into Yakym's hands.

"This means that you're taking the money, and that you'll vote for the lord from Kivkovets . . ."

Yakym wavered, but did not take the money. The chief, glancing sharply at Yakym, saw his indecisiveness. He took the banknote from the sequestrator's hand and put it back on the table.

"Leave the money—it won't be lost!" the chief said. "And as for you, Yakym, think about it—if you decide to do what we've asked, then keep the money, and if you decide not to, you can return the money to me. As for the money," he said, turning to the sequestrator, "I'll guarantee it."

While Yakym was walking his guests to the gate, Yakymykha ran quickly into the house. The money was still on the table. She reached out to take it and hide it in the trunk, but then hesitated because she feared what Yakym might say.

"I'll wait," she thought, "but I won't let the money get away. The chief was right—let the lords hold their council, but for a peasant, money will do; and the chief is a wise man, maybe even wiser than Ivan, because otherwise he wouldn't be the chief in the village, despite the fact that he doesn't agree with the priest."

When Yakym entered the house, she immediately went on the attack: "Well, will you take the money? You'd be a fool, if you didn't. It's enough to pay the taxes, and with another fiver, we could buy a fur coat as well."

Yakym was silent and pensive, but his wife kept on nattering: "Why not take it, if they're giving it to you? You didn't steal it! No one went out to rob someone. Just think—people are pleading with him to take the money, but he, like a fool, is thinking about it!"

Encouraged by her own words, Yakymykha removed a piece of linen cloth from the trunk to wrap up the money, but her husband silently pushed her hand aside, took the banknote, and tucked it away in his leather belt.

The next day, the electors were to go to town for the election. As neither the chief nor the sequestrator had come to see him, Ivan did not know about their meeting with Yakym. But he had heard talk in the village that, on the day of the election, the chief would be setting out for Yakym's home with a wagon.

"This doesn't look too good," Ivan thought, "I'd better go and find out for sure what's happening. It doesn't bode well for us if he's travelling with the chief."

Without thinking too long about it, Ivan went to see Yakym, using the excuse of the upcoming trip. He supposedly wanted to invite Yakym to travel with him, but he really wanted to find out if Yakym actually had an agreement with the chief. Yakym had not discussed the trip with the chief, and he did not know why the chief was assuming that he would be travelling with him.

"Well then, you'll come with us," Ivan said. "I'm going with the priest, and we can take a second wagon, because the priest's son will be going with us—you see, he's very interested in all of this!"

Yakym grew very uncomfortable. He felt embarrassed and did not know what to say to Ivan, or how to get out of going with them. He would have been glad to travel with them, but he felt as if something were holding him back, as if he were bound by something and could not free himself. He scratched his head worriedly and adjusted his belt—it was weighing heavily upon him, and the banknote given to him by the sequestrator seemed to be squirming in it like a worm in a rotted oak. He didn't know what to do. First of all, he wanted to get rid of Ivan. So he said he'd go in his own wagon, because there was something his wife wanted in the city; and he also had to have an iron ring put on one of his wheels because the gypsy in the village could not do it, and even if he did do it, it wouldn't be done as neatly as it would be done in the city.

Ivan deliberated for a moment. He could see only too well where this was all heading, so he initiated a conversation about how the Poles wanted to elect the lord from Kivkovets, and the Ukrainians—the lord from Lviv. Yakym felt as if he were standing on burning coals.

"Well, do you remember the name of the lord that we're supposed to vote for?"

Yakym firmly repeated the lord's name and surname. Ivan looked askance at him. "So, are you coming with us?"

"No, I'm not, thank you very much. I'll go with my own wagon."

Ivan left without saying anything more.

Yakym really had decided to go in his own wagon and to set out very early, so that the chief would not find him at home. He did not want Ivan to see him travelling with the chief, and if the chief needed him, he could find him just as easily there, in the city.

He set out with only a servant; his wife did not go because there was no reason for her to do so—even though she would have been glad to make the trip. Moreover, she was aware that Yakym had mentioned her to Ivan only to get himself off the hook.

Once Yakym had driven out of the village, he met other people along the way—there were always two, three, or even more men in every wagon. These men were electors from neighbouring villages.

"And here I am—all alone," Yakym thought, "like a fool—as if I'm someone that no one wants to have anything to do with." Yakym was sorry now that he had not waited for the chief after all. Maybe he actually had stopped in for him?

The farther that Yakym drove on, the more often he met up with the coaches and carriages of lords and priests, the small wagons of Jews, and the long wagons of the peasants. And, the closer he came to the city, the more annoyed he was with himself! He looked up and down the road to see if there was someone he could travel with, but he did not find anyone.

In the city—well, my Lord, absolutely everyone was there! A great multitude of people—all the lords, priests, and secretaries from the neighbouring villages. And there were ever so many Jews—like so many black beetles! And all of them were scurrying about and rushing around, as if salt had been sprinkled on them. Yakym tied up his horses in a secure place and began looking around for the chief. He met a man, also an elector, from a neighbouring village, and asked him if he'd seen the chief anywhere.

"No," the elector said, "I haven't seen him, but come on, maybe we'll find him."

They had taken just one step, when a tavern keeper from the largest hostelry in the city approached them. "My respects to the gentlemen electors," he said, waving his cap in the air.

The electors kept on going, without so much as looking back. The tavern keeper kept up with them. He bragged about his sausages, his head-cheese, and his bread.

"Go to the devil," Yakym grumbled. "If I want to eat, I'll manage quite nicely without you."

"But why go elsewhere to buy something, gentleman elector, when you can have it at my place for nothing?"

"Ha-ha-ha!" the two electors burst out laughing. "You'll give it to us for nothing, but you'll take our money, right?"

"Why would I take money?" the tavern keeper said. "If I say that I won't, then I won't . . ." He drew closer and lowered his voice. "Why would I take money? If the lord from Kivkovets becomes the member of parliament, there will be money. And the sausages and bread won't cost you anything. Do you understand?"

"Out of my sight, you damned loathsome creature!" someone shouted over their heads; it sounded as if a cannon had been fired. "You're trying to confuse people, are you? Judas sold Christ, and you, the faithful son of Judas, are leading people into perfidy?"

Yakym looked up and saw Malandevych. He was a local man, the wealthiest of all the burghers, and he enjoyed great fame and respect throughout the entire district. He did not like tavern keepers, and everywhere that temperance was introduced, he was the first one to be there and to lead the way with a cross. The tavern keeper was rattled.

"Lord Malandevych, Lord Malandevych!" he mumbled indistinctly, bowing down low.

"Shut up, you damned . . ."

Malandevych did not finish what he was saying, because two young priests came running up; they took him to one side and began talking quietly to him about something. The tavern keeper vanished, as if the earth had swallowed him.

In front of the district council building where the election was to be held, it was so packed that it was impossible to force your way through the crowd, and the heads of the people rippled like waves in a pond swept by a breeze. A little farther off, men stood in groups and carried on all sorts of conversations.

Yakym heard a familiar voice drifting in from farther away. The voice rose and fell, booming at times as if someone were speaking in an empty barrel and, at other times, flowing quietly and calmly, like the gurgling of water in a shallow stream. Yakym looked around. It was the priest's son. He was moving from group to group, pleading with them, calling upon them to respect themselves, to show that they were people, propertied men, Ukrainians, and not to give in to persuasion or be deceived by promises, and not to sell their votes.

"Stick together, my brothers!" he spoke out passionately. "Your fate rests in your hands; the fate of Ukraine depends on you." His voice broke off. He gazed with fiery eyes at the groups of men and read in their faces the power of his words.

Yakym could not bear to see that look, and he lowered his eyes. He was overwhelmed by the din of the voices and all the new impressions, and the worm, wriggling vigorously under his very heart, gave rise to a prolonged, insistent pain. The look of the young man confused him and made it impossible for him to move.

When Yakym once again raised his eyes and looked around, instead of the young man's face, he saw that of the sequestrator. The sequestrator was as weary as a mower at noon, and the sweat was pouring down his forehead. He forced his way through a group of men, almost bumped into Yakym, and kept on going.

Yakym looked around and saw the tall lance and cap of a gendarme. The sequestrator was whispering in his ear. The gendarme looked in all directions. Finally, the eyes of the two men focused on a group of people talking excitedly, and Yakym thought he could make out the voice of Master Nykoltsya, the priest's son.

Ivan was walking along with two men, and the taller one was talking loudly: "Phooey! The devil take it! One man says this, and the next one says that. They all babble on and on until your head is ready to burst. A man just doesn't know what to do anymore."

"That's what the mind is for," Ivan said, "so that a man can know what to do."

"A mind is one thing, but in the midst of such roguery, even a mind won't help! They keep saying—he's one of ours, he's one of ours but, at the same time, they tell us to elect a lord."

"But you don't understand what they're saying! It isn't about whether or not he's a lord; the lord from Kivkovets is a Pole, while the one from Lviv is a Ukrainian."

"So, of what benefit is that to us?"

"You're really strange! Just think—if you sue someone, and you can't be in court yourself on the appointed day, who do you delegate as your proxy? The one with whom you are in litigation, or the one who is defending you? And with whom do we have more litigations than with the Polish lords? Where have our forests and pastures gone? The rights of the peasant are being lost everywhere because he's ignorant, unenlightened. It's only the priests and the Ukrainian lords who stand up for us. Let's take the situation that we have right now," Ivan continued. "Tell me yourself, my good man, if you had the law on your side, would you have to bribe witnesses?"

Blood rushed to Yakym's face. In his belt, the small piece of paper, folded over four times, made a hissing sound, while the distinct round numbers on it blazed like the eyes of a snake . . .

The election began. Master Nykolstya stood almost at the very door of the council building, encouraging and emboldening everyone who passed by. Someone shoved hard against Yakym. It was the same gendarme who had been talking with the sequestrator.

Drawing himself up as straight as a candle, he formally addressed Master Nykoltsya: "I'm arresting you in the name of justice!"

"Who? Me? For what?" Nykoltsya asked in a confused voice. His pale face grew paler, and his eyes flashed in anger.

"You? Me? For what?" he shouted again with all his might. "For telling the people what they themselves should know? Why don't you arrest those who try to lead them astray, who are bribing them with money?"

And when he was being led away, he turned around and said once more: "My good men, stick together!"

His voice sounded strange and, beneath the encouraging words, a different note could be discerned: "All is lost now!"

The people fell into a panic. Yakym felt as if a knife had been scraped over his body. He was struck dumb. It seemed to him that everyone was looking at him, pointing at him with their fingers, and that it was he who was the confused, bribed villain.

"Well, Yakym, who will you be voting for?" the chief unexpectedly asked him from behind.

Yakym looked around, but he did not say so much as a word.

"Well, let's go! It's time!" the chief said, moving on ahead.

Yakym followed him, just to avoid staying in one spot. In his heart, however, a different, confident, and firm thought was emerging—to rid himself of the terrible enemy that was drilling in his mind, piercing his soul, and burning in his breast.

Everything was confused in his head; his temples were throbbing, his ears were ringing, and a single thought was whirling, pressing in on him like smoke in a chimney.

One thing was clear—in one way or another, he had to get rid of the damned money that was flaming like glowing embers, hissing like red-hot iron.

Sweat was pouring down his forehead, and his heart was pounding furiously. He looked at the men who were present and saw every face and every movement, but why things were as they were, and why people were not behaving as they should—he did not know. But then, he no longer cared about this; he was preoccupied by a single thought that made him shudder with disgust.

"Yakym Machuk!" the voice from inside the building—the one that had called out to others—was now calling him.

Yakym went inside and stood in front of the table behind which the commissary was sitting.

"Who are you voting for?" a corpulent, heavy-set lordling asked.

Yakym remained silent.

"Who are you voting for?" the young lord repeated impatiently.

Yakym remained silent; he was breathing heavily, his whole body was shaking, and even his hands were trembling. He pulled out the money and put it on the table.

The gentlemen on the commission were aghast.

"What's this?" one young lord asked, jumping to his feet.

Yakym felt as if a stone had been lifted from his heart. He stated in a clear, ringing voice: "I was given this money, but I don't want it; I'm putting it down here in front of the entire commission, and I'm voting for the Ukrainian candidate!" And he gave the name and the surname of the lord from Lviv.

A hushed, prolonged hum broke out in the room . . .

"Hurrah! Hurrah!" a few voices called out.

The district chief turned red as a beet. "Agitating is not permitted in the building!" he shouted furiously. "If you don't stop, I'll have you removed!"

The voting did not last much longer. The votes were counted—and there was a twenty-vote majority for the Ukrainian candidate.

There were some sharp discussions among the members of the commission. A few votes were discarded—in those cases where the name and surname had not been pronounced distinctly. Nevertheless, the majority was retained by the Ukrainian candidate. None of the manoeuvres of the friends of the lord from Kivkovets were of any avail—everything had been done strictly in accordance with the rules.

All the other people who had impatiently awaited the outcome of the election now mingled with the electors. The noise and the merriment were vying with each other. Everyone wanted to know all about even the slightest detail, and so, individually, and all together, they excitedly described the moments they had just experienced.

The telegraph office could not cope with all the messages, and the happy news flew throughout the world.

The Jews, as if they were losing their minds from happiness, began shouting: "Hurrah!" Among them, the electors could spot those who had only recently been chasing after them for the lord from Kivkovets, inviting them to eat their head-cheese and sausage.

Yakym heard his name being passed from one set of lips to another.

"Where is he? What's his name? Where's he from?" everyone was asking from all sides. Some took out pieces of paper and wrote down his name.

"He's my parishioner," the elderly priest stated proudly, as he led a few friends and some young lords to meet Yakym.

The priests and the lords began wishing Yakym all the best, and some even exchanged kisses with him. One of them, tears brimming in his eyes, pressed Yakym's hand, and said: "If we already have peasants like you, then Ukraine will not perish, but its enemies will perish, for the Ukrainian people are beginning to comprehend who they are, who they should be."

Yakym could not come to his senses. He was bewildered, and he saw himself as an enigma. What kind of "comprehension" the people were talking about—he did not understand. He only felt that an indistinct foreshadowing was beginning to reverberate within him—some hitherto unknown voice.

"Why were all these people striving so hard; why were they struggling and weeping? Was there something greater hidden in all this than he had previously imagined? Was there an invisible mightier power that was uniting these people into a single soul and awakening a new life within him, as well?" All of these feelings, however, were overwhelmed by the joy that he felt, and by an inexpressibly deep satisfaction.

He returned home, feeling as though he were intoxicated, even though he had not touched any liquor. His wife was waiting for him. "What will Yakym do with the money?" This question had been impatiently burning within her for the past few days. When she heard that he had returned the money, she was outraged.

"You've really gone and outsmarted yourself this time!" she said wrathfully. "People would be happy to get money from somewhere, but when you had some, you threw it into the jaws of the devil!"

"Oh, leave me alone, wife!" Yakym said, furrowing his brow. "You don't know what it's all about, and you don't understand it, so don't get involved! That money wasn't honest money . . ."

His wife calmed down. She did not want dishonest money. It was said that what is stolen will disappear fourfold, while an evil sin could bring ruin down upon the entire household and farm.

When Yakym woke up the next day, his first thought was to go to the priest's home to inquire about Master Nykoltsya. However, it was a little too early; it was barely dawn, and the dark night shadows had not yet completely lifted.

He went outdoors. Since Sunday the wind had been interfering with the seeding by starting up at sunrise, but now it had died down, and he hoped that if it had not come up in the morning, then it would not arise during the day, or at least not until noon.

Yesterday had been a loss as far as the farm was concerned—and he had to make up for it. He called his wife, and they both got down to work.

The sun was quite high when Yakym drove his wagon out of the farmyard. He had a sack filled with seed on the wagon, and an iron harrow tied above the ladder. The road led past the priest's residence. Yakym shouted to his helper to go on to the field, while he stepped in to see the priest. On the threshold, he almost bumped into the young master, who was holding a newspaper in one hand and a hat in the other.

"Oh, it's a good thing you're here," he said to Yakym. "I was just going over to your place to read you what's written in the paper. Listen!"

Yakym listened, and could not believe his ears when he heard what kind of abuses had been perpetrated during the election; but all of this roguery had been overcome by honest electors who, with only a few exceptions, had stood together as one man. A few were named, and among the very first ones stood Yakym's name; he was touted as an indefatigable fighter who had publicly shamed the enemy and thrown a money bribe back in their faces.

Yakym's head began to spin, and he turned his eyes away in embarrassment. He could scarcely remember why he had come, that he had wanted to ask about what had happened to the young master.

Earlier on, while cleaning the seed grain, he had been completely calm, but now his blood was racing through his veins once again. Deeply preoccupied with his agitated thoughts, he reached his field almost before he realized it.

He, who until recently had been a man who was not known to anyone outside of his own village, was now renowned throughout the world! People were writing about him, talking about him, and praising him as an honest and good man! He recalled, with terror, those uncertain moments, those dark moments, when his thoughts had cast about in all directions, when he had not known what to do, and when he could just as easily have done the opposite.

It was not only Yakym's name that emerged from a quiet nook—a similar transformation was occurring in his soul. It was as if he were hearing things anew, as if he were seeing them anew. He realised that the soil on which he walked, and on which his home had stood from the time of his distant ancestors, and the green meadows, hills, valleys, and the ploughed field on which he was casting the seeds—all this was one great Ukrainian land. And he, its rightful owner, its native master, was supposed to care for it, to demand its rights for it!

The sun, veiled with a thin cloud, was casting down its warm rays. The mighty powers of spring were burgeoning, gaining in strength. Everywhere, life and work were seething—everywhere, something was moving, buzzing over the plants, the grass, and the water. From the freshly ploughed furrows, emanated a strange odour—an odour well-known to Yakym.

Yakym shuddered. It was the odour of peasant blood and sweat. This odour overpowered all his turbulent thoughts and, with its ancient right of rule, asked if the lord from Lviv who had received Yakym's vote would wipe the bloody sweat from the peasant's brow, if he would lower the taxes and the imposed payments, if he would return to him the rights to the land he had lost, to the meadows, the riverbanks, the forests, and the pastures?

Yakym lowered his head and fell deep into thought . . .

And, his lips twisting strangely, he murmured: "I wonder . . ."

Yadzya and Katrusya
(1890)

Who does not know our delightful province of Pokuttya at the
foot of the Carpathian Mountains—the mountains that rise
riotously to the heavens and vanish in the bluish mist of the
clouds? Who does not know those swiftly flowing streams that
leap noisily off steep slopes and swirl agitatedly over expansive,
gravelled river beds? In places, as if to spite the agile stream, a
thickly overgrown meadow stands in the middle of a bed, and the
stream—angry at being forced to go around it—foams and
splashes over stones and pebbles.

Here and there, a small grove of oak trees appears and, farther
off, a level expanse of unbroken fields stretches as far as the eye
can see: wide meadows and narrow grainfields with high hedges,
gleaming with golden wheat and barley, silver spikes of rye, and
supple, undulating oat stems. Wide-leafed tobacco plants spring
up next to tall tasselled corn, and an occasional patch of green
swampland shimmers with red, blue, and yellow flowers, like a
miniature carpet woven by the hand of God.

However, the village we are approaching is not marked by an
exceptional attractiveness. Here, the distinct features of the
highlands fade, and the village assumes an appearance more like
that of villages in the province of Podillya. Lying in a valley in
the middle of a broad plateau, both sides of which stretch up to
tall hillocks, it has the appearance of a child sleeping in a trough.

Through the centre of the village flows a small stream, and its
turbid water rolls lazily over the silt settled on the riverbed. The
eternal tranquillity of the gloomy stream is ruffled only when the
winter snow melts and flows into it in rushing, muddy rivulets.
The liveliness of the tiny rivulets energizes the stream, so that it
roars and overflows its banks, sweeping away everything in its
path, and carrying it all to its exuberant neighbour, the river Prut.

In the autumn, the village women soak hemp in the murky water of the stream. At those times, the stream looks even gloomier, and its water becomes still darker and muddier, while around it spreads an unpleasant odour that lures the village children, who gather in throngs to catch the fish poisoned by the hemp.

A narrow village road stretches alongside the stream, arches over it like a little bridge, and then continues clambering upwards into the distance. On the other side of the bridge protrude tall barren hillocks covered only with sparse low grass partially scorched by the sun. In places, the earth has cracked, and its deep, yellow fissures gape from afar.

Across from these hills—where the road, rising high on a slope above the village, disappears from view—stands the lord's manor. It looks down haughtily at the little village lying in the valley, at the small church with its three domes, and at the priest's residence and orchard nestled near the church, above the turbid stream. The entire village seems to be stooping to escape the imperious glare of the lord's manor. Only the tavern, situated at the opposite end of the manor yard, stands boldly, smiling insolently through its long row of triple-paned windows.

The large manor, old, but well-maintained, has a veranda that rests on columns and a high foundation. In the spacious yard in front of the veranda there is a small lawn, and beyond it are the outbuildings. Pressing closely to one side of the manor there is a large flower bed that leads into a large orchard.

The garden is laid out in the formal English manner; the green lawns are graced by a large assortment of flowers planted in meticulously shaped beds, many varieties of foreign shrubs and grafted roses and, in the very centre, an American pine tree with widely spreading branches. A high wattle fence is screened by densely leafed lilac bushes and spiraea, while the corners of the enclosed garden are shaded by groves of young pines and elms.

A young couple was slowly strolling on the winding paths of the garden. The woman's attractive face was as pale as the first flower of spring, and her blue eyes seemed to be veiled by a cloud. The man was gazing sadly at his pale companion who, not at all cheered by the beauty of nature, was shivering in the fresh air.

They walked silently under the shade trees, through the artfully created groves, and past the carefully sculpted beds brimming with flowers.

Scattered under the widespread branches of a pine tree, clusters of blue and white anemones bloomed, enticing one from afar with their sweet fragrance. But the young woman looked indifferently at the radiant beauty of these plants, just as she looked at all her surroundings, in spite of their vigour and vitality.

It seems, however, that the man could not resist the beauty of nature; he picked a few anemones and held them out to his companion. Out of habit, she extended her hand and took the flowers from him; then they continued walking down the winding path. One of the tiny anemones had two buds on it, and a freshly formed seed-pod.

"Oh," the pale woman sighed, turning to her companion. "It's such a tiny thing, but it will be reborn in a younger generation and rejoice in a new life. My God! It's such an elementary law of nature—but that good fortune is denied us." The young woman burst into tears, and the man clasped her to his bosom. Tears were choking him as well, but he forced himself to hold them back.

They had been married for ten years, and God had given them two children—but He had taken them back as soon as they were born. And so now, when they were awaiting another little guest, they feared that fate would not permit them to rear this child.

"Perhaps you should see some doctors," the man finally suggested in a hesitant voice.

"What's the use," the woman responded resignedly. "Haven't I seen enough of them already?"

And they once again walked down the long garden paths.

"You know," the woman said after a long pause, raising her teary eyes to her husband, "a long time ago, I heard from my granny that there's a custom among the peasants—if they don't have any luck with their children, they take the lowliest beggars as godparents, and it's supposed to help."

"Hm, there are things in this world that even philosophers haven't dreamed of," the man stated. "Who knows—perhaps there is something to what you're saying," he added. And he fell deep into thought.

This conversation had a practical outcome. When the child—a little daughter—entered the world, the parents did not select godparents from among the lords. But, neither did they seek out the lowliest beggars; they chose decent, upstanding peasants, Vasyl and his wife Vasylykha, the leading householders in the village. Nonetheless, it amounted to the same thing—because a beggar is to a peasant, what even the very best peasant is to a lord.

Vasyl and Vasylykha, of course, saw things differently. They boasted among their peers that they were now on intimate terms with the lords and, from that time on, they began visiting the manor. Vasyl, however, soon stopped going—he realised that these visits were uncomfortable both for him and the lords. Vasylykha continued the visits for a longer time, but she went less frequently.

Her goddaughter, Yadzya—a name that Vasylykha always found difficult to pronounce—remembered her well, and when she became a young lady, often related humorous anecdotes to her circle of friends about the visits of her godmother, a tall, dark woman. She recalled her mother inviting the woman to sit down, and the latter complaining that something ached under her heart. Pressing her hands to her chest, she would groan: "Oh! I'm sick, so sick, my dear kinswoman." And her mother would hardly be able to restrain herself from laughing.

After a while, Vasylykha also stopped visiting them; perhaps she came to the same conclusion as her husband—that it just did not feel right. After all, lords are lords, and peasants are peasants.

Even though the lady desperately wanted the child, she did not nurse her. For one thing, breast-feeding greatly fatigued her, and for another, it was better for the child's health to hire a healthy peasant woman as a wet nurse. There happened to be two unmarried mothers in the village, both of whom could have performed this function, but the lady feared to entrust her child to them.

"The deviancy of women such as these is already present in their blood, and it could be passed on to the child," the mother said to her neighbours from the nearby villages, all of whom heartily concurred with her point of view.

Finally, a woman was found whose husband had died and left her with a month-old infant. The poor woman gladly agreed to be a wet nurse, even though she regretted having to abandon her tiny, whimpering infant to the care of others. She had no choice, however, as she was poor, lived only on what she could earn, and had an older daughter to care for. And so, placing both of her children in the care of her brother, who had married a woman with some land, she hired herself out. Her infant, whom she could no longer nurse, did not live long; the poor thing withered away, as if it were overgrown with moss, and fell asleep forever. The lord's child, however, thrived.

Having lost her own infant, the wet nurse transferred her love to the one who nestled at her breast and smiled at her beguilingly with its tiny lips. The child became very attached to her, bonding with her so closely, that when she stopped nursing her, she had to stay on as a nanny for a few more years.

Yadzya cried for a long time when her nanny finally left and was replaced by a French nursemaid who jabbered away at her in a language she did not understand. The child found her new companion so annoying, that her mother, feeling sorry for her poor little daughter, came up with the idea of inviting a girl from the village to come and play with her occasionally. She asked that the former nanny be summoned, so that such a girl could be found.

"Why, my own daughter can come as often as you like," the nanny said, only too glad that she would once again have closer ties with the manor. Of course, when you are poor, you are happy if your child is given so much as a crust of bread.

The next day the nanny brought her young daughter, who was two years older than Yadzya, to the manor. There was no formal agreement—Katrusya was to come whenever Yadzya wanted to play with her, or whenever she became fed up with the French nursemaid. The village girl was brought to the manor in a heavy, full-length shirt that she wore with an apron instead of a skirt. As this attire was not appropriate for the home of a lord, the lady saw to it that Katrusya was given one of Yadza's fine linen shirts and a skirt sewn out of one that had been discarded.

"That's much better," the lady said when Katrusya was brought to her in her new attire.

The young girl was delighted with her new clothes; she proudly examined the buttons fastening the shirt sleeves that were too short on her and admired the little skirt that had to be let down several inches. When she went to see her mother in these clothes, however, all the neighbours' children laughed at her, and Katrusya felt ashamed. She took off the shirt and skirt given to her by the lady, put on her own coarse, unbleached shirt, and said she would never again go to the manor. It was all her mother could do to convince her to go back. Even so, Katrusya refused to have the village children see her in her new clothing; therefore, when she was at home, she wore her own homespun shirt.

Yadzya truly did play much better with Katrusya than with her nursemaid, but it was the lady who had to oversee their playtime. In addition to speaking in her peasant dialect, Katrusya did not always know how to behave around a lord's child, and she often used words that were not too polite. The nursemaid could not stop her, of course—she did not understand a word of what was being said.

This arrangement pleased the nursemaid, as it made her work easier. She was happiest when the children went to play in the garden; after ascertaining that the lord and lady were otherwise occupied, she would take some time for herself, leaving the children to play by themselves.

One day, waking up with a start from her afternoon nap, the lady was seized by a compelling need to check on the children. Her maternal instinct was truly powerful, for at that very moment, she heard a child's terror-stricken screams in the distance. Yadzya was lying on the ground, and Katrusya was pounding her with her fists. The lady did not look for the pathway, nor did she pay any heed to the lawns and flowers; catching her gown on the bushes and border flowers, she hurtled straight towards the children. Completely beside herself, she tore her child out of the brutal clutches of the peasant girl, who had the upper hand. Yadzya was deathly pale, and a stream of blood from her injured nose gushed over her hands and her mother's clothing. On the ground lay a broken doll and a torn string of coral beads—visible evidence of the misunderstanding between the children.

"Water, water! For the love of God, some water!" the hysterical mother shouted.

Upon hearing this shout, servants came running from all directions, and the terrified nursemaid flew out of the thicket; the lord bolted out of his study, and the steward, covered with flour, rushed up from the mill. The lady was already pouring water over Yadzya, scarcely able to relate in what a shocking state she had found her child.

The lord sharply reprimanded the nursemaid and told the steward to take Katrusya and punish her, even though Katrusya maintained that she was not to blame, because Yadzya had attacked her first and broken her beads.

A short while later, a badly shaken Katrusya, her face livid and her lips twisted, tore across the gardens from the manor to the village. Tears streamed from her eyes, and her small chest heaved with spasmodic sobs. She ran all the way home like this, but she was too scared to go into the house, so she crawled into some clumps of tall weeds by the fence and spent the night there.

Her mother was not worried in the least—she thought that Katrusya had stayed at the manor. It was only the next day that she learned what had happened. The poor woman clutched her head in despair. Overcome with grief and anger, she wanted to give Katrusya even more of a beating, but her pity for the girl stopped her. Instead, she went to the manor and apologised for her disobedient child who, from birth, seemed to be possessed by the devil. But Katrusya never went to the manor again.

Not too long after this incident, Katrusya's mother died, and the young girl was left an orphan. Except for a few pieces of clothing, she did not inherit anything from her mother, as the latter had been an indigent lodger all her life. Katrusya's uncle took the clothing for safekeeping and hired out the young girl as a servant.

With the departure of the nursemaid, Yadzya passed into the care of a governess, who was responsible not only for looking after her and conversing with her in French, but also for teaching her various school subjects, music, and women's handiwork.

Yadzya's parents rarely went anywhere. People said that in the old days, during the lifetime of the lord's father, hardly a day went by without guests being entertained at the manor. But times change; the farm was not showing a profit, and so it was only for old time's sake that a gala name day feast was celebrated on the Feast of St. Julian and St. Julia, the saints in whose honour both Lord and Lady Solyetsky happened to be named. The parents, therefore, had plenty of time to devote to the rearing of their daughter. This was especially true of the mother; the farming operation made heavy demands on the father's time.

As Yadzya matured, she was supervised closely by her mother and governess, because it was deemed more dangerous for a maturing young lady than for a child to mingle with the common people; her mother kept a close eye on her in this regard. The young lady was permitted to address the servants only when she needed something and, even then, she could speak only to the housemaids; she did not have anything at all to do with the other servants who worked for her parents—she did not even know them. In the evenings, however, when her father joined the company of the ladies, she heard a lot about the laziness and thievery of the servants, the enormous problems their behaviour caused her father, and his ongoing struggle with those morally defective people.

Yadzya was making such good progress in her studies that before long the governess became superfluous. It was with true pleasure, therefore, that Yadzya took over the room of the governess and, with her mother's assistance, worked out a new schedule for her studies. The most time was devoted to playing the piano—she played it for several hours a day—and to improving her knowledge of French by reading French books in which her mother had marked some pages she was not to read. She enjoyed a greater freedom when it came to Polish books and, at her request, a bookcase filled with books was moved from her mother's room to hers.

She began to assume some of her mother's household tasks—ensuring that the rooms were kept neat and clean, and doling out butter to the cook; the remainder of her time she spent doing exquisite handiwork, the pastime she enjoyed above all others.

From a pretty child, she had grown into a tall, supple young woman with pleasing facial features. Her dark blond hair harmonised beautifully with her pale white face and dark blue eyes. Her shapely figure attracted universal attention and was the subject of unconditional admiration by the neighbouring nobility and the intelligentsia in the nearby town, to which she travelled every Sunday and Feast Day to attend the Roman Catholic church. The local Don Juans glanced timidly at the beautiful girl as she walked with her mother to the front pews where the cream of village society usually sat.

When she became a young lady, the home of her parents was much livelier; guests came more frequently, and the name day celebrations were celebrated with even more revelry. Most often, however, the Solyetskys exchanged visits with one particular family in the neighbourhood. The son of this family, Master Vatslaw, was especially attentive to the Solyetskys, and people predicted that it would all culminate in a marriage dance.

But things did not work out as predicted. Master Vatslaw truly did visit the Solyetskys frequently, but he ended up marrying a young lady in the province of Podillya who was twice as rich as Yadzya.

This traumatic rejection changed Yadzya forever. She could not live down this insult, even though she masked her feelings and put on an appearance of being even haughtier and happier than she had been prior to this unhappy turn of events. Her offended pride sought solace in her beauty. From childhood, she had been taught to take great pains with her appearance, and now, a preoccupation with her beauty became the primary focus of her life.

She spent hours on end arranging her hair, applying a delicate powder to her already pale and attractive face, trying on dresses, and manicuring her nails. But when she stepped in front of a mirror after completing her toilette, her fine lips involuntarily twisted into a bitter smile. Whom were her lovely eyes supposed to impress? And whom was her shapely figure to charm when, in the entire district, there was not a single suitor worthy of her hand?

This set of circumstances grieved the parents even more; therefore, after lengthy deliberations and secret discussions, they decided that it was imperative that they go to a larger city for the pre-Lenten season. As a result of this decision, the mother took the daughter to Lviv for the entire season; it was not possible to abandon the household completely, and so the father came in only occasionally to escort them to some of the major social functions. Yadzya was very pleased and happy with this turn of events; her beauty attracted many admirers, and she enjoyed great success at the socials and balls.

The prospect of a good marriage cheered the mother's heart, and she spared no cost to enhance the elegance and attractiveness of her daughter. Praise for Yadzya's loveliness, her elegance, and her overall appearance often floated to her ears, and—just as a tiny bird is carried away to distant lands on the wings of a companion stronger than itself—she was carried away with the fondest hopes for her daughter's future. Before long, however, some dissonant notes were added to the pleasing ones. From her good friends, who were rapturous in their praise of Yadzya, she occasionally heard a word or two that destroyed her good humour and dashed her hopes.

"My goodness, how lovely Yadzya looked at yesterday's ball—just like a goddess," a friend from Lady Solyetky's childhood days said to her one day. "Everyone was charmed by her, and Arthur was more attentive to her than ever. Yadzya has really made quite an impression on him. And he's such a handsome and witty young man. Just the other day, at another social, he sat down beside me—Yadzya was dancing just then with Master Zygmund L.—and said: 'Oh! Why is it that beautiful women don't have money?' He said this as if he were joking, but I could see that a sad shadow flitted across his face; he sighed and went straight to Yadzya, who had just completed a round with Zygmund."

A sad shadow crossed the face of Yadzya's mother, as well. Their presence in Lviv, their toilettes, and their overall living conditions in the city did not testify to an overly large fortune, and it was possible, therefore, that the young people—especially those in whom Yadzya was most interested—could already be talking about this. These barbs struck her right in the heart.

Foreseeing that their beloved daughter's future could be ruined, the lady strove to increase the brilliance of their home and eradicate any insufficiencies that could bring down upon them even the slightest hint of shame. With every passing day—or rather, with every evening, and with every ball—Yadzya's admirers increased in number, but not one of them made any definite overtures.

The pre-Lenten season ended. Yadzya came home with a mellow heart, a head intoxicated with compliments, and trunks filled with dresses, cotillion nosegays, and other carnival trophies, but without any tangible results—except that their small fortune was greatly diminished by their expenses in Lviv. And rumours spread noisily about Lady Solyetska's savings, over the years, on cabbage and milk, as she always looked after this particular source of income herself.

All the same, they did not give in to roguish fate, and the following year they once again spent the pre-Lenten season in Lviv. This time, as well, they returned empty-handed. The young cavaliers twirled around Yadzya, enjoyed themselves, but not one of them proposed to her.

To make matters worse, the father presented the family budget to the two women in such gloomy terms—their expenses were considerably greater than their income—that it was impossible to consider any such trips in the future. This news was a terrible blow for the two women, but they tried to bear it stoically so that the father would not be overly aware of their disappointment. The mother's eyes, however, often filled with tears when she looked at her daughter's pallid face.

"My God!" she thought, her heart breaking with grief, "why be blessed with so much beauty, and so many admirable physical and spiritual qualities, if they're to be buried, without fate and fortune, in this backwater, this cursed, remote corner where there is absolutely no hope of circumstances changing for the better." And she could not hold back the lament that issued from her heart: "This greatly desired child, given to us by God in answer to our prayers, will, like a flower in a dense forest, wither and die—her beauty wasted!"

But this cry of her aching heart terrified her. She kneeled down and raised her arms to the heavens, so they would not be angry with her because of her sinful thoughts. For who was she without that child—the child who was her whole world, the light of her life! And she felt, even more keenly, her inadequacy, her powerlessness to help her beloved daughter.

Lord Solyetsky did not suffer any less; more than once, as he gazed at his daughter, he looked like the father of Mariya—in the poem by Malchevsky, the Polish poet—who would have preferred to wear the chains of the Tartars and Turks, than to see his daughter wither so pointlessly.

To replace, at least partially, the pleasures of Lviv for Yadzya, the Solyetskys tried leading a more active social life with their neighbours; however, not only did these visits and balls prove to be almost as expensive as the costs associated with the carnivals in Lviv—they held out no prospect of obtaining the desired results. Moreover, Yadzya did not enjoy going to these functions. After the balls and other events in the city, the village socials seemed boring and dull. Furthermore, the failure of their trips to Lviv could not go unmentioned in the various levels of village gossip. This fact discouraged her even more, and she withdrew almost completely from social activity.

Her monotonous life—without any lively impressions, youthful impulses, and movement—played havoc with her sensitive soul and negatively affected her youthful organism. She pined away, grew more pale, and lost weight. Her parents, concerned about her health, turned to doctors for advice.

The doctor who was supposed to sustain the declining health of Yadzya lived in a nearby town; he had a well-developed practice and a reputation as a good physician. He had not distinguished himself with great ability in his medical studies, but he had the attributes that generally bring a doctor a good name. In addition to having a medical diploma, he was handsome and, even though he had turned thirty-five, was still unmarried. It is no wonder, therefore, that he was the object of the ardent affections of all the members of the fair sex in the little town who wanted to get married—and he seemed even more desirable because he appeared indifferent to all the efforts of the young ladies and their parents.

"If one is to marry, then one should marry wisely," he often said within his circle of friends. "If I were to marry, it would only be with a lady from 'high society.'" In his view, young ladies of that extraction had a better upbringing than city girls, and it also made more sense financially. "What kind of a dowry," he added with a smile, "can even the most highly placed government official give his daughter? At best, only a few dresses and a parental blessing— and this is too little for a man of my position. It could not support the great services to humanity that every great physician has to provide!"

The neighbouring nobility ridiculed the doctor's pretensions but, at the same time, they invited him to their homes whenever the opportunity presented itself, and often sought the doctor's advice, even in instances where it was not really required. These ploys were used most often by the lord who owned one of the smaller villages and had four unattractive daughters—all of whom were getting on in years.

Yadzya's beauty had made a great impression on the doctor when he had only a fresh diploma in his pocket and no position in the district, and he was among the local Don Juans who looked timidly at the proud young lady as she walked through the church, her head up in the air, and made her way to the front pews. Now Yadzya seemed even more attractive to him, and he occupied himself feverishly with his new patient, while the whispered rumours about the unsuccessful trips to Lviv awakened in him the most daring conjectures.

Yadzya did not pay attention to the advances made to her by the doctor; she may not have had any luck in having her wishes fulfilled—wishes that did not go beyond the normal demands of a beautiful woman—but she was accustomed from her pampered childhood to having everyone around her try to satisfy her every whim.

This expectation brought to naught the very best laid plans of the doctor, who wanted to show her that his efforts on her behalf were more than merely a doctor's diligence, that there was more to them than met the eye. He waited for even the slightest opportunity to reveal his state of mind and, one time when Yadzya happened to say that she would like to read a certain book, he brought it to her within a week, still smelling of fresh ink.

"How thoughtful of you, doctor!" Yadzya said, as she leafed through the pages. "You really are very considerate," she added after a moment, "and you've made me very happy, because this book has interested me from the time that it was first announced in the newspapers."

The doctor's heart thumped more loudly. "My consideration for you would be unlimited, my dear lady," he said, "if such were your desire, and if you would permit me to gratify your wishes." But at this point, his voice broke off.

Yadzya glanced at him with such a questioning and cold look that the doctor felt as if he had been doused with cold water. After that incident, Yadzya did not change in her behaviour towards him—she may even have become more affable—but despite this, he could not detect even the slightest nuance of a hint that would reveal so much as a shadow of a desire that he could fulfil. What annoyed him most was that he did not know if this behaviour on her part was spontaneous or deliberate.

After a lengthy and assiduous consideration of the matter, his observations convinced him that her treatment of him was deliberate. This made him lose patience and, more than once, he thought it would be the better part of wisdom to forsake his intentions vis-à-vis Yadzya; however, it appeared to be too late for that. Yadzya had entered his thoughts and feelings to such an extent that it was almost impossible for him to give up his dreams voluntarily. As it was proving too difficult to come to an understanding with Yadzya, he resolved to resort to other means.

Yadzya's mother, worried about her daughter's indisposition, often asked the doctor what he thought about the state of her health. The doctor was determined to take advantage of her concern and, at the very first opportunity, he informed the mother that the state of her daughter's health required a complete change in the way she lived.

"Are you advising me, doctor, to take her to a spa, and do you consider this to be absolutely essential, mandatory?" Lady Solyetska inquired. She was greatly alarmed, but she attempted to speak calmly.

"I do consider a change in her way of living absolutely essential and mandatory, my lady, but I did not mean to imply that it was necessary for her to go to a spa . . ."

The doctor continued speaking in this vein ardently, and at length, even though Lady Solyetska was not at all pleased to have to listen to him. The mysterious mien of the doctor irritated her, and she feared that the question of their finances might be touched upon. This reserve on the part of the mother did not coincide with the doctor's plans, but abandoning this attempt would mean to resign completely from his intentions, and he neither could nor would do so.

Just when these thoughts were torturing him, an unexpected incident opened another avenue for him. The wife of Mendel— the lessee of the tavern in the village belonging to Lord Solyetsky—fell ill. The doctor went to see her a few times, and later, when the woman's health improved, Mendel travelled to town himself to report on his wife's condition. Her recovery was certain, and Mendel, exceptionally happy, had boundless words of praise and best wishes for the doctor.

"God grant you good health, O most esteemed doctor, for saving my wife's life; everyone says there isn't another wise doctor like you anywhere. With God's help may you become still wiser and richer, and may you have the kind of wife that you desire!" As he said this, Mendel closed his eyes and kissed the tips of his fingers. The doctor laughed merrily and, like a man who falls unexpectedly into a good mood, initiated a light-hearted conversation.

There was a village for sale in the district.

"Tell me, Mr. Mendel, are you buying the village of Halanivka?" the doctor inquired, lighting a cigarette.

"If I had the money, why wouldn't I?" Mendel replied, maintaining the casual tone of the conversation.

"Are you saying you don't have the money? You probably have more money than your lord," the doctor said with studied carelessness.

"Maybe more, and maybe not; he has the village, and I have only the tavern, but," he added, lowering his voice, "I wouldn't want to have that village and all of his problems."

"What kind of problems does he have?" the doctor asked in the same indifferent tone. "He doesn't associate much with anyone, or go anywhere, or hold balls . . ."

"What kind of problems?" Mendel repeated slowly. "He inherited a lot of problems from his father, and then, for two years in a row, both ladies spent some time in Lviv—do you suppose he's been able to put that behind him?"

"Why, did it cost so much?"

"As to what it cost him—no one knows that as well as I do."

"Are you saying he borrowed money from you?" the doctor continued with his questions, hoping to use this opportunity to find out more about Solyetsky's financial situation.

"Maybe he did, and maybe he didn't—that's between the two of us, but I know that no matter what's troubling him, he won't discuss it with either his wife or his daughter—only with me." Mendel proudly adjusted the yarmulke on his head. There was something so comical about Mendel's self-important stance as he said this, that the doctor broke off the conversation and turned to another theme.

After Mendel's departure, however, the doctor fell deep into thought. His mind was working feverishly on another plan. Perhaps the wife and the daughter truly were not aware of all of Solyetsky's business matters. Perhaps they did not know the true state of their finances, so they were arrogant and unapproachable. Would it not be better to begin with Solyetsky? Deeply engrossed in his thoughts, the doctor paced the room, lighting cigarettes and throwing them down half-smoked; finally, he sat down at a desk, pulled out a sheet of writing paper, and began writing.

The writing did not go well; several times, he tore up what he had written and pulled out more paper. Finally, he shoved aside a sheet of paper filled with dense writing, pulled out an envelope, and addressed it to Solyetsky. Before he placed the letter in the envelope, he ran his eyes over the contents. It began with some words that assured the addressee of the high regard in which the writer held his entire family, and then he confessed to his intentions vis-à-vis Yadzya, expressing his unqualified hope that he would be able to earn her good will and her love.

The day after the doctor wrote the letter, Yadzya unexpectedly walked into her parents' room. She could tell by their faces that they were greatly agitated, and her father quickly shoved something into the pocket of his jacket.

"What's happened?" Yadzya asked, giving them a sharp look.

"What do you suppose?" her mother replied, pretending to be calm. "Just our usual household problems."

But Yadzya could see that her mother's eyes were filled with tears.

"No, you're hiding something from me," she said in the tone of a spoiled child. "You think you're doing the right thing; you think I can't see that you're all upset, that I can't guess that something important and unpleasant has happened."

"My dear child, rest assured that we never keep anything from you," Lady Solyetska said.

"All the same, your agitated faces are betraying you!" Yadzya replied irritatedly.

Her father cast a questioning look at his wife, who was undecidedly kneading a handkerchief in her hands.

"I think, my dear," he said to her after a moment, "that it would be better if we told her what this is all about, because she may think it's something much worse." And he pulled a letter out of his pocket and gave it to his daughter.

Yadzya stepped up to the window and began to read. The blood rushed to her face; then she turned pale like the wall, silently placed the letter on the table in front of her father, and walked out. After a while, her mother walked into her room and brought her father's reply to the doctor for her to read.

"At first, we didn't want to tell you about the letter," she said, "but now that you've found out about it, you should know what your father's reply is."

Yadzya rapidly scanned the brief letter in which Solyetsky expressed his regrets that he could not respond favourably to the doctor's stated intentions, and that they should both keep the matter confidential, as befits honourable people. Yadzya, no longer able to control herself, collapsed in a fit of nervous, spasmodic weeping. The mother clasped her sobbing daughter to her breast, and copious tears streamed from her eyes.

"Oh!" she sobbingly sighed. "We didn't hope for such a match for you." And tears once again flooded her face.

Some time later, the Solyetskys heard that the doctor had turned his amorous attentions to the four unattractive daughters of the neighbouring lord. A year later he married one of them.

Yadzya's situation did not change, but she became increasingly dissatisfied with herself and the circumstances of her life. Music irritated her, reading exhausted her, and so she sat for days on end in her room, either embroidering or doing some other handiwork.

"This is the one thing that calms me down," she said to her mother, as open-work doilies, embroideries masterfully executed in gold, and flowers embroidered with colourful silk threads emerged from under her slender fingers. All the tables and chairs were spread with beautiful coverlets, lamps and albums rested on exquisite mats, and cushions of various shapes and colours graced the sofas and couches.

The courtship of the doctor was not kept as secret as they would have wished, and some of the rumours were slanted to say that the Solyetskys would have very much liked to have the doctor as a son-in-law, but were unsuccessful in their attempts.

There were those, of course, who doubted that the Solyetskys would want a son-in-law who was not of the nobility, but even they predicted that Yadzya would be an old maid, because in these times a noble with a fortune of any kind at all was a rare bird indeed, and certainly he would not want to marry a young lady with a small and dubious dowry.

These rumours would have ended without the Solyetskys finding out about them—they had almost nothing at all to do with their neighbours—if it were not for some of their friends. Among these friends was a companion of Solyetsky's father, his coeval, comrade, and fellow soldier from the thirties. Having never married, he had run his property into the ground and now lived at the expense of creditors, who, not surprisingly, were becoming ever harder to find. In order not to make matters even worse, he sought relief for himself by assuming the role of a family friend who travelled throughout the district, staying first at one home, then another. He spent the most time with the Solyetskys, however, by reason of his close friendship with Solyetsky's father.

"May noble blood live forever!" he called out more than once at the dinner table, after emptying several glasses of wine. "I heard that Solyetsky was marrying his daughter to some blood-letter, and my hand began to itch—you have my word of honour—my hand began to itch when I heard this, and I would have punched the one who was telling me about it smack in the face if he, too, had not been a nobleman—a fact that saddened me greatly. I knew that the son of my comrade wouldn't do a thing like that, but I feared that perhaps the young lady's head was addled with some 'romances,' because, in these days," he said, turning to face Yadzya, "young ladies think only about getting married and don't consider anything else . . . "

Yadzya blushed furiously. "I'm not one of those," she said haughtily. "I would like to think, my good sir, that you would not count me as one of them."

The elderly nobleman peered at her with his rheumy, eyes, reddened with wine, but flashing with a spark of enthusiasm. "There's a true heroine for you! That's what I call pure noble blood! May nobles live forever, and may they defend their ideals—ideals that separate them from the rabble above which they should proudly hold their heads!" he proclaimed in a thunderous voice, draining a wine glass that had just been refilled.

Yadzya was deeply troubled by this scene. Not only had inconstancy in the views of friends come to the fore—views to which she was very sensitive—but, hidden in them, there was a still greater affront, in that she was taken to be a woman whose only desire was to get married.

Oh, how dearly it had cost her in terms of strength and self-control to stifle the impulses of her young organism when she was all alone and, despite her will, the healthy figure of the young doctor glimmered before her, but still, despite all her efforts, she had not managed to protect herself from the abominable rumours that offended her womanly honour by speaking about the lowest of human instincts . . .

Agitated to the depths of her soul, she returned to her room, opened the window, and picked up her work—her truest companion in moments of sadness and heartfelt anxiety. Because really, was she not living like the girl in the secluded room in "Grandfathers,"—a poem by the Polish poet, Adam Mickiewicz— who, thinking about her boring and trivial life, returned every day to her loneliness and her dreams, and was "like a traveller left alone in the wilderness, who takes a good look all around every morning, walks in a different direction every day in the hope of finding a human footprint, and every night returns to his cave with immutable despair in his soul."

From beyond the window she heard the sad, drawn out sounds of a folk song. The girls were weeding the garden and singing:

"Oh, out I went to the pond so fair,
And saw six ducks a-swimming there;
They swam in pairs, feeling great,
Each drake and duck with its mate.
Hey, when this scene I espied,
I bitterly wept, and then I cried:
"Is it Your will, Oh God so great,
That I've no fortune and no fate?
Is it Your doing, Oh God most pure,
That such torments I must endure?

"What a mournful song!" Yadzya thought. "Where do these vulgar, uncultured people get these deeply moving and highly poetical songs that are suited to almost every mood of even the most intelligent soul? Who taught them how to do this? Surely it can't be their own thoughts, their own feelings and experience? And this song is winging its way to me at a moment when I can hardly calm my agitated soul!"

She rose to her feet and wanted to close the window, but the fresh air swept over her face and stopped her from shutting herself up in a stuffy house. There was no interruption in the singing of the village girls; as soon as they finished one song, they began another. Yadzya leaned her exhausted head on the window frame. The girls were laughing cheerfully as they started singing a ribald song about a soldier who was teaching a young woman how to lie to her mother:

"Oh, in the field there's a well,
Grass grows near it in the dell,
A girl was fetching water there,
A soldier hurried to catch her there:
'Drop your buckets, oh my dove,
I want to teach you, my little love.'
'I won't drop them, 'cause I fear
My mean mother may overhear,
And she'll beat me, it's quite clear.'
'She won't beat you, have no fear,
I'll teach you what to say, my dear.'
The girl went home, full of dread;
Her mother struck her on the head.
'Oh, don't beat me, mother dear,
I'll tell you what you want to hear.
Geese flew up from the river bank
And stirred up the water with the sand.
While the sand settled in the well,
I dallied with a soldier in the dell;
We talked beneath a maple green
I and the soldier, so young and keen.'"

Yadzya considered the song thoughtfully. In her view, this song should not cross the lips of a decent girl, but these uncouth village girls were singing it freely, without any hesitation! This song lacked the more refined feelings of the first one; the relationship in it was completely primitive, and the biggest obstacle was the mother's fist. It was not surprising, however, that this obstacle could be overcome in such an easy manner. Where were the complicated reflections of the more intelligent social stratum that entangled ideas and feelings like a fine cobweb?

"In all likelihood, not one of those coarse girls would be offended by the words that were flung so insultingly in my face at the dinner table today," Yadzya thought, pressing her lips closely together. Exhausted, she shut the window and picked up a carpet she had begun working on some time ago.

A branch of a grapevine, twining its way up the wall, lowered itself on the window, as if it wanted to peek into the room. Clusters of red roses broke through the thick branches and leaves of the lush garden shrubbery; a tall, supple lily unfurled its pure, white, fragrant blossoms; and the large crown of a delicately leafed acacia embraced rows of blue lobelia in its shadow. All of them appeared to be whispering and conversing, responding to the touch of the soft light breeze.

Everything was happy, amusing itself, enjoying life. Delicate butterflies, like plucked flowers, soared in the air; a bird chirped incessantly; a small flock of merry sparrows flew from tree to tree; and the loud laughter of the girls bounced off the closed panes of the young lady's room. But Yadzya did not see or hear any of this; the needle moved mechanically in her hands, and neat, symmetric stitches covered the background of the large carpet in a dark colour.

The symmetric pursuits of Yadzya's symmetric life—a life that stretched unvaryingly through the long days—included a habit of glancing through the newspapers when her father and mother finished reading them.

One time, while looking at one of the national papers, her interest was sparked by a project initiated by upper class ladies in Lviv; they were organising a mammoth lottery to assist the poor. When one of the ladies, a family acquaintance, invited both her and her mother to participate in it, she enthusiastically agreed.

Yadzya sent her a number of her finest and most aesthetically pleasing pieces. Her excellent taste and flawless workmanship attracted everyone's attention, earning her public recognition in the newspapers and the gratitude of the committee, which sent her a personal note of thanks.

This incident assumed a great significance in Yadzya's monotonous life. Producing her works in numbers that far exceeded the requirements of even a lord's house, she was in a position to donate many of them without detracting from the decor of her own home. And so, encouraged by what had happened, she began to send embroideries to public sales organised for charitable purposes.

She liked to think, in the goodness of her heart, about the poor, distant people she was helping with her works. In her imagination arose very touching scenes from her favourite novels. She saw an unfortunate mother who, in a fit of utter despair at having nothing to give her children to eat, was about to take her own life and the lives of her children when, unexpectedly, help arrived from an unknown benefactress. Oh, what gratitude filled the hearts of these poor people, what a happy smile beautified the face of the impoverished woman, how brightly the eyes of the poor children shone!

Or perhaps, in some dark little room, an elderly man, his noble features contorted by a horrible illness, was lying in a pauper's bed. A young woman, weeping inconsolably, pressed her head to the edge of the bed. But there was no way to find the money to save the precious life or, at the very least, to ease the suffering. Then, suddenly, the door opened, and a doctor entered with the required medicine. No amount of pleading could make the doctor reveal who had sent him, and the unfortunate people surmised that it was the act of some unknown benefactress.

Her imagination caught fire. From a dark underground passage, she could feel a stream of cold and repugnant decay issuing from debased people, shoved into that abyss by a crushing poverty that deprived them of the bare necessities of life. Then, an angel-consoler miraculously appeared and led the wretched souls out of the dark alley and dank air into the broad daylight of God's world.

She had no sympathy, however, for poor people who approached the door of her home, because she was accustomed from childhood to view them as tramps who preferred begging to working. She had often heard that, in taverns far removed from the villages, all the beggars from the district gathered to drink and enjoy themselves with the money they had begged. At those times, the cripples were transformed into able-bodied people, the blind could see, and the mutes shouted and sang the loudest of all.

She herself knew one mute who often came to their home; it was said that he could talk as well as any man, and that he pretended to be mute to earn peoples' sympathy. It was also said that a certain blind woman beggar had to try very hard to keep her eyes closed when she asked people to lead her around. This deceitfulness offended her so greatly that if she did not actually shove those tramps away from herself, it was only because of the Christian tradition of mercy to which rich ladies have laid claim from time immemorial.

There was still a third category of the poor, but these people interested her least of all. They were the indigent peasants who could not survive either on their land or on their earnings. Even though it pleased her to imagine herself in the traditional role of the peasants' guardian—someone who rushed from one thatched cottage to another with a basket in her hands, bringing all sorts of help and joy—much of what she had heard about these poor people was even worse than what she had heard about ordinary beggars; it was said that their laziness and carelessness exceeded that of common vagabonds. Yes, she had often heard that entire families would rather freeze and go hungry than work. More than once, she saw her father fall into despair when he could not find workers, and she involuntarily considered the peasants to be partners in crime in the ruination of her father's fortune.

"What evil, demoralised people they are," Lady Solyetsky said one day as she entered her daughter's room. "Just imagine, my dear child—they took their money in the winter, and now, in the spring, they have no intention of working to pay it off! Daddy got angry and shoved the old foreman through the door because he didn't find him a single worker for tomorrow—so many of them have left the village to go, God knows where, to earn money. Oh, scenes like that upset me terribly—I simply can't stand them. Now my head aches so badly that I can hardly see. Almost all the money that our farmstead brings in goes to those workers, but it's still not enough for them—they're looking for better pay elsewhere. Maybe they think they'll get money without working for it!"

Yadzya was sitting in her usual spot, embroidering a white velvet antependium for the church in town. The window was half shut, even though the spring sun, shining in all its beauty, was melting the snow, drying the mud, and prying into every nook and cranny, awakening the smallest worm and the tiniest insect to new life.

Lady Solyetska, groaning and holding her head, sank into a small sofa opposite Yadzya. After a moment, a butler walked into the room and told them that old Lukynykha, whose daughter worked as a kitchen maid, had come to see her.

"My God, they don't give me a moment's peace," groaned Lady Solyetska. "If she's come, then let her wait."

Several minutes went by, and then the butler once again came in and asked if Lukynykha was supposed to wait.

"I said, go and tell her to wait," Lady Solyetska said irritably. "She's probably come to get some money for her daughter," she said to Yadzya after the butler had left. "These peasants are strange parents—everywhere else, parents take care of the children, but in a peasant family the children have to work to support the parents. They hire out a child and take all the money she earns, and then the girl becomes ornery, as if she's working for nothing. And, before you know it, that blockhead of a foreman, Matsey, comes crawling to me to complain about her. Oh," wailed Solyetska, "I've got such a pounding headache, and here I have to go and ask the old woman why she's come."

"If you can't go, then I'll ask her," Yadzya said, without raising her head from her work.

"Why should you get involved in these matters—isn't it enough that I'm plagued by all this unpleasantness?"

Yadzya, however, rose to her feet, rang for the butler, and told him to tell Lukynykha to go into the antechamber. This time, Lukynykha's request was not about money; she stated sorrowfully that her husband was so ill with the ague that she did not know what to do. She had gone to the fortune teller, and done everything that anyone had told her to do, but nothing seemed to help.

"Well, what is it you want?" Yadzya asked.

Lukynykha did not know how to begin her request. After a moment, she said: "Well, you see, my dear young lady, my daughter told me that, last year, the lord—may he be protected from the evil eye—also had the ague, but God saw to it that he was given something to save him, and so I came to see if maybe the lady would help my old man, because the ague is eating him up." Lukynykha grimaced, as if she were going to cry.

Yadzya listened silently and then relayed the message to her mother. "She says her husband is ill with the ague, and so she's asking for some medicine," Yadzya said, speaking as if she were making a report.

"What kind of medicine am I to give her?" her mother said irritably, shrugging her shoulders.

Yadzya was on her way to pass on her mother's answer to the old woman, when she remembered something, stopped halfway there, and turned around again. "Perhaps we could give her daddy's prescription from last year?" she asked her mother from the adjoining room.

"Where is a peasant going to buy some medicine? If there's any quinine powder that daddy didn't use up, you can give it to her, but that means you'll have the trouble of looking for it . . ."

Yadzya, however, touched by Lukynykha's grieving, did not begrudge the effort. And she actually succeeded in finding three doses of quinine. She gave them to Lukynykha, instructing her to give her husband one dose in the morning, another at noon, and the third one at suppertime on a day that the fever made him shake.

Two weeks later, spring, with an exuberant, youthful mischievousness, began laughing at the top of its lungs, and everything rejoiced and was happy.

"Why are you always sitting in this hole?" Lady Solyetska said to her daughter. "It's such a nice day—you should go out into the garden for a little while! Are you aware how bad it is for your health to sit around like this?"

Taking heed of her mother's suggestion, Yadzya stepped outdoors. Spring had already arrived, but it had not yet adorned itself in all its beauty. The grass was just beginning to turn green, and the trees were still bare, even though their buds were already well filled out. Without the dense wall of leaves that usually fenced the garden from the street, the entire street was visible—as if it were laid out on the palm of your hand. Wandering aimlessly, Yadzya approached the low gate and looked indifferently at the peasants who greeted her as they passed by.

"May God give you good health, young lady!" an old woman called out and, walking up to the gate, she grabbed both of Yadzya's hands and began kissing them.

"Oh, is it you, Ivanykha?" Yadzya asked.

"Lukynykha, Lukynykha, if you please, young lady," the old woman corrected her.

"How's your husband?" Yadzya asked, smiling at her own mistake.

"Oh, my dear lady, it was as if someone waved a hand over him and took his illness away. May God give you good health and a good life! He took it, and the fever was gone, as if washed away."

"Did you give it to him three times during the day, as I said?"

"No—all at once. There was only a tiny bit in each of the packets, and the old man said there was nothing even to look at three times, and so he swallowed it all in one gulp. Oh, but it tasted awful, really awful! He said that God should protect anyone from having to take it!"

That year, the spring brought a lot of ague, and when word spread through the village that Yadzya had medicine for it, not a day went by without someone coming around to beg for some. Yadzya's conscience did not let her refuse; she got several doses of quinine on her father's prescription and gave it out to those who asked for it. In doing this, Yadzya did not even stop to think that she had fallen into the role of benefactress of the village. It was the role she had long imagined in her dreams, and which she thought of as belonging to a bygone era—a time barely retained even in the memory of the older generation—when people were not yet demoralised.

Encouraged by the unpremeditated succour she was able to afford the sick, she came up with the idea of setting up a traditional pharmacy like the one her great grandmother had been known for. The patients came, often causing her many problems when they tried to describe their illnesses. Mostly, they complained—just as her godmother used to—that something pained them under their heart and stopped their food from going down. Yadzya gave them bitter herbs to drink, but they helped virtually no one.

The women usually came with the request that the ill person wanted to have some milk or cheese, and when Yadzya disallowed that and gave them medicine instead, the women accused her of being stingy. They said she gave out only drops and forbid them to eat, without so much as asking if the sick person even had anything to eat. They believed that if the patient had some good food, he just might get well, but all she said was that it would hurt him—as if food could ever hurt a man; as if a God-fearing Christian could live, if he did not eat. Perhaps this was why the number of Yadzya's patients decreased; after a while, not nearly as many came as had come at first.

These new interests engaged Yadzya's attention for some time, but they were not capable of reviving her waning energy. A quiet sadness settled in her soul and was reflected on her mournful face and pensive blue eyes. Her movements were lethargic, and only rarely did a smile flicker on her pale lips. Time passed joylessly, drearily.

For Yadzya, winter was the most depressing season, especially the pre-Lenten period. While the world rejoiced and enjoyed itself, she swallowed her tears as she glanced through the write-ups in the newspapers about the grand balls, the banquets, and the outfits worn by the women. In that festive season, filled with so many special occasions, Yadzya had to satisfy the demands of her young body for activity with subdued walks in the fresh country air with her mother.

It was already the middle of February. The air was calm, the sun was casting its pale rays across a misty sky, roofs and branches were covered with a thick layer of clean, white snow, and even the fence pickets seemed to be wearing tiny white caps. There was no wind, and it was the birds that knocked fluffy white handkerchiefs from the trees as they flew by.

Dressed lightly but warmly, Yadzya and her mother were conducting a highly animated conversation as they walked down a road well-packed with snow. The mother had revived an idea that had taken root at the time of the doctor's wooing of Yadzya, but had since remained dormant—a trip to a spa. She had not been in a financial position to think about it for quite some time, but now that her savings from the milk and cabbage had accumulated into a tidy sum, she could afford—with some minimal help from her husband—to take Yadzya out of the village for at least one season.

"I'd like to go somewhere to a spa with you," she said to her daughter. "It's not so much for the sake of one's health, but simply because continuing to vegetate in this village is intolerable."

Yadzya shrugged impatiently. "I can guess at your intentions," she replied in a slightly irritated tone. "You plan to put me on display once again, in the hope that I'll appeal to someone. But, if you weren't successful in your attempts during the May carnivals, then the spa season will be even less fruitful."

Her mother fell silent. Yadzya knew that her harsh words had hurt her mother, so she continued the conversation in a more gentle tone. What she said, however, revealed still another painful facet of her emotional state—namely, that it was distressing for her to be an onerous burden on her parents. This topic, such a sensitive one for both the ladies, and so complicated in its various permutations, absorbed them completely. It was only when they reached the other end of the village that they realised that they had gone too far.

What were they to do? In front of one of the peasant cottages stood a man, tying bundles of straw.

"Could you go to the manor and request that horses be sent to meet us?" Lady Solyetska asked as she approached the gate.

"Hey, Yurko!" the householder called out to his son, a husky, strapping youth, who was helping him tie the bundles. "Run to the manor and tell them to send some horses for the lady—and hurry!"

Yurko flung his jacket over his shoulders, jumped over the fence, and took a shortcut to the manor.

"He'll be there right away," the father said, following his son proudly with his eyes. Then, drawing nearer to the ladies, he doffed his cap and kissed their hands, saying. "Glory to Jesus Christ!"

"Glory forever!" the ladies responded.

"Your ladyships are taking a little walk?"

"We decided to go out; it's such a nice day."

"Well, why not—it's not cold, so that's good. Oh, he'll be there right away," he added, pointing in the direction of the manor. "But there are no horses in sight yet."

"Thank you; we'll go ahead a bit, and perhaps we'll meet up with the sleigh," Lady Solyetska said, moving away.

The peasant bowed down low and went back to tying his bundles. "Maybe you should go for a walk as well, Matrona," he said to his wife, who had come out of the house when she heard her husband talking to someone.

Matrona, a tall, lean woman with sharp facial features, shrugged her shoulders indifferently.

The ladies walked slowly to meet the horses. A few houses down the road stood a small cottage; on the earthen embankment sat a small boy, dressed only in a shirt, and holding a piece of rye bread.

"The poor child! He looks so sickly," Yadzya commented to her mother when she saw the child. "God! How can these people survive—our children would die from the cold and from eating food like that."

"It all depends on what you're used to; they're accustomed to it, so it doesn't harm them," her more practical mother responded.

But Yadzya could not refrain from talking to the little fellow: "Why are you sitting outside, my child? Why don't you go into the house?"

Looking at the lady, but not understanding her—she was speaking Polish—the child jumped up in tears and ran into the cottage. Yadzya, who was beginning to have the enviable reputation of a benefactress, was not pleased that a child was scared of her. She decided to go into the cottage to convince the child that she was not someone to fear.

Her mother advised her against it—entering a stuffy peasant's home after being in the fresh air is both unpleasant and dangerous for a person in delicate health. She did not, however, forbid her daughter to do so; the way things were, she could not secure her daughter a stimulating life in this remote village, and these acts of charity appeared to hold some interest for her.

Yadzya stepped into the cottage. On the bed lay a young woman covered with a heavy hempen cloth. Her lips were dry, her eyes were glazed, and her cheeks were flaming. A bulky, grimy pillow had slipped from under her head and fallen to the floor; the sick woman tried to raise her lowered hands, but lacked the strength. Two children were fighting on the floor over a plate of some kind, and the older boy, who had been outside, was now sitting motionlessly on the bench, peering out the window to see what the ladies would do next.

When Yadzya appeared in the doorway, the children screamed wildly and clambered up to the sleeping area atop the brick oven. The sick woman turned slowly, and her eyes fastened on Yadzya, standing before her like an apparition. Seeing the suffering of the helpless woman, Yadzya forgot all about the children and her reason for entering the cottage.

"What's wrong, my good woman?" she inquired gently and, drawing nearer, she picked up the pillow and tucked it under the woman's head.

A ray of tenderness flickered over the face of the sick woman; she wanted to say something, but could only cough and groan. The children, who had wedged themselves into a corner of the oven-bed, once again started bawling. It seemed to them that the lady wanted to harm their mother.

"Hush, children, hush!" the mother said in a barely audible voice, and she groaned once more as she clutched her chest.

"What is it? Are you having sharp pains there?" Yadzya asked.

"Oh, they're sharp, my young lady, very sharp. I've been lying here for three days, and there's no one to feed my children or give me anything." The ailing woman spoke in short broken phrases.

"Doesn't anyone come to see you?" Yadzya asked.

"My husband's sister and my kinswoman came—they placed some leeches on me and left. How can they stay with me? They have their own small children, their own work. They dash in for a moment and run off again; all they can do is give me a spoonful of water."

"But where's your husband?"

The woman gestured hopelessly. "He died a year ago." Her fever must have been very high, for it was cold in the cottage, but she was covered with only a thick hempen cloth; a crumpled coat lay at her feet.

"I'll send you some medicine," Yadzya finally said. "You have to pour a bit of it into some water. And you should burn some straw in the stove, because it's not good to lie in the cold like this."

The woman did not thank her, but two big tears rolled down her face, and this was the greatest reward that Yadzya could have received.

When she walked out of the cottage, the horses were standing on the road, and her mother was sitting in the sleigh, wrapping her feet in a sheepskin.

"You were there such a long time, my child! I'm completely frozen," her mother said by way of a mild reproach.

On the way home, Yadzya told her mother in what condition she had found the sick woman, and added that she had promised to send her some raspberry juice and at least a small bundle of straw. She was worried, however, that her father might not be pleased, because he sometimes looked askance at his daughter's philanthropic deeds when they came at his expense.

"Who is the woman in the cottage?" Yadzya asked the coachman when she was getting out of the sleigh in front of the manor.

"If you please, young lady, that's Katrusya Petryshyn, who was married to Maksym Ivanyshyn," the coachman, a peasant youth dressed for his job in a wide coat and an oilcloth cap, answered in his broken Polish.

Yadzya smiled despite herself. "That certainly helped me a lot," she said softly to herself. "These people don't even know how to name themselves properly; they keep dragging out the names of their ancestors—as if they were descended from God only knows what sort of eminent lineage."

***

While Yadzya was growing like a hothouse flower, dependent on the care of a solicitous hand and carried in a vase from room to room and from window to window, Katrusya, like a wild weed, had to rely on her own strength, and made her way in the world through her own efforts.

After the death of her mother, her uncle hired her out to care for a child. But Katrusya, quickly wearying of the screaming child and the blows of its mother, abandoned her work and fled to her uncle's home. Her uncle beat her and made her go back, but Katrusya did not remain there for long. Afraid to live in her uncle's home, she drifted through the village, going from one cottage to another. The villagers began to call her "the good-for-nothing," because she did not stay anywhere for any length of time—no matter where she found work, she left after a little while.

Finally, Katrusya did stay for some time in one household. The people in it were no longer young; their children were married, and their youngest son—they had hoped he would remain with them—had died as a youth, and so they were left like orphans. Katrusya liked being with them, because she spent whole days in the cottage by herself. The man of the house would set out with a servant for the fields and, as soon as he was out of the gate, the mistress would take a jug of milk or a freshly baked flatbread, tell Katrusya what she should do, and either go to visit one of her married children—where she would often stay until evening—or take a net and go to the river to catch fish.

Katrusya was with them for several years, and during that time she grew up into an attractive young woman. Tall and strong, her hair was as black as coal, and fine eyebrows accented her shiny dark eyes; her round, dusky face blazed with health, and her full, red lips looked like ripe cranberries. When she got all dressed up on a Sunday and stood at the gate, all the young men who strolled down the street stared at her, and if one of them started up a conversation with her, she would laugh heartily, and her laughter sounded like peas rolling around in a sieve.

"All she wants to do is stand out in the street and grin at the young men!" muttered Maksym, a youth who served with her.

"What's it to you? What business is it of yours?" Katrusya fired back at him.

"If only you did your work the way you mind the street!"

"Are you saying I don't do my work? If only you worked as hard!"

"Some worker you are!" Maksym laughed at her.

"Some worker you are!" Katrusya snapped back.

As time went on, Maksym noticed that Ivan, the bailiff's son, was beginning to hang around the cottage.

"So, it's barely got its feathers, and it's already beginning to lead the boys around!" Maksym muttered angrily, but then he just gestured in disgust because it really did not concern him.

The mistress also must have surmised that Katrusya had a sweetheart, and she began to watch her more closely. Katrusya, however, knew how to wriggle out of things. When she knew Ivan was in the vicinity, she would find some work to do outside; she either had to pick up the washed shirts off the fence, or go to the barn to see why a chicken had squawked—maybe a skunk had crept up on it—or, and this kept her the busiest, she had to make sure the pigs were all right. It used to be that the pigs ate just as God had intended them to, but now, she had to watch them closely; they would either turn over the bucket, or refuse to eat, and so you had to stand watch over them. And when everyone had gone to sleep, Katrusya quietly crept out of the cottage and stayed out with Ivan until midnight.

Maksym, who slept in the barn, often heard Katrusya cautiously opening the door as she sneaked out to meet Ivan. He could hear then whispering and laughing, and at times he was so hopping mad that he had a hard time restraining himself from jumping up and beating both of them.

This romance continued for an entire summer.

In the autumn, word spread through the village that Ivan had won the hand of a girl who was the daughter of the richest man in the village. Her father was against the marriage, but the people said that the young girl loved Ivan very much, and that she had gone to a fortune teller to have her cast a spell to change her father's mind.

"Well, Katrusya, aren't you sorry to lose Ivan?" Katrusya's friends asked her when they heard he was marrying another girl.

"Huh, he's not the only fish in the sea!" Katrusya responded, shrugging her shoulders unconcernedly.

Not long afterwards, Katrusya began to act up whenever the mistress spoke to her, and finally she said she was leaving.

"The devil knows what's got into the girl!" the mistress said to her husband. "She's been here so many years, and now she wants to leave. Well, she's an orphan, and I say she should stay, and maybe she'd learn to get along with people—but she doesn't want to, and God knows what she'll end up doing. Do you suppose someone has put her up to it, or what?"

Maksym also was surprised when he heard that Katrusya wanted to go away. "Why are you leaving? Don't you like it here? Do you think you'll be better off someplace else?"

He tried talking to her, but Katrusya gave him such a tongue-lashing that he did not utter another word.

"Could she be planning to go to the neighbouring province of Bukovyna to work in the tobacco fields?" Maksym wondered. "They're taking workers to Bukovyna now, so maybe someone has convinced her to go, or maybe she's fleeing the village because she's grieving over Ivan. Stupid girl—as if Ivan were the only man in the world!"

A week later, a small cart rolled along the wide road that came down from the mountain into the valley. The air was cold and damp; grey winter clouds were hovering on the horizon, snow lay on the fields and in the ditches, the earth was still frozen solid and where there was no snow the ground lay in frozen lumps. The cart, packed with straw—it was sticking out on all sides through the tattered top—was bouncing over the stones and sliding around on the damp lumps of earth, its cracked, worn wheels clattering noisily. An emaciated, light bay horse, whose ribs could be counted from afar, was harnessed to the beam with a strap.

On the cart, wrapped in a huge, faded shawl whose original colour could not be discerned, sat a young Jew wearing a black hat with a round brim. He was urging on the wretched horse by cracking a short whip and tugging at the knotted hempen reins. The horse, however, was in no hurry and, accustomed both to blows and to whips, dragged its battered hooves over the uneven road. It was only during the descent from the mountain into the valley that the horse started running, and then the cart bounced violently from side to side, and its wheels clattered even more loudly.

The cart drove into the village and, without turning off, stopped at the tavern. There, on the veranda supported by six bare wooden posts, was the owner, Abramko. With a pipe in his teeth, and wearing a long coat tied at the waist with a silk belt, he was pacing back and forth and looking around with large, staring, grey eyes. He saw the approaching cart but, paying no attention to it, he continued sucking on his pipe and walking about indifferently. It was only when the cart came to a stop in front of the tavern that

Abramko halted, spit out some bitter saliva, and placed the stem of the pipe back on his lips.

A nimble Jew, dressed in sturdy high boots and a short Hungarian fur coat, jumped from the cart. "Good day!" he said in Yiddish to Abramko, as he removed the harness from the horse.

"Good day!" Abramko responded. "You've come out to the villages?"

"To the villages," the newcomer replied, throwing his horse a bit of straw.

"To hire workers for the tobacco fields?" Abramko continued in the same tone of voice.

"Well, it's time—March isn't far away."

Abramko, raising an eyebrow, tamped his pipe with a thick finger. "But this year you're going to have problems with them," he said slowly, as if he were straining every word through his nose.

"Why so?" the newcomer inquired a trifle uneasily.

"Our people have decided to plant tobacco; the lord is planting ten *morgy [acres];* the priest, it seems, is also planting a bit; and the steward, who retired from working for the lord, has his own land and is also going to plant some; and two of them have their own tobacco workers."

"What are they paying?"

"The same as you're paying in the village of Hrabyntsi—thirty *rynski [dollars]* for the summer, and the girls are getting twenty-five *rynski* and a kerchief."

"And will there be whiskey?" the newcomer asked, casting an oblique glance at Abramko.

"Well, there might be at the lord's place, but it's too much of a burden for the steward, and the priest wants to stay sober."

"Well, well! Let him remain sober," the newcomer responded, and they both smiled.

"Where have you seen a peasant without whiskey?" Abramko said, after a moment's pause, and he stroked his voluminous yellowish-grey beard.

"If a peasant didn't get drunk and fight, he wouldn't consider life worth living," the newcomer said, bursting into raucous laughter.

Abramko's wide face also brightened, and his lips parted so widely that he had to hold on to his pipe to prevent it from falling.

"Klugman's steward from Hrabyntsi has come to hire tobacco workers," the people said, and the news spread through the entire village as the newcomer scurried up and down the streets. The steward rushed about as if someone had salted his tail; he ran from house to house and stopped people on the road. The village was bubbling like a boiling pot. Some of the peasants sought out the steward themselves and went with him into other homes.

A week later, the steward once again arrived in the village, but this time he came with large horses and two huge wagons with side ladders. He had come to pick up the workers who had agreed to work on the tobacco fields of the wealthy buyer in Bukovyna and take them to Hrabyntsi for the entire summer.

Maksym's prediction came to pass. Katrusya struck an agreement with the trusted steward of the wealthy Bukovynian buyer to work in the tobacco fields.

"The poor orphan, the poor thing," the kind young man thought. "No one will stand up for her; no one cares about her. 'Do whatever you want to do,' everyone will say. But she's so foolish, that she doesn't know what she's doing; she knows how things are for her now, but does she know what she'll be like by the time she returns? The village of Hrabyntsi has ruined more than one young girl. I know—I'll tell her not to go; maybe she'll listen to me, even though she's a stubborn girl who doesn't take kindly to advice."

Every year, the people who were planning to go to Hrabyntsi gathered at the tavern and the steward picked them up there. Not far from the tavern, stood a wayside cross with thick willows planted around it. Maksym, standing under one of the willows, did not take his eyes off all those that he thought would be going to Hrabyntsi. Among them were his friends, but he did not want to see them, and he hid behind the thick willow when any of them came near the cross.

The figures of two girls became visible in the distance. Maksym immediately recognised Katrusya and Yaryna. Dressed in black jackets and red kerchiefs, and carrying small bundles, they were walking along, conversing cheerfully. Because Maksym was standing behind the willow, they did not see him, but he had a good veiw of them, and he took pleasure in Katrusya's voice, ringing in the distance. And that voice was to vanish somewhere in Bukovyna and ring out among strangers instead of her own people! The young women drew nearer. The large flowers on Katrusya's kerchief caught his eye. That kerchief always hung on a hook in the corner, and Maksym would have recognised it even if there had been hundreds of young women, for he knew every leaf on it, every flower, and every bit of fringe. And he once again became sad because he would no longer see those large, round flowers, those fine, long, red fringes . . .

When the girls were very near, Maksym walked up to them; he wanted to say something, but did not know how to begin. Fortunately, Yaryna stepped into a cottage, and Katrusya was left alone by the gate.

"So you're off to Hrabyntsi, Katrusya?" he asked casually, as if he had not been waiting for her and had just happened to come by.

"Why are you asking me?" Katrusya responded curtly.

But Maksym, accustomed to Katrusya's sharp tongue, kept on talking. "I'm not asking, but I can see that you're taking off someplace."

"How do you know that I'm taking off?"

"Well, you've a bundle in your hands."

"It's not mine—it's Yaryna's."

"You're only saying that; I know you're going to Hrabyntsi."

"Even if I were, so what? Can't I?"

"Maybe you can, and maybe you can't—you have your own mind; but I just want to advise you not to go to Hrabyntsi. Why would you want to go there, Katrusya?" He was speaking in such a soft and tender voice that Katrusya, glancing quickly into his eyes, burst out laughing at the top of her lungs.

This laughter offended Maksym. "Why are you laughing?" he asked abruptly.

"Well, who am I supposed to cry for—maybe you?"

"For me, or not for me, but maybe there are those that you should cry for!"

Maksym wanted to say more, but Yaryna ran out of the cottage and waved at Katrusya, indicating that they should hurry along.

"Oh, it's you," she said, when she saw Maksym. "Good-bye; we're off to Hrabyntsi."

"Good-bye!" Katrusya added, as well, and they set out again.

After they had walked for a bit, Katrusya glanced back, grabbed a lump of earth, and threw it at Maksym. From where he was, Maksym could see Katrusya's flashing dark eyes and white teeth. All the workers who were supposed to travel to Hrabyntsi were already at the tavern, where two huge ladder-wagons were waiting for them. The steward ran out of the tavern, counted the workers, and told them to get on the wagons.

The young men and women climbed into the wagons with a great deal of noise and shouting. The youths shoved the girls, and the girls laughed, cursed, and used their fists to give as good as they got. The hubbub spread throughout the village; young men parted with their comrades, and young women with their girlfriends. Some passed along messages, while a few mothers ran out of the cottages, held back the horses, and gave their daughters or sons a fresh flatbread or a bundle of clothing.

After they left behind the little town that stood on the boundary of Bukovyna, they travelled through villages that did not differ from those on the other side of the boundary—the same small cottages and yards, except that, perhaps, more of them had roofs and chimneys.

The people, however, looked different. The men had long hair that hung down their backs, their shirts were belted with wide, woven belts, and they wore small silk kerchiefs around their necks. The women wore skirts, but they were of a darker fabric than the skirts worn by the girls back home.

The young women on the wagons found it funny that the women's hair, braided into a tight knot on the very tops of their heads, jutted high above a thin, white kerchief. And even though the Bukovynians spoke Ukrainian, it sounded strange that instead of saying: "Glory to Jesus Christ!"—they simply said: "Good evening!"

"They greet people like Jews! Either they're not christened, or they think we don't believe in Christ!" the tobacco workers said.

They laughed the most, however, whenever a Romanian walked by and said: "*Buna sara [Good evening]*!"

Katrusya could not sit still; she had something to say to everyone. She tugged Fedko, who was deaf, by the ears; he cursed her and went at her with his fists, but she leaned back just in time, and he hit the ladder so hard that it rang out, and everyone shrieked with laughter.

But there was even louder laughter and shouting on the other wagon. A small, grimy gypsy child, with black hair and coal-black eyes, and wearing an open shirt, came through the gate of one of the cottages, dragging a large fiddle behind him.

"Once a gypsy always a gypsy—it can scarcely lift itself off of the ground, and it's already grabbing a fiddle!" the young men said.

"That's the kind of child to have!" Katrusya said, roaring with laughter.

"Well, what's the problem? Anyone who wants to can have a child like that; more than one young woman has got herself one, so you can too," said Matviy, a small, dark young man who was sitting beside Katrusya.

"The plague take you! You're comparing me to gypsies? Watch out you don't find yourself a gypsy woman!"

"What if I do? Isn't a gypsy girl like any other?" the youth responded haughtily.

"Why not? A bitch is also a dog!" the steward driving the horses intruded into the conversation.

"But all the same, a gypsy is not a man!" Katrusya said in response to his remark.

"How do you know he's not a man? Did you give him his soul?" Yaryna asked.

"Because he isn't a man," Katrusya maintained stubbornly. "Look here, when Ulasiy or Fedko walk through our village, no one says it's a man walking—they all say it's a gypsy walking."

"She heard bells ringing, but didn't know where—she wanted to prove it to us, but she knows nothing about it! I swear it's not like that at all!" Matviy said. "Where do people say things like that?"

"Oh, you know everything!" Yaryna defended Katrusya.

"I'm telling you—people don't say things like that."

"Then tell us what people say!"

"This is what people say," the young man said firmly. "When they see a man and a gypsy walking down the road, no one will say that people are walking, only that a man and a gypsy are walking—but she's babbling on about Fedko and Ulasiy."

"And furthermore," another young man spoke up, "what has she got against Ulasiy and Fedko? Today, Fedko is probably in his dump, pumping the bellows and forging teeth for a harrow, while the worms finished off Ulasiy long ago."

"My grandfather remembered Ulasiy." Petro, the strongest youth in the village, became involved in the conversation. "He used to tell us that one time he was walking on the bridge, and Ulasiy was there, standing on guard. It was bitterly cold, and he was wearing only a worn little jacket. He stood there and stretched his hands towards the moon, thinking that it was the sun. My granddad asked him: 'What are you doing, Ulasiy?' And he replied: 'I'm warming myself in the sun, because I fell in the water and I'm very cold.' The frost hewed his face some more, and he said: 'One side of my face is warm now, so it's time to warm the other.' And he turned his back to the moon."

"It's easy to get along in this life if you tell lies, but if you live truthfully, you aren't allowed to breathe," Matviy, raising his eyebrows, spoke up against Petro.

"If only you weren't allowed to breathe once and for all!" Katrusya said. "Why, you're the biggest liar of all!"

"And you don't even know how to lie, and yet you lie by trying to give us some proof."

Katrusya, disgusted with all this, turned her back on Matviy.

At the other end of the wagon, a girl and a youth were sitting together, holding one another in an embrace.

Katrusya, catching sight of the loving couple, sang out in a shrill voice:

> "Oh, a sharp wind blows from the mountain above,
> Press your face to mine, let me warm it, my love!"

"She always knows how to make fun of others, but someone should sing a song about her!" the youth who was embracing the girl said.

"I'll sing one for her," Yaryna said.

"And so will I," another girl spoke up bashfully. Her name was Dotsya, and she was the quietest girl in the village.

The girls started singing:

> "Oh, the village can't be seen, just the church domes,
> In that village is my love . . ."

"That's not the way," Petro interrupted. He began to sing, and the other young men joined in.

"I can't put on my belt, I can't put on my shoe,
And, oh, my dearest darling, I can't forget you.

"Why don't you sing the rest of the song?" Katrusya inquired when the youths stopped singing.

"There is no more," Petro replied.

"Oh, but there is," Katrusya said, picking up the song:

"I put on my belt and I put my on my shoe
And, oh, my dearest darling, I forgot about you."

But, before Katrusya finished her song, everyone was occupied with something else.

An old woman, sitting on the earthen embankment abutting a cottage, was wearing a red fez on her head; strands of grey hair hung down from under it.

"What the heck is that?" Yaryna called out, pointing at the woman with her finger.

Craning their necks to get a good look, they burst out laughing.

"Holy Mother of God! What's that on her head?" Dotsya asked—she had never been in Bukovyna before.

"It's a fez," Matviy explained.

This broke the girls up even more. "It's a pheasant, is it? She's put a red pheasant on her head!"

Katrusya, who also had never seen anything like it before, stood up in the wagon to get a better look. At that moment, because there was no bridge, the wagon began rolling down into a ditch. Katrusya swayed and toppled on the steward's shoulders. The steward grabbed her by the hem of her clothing and pulled her on his knees. But Katrusya tore free of him, punching him so hard in the neck that his hat flew off his head and fell between the horses.

"Oy, vey, my hat! Whoa! Stop!" the steward shouted, trying to reign in the horses. The hat tumbled from under the wagon into the ditch, but the horses did not stop, even though the steward was pulling on the reins with all his might.

"Come on, fellows! Somebody get my hat!" the steward begged the young men.

"That'll be the day! Next time, don't get fresh with the girls!" the youths said.

"Go and get the hat yourself," Matviy added in a dignified tone.

The steward, seeing he was not getting anywhere, climbed down, picked up his hat, and brushed off the mud.

"That's the way to do it! That's what you should have done in the first place," the boys jeered at the steward, while Katrusya continued shooting dirty looks at him.

While the steward was picking up his hat, the other wagon, with the rest of the tobacco workers, got ahead of them and moved on at a good clip. The steward whipped his horses as well, and the wagons started racing each other.

"Whoa! Whoa!" both coachmen yelled at the same time, but it was too late—the wagons bumped together. There was a cracking sound, and one of the wagons tipped to one side. Everyone jumped down from the wagons. The coachmen swore and began quarrelling—the axle in one of the wagons was broken.

Now the trip was even merrier, because everyone had to climb into one wagon to get to Hrabyntsi. It was so tight, that a few of the young men preferred to walk alongside the wagon that was hardly crawling along. But, as the saying goes: "Good company and good conversation make the miles fly by," and so, almost before they realised it, they arrived in the village. They crossed a few streets and came out on a wide road that led to the manor.

Hrabyntsi was formerly owned by Armenian lords. The first owner traded in oxen and sheep, taking them to Vienna and Moldava, where he made a tidy profit; finally, he stopped dealing, bought Hrabyntsi, and became a lord. Even though his son acquired more of the attributes of a noble and lived in a lordly style, the older people still remembered that he used to sell sheepskins, cleaning and weighing the raw fleece himself. But he had become a true lord by marrying a Polish woman—not too affluent, but from the highest nobility—and, after that, everything changed.

The spacious old manor was replaced by a small palace. In the orchard, the old fruit trees were chopped down and replaced by acacias, birches, and pine trees; in the older lady's vegetable garden, large paths were laid, and many varieties of foreign flowers were planted. The younger lady did not run the household, but there was a steady stream of guests, and the gate to the manor was almost never shut.

After a few years of this kind of living, people noticed that old Klugman, well known as a usurer throughout the district, began to visit the lords more frequently. Even though he never entered the manor itself, always maintained a self-effacing manner, and waited in the servants' quarters until the lord found the time to speak with him, the people began to predict that something untoward was afoot. Later, Klugman began to appear at the lord's estate more often, driving right up to the manor house itself. And if no guests were present, the lord and lady invited him into their home and spoke with him as with an equal.

One night, the lord fell ill, and he died a short time later. Klugman, like an evil spirit, began to haunt the house that he had visited, as if he were a close friend, for so many years. He argued and yelled, and the lady cried and fainted. Finally, the relatives got together and, after some long, hard bargaining, Klugman was given Hrabyntsi in payment for what was owing to him, and a small village was bought in Halychyna—a neighbouring province—with the remainder of the payment.

After some time, everything in Hrabyntsi changed. The wide gate fell off its hinges, leaving two brick columns that seemed to to mock the former glory of the home. The fence around the garden warped every which way, and broken pickets were replaced with ordinary branches. The manor was peeling, the eaves-troughs were sagging, and the large, grimy windows gaped like the eyes of a corpse at the wide yard and the neglected buildings.

As the wagonload of tobacco workers drove up, a flock of chickens scattered in all directions from a huge mound of manure in the middle of the yard; not far from this mound, pigs were rooting mercilessly, throwing the dirt up in the air with their long snouts and digging out the remaining shrubs in the old flower beds. The long border of formerly attractive spiraea, from which individual shrubs had been rooted out, now looked like a gaping mouth with missing teeth A big, black cow, her horns entangled in the spindly branches, was angrily trying to make a path for herself through the bushes; behind her bellowed two large calves.

All around, there was the hum of farming activity. Some men were pulling wagons out of sheds, others were setting out to the fields with ploughs, while still others were carrying sheaves from the barnyard into the barn. The monotonous clattering of threshing machines came from the barn, while the wheezing of bellows and the clanging of a blacksmith's hammer issued from the smithy.

The wagon drove right up to the barn, and out of it came a tall stout Jew. He was dressed in a long coat trimmed with fur, and wore a hat slightly tipped to one side, from under which could be seen a black velvet yarmulke and hair that was trimmed to the scalp. You could tell at first glance that he was the owner, the hub of the activity that milled around him.

The steward went up and spoke to him in Yiddish. Running his eye over the new arrivals climbing out of the wagon, the owner counted them on his fingers. The steward motioned to them, and they all followed him into an enclosure attached to the manor house. As soon as they entered it, they found themselves in a large, long room with a huge pile of corncobs. Two workers were selecting the bigger cobs and throwing them into a smaller room; the cobs often struck the wall, knocking off the stucco. Adjacent to this room was a still larger one, in which rye was heaped up against both sides of the walls. Small boards were missing from the parquet flooring, as if they had been dislodged by blows from a threshing flail.

"Come along, come along," the steward said and, walking across the room with the rye, he opened the door to a fourth room that was called the office. It was clean and had very little furniture in it. In front of a tattered red sofa in one corner, stood a card table with a broken leg and a few chairs, one of which was upholstered with elegant and expensive fabric. The walls were almost completely bare except for a small tilted mirror that hung close to the ceiling; a clock with a glass cover and a gold frame jangled on the opposite wall. Over the sofa hung a small picture embroidered on a paper backing. In the centre was a goose or a duck, with tall legs like that of a stork.

In a bigger armchair sat a young shaven Jew with blond sideburns, peering intently at a book. Upon seeing the steward with the workers, he reluctantly rose to his feet, moved to a desk standing under the window, and drew a thick, long book out of a drawer. Then he lifted a straight pen from an inkstand, cleaned the steel nib on the hem of his jacket, and waited to hear what the steward had to say.

As the steward began reading the names of all the workers, the blond Jew rapidly wrote them down. The steward spoke Ukrainian well, but the Jew who repeated the dictated names garbled them so strangely, with a German-Yiddish accent, that the workers could hardly refrain from laughing.

"Don't laugh—he's Klugman's son-in-law," warned Petro, who had been in Hrabyntsi more than once.

After the names of all the new arrivals were written down, the steward assigned everyone a job. He sent some of them to help pick over the corncobs, and others to the threshing machine. He took Katrusya, two other girls, and three young men to help in the hotbeds that were set up on the lord's land beyond the village, where most of his fields were.

A tall house and well-built farm buildings could be seen from afar. But here, like in the manor yard, the stucco was falling off, and the roofs, patched with shingles, had the appearance of a piebald heifer. It was in this area that the steward was truly the master; all the workers were under his care, and they had to live and eat here during the time that they worked in the tobacco fields.

In the garden, where the hotbeds were to be built, the snow had been hauled away, and large mounds of manure had been carted in. A few workers, putting the final touches on hotbeds that were five or six fathoms in length, were placing boards around them; young men were filling the beds with manure, while girls were hauling frozen soil in baskets and wheelbarrows. Some distance away stood a tall, fairly young man, who was using a stick to measure off a spot for new hotbeds.

"Well, he's bringing more workers," he said when he saw the steward approaching with the new arrivals, "but there still won't be enough people to do the work."

"Well, now! You've really worked hard," the steward said, shaking his head.

"Why don't you try measuring with a stick all day long, then you'd know 'what the price of pepper is' and how your lower back aches . . ."

"Oh sure, tell us another one! I've probably worked harder than you today, but I'm not complaining about it."

"Yes, you probably have cheated more than one person today— and torn the skin off some Christians!"

"See here, Mykhaylo, stop kidding around," the steward interrupted him, as if he was sorry to waste time talking about nothing. "It would be better if you gave these workers something to do, because I have to place some of the others."

Mykhaylo glanced disdainfully at the workers. He was a senior tobacco worker, knew how to lay out hotbeds, and received a higher salary than the other labourers.

"How many are there?" he asked, as if there truly were so many that he could not count them.

"Six," the steward replied.

"Well, then! Young men—it's off to the manure with you," Mykhaylo shouted in a loud voice like a thunderclap. "And girls, as for you—go help the other girls haul soil."

The workers enjoyed themselves. A few of them were acquaintances from neighbouring villages, and they greeted the new arrivals cheerfully. Of course, whenever young people get together, it's impossible for them to behave. The young men who were packing manure into boxes swung their mallets at the girls, and the girls returned the compliment by heaving lumps of frozen soil at them.

A Bukovynian girl, her hair knotted high on her head, and dressed in a skirt made of two aprons tied together, was breaking up the smallest lumps of soil with a rake. There was not a youth who walked by her that she did not boldly confront. The newly arrived girls did not approve of her behaviour.

"What a girl!" they whispered among themselves. "Accosting men like that!"

The Bukovynian girl did not pay any attention to the oblique glances of the newly arrived girls and, to spite them, she began saying words that were not at all suitable for a girl to utter. Despite the girl's behaviour, Katrusya could not refrain for long from beginning a conversation with her—even though Yaryna tugged at her sleeves.

After some time, the steward brought pieces of bread for those who had just arrived. The bread, made half-and-half out of coarse rye and barley flour, was dark, full of chaff, and difficult to swallow.

"We'll raise some blisters for sure if we're going to be fed bread like this," Matviy observed, pulling out some larger pieces of chaff.

"Oh, we know how to raise blisters here," Mykhaylo responded jokingly.

"Have they raised blisters on you?" Katrusya inquired laughingly.

"Not on me, they haven't, because I'm a local man; it's only those from elsewhere who get blisters," Mykhaylo replied, eyeing the bold, good-looking girl.

Katrusya wanted to ask something else, but Yaryna shushed her.

In the evening, they assembled in their living quarters. It was a huge, long building with a hallway running down the middle and four large rooms on either side. One room belonged to the steward; the door to it was shut, but from behind it you could hear the crying and shouting of children. From time to time, the steward's wife, a stout young woman, walked out of it, unlocked a big pantry and, arguing loudly with the cook, doled out supplies.

In the kitchen, a roaring fire burned in a huge oven-stove; benches and shelves laden with pots, dishes, and spoons lined the walls. On a large table stood a few cast-iron pots filled with cornmeal mush. Under the benches, there were numerous buckets and basins filled with dishwater; two girls took out clay dishes that had been soaking in them and rinsed them with dirty water.

In the middle of the kitchen stood a sturdy woman with her head wrapped in a kerchief tied on her neck. Her sleeves were rolled up, and she held a large wooden spoon with which she occasionally stirred the boiling food.

The largest room was the one in which the workers lived. Beside the damp and peeling walls, there were wide sleeping benches standing on posts high off the ground. The ceiling was black with smoke and dirt. In the centre of the room, a coal oil lamp, flickering faintly through sooty glass, was nailed to a blackened beam; in the corners lay bundles of straw. The air was heavy, saturated with the stench of sweat and tobacco smoke.

Supper was ready. The cook poured borshch into large bowls, while the steward took up his position by the cornmeal mush and, using a string, sliced off a slab for every worker. Everyone sat down on the ground to eat. The girls who washed the dishes distributed the borshch and cornmeal. The workers pulled out their wooden spoons from their belts and began eating. The borshch was meatless, and so sour that it made their eyes water; slices of beets, thick as fingers, floated in it.

"Catch it, catch it, or it'll run away" teased one youth, fishing for a beet slice under the spoon of another worker.

"May the devil take it, it's damn sour!" another said, grimacing.

"Your eyes saw what they were buying," his companion spoke in proverbs, eating the borshch as if it were the tastiest of food.

"What's this?" a girl screamed at one end of the room, flinging a spoonful of borshch on the ground; a big black cockroach, thrown out with the borshch, splashed about in it.

There was a general outcry; a few workers threw down their spoons and said they were not about to eat borshch that had cockroaches in it.

"Damn them! They're feeding us with cockroaches!" they attacked the steward.

The steward walked about as if he was not the one to whom they were speaking. "Now, now," he smiled, "if you don't eat it, there'll be more left for the others."

When everyone finished eating, the steward yelled at the girls to gather up the dishes and help the cook wash them. Some did as they were told, but others, who did not want to listen to the steward, began arguing with him.

"I'll be there right away," a Romanian girl said roguishly, rolling up her sleeves. "Come on, who wants to arm wrestle with me!" she shouted at the young men.

"Come here!" one of them said, and they began to wrestle so hard that they staggered.

"Come on! Don't give in! Push on the other side," others encouraged them from the sidelines.

The girl was all out of breath, but she did not let the youth push her down.

"I'll show her!" Petro, a strong young man, said. "Let her pit her strength against mine!"

"Oh my! I'm really scared! I've seen better ones than you!"

Petro jumped up to the girl and grabbed both her hands. The girl mustered all her strength, but he overcame her.

One young man started to play on a *sopilka [shepherd's flute],* while others tried to get the girls to dance with them. In the middle of the room, three youths sat down on the ground under the lamp, and one of them pulled a deck of grubby cards from his leather belt. Others, with pipes in their teeth, sat down around them.

The girls turned their attention to the dishes and lazily gathered the bowls set out on the ground. One of them piled up about six and was carrying them to the kitchen when a youth, sitting in the middle of the room, purposely stuck out his foot. The girl tripped on it and crashed to the floor with all the dishes.

"Slowly! Slowly!" the steward shouted angrily, rushing to the girl with raised fists; however, he quickly regained control of himself and, picking up the pottery, he sorted through the bowls to see which ones were salvageable and threw the broken ones into a pile of potsherds.

The girl lashed out at the youth who had tripped her, blaming him for everything. The steward, without paying any attention to her, pulled out a notebook from his pocket and wrote down the number of bowls that she had broken.

"There go her earnings!" some of the workers laughed. "He's sure to deduct those broken bowls from her wages."

"It wouldn't be too bad if he had bowls like everyone else has; as it is, he'll probably charge her fifteen *kreytsary [pennies]* for each bowl!"

"Come on! What did you write down? Show us the book!" one of the youths said. "I know my numbers."

But the steward shoved the youth aside and went into his room.

The workers talked for a long time. It became stuffier in the room from the sweat of human bodies, the smoke, and the clothing that was saturated with the damp wind of early spring. A few of the young men began taking off their shoes and hanging their foot cloths—black with dirt, terribly smelly, and soaked with manure— on the benches, windows, and shelves.

A few went to the kitchen, where food was being cooked, to dry their foot cloths near the warm oven because, even though the cold was tormenting the workers, there was no heat in the big room. The cook scolded them because there were pots on the oven, and the wet foot cloths were dripping into them. When no one listened to her, she became even angrier, gathered up the foot cloths they had hung there, and flung them over the threshold.

Despite the fact that the walls were reverberating with the laughter, shouting, and noise, some of the workers had tumbled down on piles of straw in the corners and were snoring at the top of their lungs.

"Get up! It's daytime! Move it! The steward's coming to wake you!" others shouted at them, pulling their feet to the ground.

The workers who had been sleeping were angry. They cursed, but they had to get up, because everyone wanted to get at least a small amount of straw to sleep on. The girls who had arrived that day stood by a wall in a corner for a long time, not knowing what to do.

"Why are those girls standing there like chickens by a fence in the rain?" laughed one of the youths.

"Are they maybe waiting for someone to make up a bed for them?" another youth added snidely.

"Come over here, come to us!" called the girls who had already lain down in a row. But Yaryna did not dare to go there, and Dotsya took a clump of straw and made herself a bed in a corner, apart from the others.

"Maybe it would be better in the hallway!" Katrusya said, walking out of the room.

It was dark in the passageway; only slivers of light, peeking through the cracks in the doors, dispersed the darkness. Katrusya stood there for a while and began to grope around for the door leading to the kitchen, because it occurred to her that it might be possible to bed down in there.

"What are you doing here?" someone whispered into her ear, wrapping his arms around her waist tightly, like pliers.

Katrusya recognised Mykhaylo, the older tobacco worker. "Go to the devil!" she yelled loudly, shoving him so hard that he slammed into the wall.

"Phew! The girl's possessed," Mykhaylo muttered under his nose and walked away.

The moon was shining brightly, the stars glittered with a soft, gentle gleam, and the air was fresh and cool. Katrusya was even more reluctant to go back into the room raging with noise and stench.

In time, a person becomes accustomed to everything, and so the new girls did not lag behind or shun the others for long. Katrusya was always ready to laugh and joke and, in a group like that, there was much to laugh at, and more than one thing to poke fun at. On occasion, Klugman, who did not rely completely on his steward, came to oversee the workers himself and, after his departure, Katrusya enjoyed making fun of him, imitating the way he walked, talked, and adjusted his hat.

"Come on now, move your hands more quickly. And why are you dragging your feet as if you haven't eaten for three days?" Katrusya would begin to drawl like Klugman, and all the workers would roar with laughter. Everyone knew that the steward liked pretty girls—he did not wake them as early or make them work as hard. When Katrusya realised this, she began to pretend that she would not mind if he followed her around, and she played all sorts of tricks on him.

Mykhaylo did not lose interest in her either. He was married, and his wife had a reputation for being very jealous. Someone must have told her about Katrusya, so whenever she saw her anyplace, she cursed and yelled at her at the top of her lungs.

Katrusya would intentionally gather together a group of youths and girls and stroll by her house, and if Mykhaylo's wife saw her, she would throw whatever was handy—a broom, a stick, or a stone—yelling, until she became hoarse, that the so and so b. . . was corrupting her husband . . . and that because of the so and so b. . . her husband was killing her. Listening to her, Katrusya and her group would almost die laughing.

In Hrabyntsi, it was customary for the workers from one village to get together and go home for a visit.

"Come with us, Katrusya," the girls from her village would call to her, but Katrusya did not want to go.

"Who did I leave there, that I'd want to go back now?" she said.

"What about Ivan?" Yaryna inquired.

"Let him go to the devil!"

"And Maksym?"

Katrusya spit on the ground and turned away. Maksym, however, inquired about Katrusya every time the workers came home.

"What's Katrusya doing there?" he would ask the young men.

"She's being stupid! The steward is chasing after her, and so is Mykhaylo, the older tobacco worker. And it's impossible to say how many youths she's leading around by the nose."

Before long, Maksym had the opportunity to find out for himself how Katrusya was faring in Hrabyntsi. He decided to leave the householder for whom he had been working, because even though he was learning to farm, he earned very little money. And Maksym needed money. The small piece of land and the little cottage he had inherited from his father had liens against them, and had been taken over by the tavern owner for five years. He had to find another place to live during that period, and he thought he might be able to use the time to earn a few *kreytsary* which he could use to fix up his cottage when he regained possession of it.

At the manor, they were paying thirty silver coins and a hundred kilograms of grain or potatoes in kind. For Maksym, the trouble with that was, as the saying goes, that "when one man works for the government, another one carries his food around for him." But he could always find free lodgings at his brother's place, at least for a short time. Even though his brother had children, one of them could always be sent away someplace for a while.

While working for the householder, he had been paid mainly in clothing, and he had lent to others the few *levy [dollar coins]* he had been given. Some time ago, one of the young men who had gone to Hrabyntsi to work had borrowed two silver coins from him —and seemed to have no intention of returning them. Now that Maksym had some time—because even though he had an agreement with the manor, he did not have to start working there until a week later—he decided to go to Hrabyntsi to get his money back.

He went there towards autumn, just as the workers were beginning to strip the tobacco plants. When he arrived at the lord's manor, many workers were out in the fields gathering the stripped leaves, but many more, especially the girls, were in the manor yard, where they were stringing the leaves as they were brought to them.

A few of the girls were spinning; the full spindles were taken from them, unwound, and the thread braided into long, four-strand ropes to which flat needles were fastened. The workers sat in rows on the ground among the piles of green tobacco and rapidly punched the rope through them. The tall mounds of leaves kept disappearing under the swift movement of their hands, and the long ropes wound along the ground like gigantic green snakes. Other workers took away the long ropes and hung them on pegs pounded into fences, the walls of barns, and other outbuildings.

Wagons that hauled the picked leaves kept coming and going, and the leaves were laid carefully on the ground beside the workers. Katrusya sat in the middle of the yard; the leaves flashed in her hands, and her tongue worked just as rapidly. She had something to say to everyone, and her lips did not close for a moment. Laughing and joking, she did not let a single youth go by without confronting him.

Mykhaylo, the older tobacco worker, strolled among the workers, like a drake among ducks, watching to see that everything was coming along as it should.

"Why are you driving in so close with your wagon? I'll teach you how to drive, yes I will! And you—why are you dragging out leaves from the bottom and tearing them? And as for you, why are you standing around? Don't you have any work? And that one over there does nothing but grin at the girls!" his powerful voice blared like the *trembita [wooden mountain horn, three metres in length]* of the *Hutsuls [Ukrainians living in the Carpathian mountains]*.

He scolded workers who grinned from ear to ear and did not pay attention to what they were doing, but when he passed by Katrusya he tugged at her ribbons and pinched her. Katrusya turned around and laughed.

At that moment, Mykhaylo's wife, livid with rage, her apron-skirt twisted, and her kerchief askew, jumped out from behind a wagon and flung a pot of wagon-grease the size of a little pumpkin at Katrusya. The pot struck the girl in the head, and the shards from the pot scattered. Katrusya jumped to her feet. Her whole face was dripping with grease, and long black streams of it flowed down her white shirt. Mykhaylo turned pale and, rushing at his wife with raised fists, grabbed her by the neck and toppled her to the ground.

"Help! Save me!" shouted the unfortunate woman. "He's killing me, the murderer, thief, tramp, son-of a b . . ."

Mykhaylo pushed her down and began trampling her; it was almost impossible to pull them apart. When she tried to flee, he grabbed a cudgel and chased after her down the road.

At first, when the whole ridiculous scene began, everyone just gaped and did not grasp what was happening. Many did not know why Mykhaylo was beating his wife, or who had thrown the pot, but then there arose such a racket—shouting and laughter—that no one could hear what the next person was saying.

"What a girl—and what a dame! She sure smeared that girl's head! But then she sure got what was coming to her; her old man grabbed her like a hawk grabs a chicken and beat her—the way a gypsy hammers metal."

Katrusya stood without moving as the wagon-grease trickled down her white shirt. The red ribbons in her hair were completely black, and the ribbons down her back were stuck together. She wanted to wipe her head with her hands, but she just made things worse, and now her hands were blackened.

The laughter did not abate, and the steward laughed more than anyone. This enraged Katrusya. She angrily seized the broken pot and threw it at his face. The steward ducked, and the pot struck the door of the coach house, leaving a long black mark.

"This mark was put there so people won't ever forget what happened here!" the steward, doubled over with laughter, went on to say. After that remark, there was even more laughter.

"May God strike you dead!" Katrusya said, almost in tears and, grabbing a nearby bucket of water, she went into the workers' room. Here, she gave way to her tears; however, she quickly regained control and resolutely wiped her eyes with a clean corner of her sleeve. Unwinding the ribbons from her hair, she began to wash herself. The grease would not come off in the cold water. She found some warm water in a pot, took a handful of sand from beneath a bench, and began rubbing her face and hands as hard as she could.

She had to change her shirt, but she would have to go back to the village to get a clean one. The workers were not allowed to keep any clothes at the lord's manor, so most of them stored their clothing in the villagers' cottages. There was no one in the workers' room. Katrusya glanced through the window and caught sight of Maksym, who was standing nearby. She had seen him earlier that morning, but had exchanged only a few words with him; now she was as happy to see him as if he were a god; she tapped on the window and waved to him.

At first, when Mykhaylo's wife had poured the grease on Katrusya, Maksym had laughed along with the others, but then he started to feel uncomfortable. He could hear the tears in the girl's voice, and he felt sorry for her. This was why he had sat down by the youth who was hewing pegs for the tobacco leaves near the building. And he kept glancing at the window. Now, when Katrusya waved to him, he quickly ran up to her.

"Go to Yaryna, Maksym," Katrusya begged, "and tell her to run to the village and bring me a shirt. Only be careful that the steward doesn't see you, because he won't let her leave her work."

Maksym rushed off willingly to do her bidding. The steward was not among the workers; Maksym had seen from a long ways off that he had gone into his room. The young man found Yaryna, told her to bring Katrusya a shirt, and then hurried back to the youth who was hewing the pegs.

Katrusya was changing into a clean shirt when the steward's voice rang out. "Get back to work right now!" he said and, seizing her by the shoulder, shoved her out the door.

Maksym flushed. Without thinking, he rushed up to the steward and grabbed him by the hair.

"What do you want?" the steward yelled. "What's it got to do with you?" and he shoved Maksym so hard that the youth stumbled. Maksym flung himself again at the steward, but the latter pushed him aside with one hand. The steward was a sturdy man, while Maksym was small and frail, and when he attacked the steward once more, the latter caught him by the collar and tried to lock him up in the granary. Maksym broke loose and fled as fast as he could.

Maksym did not slow down until he reached the village of Hrabyntsi. A short while later the village faded behind him in a bluish haze, but Maksym did not look back. He was pondering what had happened. He had always been a quiet, even-tempered youth, and had never been interested in either quarrelling or fighting. And yet, he had flung himself at the steward like a madman, and if it had not been for the fact that the older man was stronger than he was, he would have torn him to pieces right then and there.

"The damned steward flirts with her and is ready to take advantage of her . . . Who knows what he's doing to her now?" Maksym wondered, and he fell into a rage once again.

He recalled the tears in Katrusya's eyes when she had grabbed the bucket and gone to the building; at that moment he would have jumped into a fire to save her, even though she had not so much as looked at him. When he arrived in the morning, she had hardly said a few words to him. But she was always like that—you would rarely hear her say anything serious.

Now he, for example, was going to earn thirty silver coins working in the manor, and if she were more like him, she would also save the money she earned in Hrabyntsi, and they could fix up his cottage. But she would never do that! Most likely, she would not bring home a single *kreytsar* from Hrabyntsi—she would spend all her money, and she herself would not know where it had gone.

He was walking on a narrow, well-trodden path along the side of the road; a stone rolled off a rock pile and fell at his feet. Maksym stumbled and cursed, but his train of thought was broken. He began to laugh at himself. Was he not like the gypsy who, before he even had a colt, beat his son so that the youth would not ride the colt into the ground? Who knows, Katrusya might be laughing at him at this very moment—it didn't take much to make her laugh—and here he was, fixing up his cottage with her money.

"Phew, devil! Get away from me!" Why did he keep thinking about this girl? Were there no other girls in the village? There are lots of those flowers in God's world.

There was no sense in pursuing a rich girl, because a girl with money would not marry him. But he could marry a girl who was better off than Katrusya. Take Yaryna, for example. Why shouldn't he woo Yaryna? She was quite the girl, and her mother had only the two of them—the younger daughter would remain with her mother on the small plot with the cottage, while the older one would get more than half the garden . . . And what about Dotsya? She was a quiet girl, very quiet, and maybe her father would give her a piece of land; he did not have overly much land, but he had enough.

But what did Katrusya have? Nothing, except what the folk song stated: "Dark eyes, brows so fine." But—oh, those eyes! And her lips were red—blood red.

Hrabyntsi had been assigned a late deadline for getting the tobacco to the store, and so, by the time the workers returned from Hrabyntsi, much had changed in the village. Some people had died, others had been born, and still others had married. Among those who had married was Ivan, the bailiff's son.

Ivan's wife, Ivanykha, was very proud. When she walked through the village, she held her head in the air like a horse that is too tightly bridled, strutting arrogantly, and swaying her hips from side to side.

"Hold the bulls—the procession is coming!" Katrusya laughed when she caught sight of Ivanykha in the distance. And then she would imitate the way Ivanykha walked into church, hesitated for a moment, crossed herself, and bowed deeply to the ground. Katrusya's actions were relayed to Ivanykha who, not surprisingly, became very hostile towards her.

"She's angry," Ivanykha said, "that Ivan didn't marry her. As if he had no one better to marry than someone who has nothing but the shirt on her back—a harebrained girl, a useless servant of Jews, not worthy of sweeping the threshold of a mistress or grazing a householder's swine! Let her take care that her head isn't smeared with wagon-grease once again, and that she doesn't cover someone with boils when she crosses their path—and that what's already showing up on the bellies of her girlfriends and companions who went with her to Hrabyntsi doesn't show up on her as well!"

Ivanykha was saying this because unkind rumours were being spread about Dotsya.

"How can it be," some people wondered, "that it happened to Dotsya—and you never heard anything bad about her—but it didn't happen to Katrusya who does nothing but chase after the fellows!"

"Never fear, she knows what to do!" Ivanykha said. "She knows how to dig in the ground and find what makes a rose beautiful, and she knows that you must not drink water from a whetting stone container while standing under a scythe!"

"She knew how to cast spells and how to entice and seduce the fellows, and so she thinks that everyone's like that!" Katrusya retorted. "As if people don't know that she went to a fortune teller to have her father's life shortened . . . Oh, my! Yes! What a grand mistress we've become, and how we pass judgement on the girls! She should go lick dogs' snouts instead of spreading gossip! She's vain, like a rich woman. But the rich often end up being guides for beggars, and one day she, too, may have to tap her way down the road, in rags, with bundles tied to her belt."

Someone told her that Ivanykha had talked for a long time with Yaryna about Katrusya. As soon as she heard this, Katrusya dashed right over to see Yaryna. "So, Yaryna is getting together with 'that one' and starting up lies about me! Well, let her be quiet if she wants others to be quiet about her," Katrusya thought.

"Call Yaryna for me," she yelled from the gate to Yaryna's younger sister; she did not want to meet up with Yaryna's mother.

"Yaryna won't come out; we have matchmakers at our place," the girl responded.

Katrusya stopped to think about this. "Who are they," she asked.

"It's Ilash Hawrylyuk—he wants to marry her."

"Ilash Hawrylyuk? What's Petro saying about that?"

"Oh, who cares about Petro!"

"But wasn't he courting her?"

"Well, what's the good of that, if he doesn't have anything. Ilash is signing over half his land and his cottage to her."

"But he's old, and he's a widower with four children!"

"So what? Daddy says it doesn't matter what he's like, as long as he can earn a living."

"Does she want to marry him?"

"Well, wouldn't you marry him?" the girl asked slyly.

Katrusya grew angry. "I didn't come here to have you ask me questions. Just tell Yaryna that if she tells lies about me, I'll rip her head off."

"Just you wait, my dear girl," Katrusya threatened Yaryna in her thoughts. "If you don't be quiet, you'll hear something that will make your heels turn cold!" Then her thoughts raced on: "Now she's going to be boasting that she's getting married, and she'll be getting together more often with Ivanykha to swap lies about the girls. What kind of a mistress is she, after all; just because she's getting married, she thinks that it's God knows what kind of a big deal! If I wanted to, I could get married before she does. 'He who seeks, shall find.'"

And, in her head, Katrusya began to pick through the young men who could marry her—because not all the youths who chase after girls want to get married. She was just beginning to recall all the widowers in the village, when she heard someone call her name.

"Where were you, Katrusya?"

Katrusya turned around and saw Maksym.

"Where were you?" Maksym asked again, drawing nearer.

Katrusya was once again overcome with a great rage at both Yaryna and Ivanykha, but more at Yaryna, because she had thought of her as a good friend.

"I was at Yaryna's; she's telling lies about me. She pretends she's such a good friend, but she gets together with Ivanykha, and the two of them concoct lies. They say that I dig up roses and drink water from a whetting stone bag! They better be careful—the both of them! They don't see their own problems right under their own noses, but they can spot someone else's way over by the forest."

Katrusya fired this off very rapidly, in one breath. Her eyebrows were frowning, and her eyes flashed. In her anger, she appeared so attractive to Maksym that he just gazed at her admiringly, instead of listening to what she was saying.

The fact that Ivanykha and Yaryna were talking about her did not bother him in the least—let them talk if they wanted to—no matter what, he liked Katrusya better that Ivanykha, or Yaryna, or any of the other girls in the village. And ever since he had attacked the steward because of her, she seemed to have become closer to him, and the thought that maybe he might marry her kept creeping into his mind.

Even though he was annoyed with himself, he was more annoyed that Katrusya was indifferent to him, as if it did not matter to her what he thought about her. Nevertheless, he did notice that ever since the incident with the steward, Katrusya seemed to have become more favourably disposed towards him. It used to be, that if he said anything at all to her, she would answer angrily, and then there would be no point in continuing the conversation, about what this girl or that one had said, or what that youth had replied.

All these thoughts crossed Maksym's mind as he gazed at the comely girl. The only impediemnt to courting Katrusya was the fact that she did not have a dowry—and he was not a rich man. And when two poor people marry, they are destined to live in poverty the rest of their lives. Just now, however, that fact did not seem very terrifying to him.

"Katrusya," he finally said. "I'm going to tell you something— I'd send matchmakers to you if I knew that you'd marry me!"

The gloomy face of the girl brightened at once; her eyebrows lifted, and her eyes flashed merrily.

"Well? What do you say?" Maksym asked once again, when Katrusya did not reply.

Suddenly, Katrusya laughed loudly and turned away from Maksym, leaving him alone on the road, just as she had when she left for Hrabyntsi.

She had found Maksym so amusing that she kept smiling to herself as she walked along. How could you not help laughing? "Talk about the devil, and there he is!" She had been thinking about the young men that she might marry—and, quite by accident, he had crossed her path. That would be proof enough that she had not drunk water from "a whetting stone bag." And then the people would know that the two women had been lying, and as for the fact that they were putting on airs because they were rich—who cared! Poor people also live on this earth and are mistresses in their own homes.

Mulling over her thoughts, she made her way to her uncle's home; since her return from Hrabyntsi, she was staying there until she found another place.

Yaryna did not know that people's rumours had caused a rift between her and Katrusya—that Katrusya was threatening to get even with her because of some lies. She was not too terribly happy to be marrying old Ilash and, wanting to be with her girlfriends for a little while longer, she invited them to a *vechernytsi [an evening party with singing and dancing]*. When she came to Katrusya's house, the latter attacked her with her fists.

"The devil take it! Vanish into the slimy swamp, into the mud! What do you want with me?" Yaryna said, trying to calm Katrusya down. When she found out what the problem was, she crossed herself in shock and dismay. "May I not live to see God's world, may I never get married or walk on the earth if I ever got together with Ivanykha; may I never hear bells ring if I heard her voice; may my tongue wither, may I never move from this spot, and may I never bring a spoonful of food to my mouth if I ever said anything about you, Katrusya."

Katrusya finally calmed down and promised to go to the party.

There were not too many girls at the *vechernytsi*, and it was quite late by the time a few young men came by. Before their arrival, the girls had sung all kinds of songs, but with their appearance, they seemed to become shy and stopped singing—even though they all began talking and laughing at the same time.

For Yaryna, however, the sad songs of the girls were more pleasing than their cheerful jokes and their banter with the young men; time and time again, she pleaded with the girls to sing. Katrusya laughed and sang alone:

"Oh sing, dear girls, sing and take your turn, just so!
So the mean old mistress won't chase you with a hoe."

After this, everyone began to joke and laugh even more. The youths teased the girls, wondering what it would be like if the mistress took after them with a hoe, and which girl would be the first to run away.

"Or which young man," the girls responded.

"A hoe—that's a woman's tool—it has no power over a man!" Matviy said.

"Oh, yeah? Men don't fear anything like they fear a hoe!" Katrusya prattled. "Go on, ask Toma Hrynchyshyn if he's afraid of a hoe."

Everyone knew that Toma did not beat his wife—she beat him. And they all burst out laughing.

"If one man's a fool, it doesn't mean that everyone else is," Matviy added gravely, just to have his own way.

At that moment, heavy footsteps were heard outside the window.

"Uh-oh, those aren't girls' footsteps!" one of the girls said, glancing out the window.

Petro and Maksym entered the house. When Yaryna saw Petro, she became all flustered. Petro felt uncomfortable as well, even though he did not show it.

"Glory to Jesus Christ! God be with you! What are you doing, girls?" the youths greeted the young women.

"Why, can't you see?" the girls replied. "We're spinning."

"The kitty cat spun forty skeins of thread; the tomcat ran and tore them to shreds," chanted one of the youths.

"And the girls don't want to sing," Matviy added.

"We didn't want to sing for you, but we'll sing for them."

The girls exchanged glances, whispered among themselves, and a moment later began singing:

"Rolling down a hill, the wagons broke their wheels.
'Where are the *vechernytsi*?' two youths clicked their heels.
'The widow's *vechernytsi* clearly have the edge,
Four horses on a tether, magic potions on a ledge.'"

The girls peeked furtively at Petro and smiled to themselves.

"Horses are one thing," Maksym said gravely, as always, "but there should be charms here somewhere." He got up on a bench and groped around with his hands.

On the shelf in the corner were Yaryna's coral beads and *zharda [beads interspersed with coins]* tied in a handkerchief. He waved the small bundle triumphantly and showed everybody Yaryna's charms.

Yaryna became angry, grabbed the handkerchief, and flung it into her trunk. Petro pretended that none of this had anything to do with him, and Yaryna did not even look in the direction where he was sitting.

From the moment that Maksym entered the room, all he did was watch Katrusya—how she spun, twirled the spindle, and wound an even thread. Katrusya noticed this and looked at him with such burning, laughing eyes that, unable to face her, he turned to look out the window. This amused the mischievous girl even more. Twirling the spindle energetically, she sang:

"On the hill grows periwinkle, periwinkle grows,
It's such a joy to watch you, Heaven only knows,
It's such a joy to watch you . . ."

"No, not that one," the girls interrupted her, "Let's sing the one that starts with the words 'In Bukovyna green leaves are unfurling.' Let's remind Yaryna she won't be leading the life of a girl much longer—nor enjoying a girl's freedom."

The girls began singing:

"Oh, sing, if you can sing, sing my dearest girl,
And here in Bukovyna, may green leaves unfurl,
May all the leaves unfurl, together with the grass,
It's better not to marry, better to stay a lass.

A wedded woman is a slave—she cries where'er she goes,
A lass is like a *kozak [cossack]* free—she skips on nimble toes.
A wedded woman is a slave—she frets, no matter where,
A lass is like a *kozak* free—she sings a lively air."

Yaryna sighed as she listened to this song.

"That's a sad song," Maksym said. "Yaryna will soon be crying."

"Do you want a happy one?" a few of the girls asked.

"I'll sing one for you," Katrusya said, and she began a *kolomiyka* [*a fast, dancing song*]:

> "A servant I won't marry,
> He shies away from work,
> He strolls from barn to bakehouse
> To light his pipe, the jerk."

"Now, now! Don't sing so confidently," Matviy spoke up, "because, before you know it, they'll sing one for you."

"Go on, sing it! Let's hear it!" the girls taunted the young men. Yaryna filled bowls with borshch, put some *holubtsi [cabbage rolls]* on the table, and invited everybody to have some supper. Soon afterwards, the guests began to leave. They walked out of the house together, but at the gate they split up into two groups— one going in one direction and the other in the opposite one. The girls who were going the same way as Katrusya noticed that Petro had stayed behind.

"He's stayed behind. Honest to God, girls, he's still at her place," the girls whispered among themselves. "That's really something! She's marrying one man, but carrying on with another one. She thinks that the old man won't find out about her *vechernytsi* and her sweetheart. He'll remind her about it one day."

"Of course he will, my dears; he'll really remind her about it: 'You were about to marry me, but you still cavorted with sweethearts.' He'll knock some sense into her—she'll taste more than one fist for this evening."

"Good night!" first one girl said, and then another, as they approached their homes. The young men were also left behind along the way. Maksym should have stopped at his cottage, but he wanted to walk Katrusya home, and she had the longest way to go.

"Katrusya," Maksym said when they were left alone, and his voice seemed to be choked in his chest, "Did you have me in mind when you sang the song about not marrying a lord's servant?"

"Even if I was, so what?"

"So you really won't marry me? Tell me the honest truth," Maksym pleaded. Maksym's voice became still more choked up. This amused Katrusya greatly, and she laughed more uproariously than ever. But this time Maksym did not let her escape, and when they were near her house, he seized her hand.

"Why are you asking me?" Katrusya finally said. "Am I a young lady that you're asking me? Send matchmakers, and you'll know."

A week after this conversation, Maksym sent matchmakers to Katrusya. It had not even occurred to Katrusya to be serious about what she had said, and she really did not think that he would take her at her word and actually send matchmakers. So now, when they came, she did not know what to say.

At first she wanted to refuse him—she was sorry to lose her freedom as a girl. She started out protesting that she was an orphan and did not have anything, but she ended up saying that the chance coming her way was a good one, that she would have her own house and would not have to ask favours of anyone, and even though they would not be rich, they were both young, healthy, and able to work. But a certain neighbour provided the most convincing argument—she had married a younger brother and was the second daughter-in-law in the house.

"My girl," she said to Katrusya, "if you have the chance to be the mistress of your own home, then kneel down and kiss the ground—don't end up in a situation like mine."

"It's true that I'll have my own house," Katrusya thought. "And no one will be telling me what to do and when to do it—and I'm not afraid of work."

Preparations were begun for the wedding. Maksym was absolutely delighted when he found out that Katrusya still had ten *rynski* from her earnings in Hrabyntsi. The mistress where Katrusya served gave her pillows and a coarse wool bedcover, and her uncle gave her the little bit that had been left after her mother's death. Maksym took his wages from the manor, and they had a wedding.

Even though they did not have the money to rebuild the house, Maksym fixed it up, so that, with caring owners, it could stand for another few years. A true householder won't allow the roof to leak, and a good housewife won't let the walls peel.

Katrusya had three silver coins from the money gifted at the wedding, and Maksym had two, so they went right out and bought themselves a piglet. There was a bit left over from Maksym's pay in kind, so there was enough to feed both of them and throw something to the piglet as well. Maksym finished off his year at the manor and bought a heifer with the rest of his pay.

The next year, Maksym decided not to go to work in the manor—he was very clever with an axe, and people began calling upon him to help with their carpentry work. The main reason for his decision, however, was an altogether different one. When Maksym worked in the barnyard or by the barn, Katrusya brought his food there, and he would sit down on the ground and eat it. There were usually servants in the manor yard. One of them would laugh, another would tell a joke, and Katrusya could not refrain from replying. This angered Maksym, even though he did not want to admit it.

Katrusya did not like going near the manor house, and she rarely had to. Sometimes she saw either the older lady or the younger one at a distance, strolling in the garden, but they never came near the barnyard. At times, the lord would fly out to the workers as if he were scalded, but at those time he yelled at everyone and did not look at anyone in particular.

No one would have recognised Maksym's old cottage after Katrusya finished fixing it up—it seemed to have become taller, as if the ceiling had been raised. Maksym built a little shed, constructed a small barn, and put up a wattle storage bin for corn, because they worked in the cornfields for one-third of the crop.

Katrusya had more than enough to attend to—often she worked without stopping, from morning until night, either in the fields, or at home. Two years later, God gave them a son, then a little girl, and the third was on its way when Maksym took sick.

It was harvest time, he was mowing oats and, as it was very hot, he lay down on the ground and greedily drank water from a spring. People said he must have swallowed a frog while he was enjoying his drink, because he kept saying that something was knocking about in his stomach. The villagers remembered that, long ago, the same thing had happened to a certain rich man, and he had gone all the way to Lviv, where the doctors had removed a decayed frog from his stomach. And they said there was another man who had a frog fly into his brain. When the doctors cut open his forehead, the frog leaped out alive.

Katrusya was so worried by Maksym's illness that she looked like a jackdaw. Because he could do nothing, she had to do everything herself. Moreover, she had no money and could not find help anywhere. She took Maksym to a doctor in town, and the pharmacy alone cost her two silver coins. She walked three miles to see a fortune teller and did everything she was told to do, but nothing helped in the slightest. Maksym ailed and withered, and finally, he died.

It was very difficult for Katrusya to give Maksym a decent burial—she did not have much of anything, and no money had come in during his illness. But he had to be buried properly. After all, he had been a householder! What would people say if there were no funeral? And she herself did not want to bury him in a haphazard manner, without the respect due him.

He had been a good husband; he had not mistreated or beaten her—no matter how much she quarrelled with him. And as far as being hardworking—well, he had no equal. But what good was that, when what little money they had saved was spent during his illness, and now she had to scrape together whatever she could to bury him as God willed it.

And the deceased himself, when he saw that there was no hope, had said: "See that you bury me properly, like a householder; and later, you'll manage somehow!" She was young and able to work, but when there is no man in the house, it is difficult to manage, even if you are well off, let alone if you are poor.

In the village, it was known that she was a hard worker, that she did whatever she set out to do, and so, for a time, a widower with two children courted her.

"Wouldn't it be smart of me to bring together so many children! Besides, aren't I worthy of a young, unmarried man?" she said.

A young man courted her as well, but she did not want him. He was called Mule because, one time at the market, he had bought a mule instead of a horse. Katrusya joked that she wanted to drive with horses, not with mules. She was prepared to suffer for a while, even though life was very hard, until God sent her someone that she herself wanted.

That is what Katrusya thought. But no one knows what fate has in store for him tomorrow or, as the saying goes: "Your thoughts may be soaring beyond the mountains, but death is lurking behind your back."

One time there was a severe cold spell; the frost was so strong that birds froze in flight. Katrusya was left without a bit of flour in the house, so she hired herself out to wash the neighbour's clothing. She was strong, and work had never bothered her. Even though her feet froze to the ice, she did not step back from the ice-hole and kept beating the clothes with her washing beetle. There was a lot to be washed, and she had to hurry, because a winter day is very short.

That evening, she felt a pain in her side. The next day the pain did not abate, and then her chest ached more and more, until, finally, she could not get out of bed.

That was when God sent to her the young lady from the manor. Katrusya said more than once, that if the young lady had not come and given her some medicine to drink, who knows if she would not have been claimed by death. She did not lie in bed for long, of course, because a poor person cannot afford to take the time to convalesce, but she could not regain her strength for some time.

More than once, it occurred to her that if she went to the manor, the young lady might give her some other medication; but when she recalled her childhood days, she dismissed the thought with a wave of her hand. She had done without her help thus far and, one way or another, she would manage now—if only she regained her strength, and God blessed the people with a good crop.

And, praise the Lord, everything looked promising this year—there would probably be enough grain. The spring had been early, the rains had fallen, and now it was up to God to ensure a successful harvest.

Katrusya had taken two *morgy* of corn to work for a third share. It was more than two people could reasonably cope with, but she had taken it on all by herself. She would jump out of bed at the crack of dawn, leave the children some cold leftovers or a slab of cornmeal, take along some bread for herself—if there were some—lock the sleeping children in the house, and go into the fields. At noon she would run home, cook a bit of borshch for the children, let out the chickens, tell the older boy to take care of the house and the children, and then race off into the fields again.

The grain was already in leaf, and some of it was even heading, but Katrusya and others were still busy with the hoeing.

It was very close to dinnertime. Katrusya left her hoe in the cornfield and ran home to check on her children.

The sun was searingly hot; its brilliance dazzled the eyes and made everything sparkle and glitter. The green wheat, the even greener grass in the ditches, the purple pasqueflowers, and the blue cornflowers shimmered brightly, while the crimson poppies flamed in the thick wheat. But even though everything was shining lustrously, almost every flower seemed to have lowered its head, every leaf was drooping slightly, and the riotous stalks of the potato plants had wilted.

"Oh, it's burning hot!" the people said. "Even the potatoes have wilted. May God protect us from evil!" And they gazed in terror at the sky. But the sky was clear and calm, and its azure blueness glistened in the sun.

Katrusya walked swiftly along the stream to the village. The sun illuminated the murky water that scarcely covered the gravel and slime. In some spots the water dipped into deep holes where plants, attached to the riverbed, spread their long leaflike stems, tadpoles crawled, scum swirled, and eels glistened in the sun. Along the bank, in the rushes and horsemint, frogs warmed themselves in the sun and splashed noisily as they leapt into the water.

Before Katrusya unlocked the door, she once again glanced up at the sky, but it was clear, and only the occasional little cloud floated, like a feather, across it. Katrusya walked into the porch and sent the children outdoors to break off some of the wattle fence for firewood. They were slow to return, and she went out to get them. She looked around—and shuddered.

The little white clouds, that had so recently been transparent, were now amassed into a heavy cloud that was rapidly covering the bright azure sky. A strong wind blew in from the west, shook the windows of the cottage, bent the willows down to the road, and swept up the dust and small pebbles. Lightning pierced the clouds like arrows, and one thunderclap followed another.

Katrusya stood in the cottage by the window and fervently crossed herself. "Lord! Lord have mercy! Dearest Lord, have mercy upon us!" she prayed to God, while the children, crying, clung to her.

There was a rustling noise up above; at first, a chunk of ice came flying down, and then large, thick hail fell in buckets. To the din, the roaring, and the crashing was added the muffled sound of bells ringing. Women threw hoes, spades, and willow branches out of their cottages, burned herbs that had been blessed, gathered the hail pellets, and dropped them into holy water.

The tempest ended. Not one pane of glass was left unbroken in the village, the ground was white, and broken branches hung from trees. And what had happened in the fields?

The sun smiled and cast long warm rays; the water soaked into the ground; the distant mountains, as if spread with a light coverlet, distinctly mirrored the clear sky; and, here and there, the earth was steaming. The torn leaves, the trampled grass, and the broken flowers looked as if they had been washed in pristine water. There was a fresh breeze in the air; birds, emerging from hiding places under the branches, stretched and flapped their drenched wings in the sun, and the occasional white butterfly flashed by on wings already dry.

It was only the people in the village who had lost all hope. Their rough, callused hands fell in numb despair. All was lost—their blood, sweat, and bitter toil . . . The manor lord was also in a state of shock, even though the larger part of his crop was covered by insurance—something that the peasants, having a hard enough time paying the taxes, could not afford!

Katrusya ran out into the field. The grain was lying in utter disorder; the ground was black. There was no reason to finish hoeing the cornfield—everything was levelled to the ground; only the hoe was lying sadly abandoned in the middle of the soaked field. Katrusya picked up the hoe and returned home; she walked into the house, threw the hoe under the bed, sat down on the bench, and wept bitterly . . .

The children, happily playing with a broken pot, cast covert glances at their mother—the poor things did not know that, later, they too would be in tears when they begged their mother in vain for bread.

Three villages fell victim to the hail.

The misfortune that befell the peasants deeply affected Yadzya, and she conceived a plan to organise a far-reaching assistance program among the district nobility and intelligentsia in benefit of the devastated peasants. This time she demonstrated an exceptional amount of energy. She convinced a few lords and ladies from the neighbouring nobility to form a committee, drew into it all the more important intelligentsia from the nearby town, and set up a forfeit lottery for which she donated half of her artistic creations. The committee also held a whole series of socials, with dancing.

And, as if all of that was not enough, she struck up a friendship with the doctor's wife—an obvious compromise between the nobility and the upper intelligentsia—and travelled with her to almost all of the more important homes in the district.

The two ladies were accompanied in their travels by Adam B., who, as a representative of the male members of the committee, fulfilled the role of knight and defender of the weaker sex.

Lord Adam was a scion of a good noble family, and he had just leased a village that adjoined the one in which the Solyetskys lived. Even though he did not have a large fortune, and was not doing all that well with his new lease, he was, nevertheless, a welcome guest in every home. And when he toured with the ladies, his very presence, especially in homes where there were daughters of a marriagable age, noticeably increased the size of the donations.

Throughout the entire district, the county, and even beyond it, people were talking about Yadzya and her philanthropic bent; and, wherever she went, she was greeted with the most exalted compliments. But when the door closed behind her, the mood of the donors changed.

"These are difficult times," they said, "and demands are being made on us from all sides; it would be fine if it were being done out of altruism, but it's all just to show herself off and to figure prominently in the newspapers."

And a few of the ladies were confident that Yadzya was travelling around and gathering donations with the sole intention of establishing a more intimate relationship with Adam B.

These accusations were refuted by the facts; she had always taken an interest in the welfare of the poor, and this was her defence against peoples' evil conjectures.

In all honesty, however, she could not deny, even to herself, that the courtesy and the attention of Lord Adam boosted her strength and energy so greatly, that she was much more able to overcome obstacles and tolerate unpleasantness than she had been in the past.

The peasants, upon hearing that the lords and ladies were trying to help them, began to take heart that it would be easier for them to live through the difficult times. The problem was, however, that it was taking a very long time; the winter was over already, and it was time to seed the fields again, but they still had not received any help. The people feared they would be late with their spring work. They had to find some way of getting seed grain; the price of grain was high, and they had to scrape together everything they had to buy some. The local tavern keeper filled a whole room with pawned articles and loaned out hundreds of *rynski* at an exorbitant rate of interest.

There were those who said: "If we have to wait, we'll wait; we've waited this long—we'll wait a little longer."

Katrusya also heard that the lords wanted to assist those who had been hit by the hail, and even though she had never relied on help from anyone, preferring to earn whatever she could, she hoped that the lords could be of some assistance.

She finally got what she was waiting for.

The peasants were summoned to the manor. Despite the fact that the yard was fairly large, it looked as if it had been thickly sown with people.

Yadzya, sitting on the high veranda, was looking after everything herself. All around the veranda stood sacks filled with grain, and the steward, assisted by serving men, was doling it out to the peasants. Each peasant was allocated four litres of grain and ten *kreystary*. Yadzya gave out the money herself.

The peasants bowed and kissed Yadzya's hand, but a muffled grumbling could be heard in the crowd.

"What you're giving us won't make any difference at all!" a woman's voice suddenly erupted above all the others.

The peasants shushed Katrusya, and she glanced fearfully at the veranda to see if those on it had heard her voice.

Yadzya did hear it; she swept her eyes over the crowd and saw the woman in whose cottage she had been, and whom she had helped during her illness. Her face contorted painfully.

The peasants began to disperse. There was no need for Katrusya to wait any longer; she went home, looking sadly at the small bundle and the ten *kreytsary* in her fist . . .

"Well, Katrusya, did you receive a lot of help?" Abramko smilingly taunted her as she walked past his tavern.

Katrusya continued walking without replying.

At that moment, Lord Adam drove up to the lord's manor with handsome, light-bay horses.

Yadzya greeted him with a pale face. She was very distraught. The woman's words had hurt her to the quick. So much effort, so much unpleasantness—and she had not heard a word of gratitude!

She was not able to calm down for a long time, even though her parents and Lord Adam tried their utmost to soothe her.

And, after all was dark in the village, the lights burned for a long time in the lord's living room, and the conversations focussed almost exclusively on the indifference, laziness, drunkenness, arrogance, and ingratitude of the common people.

In the following days, the villagers often saw Lord Adam's spirited horses driving up to the manor.

Then, suddenly, there was a rumour that the young lady was getting married.

The rumour reached Vasyl and Vasylykha, and they debated for a long time whether or not they should go to the manor to bring the lords their "well wishes."

Finally, they decided to go. They milled one-quarter of a litre of grain as if it were gold, and Vasylykha baked *kalachi [braided circular ceremonial bread]* because it was not fitting to go empty-handed, even if it was the lord's manor they were visiting.

The lord welcomed them happily, and the lady was even more delighted; she plied them with food as if it were a Feast Day, and when the visitors began reciting the traditional, time-honoured good wishes appropriate to such an occasion, both the lord and the lady shed tears of joy.

The young lady, however—and they found this very strange—had changed completely. She had always been friendly and outgoing, but now it seemed she had to force herself to talk to them, and there was no joy to be seen on her face.

And it was not only Vasyl and Vasylykha who made this observation. Some of the servants noticed that she had tearstained eyes, and the chambermaid said that, earlier on, when the lord was still courting her, the young lady had walked from window to window as she watched for him. When everything was settled, however, it was as if she became another person, and the older lady often had to plead with her to come out of her room to see her betrothed.

All the same, after some time, the manor hummed with a wedding. When the young couple were driving to church, the entire village gathered to see them. There were crowds of people—men, women and children—by all the gates; it was only Katrusya's cottage that had a padlock on the door, and no one looked on from her yard.

It was common knowledge in the village that she was in Hrabyntsi. After hiring out her two older children to people in the village, she had set out, taking the youngest child with her, to work in the tobacco fields. They were surprised, however, when she was not among the workers who returned. But when they were told that she had carried on there in the same way as she had behaved when she was still a girl, they realised that her nature had not changed.

The Soothsayers
Based on folk tales and stories
(1894)

Dedicated to Mykhaylo Drahomanov
on the 30th anniversary of his writing career.

The day was ending. The sun was sinking, and its final rays were
bidding the earth farewell, leaving in their wake a broad swath of
crimson clouds that gradually faded and grew dark. On the wide,
dusky horizon, pale stars, breaking through a heavy, murky curtain,
cast their eyes down ever more brightly on the impenetrable
darkness veiling the earth.

Night was encroaching on a small village nestled at the foot of
a mountain. A wooden church, with a metal roof that a short time
ago had been gleaming in the radiance of the setting sun, had
almost completely disappeared; the low, white walls of peasant
cottages were becoming indistinct; and thickly growing orchards
were fading from view. The lively din of people, cattle, and
domestic fowl was dying down, streets were almost deserted and,
except for the odd cottage where the bustle of daytime activity
persisted, the little village was falling asleep, along with the sun.

Two travellers were trudging slowly down the road, casting their
eyes about in all directions, hoping to find a place to sleep in the
village.

"Perhaps we should turn off here," one of the men said, pointing
at a well-maintained property with a large cottage and neat yard.

"Fine with me," the other responded. "Let's hope there's
someone there to ask if they'll take us in."

They entered the yard, and the owner, a robust young man,
walked out of the house.

"Glory to Jesus Christ!"

"Glory forever!"

"Would you, kind sir, let us spend the night here?"

"I'd have nothing against it, if I had room to put you up," the owner said. "You see, my wife's due any day now—it could happen at any moment."

"We can bed down anywhere at all, even in the yard; it's summer—we won't freeze."

As he led them to a haystack, the owner told them that God had already given him three children, but not one of them had lived past its fourth year.

"Perhaps God will grant you happiness with this one," the men said.

The owner thanked them and returned to the house, leaving the travellers by the haystack.

A misty light tinged with azure and silver flooded the village, the cottage, and the haystack where the travellers were sleeping. The metal roof of the little church gleamed with a new lustre, and the stream—a sparkling, narrow band in the enchanting moonlight—hugged one side of the garden and ran off far into the field.

The fragrance of green grass permeated the air; the bluish light trembled with a power of its own and seemed to be swaying a tall crane that was staring into the deep framed well near the cottage. From the cottage came the shrieks of a young woman.

A light cloud tore itself away from the moon and settled on its surface. The travellers spotted two silvery grey birds that noiselessly flapped their wide wings and alighted on a window of the cottage.

"Well?" one bird asked the other, and its voice sounded as if someone were playing a *sopilka [shepherd's flute]* far off in a field.

"It hasn't been born yet," the second bird replied in the same voice.

"What would happen if it were born in this hour?"

"Whoever is born in this hour," said the first bird, "will live for many long years and will have untold wealth."

The birds flew away as silently as they'd flown in.

After some time, a faint shadow appeared in the distance, and the birds alighted on the window once again.

"Well?" one bird inquired.

"Nothing has happened yet."

"What would happen if it were born in this hour?"

"If it were a boy, he would become a notorious criminal, and if it were a girl, she would bring great shame to her mother," the first bird replied, and the birds flapped their wings and flew away.

When they flew in the third time, the child was already born. "What kind of hour is this?" one bird asked the other.

"It's the kind of hour that the new-born will live only three years longer than the previous children, and it will meet its death in the well that is right here in this yard."

The travellers heard all this. In the morning, they got up and told the owner that it was thus and so; some birds had flown in during the night and stated that the new-born child would live only three years longer than the previous children, and that it would meet its death in the well that was in the yard.

The master of the household felt as if someone had cut him down with a knife.

The child grew for a year, and a second year, but the father felt no joy. He filled the well with stones and boarded it over. And both he and his wife never let the child out of their sight.

One day, when the child was seven years old, the parents suddenly noticed that it was missing. They ran to the well and found the child lying on it; they rushed up to it, but the child was already dead.

It happened exactly as the birds had prophesied—the child met its death at the well because it had been born in that kind of hour.

***

Some soldiers were given a leave of absence to go home. One soldier was on his way to his native village, but there was such a heat wave, that God forbid! It was as if the sun had gone berserk, for there was not a single corner, nor a single crack, that its searing rays had not penetrated. It beat down on your head from above, and scorchingly hot stones burned you from below. And, with every step you took, the dust swirled, blinding your eyes, forcing its way into your mouth, and flying up your nostrils.

The soldier kept spitting, wiping the sweat from his brow, and swearing for all he was worth. Arriving in a village towards evening, he stopped at a cottage and asked if he might spend the night there.

He bought some milk curds from the mistress of the home, had a bite to eat, stretched himself out on a bench, and fell asleep.

As he was trying to sleep, he heard shrieking, screaming, and much running around in the adjoining room. You see—please excuse me for saying this—a woman was giving birth to a child.

"Well, I've sure found myself a place to spend the night—may the devil take it!" the soldier swore, turning over on his other side.

A penetrating brightness was breaking in through the window. He opened his eyes. The moonlight was radiant; it seemed like daylight, and two grey birds were flying around by the windows.

"Well?" one bird inquired, and its voice sounded like the rustling of leaves on a tree. "Has it been born yet?"

"Not yet!" the other bird replied.

"What kind of an hour is this?"

"It's the kind of hour that, whoever is born in it, will not have good fortune on this earth."

The birds flew away, but returned immediately.

"Psst! Psst!" one bird said to the other. "It's being born now."

"And what is it?"

"It's a girl."

"What kind of fate awaits her?"

"Her fate is the soldier who is sleeping by this window."

At this moment, the cry of a new-born child was heard.

The soldier wanted to fall asleep, but he could not. He sat up on the bench and rubbed his eyes. There was no trace of the birds; only the moon, floating like a shadow over the earth, beamed through the window. It seemed to be laughing at the soldier, because even though he had already seen so much of the world, his fate was only now forcing its way into it.

The soldier was infuriated to think that this screaming little brat was to be his wife!

"Why are you laughing?" he growled at the moon, which was gazing down curiously upon him. "Do you believe the birds? Oh, you won't live to see the day!"

After everything had quieted down, and everyone had fallen asleep, the soldier rose to his feet and walked softly into the room where the woman who had given birth was lying. He grabbed the child and carried it outdoors.

It was a wealthy household, and the entire yard was surrounded by a high, sturdy picket fence. The soldier, without pausing to think, impaled the child on a stake and continued on his way.

Time passes by like flowing water, and people have to experience much in their lives. And it could not be otherwise, for it is God Himself who gives us both fair weather and storms, warm weather and cold.

In the sky, there appeared a huge red star with a long tail like a broom. People were alarmed. "This does not bode well," they said to one another. And when a dog lifted its head and started howling—as if he had been hired to howl—the people became even more terrified. And their fears were justified—they heard that the kings had quarrelled among themselves and declared war.

There was a general conscription. Not only were young men called up, but older soldiers as well. For a long time, the kings defended themselves with their armies and won victories over one another, until, finally, they made peace. They no longer required the soldiers, so they sent them home again. Not all of the soldiers returned—many had been slain in battle, and many were crippled. But there were also those who had been protected by God from all evil and were returning home with money in their pockets.

Almost sixteen years had passed from the time when a soldier had slept in the house where an infant girl was born.

One day, when the master of that home was in a tavern, an older soldier came up to him. They struck up a friendship, and the soldier talked about the war and the triumphs and trials of being a soldier.

The master took a liking to the soldier. Loathe to part with him, he began persuading him to stop over at his place for a while.

"It's all the same to me," the soldier said. "so much time has gone by already, that another day or two won't make make any difference."

As they approached the house, the mistress came out to meet them. She was accompanied by such a pretty girl that the soldier smacked his lips. Neighbours dropped in; the soldier drank whiskey and made advances to the girl. She was embarrassed and covered her face with her sleeve; the neighbours quipped; bottle after bottle was drunk—and, before long, it was midnight. The master asked the soldier to stay the night.

The soldier spent the night there, and he stayed on for a day, and then for another one, and soon the third day was passing by, but the soldier gave no thought to leaving. From their conversations, the master found out that the soldier had a lot of money and liked his daughter. And so, after discussing this and that, they came to an agreement and began preparing for the wedding.

One day, after the wedding, when they were all having supper and talking about one thing or another, the master began telling the story about how a soldier had spent the night in his home when his daughter was born, and how this soldier had wickedly impaled the infant on a stake. Fortunately, the infant's diaper had snagged on the stake, and the infant was left dangling from it. When the soldier heard the story, he was astounded.

"But it was me, good people!" he said. "I'm the one who did it."

And he related how he had been sleeping, how the birds had flown in, what they had said, and how he had become infuriated with them.

But all the same, he did not avoid his fate—what was supposed to happen, did happen. A person's fate depends on the hour in which he is born.

***

It was winter. An old woman lived in a small cottage at the edge of a village. She lived there, but the winter was fierce, and she had no wood to heat her cottage, no warm food to eat. There was no way out—she had to seek help. She wrapped herself up in whatever she had, picked up a walking stick, and trudged down the street. Even though there were still a few people who cared about her, she liked, best of all, to call upon her sister's daughter—a rich, childless young woman. This woman never sent her away empty-handed—she would give her this and that, and then she would ask the old woman to pray for her, so that God would send her a child.

Finally, God took pity on the young woman, and she became pregnant. And, because of this, the old woman was given even more than she had ever received before.

Just when the old woman, with her walking stick in hand, was trudging along to this young relative's home, the latter went into labour—and she was suffering so greatly, that God forbid! At a time like this, the old woman was needed, and so she stayed the night. It was late already, but she could not sleep. She sat in a corner and prayed that God would help her niece to give birth successfully.

It was so bright outdoors, that it seemed like daylight. The moon was strolling with a leisurely gait among the stars, and the latter were winking their bright eyes and smiling at him, as girls smile at a young man. And the snow, glittering with thousands of sparks, looked like lace tatted with silver thread in the most enchanting stars and circlets.

Something made a soft sound, like snow sliding off a roof. The old woman glanced up and saw two large white birds with silver-tipped wings.

"Well? Has it been born?" one of the birds asked, and it sounded like a gust of wind.

"Yes, at this very moment."

"It's a sad hour. They didn't have any children until now, and it would have been better if they hadn't had any, because that child will be their death."

Before the old woman could come out of her trance, the birds disappeared.

When the old woman saw the joy of the father and mother, her heart broke, and she deliberated for a long time whether or not she should tell them what she had heard.

When she told them, their joy was extinguished, never to return.

The little boy grew up, and he was very handsome and obedient. He never did anything naughty, and not a single bad word was heard from him—but his parents took no joy in this. They sent him to school, and he learned everything better than all the other children. And he wondered why his father and mother were not like other parents, why they never laughed or took any pleasure in anything.

When he was grown, he began to press his parents for the reason for their behaviour. Why was it, that no matter what he did, and no matter how well he did, he could never make them happy? His father did not want to tell him, but his mother could not refuse her only child, and so she told him—it was thus and so; he had been born in such an hour that he was to be the death of his parents. Birds that had been outside the window when he was born had said so, and a certain old woman, who had been dead for many years now, had heard what they said with her own ears.

Upon learning this, the son also became very sad, and he wept bitterly. For a long time, he was more heavyhearted than his parents, and finally he said: "You know what? If that's how it is —that I am to be the cause of your death—it's better that we should part. Give me whatever you'd planned to give me, and I'll go out into the world and never return."

They talked the matter over and finally agreed to do as he wished. Selling whatever they could, they gave all the money to their son, leaving themselves only enough to live out their lives. They said their farewells, and the son departed.

The son was young, rich, and handsome, and he found it easy to make his way in the world. After some time, he married—and, in so doing, further increased his fortune. He was able to set himself up very comfortably and live like a lord. He had a good, faithful wife and all that he desired, but there was one thing that caused him pain—the fact that he could never again see either his father or mother. His wife often asked him who he was, where he was from, if he was an orphan, if he had parents, and, if so, where were they? She began to torment him about all this, dragging the answers out of him one word at a time, and after a while she found out everything she wanted to know.

The young man was a good archer, and he often went hunting in the forest. Once, when he was away from home for a longer period of time, his wife wrote his parents a letter as if it were from him. She told them where he was, what he was doing, and how he was getting along. And she invited them to come for a visit.

Of course, the parents, like all parents, were so happy, that they forgot all about their unhappy fate and set out to visit their son.

When they arrived, they found only their son's wife at home. The daughter-in-law bowed down low before them, kissed their hands, treated them to the best of everything, and kept running to see if her husband was returning; she was very happy that she was going to bring him such joy. Evening came, but he still had not arrived. She put fresh linen for his parents on the bed where she usually slept with her husband, and went to another room to sleep.

During the night, there was a thumping—thump, thump!

The husband came home, but his wife was sleeping soundly and did not hear anything. A sleepy servant got up to open the door.

Without asking anything, the husband went into the bedroom; the moon was shining through the window, and when he glanced at the bed, he saw a man sleeping beside his wife. The blood curdled in his veins, a fierce snake wound itself around his heart, and his teeth clamped together. With a trembling hand, he grabbed an arrow and aimed, first at the man, and then at the woman lying beside him. When his wife heard the noise, she ran in, wringing her hands.

"What have you done?" she wailed at the top of her voice. "It's your father and mother."

The archer toppled to a stool, as if he were dead. He had been born in such an hour that he was to be the cause of the death of his father and mother, and it had come to pass.

***

The night was dark, and there was a scent of rain in the air. The wind was chasing dark clouds across the sky; it roared though the branches of trees, stripping away their withered leaves. Here and there, a light flickered, then it turned gloomy, and then a clear, vivd flash illuminated everything again. At times, thunder crashed, and bright red arrows ripped apart the black clouds. In the darkness, something appeared over the treetops and became entangled in the leafless branches. A thunderbolt shook the heavens and the earth, and its fiery light reflected on the wings of two black birds that flew down over the roof of a peasant's cottage and alighted on a window.

"Well?" one of the birds inquired.

"It's been born already."

"And what kind of an hour is it?"

"It's an hour when witches are born," the other bird replied. Its voice was lost in a deafening crash of thunder, and the birds vanished in space.

No one saw them or heard them, and no one knew that a witch had been born in the village.

The witch grew up; she matured and married. That was when things began to go awry in the village, and even though the villagers did not know there was a witch in their midst, they began to suspect that something was wrong.

First, in one household, and then in another, cows that used to give normal amounts of milk suddenly either went dry, or began to produce only whey—not a bit of cream formed on the milk's surface. And, as the presence of a witch can be detected most readily by the milk that cows give, the villagers knew there was a witch among them, but they did not know who it could be.

Well, one time, when a young man was chopping wood, a whole knot flew out of the log. He had heard long ago, that if you looked through the hole in the log where the knot had been, then, if there were a witch in the village, she would appear before you. He grabbed the log, looked through it, and saw the richest woman in the village standing in front of him.

"Why did you strike the log so forcefully, and why have you called me here? Of what use is it to you to know that I'm a witch?" she asked. "Tell me what it is you want, and I'll do it; just don't hold me up to ridicule by the villagers."

"What can you do?" the young man asked.

"I have the most power when it comes to milk, but if you want me to, I can give you a *sopilka*—the kind that when you bring it up to your lips, it plays by itself."

You see, the witch knew the young lad really liked to play the *sopilka*, and she smiled when she saw his eyes light up when she mentioned it to him.

"When can you give it to me?" he asked the witch.

"At the time of the full moon, go at dusk into the forest; break off a branch, sit down on it, and say: 'Above the forest,' and you'll get what you want."

The young man did as he was told. When there was a full moon, he went at dusk into the forest, broke off a branch, sat down on it, and said: "Above the forest."

The wind blew and lifted him up like a hawk; he seemed to be flying straight to the moon that was hanging like a sickle over his head. The tips of trees flashed like grass beneath his feet, and a dull, prolonged roar rose from the depths of the forest; from time to time, a small meadow, with either a doe or a swift-footed rabbit running across it, could be seen. The forest began to thin out, and a thick fog spread widely, obscuring the river below.

He was carried down the length of the riverbank; fish were splashing in the water, and ducks rustled in the tall reeds on the banks.

Finally, he flew to a high mountain called *Lysa hora [Bald Mountain]*. The roar that was carrying him ceased and, in its place, he could hear something like the bellowing of a cow, like cruel, inhuman laughter. His head began to spin, even though he realised that he had stopped flying and was standing still.

"How are you feeling?" the witch inquired. "Was it a good ride?"

The young man rubbed his eyes, as if he were awakening.

Lord! There were hordes of evil spirits here! Devils were drinking, dancing with witches, and engaging in all sorts of pranks.

"Come and dance with me," the witch said to him.

"Fine with me!"

Well, they danced and they danced, and they drank and they drank, but finally the strength of the fiends began to abate; the roosters might crow at any moment—it was time to disperse.

"But where is my *sopilka*?" the young lad asked the witch.

"Don't worry," the witch said.

She waved her hand, and the "enemies"—may the evil spirits not hear their name—came running up. They gave him a golden *sopilka* and, in addition, a measure of gold. Then they sat him down on a branch and told him to say: "Over the forest."

The young man had become brazen; he wanted to outdo the power of the devils.

"I've already seen," he thought, "what there is 'above the forest.' Now I want to see what will happen if I say something else."

He sat down on the branch and said: "Through the forest!"

Well, he was blown away, carried off, and tossed from tree to tree! He was pounded up so badly that his soul was almost shaken out of him, and he was barely alive when he was thrown down at the edge of the forest.

Before another human being happened to come across him, he had given up the ghost. All that the people found near him was a horse's bone and a horse's hoof.

The witch was very happy with the outcome, because no one in the village had found out that she was a witch.

One day, a man from her village was going to town to sell brooms. He set out at daybreak—the stars were just beginning to fade, and daylight was approaching. As he walked, he noticed a sieve rolling along ahead of him. He tried to catch this sieve, but it kept running away; he tried to grab it, but it spun away into the swamps and marshes. The man, however, was big and strong; he stretched his legs, and—"Aha!"—he caught the sieve. "Be gone, fiend! What's a sieve doing here?" he pondered. He attached it to his leather belt and continued on his way.

After a while, he glanced down and saw that it was not a sieve, but a woman that he knew—the richest woman in the village.

"My good man!" she said. "Let me go, and don't say anything to anyone, and you'll have all the milk you want."

He had a pile of children, but only one cow, and so he thought: "Perhaps I should let the fiend go, and maybe I'll have more milk. What good will it do me if I hold her up to ridicule?"

He detached her from his belt. She changed herself into a black cat and raced back to the village.

In the evening, the man's wife went to do the milking; the cow kept giving more and more milk, as if it were a different cow. The woman was overcome with amazement; she could not understand what had happened. The husband did not say anything, because he was afraid the witch might take away the milk she had given them.

Well, it so happened that his kinsman's cows were losing their milk. The cows used to give milk as they were supposed to, but now the milk was so thin that there was nothing to look at; it was like water, and cream did not form on its surface, and it did not form curds and whey. The mistress of the house was worried; she asked people for advice, and she did everything they told her to do—she gathered stones along the road, got beetles from the gypsies and steamed them in boiling water, fumigated the cattle with herbs that were blessed on St. John's Eve—but nothing helped.

"Well, let's see now," an old woman said to her, just before Easter. "When you get home from church on Holy Thursday, have your husband go to the barn, seat himself behind the door, and wait until he sees something."

The housewife told her husband what to do. He obeyed her and, after the liturgy on Holy Thursday, went to the barn and sat down on a stool behind the door. Well, he sat and sat; it was after midnight already, and the roosters had crowed, but he still hadn't seen anything.

Easter went by. One day, the housewife happened to encounter the same old woman and told her that her husband had sat there, but had not seen anything.

"Well, let's see now!" the old woman responded in her usual manner. "Have your husband sit there once more, on the Feast of St. George; that's when witches are most likely to be roaming around."

On the Feast of St. George, the husband went to the barn, sat down behind the door, and waited. He was dozing off already, when he heard something rustle. He hid himself, but his head was swimming, and when he looked—there was nothing anywhere. Only a washing-beetle, used to beat clothing in a stream, was lying under the cow. "Phooey! The devil take it! How did a washing-beetle get here? There must be a reason for it!" he thought.

He took the washing-beetle, pierced a hole in the handle, and hung it under the icons. He had hardly stepped away, when the washing-beetle changed into his kinswoman, the richest woman in the village.

"Oh, my kinsman!" she said. "Let me go, and don't say anything to anyone, and you'll have as much milk as you want."

So, he let her go and did not say anything to anyone; and their cow gave them so much milk, that his wife could not find enough milk-pots.

But there was a mark left on the witch—the hole that the husband had made on the handle was left on her nose. The villagers often wondered: "How is it that she got a hole in her nose? There has to be an explanation for it!"

A few of the women noticed that some article of her clothing was always turned inside out—her kerchief, her skirt, or her apron. They also noticed that when the church procession began to circle the church, she never walked around the church three times as the others did; instead, she would lean against the fence and wait until they were finished. The neighbours began to be on their guard with her, as they would be with fire.

One day, a woman was whitewashing walls in her cottage and threw out an old brush made of twigs. Quite unexpectedly, the witch showed up, talked about this and that, visited for a while, and then left.

The woman remembered that she had thrown the brush outdoors without untying it—and she knew that you should not throw away an old brush without untying it first. She searched for the brush, but it was nowhere to be found.

"Aha! Something out of the ordinary is going to happen!" she thought. "Something 'deviant' will appear in the village."

In the meantime, the witch blew on the brush, made a child out of it, and waited for an infant to be born in the village in order exchange it for hers. But the villagers were on guard. They kept a light burning in a house until a child was christened, and no woman ever turned her back to her child, because everyone knew that a witch would immediately replace it with a changeling.

There was only one young woman—one who had just given birth to her first child—who did not know about the witch. Once, when her infant was lying beside her on the bed, and there was no one else in the house, she turned her back to the child. When she looked at the child again, well, God forbid!—it was neither a person, nor a dog. Its head was as big as a pumpkin, and its little feet and hands were like those of a puppy.

One month went by, and half a year, and then—yes, indeed—a year, and then a second one! But the child did not grow, nor did it develop mentally.

"It's Korchykha who has done this, and no one else," one young man started saying.

"How do you know?" people asked him.

"Don't ask me how. I just know."

One time, when they insisted, he told them that when he had been grazing horses on St. John's Eve, he saw Korchykha run out naked—without so much as a shirt—into the field at dawn, and start to whisper and gather the dew.

"I strained my ears," he said, "and she was saying: 'Whey for the people, and milk for me; whey for the people, and milk for me.' I was lying on the boundary, holding a feed bag in my hands, and when she said: 'Whey for the people, and milk for me,' and began gathering the dew, I began collecting the dew in my feed bag; and, whenever she said: 'Whey for the people, and milk for me,' I immediately said: 'May I have what you're wishing for yourself, and may you have what you're wishing for others.' On the second or third day, when I didn't take the horses to the pasture, I hung the feed bag on a hook in the barn and lay down to sleep. While I was sleeping, I could feel something dripping on me—drip, drip. I looked up and saw that milk was pouring out of the feed bag."

The people listened and shook their heads: "Maybe what he's saying didn't happen, but maybe it did."

For example, everyone knew that Korchykha could never retain servants in her home. If someone hired himself out to her, he would stay for a while and then move on. The people noticed that even if a young man was as ruddy as a beet when he began working for her, in a short time he would turn pale, then green, and then he would become stooped and shrivelled.

"The rich woman is stingy; she probably doesn't give them enough to eat," some of the villagers said. But others exchanged meaningful glances.

It was only one outsider who remained at her place for an entire year and then stayed on for a second one, but he also became just a shadow of his former self.

One day, this servant went to the young man who had not let the witch take away the people's milk.

"My good man," he said, "you were able to cope with my mistress and prevent her from taking away the milk from the people, so maybe you could give me some advice as well?"

"What do you need to know?" the young man asked.

The servant told him that every time there was a new moon, the witch drove him to distraction. "As soon as the moon rises, she gets up, takes a broom, and lays it down next to her husband—and the broom changes into a woman that looks just like her; then she takes a feed bag, comes to me, and throws it on my head. And when she puts it on my head, I immediately change into a horse. carry her up through the chimney, and fly to *Lysa hora*.

"Fine," the young man said. "When it's time for this to happen, you come to me; I'll teach her a lesson."

When the new moon rose, the servant called the young man.

"She'll be off on her journey tonight," he said. "And I quake all over when I call to mind the torments I'll have to suffer."

"Don't be afraid," the young man said. "Take your things and go back to where you came from. And lead me to your bed. I'll cope with her."

The servant did as he was told; he led the young man to his bed, while he himself went away and never returned

The young man lay down on the bed, put his hand on his head, and pretended to be sleeping. He heard the witch get up, take a broom, put it next to her husband, and then come towards him. She was just about to place the feed bag on him, when he jumped up, grabbed it from her, and threw it on her neck; as soon as she felt it on her, she whooshed up the chimney and flew to *Lysa hora*.

When they arrived, she said to him: "Come, take the feed bag off me, and we'll have a good time."

But he was not foolish enough to dismount and take the feed bag off her. "No," he said. "I'll have a good time like this."

He looked and saw some figures that appeared to be duelling. They were saying: "Slash, don't touch; slash, don't touch."

He watched and listened; finally, he grabbed a sword and attacked them. He swung and he swung—first in one direction and then in the other, and he kept saying: "Slash, slash right through; slash, slash right through."

His sword slashed through whatever it struck—a foot, an arm, or the tail of a witch, or the horns of the unclean ones, until they began to beg for mercy.

"We won't do anything to you," they said, "just don't slash us!"

"Take me back," he finally said to his mare.

She whooshed up into the air with him so quickly that the wind whistled, and she brought him back home.

"Just wait," the young man said, "I won't let you off this easily."

He dismounted, but did not remove the feed bag. He led her to the blacksmith and told him to shoe her. Then he brought her back home and took off the feed bag. As soon as he pulled it off, she changed back into a woman; but the horseshoes stayed on her hands and feet, and she was so tired, she could hardly crawl into the house.

It took her a long time to regain her strength; she stayed in bed for quite a while, and there was no servant in the house. She sent for her married daughter, who lived in another village, to come and help her. The daughter did a bit of this and a bit of that—of course, being a daughter, she had to help the witch. She had the most work with the milk; she had to do the milking, then strain the milk and pour it into containers.

"Oh, mother," she said. "You have so much milk! Why don't you do something, so that I too will have as much?"

The witch did not reply, but she told the daughter to bring a lump of butter from her home. She took a similar lump from her own home and, mustering all her strength—she was still quite weak—she went with her daughter to the river and threw her butter into the water.

"Now, throw yours," she told her daughter.

The daughter threw her lump, and they saw that the daughter's lump lay untouched where it fell, but all sorts of abominations—worms and bloodsuckers—crawled to the mother's lump and, in a moment, it was all gone.

"There, you see!" the witch said to her daughter. "You have only a little bit, but it's pure. And your soul is also pure. But after my death, my enemies will carry off my soul, just as the water worms took away my butter. But it doesn't help me that I know this, for I have to be what I am."

After some time, the witch regained her strength, and her horseshoes vanished; she must have flown on an oven-rake to *Lysa hora* and had the unclean ones remove them.

And then, out of the blue, there was a terrible drought. It was in the spring, and everything was begging for rain, but there was not a single drop. The grain turned yellow, the grass was burnt, and there was nothing for the cattle to graze. Everyone worried and complained. When things reek of hunger, it is no joking matter.

All the people were saying that it had to be a witch that stopped the rain; moreover, one night, a young man—the one who had spied on Korchykha as she gathered dew—saw her climbing feet first up a cross.

Even before hearing this, the people had long suspected that Korchykha was a witch, and now they were sure, because no person in his right senses would climb upside down on a cross.

They discussed it at length, but they could see no way out except to seize the witch, bind her little finger to her big toe, and cast her into the water.

The community elders assembled and went to see Korchykha. At first, they tried to justify themselves, so they asked her why she wandered about the fields at night and climbed upside down on God's sign!

The witch swore by all the saints that she wouldn't dare to go into the fields at night, let alone climb a cross, especially upside down.

"No," the elders said. "You had a reason for doing so. Come along with us."

Taking the witch, they led her to the river. She was shaking with fear, and crying in anger and shame. As they led her away, her husband rushed from the house and ran at top speed to the priest. He started telling him that it was thus and so—they were vilifying his wife, saying she'd stopped the rain, and they had stormed the house and were dragging her to the river.

The priest had heard, more than once, that rumours like this were circulating about Korchykha, but he could not permit such heathen acts to occur. He took his cross and walked out to confront his parishioners.

"Listen, people!" he shouted. "Come to your senses! What are you doing? Nothing in this world exists, or can exist, without God's will. It isn't the witch who has stopped the rain; God is punishing you for your sins. Come to the church, pray, and God will take pity on you."

Upon seeing the priest, some of the people ran away; others went with him to the church to pray, and the witch—as if she were trying to show that she was not a witch—prayed feverishly and prostrated herself on the ground. The people looked askance at such hypocrisy, and if it had not been for the priest, they would have killed her on the spot.

The witch saw that it was no joking matter, and so, during the night, she let the rain come down.

"Praise God for the rain!" the people said. They calmed down a bit and forgot about the wicked deeds of the witch.

But the witch did not forget the terrible shame they had inflicted on her, and she decided to seek vengeance. "If I didn't have any luck with the rain, I'll show you a thing or to with the frost. If things didn't work out in the spring, then they'll work out in the fall."

Prior to the Feast of The Dormition of the Mother of God, the witch went to town, bought four new pots, and cooked some buckwheat gruel in them. As soon as it turned dark, she took these pots and went into the fields with them.

But the young man who had travelled with her to *Lysa hora* and who had seen her gathering dew and climbing upside down on the cross was keeping an eye on her. He was grazing his horses when he saw that the witch was burying something on the boundary. She dug on one boundary, on the second, the third, and—what's more—on the fourth; she dug in all four directions—where the sun rose, where it declined, and on the north, and the south.

As soon as she went away, he ran up to these spots and began digging; in the first spot, he dug out a pot with buckwheat gruel; he went to the second spot—and pulled out a second pot; he went to the third, and the fourth, and pulled out all four pots. Then he went to her house; the witch was sleeping, and it was dark and quiet all around. He took the four pots and buried them in all four corners of her cottage—one pot in the first corner, another one—in the second, and the same with the third and fourth; he buried them on all four sides, and then he waited until morning to see what would happen.

When morning came, the house was filled with frost. It was such a terrible frost that the entire house turned white, and the witch and her husband froze to death.

And so, the witch died—the witch who had to live and be as she was, because she had been born in such an hour; and her husband died with her, probably because he had defended a sorceress.

The Soul
A Psychological Sketch
(1895)

"This is Father Urbanovych, the young clergyman recently appointed to our parish." Savyna presented a young man, no more than twenty-six years old, dressed in clerical clothing, to Lady Yevheniya.

He was fairly short and slight of frame. He could not be called handsome, but there was something about him that was very attractive, and his large, dark, and wise eyes were especially appealing.

"Your ladyship must have arrived for the summer season. At this time of year many people come to rest in the fresh air of our little town."

"Actually, I wanted to visit my family, but I don't deny that I came during the summer to escape the oppressively hot weather in the city."

"It truly is difficult to tolerate the summer heat in the city."

"Especially in Vienna—it's an absolute inferno there."

"Does your ladyship live in Vienna?"

"Yes, Vienna."

"I recall the Viennese dust-clouds only too well!"

"So you know Vienna, Father?"

"I'm a Viennese seminarian."

"Then you must have been among the last graduates of the Institute that was recently closed?"

"I'm 'The Last of the Sekerzhynskies,'" the young cleric replied merrily.

"In theory," Lady Yevheniya continued, "the disbanding of the Institute is itself of no great significance; but, in reality, our enemies have dealt a barbaric blow against the higher education that our clergy inevitably absorbed in such centres as Vienna."

"You're absolutely right. Our enemies realised that the priests educated in Vienna acquired a much broader education than just dry theological learning—they became familiar with the progressive strivings of knowledge, with its ideals."

"Now one truly won't be able to expect priests to be well-educated, not if they're trained in private institutions in provincial towns."

"That's why this scheme was conceived, so that the graduates would be ascetics and of little value to their native land," Urbanovych said.

During this conversation, Yevheniya had placed on a side table the book she was holding when Savyna led in the young priest.

Father Urbanovych glanced curiously at the title of the book, which he could not read from where he was.

"Will your ladyship permit me to look at it?" he inquired after a moment, taking advantage of the first longer pause in the conversation and reaching for the book.

"Please do. I too am one of those people who can't refrain from looking through a book when they see it."

Father Urbanovych quickly leafed through the book, and his eyes shone eagerly as he did so.

"I've wanted to read this for some time now, but once I left Vienna it was impossible to get a copy."

"It's not a new publication; one can find it, not only in every bookstore, but also in shops that sell used books."

"All the same, one has to have the money," the young man laughed.

"It's not expensive."

"That depends for whom. When I was still an aspirant to the spiritual profession, I had no desire to acquire riches—which are so contrary to a priestly calling—and I have even less of a desire for them now that I am a priest."

"You, undoubtedly, are married?"

"Of course. It seems, however, that celibacy will be an inevitable consequence of the newer school."

"So, it appears you did not take the practical approach of young men nowadays, who try, above all, to improve the state of their coffers with their wife's dowry when they enter the state of matrimony."

"On the contrary. I believe I provided proof of my practicality because I did not look for riches. I married without gaining a fortune and thus was spared the disillusionment that so often befalls a man when he marries for money."

They both enjoyed a good laugh.

"If it would please you, I could lend you this book."

"It would more than please me—it would be a great favour, because, judging from the local situation, it wouldn't be difficult to forget how to read altogether in this town."

"Well, I hope that at least while I'm here, you won't forget. I've brought some works that are even more interesting."

Yevheniya reeled off the titles of several recently published books. Father Urbanovych was not familiar with any of them.

"I'll fetch them and show them to you."

Before Father Urbanovych could come up with a polite phrase to the effect that she should not trouble herself in any way, she rose to her feet and went off to her room.

"She's an unusually charming lady," Urbanovych said to Lady Savyna who, after introducing him to Yevheniya, had left them alone, and only now re-entered the parlour.

"Nevertheless, it's evident that life has not always smiled upon her. A sadness of some kind is visible in her every glance and gesture, even though she appears to speak and laugh merrily," he added emphatically.

"A person's life is not all sweetness and light," Savyna nodded in reply. "The sadness that, as you say, is visible in her every glance and gesture, has marked her since she lost her son, her only child."

Their conversation was interrupted because, at that moment, Yevheniya came back with some books and placed them before Urbanovych.

Father Urbanovych, having glanced through the books, observed jokingly that they were not necessarily the best reading material for priests and ladies. Until recently, priests had been the sole leaders of women, but now women were leading them—the priests—astray!

"It would appear that the new currents of the times are indeed strong if women are able to take in tow that formerly mighty phalanx," Yevheniya replied in the same tone.

Urbanovych selected a few books and said his farewells.

From then on, he often dropped by, and his visits were the most pleasant moments that Yevheniya spent in the home of her relatives. They touched upon questions of principle, as well as matters that were more mundane, but mostly they discussed the contents of the books they read.

Occasionally, Urbanovych came with his young and pretty wife, whose sky-blue eyes and angelic glances quickened one's heart. However, at those times the discussions limped along, for they had to change the themes of their conversation and confine themselves to those in which she could participate. Urbanovych must have realised this as well, because, more often than not, he came alone.

There was one time when Yevheniya guessed correctly that he had some important matter to discuss with her. When, as so often happened, they were alone, his face assumed a conspiratorial look, and he pulled a bundle of papers from his side pocket.

"What are you bringing me that's so interesting?" Yevheniya inquired.

"I don't know if it will be interesting to you. It is of interest to me to know what you will say about it."

"What is it?"

"It's some attempts at writing."

"Ah!" Yevheniya said in surprise, stretching out her hand for the bundle. "This is truly most interesting. Will you leave it with me to read?"

"No, I'll read it to you myself, and you will be good enough to tell me if it is worth anything."

He began to read the brief sketches he had written—vivid descriptions of a young cleric's arrival in a small town parish and episodes characterising the beginning of his new life.

Yevheniya was touched. The writing of the young author revealed undeniable talent. But when the author explicitly requested that she point out his shortcomings, she observed that perhaps he delved too little into the thoughts and feelings of the characters he introduced into his story.

"This is exactly my intention," the young writer responded. "If I want to write the truth, then I can write only what I see and hear. I regard as blatant liars those writers who endeavour, as it were, to enter into the souls of others. A person can know only what is happening in his own soul, not what is transpiring in the soul of another."

"But this is exactly the principal merit of talent. I would say that talent is nothing more than the great gift of penetrating into the souls of others."

"So, you're saying that I have no talent?"

"On the contrary, I am thoroughly convinced that you are talented. Your powers of observation are very acute, but you have not developed the psychic nature of man, and this, I am saying, is the main characteristic of talent. Having said that, I think your sketches are so good that it might be necessary to concede that some talents can dispense with psychological analysis."

From that time on, the conversations of Yevheniya and the young cleric became even more frank and heated.

"I have something new to read to you," Urbanovych said one day, as he settled down in the veranda where Yevheniya spent most of her time.

He read her a short sketch entitled "The Soul." A young clergyman is awakened to go to a sick person. He goes and hears the confession of an elderly woman, who dies shortly after orally bequeathing her humble possessions to her children. At the funeral, the clergyman engages in a conversation with one of the parishioners. The peasant asks the priest: "Is it true that the soul of the departed follows the funeral procession?" The young cleric, happy as he would have been to refute this belief with theoretical proof, felt that this might have a negative effect on the practical side of his "profession." After all, a peasant might conclude that "if the soul of the departed does not see the impressive show that is put on for it, then perhaps a funeral is not needed."

This sketch appealed greatly to Yevheniya. It undoubtedly was his best effort. All the same, she could not refrain from objecting that the scene with the dying woman was written dryly, in a perfunctory manner—as a duty of the priest—and it was suffused with a somewhat mocking tone. No matter what one thought about psychology, this contradicted the serious—indeed, tragic—theme.

"You're telling me, once again, to describe another person's soul, which I am not able to see, for no one can see it," Father Urbanovych stated.

"Not to see it, but to feel it."

"No one can feel another person's soul," the young author stoutly defended his point of view. And once again they began a spirited argument.

Yevheniya was trying to make the point that even if the author does not enter into the state of a dying person's soul, he should at least describe the impression that the scene makes on those who are present, for such a moment must have a profound effect on all who are close to the dying person, even if just for the natural reason that death is claiming a victim from among them.

"You know, Father Urbanovych hasn't been here for two days," Yevheniya observed one day during breakfast.

Savyna also found this somewhat strange, and she immediately sent a servant to the priest's home to inquire why Father Urbanovych had not been at their place for a while. The servant returned with bad news. Father Urbanovych was confined to his bed; the doctor had been called during the night.

"What the deuce! What's happened to him?" the master muttered. "Not long ago he was as healthy as a horse."

"Well, he never could boast of having the health of a horse, because he never was overly healthy," Savyna observed. She always liked to correct the observations of her husband, and he had long ago become accustomed to this tendency of hers, accepting it as a sign of her affection for him.

"Perhaps I should go see him?" he added a moment later.

"Of course you should. Go and find out what's wrong. And, as soon as I've tended to my household chores, I'll go too."

"We'll both go," Yevheniya picked up the conversation. "I feel lost when I don't see him for some time; I've really become accustomed to his visits."

Savyna's husband, who had been sent off to visit the priest, returned in an hour and calmed the fears of the women.

The priest was indisposed with an upset stomach and a headache. The doctor had told him to stay in bed, but the illness was not serious. The women felt reassured and did not set out to visit the patient until the afternoon. The illness did not seem to be threatening, even though Urbanovych's wife said that he had been very ill at night. The patient was almost cheerful. He described his nocturnal cramps with his usual good humour and complained of a slight pain in his ear.

Yevheniya dropped by almost hourly to inquire about the health of the patient. Sometimes things were better, sometimes worse, but the illness did not abate.

She often came alone, and this made the patient very happy. He found it boring to lie in bed. The doctor's diagnosis was a severe stomach cold, and because dysentery was rampant in the little town, some of his acquaintances were afraid to visit him.

Two weeks after the priest became ill, Yevheniya received another shipment of books from Vienna. They were the newest publications, and she was delighted to be able to share this treasure with him; however, unexpected interruptions during the day prevented her from visiting him until evening.

It was almost seven o'clock, but as is usually the case during the longest summer days, it was still quite light outside. Taking along a book—the contents of which seemed to her to be especially interesting—and revelling in the wonderful summer air, she slowly drew near the home of the priest.

In the waning daylight, she was unpleasantly disturbed by the yellowish glare, like the glow of a lamp, that penetrated the curtain of the tightly closed window. She walked up to the house. It was quiet everywhere. She entered the kitchen. It was empty, and the door to the bedroom was opened wide.

Urbanovych's wife stood in the middle of the room in which the patient was lying. She seemed completely calm, but somewhat startled by Yevheniya's arrival. A servant, standing a little to one side and holding something in her hands, was screening the patient.

"I've come at an inopportune time," Yevheniya said.

Urbanovych's wife did not reply. At that moment, the servant turned away, and Yevheniya was struck dumb.

The patient was neither sitting nor lying down; his limbs were tautly tensed, and it was obvious that he was attempting to crawl out of bed. His face was pale and distorted, and one of his eyes was dilated, bulging out of its socket, and looking in terror at what was happening around him, as if it were asking: "Is this really death? Cruel, inexorable death?"

The life force that Yevheniya brought with her could not be reconciled with its terrible enemy—death. "No, he has not died yet! Help! Someone, please help!"

Without stopping to think, she ran out into the street. It appeared to be empty, but the shadows of three men flitted by in a bend of the road. Yevheniya ran as fast as she could. It really was three men she knew.

"For the love of God! Stop! Father Urbanovych is dying, but he's still alive. Run and fetch a doctor; perhaps he can still be saved."

Two of the men, without asking any questions, sped like arrows in opposite directions. The third remained with Yevheniya; he wanted to talk with her, to ask her some questions, but she was in no mood for talk. She saw that she was in front of the house of a good friend of the Urbanovyches—a Lady Hramska, who lived there with her elderly mother.

"I must tell her to go to the Urbanovyches, and then I'll run home. My brother-in-law knows the Urbanovych family, so he can notify some of them." As all of this rushed through Yevheniya's mind, she bid the man farewell and dashed into Lady Hramska's house.

"What's happened to you?" Lady Hramska cried out in alarm when she saw Yevheniya.

"Go! Go there! Don't leave her alone!" Yevheniya said, gesturing with her arm in the direction of the street where the Urbanovyches lived. Her arm was shaking like the leaf of an aspen.

The elderly woman rose abruptly from her chair. "What is it? What's happened?" she asked, scared out of her wits.

This reaction calmed Yevheniya a little. She took Lady Hramska by the arm and led her out to the porch. "Go to the Urbanovyches. It appears he's dying, and she's all alone; there's only a servant with her. I'm going home to inform some members of his family."

When she was out on the street again, a small carriage flashed by. She recognised the doctor and realised that he must be going to see Father Urbanovych. This meant that there would be help for the patient; Lady Hramska would be there with Urbanovych's wife; and she herself had to get home as quickly as possible to ensure that his family was informed.

But when Yevheniya wanted to increase her pace, her feet felt rooted to the ground. What was happening? Why were her legs refusing to obey her? And just at the very moment when it was necessary to save the life of a man, the husband of a wife, and above all, a talented writer who could bring honour to his native land—for he undoubtedly did have talent—a talent that death would destroy along with his life. Oh, my hapless country! A terrible fate hangs over you and snatches away your greatest talents!

Yevheniya, fearing that the news she was bringing would distress her relatives, entered the house through the kitchen.

"Why is her ladyship so pale?" the surprised servant asked.

"It's nothing! Hush! Father Urbanovych is very ill—he's dying. I'm afraid that the master and mistress will be very upset; I have to broach the matter gently."

But Savyna, hearing Yevheniya's voice, came into the kitchen; her husband followed her. They were both more alarmed by her appearance than by the news she had brought.

"Come into the living room, rest a while! Perhaps you'd like a drink of water?" They were both very solicitous.

"No, that's not necessary! Don't concern yourselves about me; inform someone from the Urbanovych family, for it's dreadful for her to be alone now, among strangers."

"But I'm not at all sure whom she'd want to inform, and even though I do know some of them personally, I don't know exactly where they live," Savyna's husband said.

Yevheniya saw that she had erred in her expectations. She decided that all three of them should go as quickly as possible to the Urbanovyches' home.

When they arrived they found the house full of people—two doctors, the blood-letter, Lady Hramska, a few men, several ladies, and some neighbours, as well as the cantor and the sexton.

The doctors and the blood-letter were occupied with the patient and kept giving new orders; first, they needed some ice, then some vinegar, handkerchiefs, sheets, glasses and plates for the bloodsuckers, fresh water and ice for the blisters, and so on.

The patient was lying with his eyes rolled upwards; he was breathing harshly. Everyone walked softly and talked in whispers.

Urbanovych's wife, wrapped in a thick shawl as if it were the middle of winter, was sitting with two ladies in a corner in the adjoining room. She was shaking violently, and the ladies were doing their best to calm her.

At last, one of the doctors stepped away from the patient, flung himself in an armchair in the next room and, propping his head on his elbow, leaned on the table.

"Well? Is there no hope? What's wrong with him, exactly?" the onlookers asked, as they surrounded the doctor.

"There's absolutely no hope! He had a polyp in his ear—it wasn't taken care of soon enough—and now it's gone into his brain, and he's paralysed."

"But perhaps there is some kind of cure for it?" several people demanded of the other doctor.

"Nothing can be done for this kind of illness," he replied, shrugging his shoulders helplessly.

After some time, the doctors exchanged glances and prepared to leave. Some of the others followed them. Only the blood-letter and the sexton remained with the patient.

It was also time for Savyna to leave. "Let's go home," she said to Yevheniya. "There's nothing more that can be done here now. Popovych will send a telegraph to the family; we've discussed this matter with him."

"You go, but I'll stay here," Yevheniya replied with firm resolve.

"But it's not something your nerves can take, Yevheniya," Savyna tried to convince her.

"No, no! I won't leave these people! I came here at a most critical moment; I know what such moments are like, and this is obviously an opportunity to pay back what I owe others."

A few more people left. Only the sexton remained with the patient. The two ladies still sat with Urbanovych's wife. Popovych approached her, a paper and a pencil in his hands. She loudly recited the addresses of some relatives, including her husband's mother. Hearing this, Yevheniya shuddered and moved towards the porch.

A large mirror on the opposite wall reflected the bed and the entire figure of the patient. His face had become calm, but it was still deathly pale; his eyelids were wide open, and his vacant, stupefied eyes stared unseeingly, indifferent to everything that was happening around him. The frenzied flies caught scent of their quarry and were swarming on the patient's pale face, and the only task that the sexton now had was to chase them away. And his mother was to witness all this.

Yevheniya's temples were throbbing, her chest was constricted, and she began sobbing hysterically. Almost immediately, however, she dried her tears. She had not come here to cry; she had come to help! "Help?" she thought. "What kind of help? Human help is of no avail here! Only some supernatural power could help, but it seems that there is none."

A deep silence settled all around. The dark night enveloped the house and stuck fast to the windows, like an opaque blind.

Those keeping vigil sat silently, without moving, exhausted by their agitation and the lateness of the hour. Only Lady Hramska was still bustling about, walking here and there, putting things away, and locking everything up with the keys she had taken from Urbanovych's wife.

Something thumped in the attic, as if someone had taken a step, and then all was silent again.

"Someone's up in the loft," one of the ladies observed.

"That's the way it's always been," Urbanovych's wife stated. "It's walked and walked, and now it's come for my husband."

One of the ladies started to tell them how something had walked and thumped in the house when her mother was dying.

"When my husband's father was dying, something wept at the window," the other lady added.

The conversation continued along these lines, as the ladies tried to outdo one another in describing terrifying omens.

After some time, a light step was heard in the loft, and then something seemed to fall from the rafters.

Urbanovych's wife shrank and curled herself up into a ball.

"It must be the cat chasing some mice," Yevheniya said.

"But we don't have a cat," Urbanovych's wife retorted, almost angrily.

Yevheniya fell silent. She explained the mysterious thumps to herself as caused, if not by a cat, by some other night animal. All the same, at this critical moment these sounds began to take on some other meaning, and they jarred her nerves badly.

"Perhaps someone took advantage of the confusion and crawled up into the loft," Lady Hramska observed, after a moment's pause.

This appeared to be the most likely explanation to Yevheniya, and she said that someone should go up into the attic to find out for sure. Lady Hramska took a candle and went first, and Yevheniya followed. They were already on the first steps leading up to the loft, when Lady Hramska stopped.

"Go and call Popovych, for if it really is some thief, what will we do by ourselves?"

Yevheniya did as she was bid. Popovych did not refuse, but he looked unhappy, as he rose to his feet and followed the ladies.

"Bring the sexton as well," Lady Hramska kept issuing orders.

There was no one in the loft. As if to confirm Yevheniya's hypotheses, there was only a scattered pile of corn and some other grain stored as feed for the chickens.

"Well, what was it?" Urbanovych's wife and the two ladies asked when the four came down from the loft.

"Nothing," Popovych replied curtly.

Urbanovych's wife wrapped herself more tightly in her shawl; triumph gleamed in the eyes of her companions.

Popovych, observing these triumphant looks, added, in a slightly impatient voice: "When it's quiet in the house, it seems as if someone is walking about, even if it's only a crow that alights on the roof."

"It may or may not be a crow, but it won't reveal itself to everyone," the sexton observed, joining the side of those who tended towards mysticism.

At last, the ladies who were sitting with Urbanovych's wife began getting ready to go home. One of them could not leave her children alone any longer; the other one had a mean husband and feared he would upbraid her for being away from home for so long.

Only Yevheniya, Lady Hramska, Popovych, and the sexton were left.

"What is it that smells like that?" the sexton asked after some time had elapsed. Judging by his bowed head, one could see that he had been deeply bothered by the mysterious thumps in the loft.

A strange smell was, indeed, spreading through the house, and both Yevheniya and Popovych noticed it as well. Lady Hramska went into the kitchen and stoked the fire. It seemed to her that it must be some firewood that had not finished burning.

The silence that descended after the departure of the two ladies weighed even more heavily on the nerves of those who remained. Popovych's cigarette holder dropped from his hand, and Yevheniya jumped, as if something untoward had happened. Mice were rustling in a corner, putting everyone on edge. A cricket chirped in another corner, and something once again stirred in the loft.

The wife of the dying man was enveloped in a despairing uneasiness. She kept leaping to her feet and running into the patient's room; however, she did not approach the bed and, as if overcome by fear, she hurriedly returned to her place.

The dying man continued breathing heavily.

Evidently, it was this sound that was tearing his wife's soul apart, for she suddenly rushed from the room into the kitchen and, throwing herself on a cot in a fit of paroxysmal weeping, stopped her ears with her hands.

Lady Hramska tried comforting her with the usual trite phrases that are uttered at moments like this, but her efforts only upset the distressed woman even more.

Yevheniya and Popovych exchanged glances and began to talk about the most ordinary matters as loudly as they could. They were successful in their efforts. The unfortunate woman became drowsy, and in a few minutes, exhausted by her husband's illness, she was fast asleep.

Whenever their conversation stopped, she woke up abruptly. Yevheniya began to pace the room, trying to block out the sound of the dying man's rasping breathing, as much for herself as for the wife.

Oh, that rasping, that heavy breathing! It reminded her of the terrible event in her life that only time had eased. Only time had taught her how to control her mind and to think about everything except what was most painful to her.

"No, no!" she kept repeating to herself with acquired firmness. "It was not like this; it was completely different!"

The sexton, for no good reason, kept calling her and Popovych to come to the patient. It was obvious that he found it difficult to sit, without any healthy companions, at the side of a man already half dead.

At those times, Yevheniya tried to gaze calmly at the patient. This death, this terrible death about which she could not bring herself to think, was not at all as terrible as the one engraved in her memory by the loss of the one who had been dearest to her. Nonetheless, this comparison wrenched her heart so badly, that she once again had to summon all her strength to divert her thoughts, to convince herself that what lay in the bottom of her heart was entirely different from what was happening before her now.

The struggle was exhausting her, and it culminated in a single, overwhelming desire to have everything end as quickly as possible. She read the same desire on the faces of the others, including Urbanovych's wife.

The young woman kept getting up from the cot, then lying down again. All her thoughts were focussed on her brother, who was likely to arrive before her other relatives. Even though it was still dark outside, she kept running to the window and asking what time it was.

"Do you have any coins?" Lady Hramska whispered to Yevheniya. "One should buy the sexton at least a measure of whiskey. I'd send a maid to the nearest tavern, but I don't have so much as a *kreytsar [penny]* with me. Sitting all night beside a sick man—that's not easy . . ."

Yevheniya was already reaching into her pocket, when it suddenly occurred to Lady Hramska that it might be better to heat the samovar and make some tea, which would also be good for Popovych, as he too, was exhausted. In a short while, the samovar came to a boil, and Lady Hramska managed to find some bread and butter.

It was a most fortunate thought, for the tea truly did revive the two men. To keep them company, or perhaps out of a physical need, Lady Hramska poured herself a cup of tea as well.

"Aren't you going to have some tea with us?" she asked Yevheniya.

Yevheniya shuddered. It was not so much the fact that they were eating and drinking that was strange and revolting to her, as the fact that people ate at all.

The patient was growing weaker. His convulsions were not as strong; he was breathing more freely, and his eyes were wandering, as if he were searching for someone.

"There's no holy picture here, that's why his eyes are staring like that and are unable to die. Bring in an icon or a cross," the sexton said to Yevheniya.

Having almost lost the power to think independently, she acceded to the will of the sexton. She walked into the adjoining room and looked around the walls, trying to find a holy picture. She saw an icon of the Mother of God and wanted to take it down, but her hands were shaking so violently that Lady Hramska had to do it for her.

The heavy breathing of the dying man was abating; it was obvious the end was coming soon. Yevheniya felt that her nerves were painfully strained, and that they would become still more unstrung before the crash of the final tragic chord.

It was dawning.

Urbanovych's wife walked out into the porch; it seemed to her that her brother had driven up. Lady Hramska, who was very concerned that none of the family had arrived, followed her.

"What will we do if the end comes before anyone gets here?"

Yevheniya was sitting limply, her hands on her knees. Popovych was gazing stubbornly at the bluish panes of the window, in which the yellow light of the sooty lamp was dimly and ominously reflected.

Through the doorway which opened into the yard, the even voice of Lady Hramska and the nervous and agitated sobbing of Urbanovych's wife could be heard.

A rooster crowed in the yard—a prolonged, shrill cry—and dogs howled in the distance.

The tall figure of the sexton appeared on the threshold. Popovych turned from the window. Yevheniya cast a long, questioning look at him.

"It's all over," the sexton said, almost in a whisper.

Yevheniya leapt to her feet, but Popovych rushed ahead of her to the room of the deceased.

The dreadful agony had changed into a picture of quiet, peaceful sleep. There was, however, something so powerful and grand in it, that the two who were entering stopped in the doorway and did not dare to approach any closer.

After a moment, Popovych took a few steps forward and crossed himself. Yevheniya, feeling as if something was lifting her hands, blessed herself three times, in keeping with the rituals of her church.

"What are we going to do now?" Lady Hramska spoke up behind her. "Her brother still hasn't arrived."

Yevheniya was outraged to the depths of her soul. This mundane concern was so contrary to what was now occurring before her in all its grandeur and dreadfulness. She stared fixedly at a spot in the ceiling where the plaster had fallen off in a few places, and she could clearly see the image of a light, transparent little cloud rising upwards above the deceased, breaking away, and gradually dissipating. Only one more moment was needed, just one moment, for what she was looking at to lift itself up and fly away.

The loud wailing of Urbanovych's wife, resounding in her ears, roused her out of her trance.

Popovych and Lady Hramska began to confer about what should be done with Urbanovych's wife. The poor woman could not be left here while the deceased was being prepared for burial. Yevheniya, preoccupied with something else, listened dully. At last, Lady Hramska decided that Yevheniya should take Urbanovych's wife to her place and leave her in the care of Lady Hramska's elderly mother.

It was no easy task to get her to leave. The distraught woman protested, and it took a long time to convince her. Finally, Yevheniya managed to take her away.

One look at Urbanovych's wife, and Lady Hramska's elderly mother realised that it was all over; she embraced her and kissed her on the forehead, with obvious respect for her sorrow. Yevheniya was extremely tired. There was nothing more for her to do here; she said her farewells and went home.

The beautiful morning sparkled bewitchingly. The rays of the brilliant sun rose above the horizon, and the sun itself, half-covered by a red cloud, cast bright streaks across the sky, gilded the houses, and poured a radiant purple over the tops of the mountains that ringed the little town. The town was coming to life after its nocturnal rest, windows and doors were being opened, and people appeared on the street. The air was pleasant, even though it was cool and damp from the dew.

The freshness of the morning revived her and shook off the impressions of the night. What had happened? What had she seen? Was it true that she had searched for night terrors, that she had taken down icons and crossed herself? Was it true that all this had happened because of him, Urbanovych, who was no longer among the living?

What she had experienced this night was painful proof that the death of a person is something so immensely tragic that it could not be discounted as easily as Urbanovych had dismissed it in his sketch "The Soul." But with whom could she share this insight? For what she had been trying to prove had befallen the one with whom she had been arguing the point.

Was this also not a tragedy?

Other details of the sad event swam into her consciousness. She recalled how Popovych, deathly pale, had crossed himself. What feelings had gripped him at that moment? Were they similar to the ones she had experienced? She resolved to ask him about this at the very first opportunity.

The opportunity came quite soon.

"Did I cross myself?" Popovych asked in surprise. "I don't recall that at all."

Yevheniya could not discern if he were speaking sincerely, or only pretending to be a free thinker.

The Rose
A Sketch
(1897)

"Ha-ha-ha!" the silvery sound of a young woman's laughter echoed down the long street of the far-flung village.

The sun was setting, leaving behind red mountains of clouds with gilded tips and deep, jagged notches. Everything was bathed in its crimson shadow—the village, the lengthy street, and a group of young women, walking along with distaffs in their hands, laughing loudly, and boisterously exchanging comments.

"You better believe it! Anna will be really happy to have so many young women at her *vechernytsi [evening party with dancing and singing]*."

"That's nothing new for her, is it? There are always a lot of girls at her *vechernytsi*."

"And she also attracts the most young men."

"That's true! There are more young men at her *vechernytsi* than at anyone else's."

"She must brew lovage and give it to them to drink."

"Huh, you're talking as if the young men actually come to see her. As if they had no one better to run after than an old woman like her!" a tall blond girl said.

"Well then, why do they go to her place?"

"To see the young women who gather in her home."

"But sometimes young men prefer to chase older women and don't even want to look at younger ones!"

"There are girls that they don't chase, but there are also those that they do." The girl who said this was walking calmly and confidently. Her eyes sparkled merrily, and her long blond braids, tied with scarlet ribbons, peeked out from under her crimson kerchief.

A grey, smoky haze veiled the blue mountains of clouds. A darkening twilight spread over the village and flowed down the long street like a river.

Two women were standing by a gate.

"Oh, oh! There goes Maryna Lukiyanova—hurrying to a *vechernytsi*," Mykhaylykha observed to her kinswoman Protsykha.

"The granddaughter's rushing off to dance—and her grandmother's feet haven't even turned cold in her grave."

"Do you suppose she's thinking about her grandmother? All she's interested in are young men and good times!"

"And she really leads them on, she really does! There probably isn't a single young man in the village who hasn't chased after her!"

"God help her! Let's hope things work out for her."

"She's made her bed; she'll have to lie in it!"

"Lordy Lord!—that's some mother she has!"

"There's no doubt about it—a mother like that should be skinned alive!"

"You're right about that, my dear kinswoman. And let me tell you this—her mother, Lukiyanykha, actually takes pride in having such a spirited daughter. Not so long ago, she told me that even if Maryna were bound with a chain, she'd break loose and run off to dance."

"My, my!"

Muted whispers drifted down the street. The wind raced along the ground, tearing off tufts of weeds and scattering them like fluff; it rolled the tips of the dill plants under the fences and swayed the long branches of the willows that stood on both sides of the street, looking as if they were pondering something in their voluminous heads. In the dark blue sky, a star flashed—like a girl who dashes out beyond the gate to watch for her beloved.

And there he was . . .

Bright and cheerful, he crept out stealthily from behind the mountains and floated out into the clear blue sky. With his arrival, everything rejoiced and glowed. The hills and trees, laughing happily, attired themselves elegantly in sumptuous vestments embroidered with silver.

Grey and black clouds huddled in thick masses and, like jealous old women, eavesdropped on the sweet tête-à-tête of a young couple in love. Observing this, the mischievous wind pursued them with a light, whistling sound, and dispersed them into smaller clusters.

Then, it swooped to the ground, blew down the length of the street, shook the willows, rustled the weeds, and sped after a group of young men ambling down the road, tugging at their tall hats, flipping back the brims, and lifting the hems of their garments.

"The wind is very playful today," one of the young men remarked, holding on to his hat.

"Yes, it's really having a good time; it's racing down the street so quickly that it's raising the dust!"

"Perhaps it doesn't have a date and is hurrying to the *vechernytsi.*"

"It's certainly in a hurry, there's no doubt about that. It keeps rushing on ahead."

"Well, there are those among us who are doing likewise," another young man remarked.

Everyone guffawed good naturedly. The only one who did not laugh was the young man in the lead. He furrowed his eyebrows in a sullen frown and absentmindedly shifted his coat from one shoulder to the other.

"I wonder if Maryna Lukiyanova will be at Anna's this evening?" one of the youths tossed out innocently after a pause, and once again, everyone roared with laughter.

"Whoever has been pursuing her the longest is sure to know that best of all," the gloomy young man finally said, and he glanced out of the corner of his eye at the rather small, skinny youth who was walking along beside him.

"Well, I chased after her only for a while, but now—let the devil chase her. I sure won't be that stupid any more," the skinny one shot back.

"Just don't renounce her, don't forswear her, because we've seen your kind before," the youths laughed at him.

"Whoever doesn't want to forswear her, doesn't have to, but I can forswear her, because I've had enough! She leads everyone around by the nose! At first, she puts on an act that she likes you, and then she makes a laughingstock of you!"

"That's what you're saying now, but what about the time that Vasyl wanted to make her leave the dancing because of her fickleness? Weren't you the one who got into a fight with him?"

"Yes, I fought with him, because I hadn't got to know her yet, but now I know her all too well."

"You thought you were going to be the best, but better ones turned up," a few of the young men snickered, glancing pointedly at the youth with the furrowed brow, who was still walking on ahead. His handsome face became even more downcast.

The street was coming to an end. The gloomy youth clenched his fists and turned abruptly to his companions.

"Listen," he said in a choked voice. "There probably isn't a single one among us who hasn't wooed Maryna Lukiyanova, and who hasn't been made to feel the fool. It wouldn't be a bad idea to bring her down a peg or two and show her that we're nobody's fool."

The young men were all ears.

"Let's do it like this," the youth continued. "Starting tonight, not one of us will talk to her; we'll all act as if she isn't there."

"It's a good idea," the skinny youth quickly agreed.

"Let's try it; it won't hurt to try," some of the others observed.

"Let's, and we'll see what will come of it," the other young men agreed.

They were drawing near a house that stood by the side of the road, on the outskirts of the village. The house was large; it had a chimney and was shingled, but the shingles were ripped off in places, and peeling walls gleamed in the moonlight. Clusters of weeds, scattered by the wind, clung to the broadly spreading branches of an old, hollow pear tree.

The barn was wide open, the door to the stable lay on the ground, and the wind was swinging a loose board on the gate. The property still showed signs of prosperity, but there was no one to look after it. The man of the house had died, and his widow did not bother to keep things up.

"I've had enough of working hard, with no time to enjoy God's world," she often said.

Her husband, albeit a good householder, had been a severe man who kept her under his thumb. After he died, his widow had a great time; she held *vechernytsi*, gave the young men plenty to drink, and paid no attention whatsoever to her property.

"Glory to Jesus Christ! God help you! Good evening!" the youths shouted, as they walked into the house.

"Glory forever. Thank you for your kind words!" the young women responded cheerfully.

"Please, come in," the hostess invited them.

"Don't invite us so nicely, because not everyone may be happy to see us!"

"Oh, just look how vain they've grown! Now, they want the girls to throw themselves at them. Where would you find young women who aren't happy to see young men?"

"You think all women are like you, Anna," Maryna chimed in.

The girls laughed, but the youths did not react.

"Well, isn't it the truth? Just try saying that it isn't true! Who would believe you?" Anna shot back.

"Yes! That's Anna for you! Even if the woman were seven miles beyond hell, she could still tell you off!" the young men said ingratiatingly.

"Like-minded people always praise one another," Maryna intruded once more.

"Well, what's true, is true!" the girls said laughingly, nodding their heads in agreement.

But the young men once again acted as if they had not heard anything.

"You're wrong, and I'm right," Anna stubbornly defended her point of view.

"That's the way it is—Anna's truth always wins out," the youths continued.

"You're absolutely right. But do sit down! Why are you standing?" the hostess entreated them.

"Thank you, let the holy ones sit down—we'll stand!"

"Perhaps you'll grow taller," the girls snickered.

"Well, some may or may not need to, but it certainly wouldn't hurt Petro to grow a little," Maryna once again interjected, glancing flirtatiously at the skinny youth.

Petro pretended that he did not hear her, or even see her.

Finally, the youths began to make themselves at home; laughing and joking, they sat down beside the girls, but not one of them so much as glanced at Maryna. Whenever a conversation began, and

Maryna took part in it, they all immediately fell silent. If she said something funny, the girls laughed, but not one youth so much as twitched his moustache.

"What's going on? Have they all gone deaf, or has something else happened to them?" the scorned girl thought. She indignantly turned her eyes away from the gathering and stared fixedly out the window.

It was dark outside, and the wind, rustling in the mounds of weeds, wailed a sad song. The old pear tree creaked mournfully.

Maryna kept her eyes glued to the black windowpanes, but her heart seethed with anger, and dark, fragmented thoughts swirled in her head, whirring like the wings of wild birds.

"If only at least the devil would come and speak to me," she thought crossly.

"If only at least the devil," the wind whistled and, shaking the windows, it wailed in a wild groan, moaned in the chimney, and blew open the door with a crash.

"Oh! Away with you! Be gone!" almost everyone in the house exclaimed in alarm.

"Shut the door!" the hostess shouted.

But the door slammed shut all by itself, with the same crashing noise; something rustled through the house, and the old pear tree groaned woefully.

Maryna looked up and saw such a handsome young gentleman standing beside her that she was struck dumb. Tall and slender, he was dressed in a short jacket and a small hat with a feather in it. His hair was black as a raven, and his eyes seemed to be burning with a black flame.

He sat down beside her and began talking and joking. She also joked and laughed, delighted that she had someone to enjoy herself with.

"Who are you talking to? Who are you laughing with?" Anna inquired.

Maryna shrugged her shoulders.

"Really, who are you talking to?" the young women wanted to know.

"What's the matter? Have your eyes crawled out of your heads that you can't see the young gentleman?" Maryna replied irritably.

"A young gentleman? What young gentleman?"

They exchanged uneasy glances.

Maryna did not say anything else after this. Of what concern were all of them to her? The young gentleman was handsome and cheerful, and he was sidling up to her, hugging her, laughing, and whispering sweet nothings into her ear.

The blood raced in her veins, throbbed in her temples, and flooded her heart with unspeakable joy.

He was whispering softly: "Be mine, and you'll be a fine lady, and everyone will bow to you. You'll wear silk, travel by train, sleep on light down, swim in wealth, and glitter in gold and silver."

She pretended not to listen, acted coy, and turned away from him. He seized her hand and tried to slip a gold ring on her finger.

She withdrew her hand and inadvertently knocked her spindle to the floor. When she bent over to pick it up, she caught a glimpse of something and froze in fear . . . She looked again—the young gentleman had horse's hooves.

"Oh! I'm doomed!" she cried in an unearthly voice and, leaping to her feet, ran straight for the door.

At the gate, some young men cut her off and tried to stop her, but she wrenched herself free and tore down the street. Her kerchief slipped from her head, her shirt flapped behind her, and her long braids came undone as she ran.

He was racing right after her, clattering along on his horse's hooves, and asking in an ear-splitting whistle: "Why, oh why, don't you want me?"

She felt so light that she did not bother looking for the door— she flew into the house through the window. The shattered pane crashed in splinters behind her, and blood gushed from her arms.

With a heavy groan, she hurled herself into a corner and stopped up her ears, so she would not hear the terrifying whistling: "Why, oh why, don't you want me?"

A thick, dark fog, billowing upwards and creeping forward like threatening black phantoms, swathed her in an opaque mist. A man who looked like her father was beating his breast, but she could not tell who it was, no matter how intently she looked, or how hard she rubbed her eyes.

Her hands were wrapped in white cloths, there were drops of crimson blood on her apron, her ears were ringing, and her chest was burning. A fierce black spectre, seizing her neck with its long, serpentine nails, strangled and choked her.

Her strings of coral beads broke, scattered on the floor, and blended with her mother's tears that, like little round peas, fell to the floor and rolled away.

A large, thick bead flashed like a silver circlet. No, it was not a bead; it was the ring that the young gentleman had wanted to put on her finger. He was standing by her even now, piercing her with the flames in his eyes, grinding his white teeth, pleading, threatening, and asking: "Why, oh why, don't you want me?"

With a great effort, she pushed him away, stopping up her ears so she would not hear the voice rending her soul, even though it was hushed to a soft whisper: "Why, oh why, don't you want me?"

She wrung her hands in despair, tore at her hair, and ripped her clothing. Exhausted, she collapsed at the head of the table. Her mother, sitting next to her, was placing a wreath on her head, and on the table there was a green marriage tree adorned with scarlet cranberries. Young women were singing:

> "When it was felled—it rang out,
> And when it fell—it sang out."

And the tree was flying, ringing, and resounding against the old bell tower on the hill. An old woman was being carried into a church; the church was crumbling and swaying, and crosses were crashing to the ground.

The cross from the very tip of the church fell and struck her on the head. Some people picked it up, kissed it, and gave it to her to kiss.

With a scream, she turned away and spit. Drops of cold sweat beaded her forehead, and molten lead flowed in her veins, distending her chest. There was a bloody stain in front of her eyes; people no longer appeared as people, but as animals with gaping mouths and red-hot tongues, while all around there was a dull roar, a grumbling, and a strange, chaotic hubbub.

"She's gone mad, gone mad, mad!"

Once again, it felt as if a stone had been placed on her head, and she did not hear or see anything; she was breathing heavily, with a rattling sound, and dreadful, incomprehensible words tore out of her breast.

She awoke.

There was music playing, and the girls and youths were gathering for a *vechernytsi*. And over there, a distaff was leaning against a bench, a spindle was spinning and turning, and a ball of yarn was winding itself up.

"Wait, wait, I'll go with you," something was saying in her voice. But he was standing here as well, calling her to go with him.

"No! You won't live to see the day!" She grabbed the ball of yarn and threw it at him. The ball bounced and fell into the pocket of his short jacket.

The wind whistled; the thread was unwinding, hastening away, stretching itself out—and she hurried after it. It tumbled over fences, houses, stiles, swept over deep ravines, spread over steep paths, and flew aimlessly.

And the farther it went, the more the thread unravelled and, gaining speed, wrapped itself around trees, crosses, graves.

Beside one grave, something scurried into a crack; the earth groaned, the clouds staggered, and thunder rumbled. She wanted to strike the crack with her heel, but the wind seized her and carried her off with a roar over dark forests, endless fields of stubble, and banks covered with reeds.

The raging wind pursued her, and she ran without looking back, without touching the ground. Behind her, there was a cackling and a roar; thunderbolts crashed, owls lamented, crows cawed, wheels clattered, and stones flew far wide, flung aside by galloping horses' hooves.

A lake burst into view, and she was carried over its glittering, glassy surface. The water, rolling in silver waves, was clear as a tear. In the middle of the lake, a man was up to his neck in water; the water was pouring into his mouth, but he kept shouting: "Drink, I want to drink!"

She stretched out her hands to him, but a blast from the wind carried her farther away, over fallow fields that stretched into infinity. The grass rippled in an exuberant greenness, but sheep bawled hungrily, and people who had taken their own lives flew through the air, pleading for a burial cross.

The swamp gurgled, the bog heaved and rumbled, and under it a man could be heard driving his oxen. And the bells were ringing, as if it were Easter Sunday.

And, once again, everything disappeared, engulfed by a thick fog. From above and below, she was hounded by sighs, weeping, screams, and the thundering of horses' hooves.

Far beneath the dark forest, a star flashed. Gasping for air, the girl made a desperate effort to reach the glittering glow.

The wind tore along the ground as if it had gone mad. Hawthorns and bramble bushes tugged at her hair, tore at her face, and ripped her hands and feet.

But let the white flesh be torn, let the blood flow. She had only one thought, one wish—to reach the bright star.

The pounding of a horse's hooves was almost upon her when she overtook the golden splendour of the star . . .

It was a completely empty house—there was only a corpse lying on a bench. At the head of the corpse a candle was burning, and on the wall hung an icon of the Mother of God.

The Mother of God was all in gold; two angels were holding Her exquisite crown, and other angels were trumpeting in the clouds. Her hands raised high, she spread out Her holy vestments, under which the saints and those who obeyed God were hiding.

"You may also come here," the Mother of God said to the girl, who could hardly breathe.

Maryna huddled against a wall, but the Mother of God covered her with her magnificent transparent garment.

On the threshold, a horse's hoof cracked, and flames flashed from burning eyes. Sparks showered through the house and flew in all directions, but they grew dim and were extinguished when they reached the golden garment of the Queen of Heaven.

A wild cry shook the corners of the house, the roof creaked loudly, the candles broke, and the corpse rose from the bench.

"You look for her as well," the devil screamed at the corpse.

And a frenzied, fiendish dance began in the house. They whirled through the corners, tumbled over the floor, clambered up the walls, examined every speck of dust, and peered into every crack.

And when they had finished going over everything once, they did it a second time, and a third, without ceasing, without tiring.

Suddenly, a weakness overcame them; this enraged them all the more, and they thrashed about and searched for the hidden girl with an even fiercer anger . . .

It struck midnight.

The rooster flapped his wings and crowed. The insane laughter died on the lips of the devil; he staggered and dissolved into stinking tar, and the putrid body of the corpse toppled into it.

"Come out!" the Queen of Heaven then said to the girl.

Trembling like an aspen leaf, Maryna stood before the face of the Virgin Mary.

"Fear not!" the Mother of God said. "He has lost his power over you, but since he once had access to your soul, it no longer can be saved."

The girl toppled to the ground like a broken lily and weepingly begged the Mother of God to help her.

"Do not turn Your immaculate face from me, O Mother of God," she pleaded. "If I once had the pride of the devil within me, then I will expiate this sin with my life and my death. Just let me be with You, O Holy Mother!"

A strange, wonderful radiance illuminated the face of the Queen of Heaven.

"You want to serve me with your life and your death, my poor child of the earth!" the voice of the Virgin Mary resounded in the heavenly tranquillity.

"With your life and your death," the words were carried as an echo into the infinite expanse of the universe. "With your life and your death," all the angels in heaven sang.

All the bells of the world rang, and the Mother of God commanded: "Go to the ones who gave birth to you; ask them to place you in a coffin and bury you alive at a cross-roads in an open field."

In the middle of a field there stands a tall mound, and under it sleeps a young woman, white as snow, and pink as a blossom.

With her arms crossed, in a golden wreath, with long, blond, unbound hair, she sleeps the deep sleep of death.

She hears neither singing, nor music; the passionate kiss of a beloved will not awaken her, and the tears of her mother will not revive her. In the embrace of the damp earth, under a white covering of light down, she sleeps forever.

And she sleeps amidst a mute silence; only flurries of tiny, crystal needles—like visions in a dream—race across the wide expanses, and fly, like a white fog, right up to the distant blue mountains, up to the village covered with mist . . .

A shaft of warm rays fell from the sky; the earth heaved and cast its sleepy eye all around, and the white glow of the mist dissolved under the warm breath of the sun.

Water flowed in turbid streams, cranes flew back from distant climes, a cuckoo called forth in the green grove, and the songs of meadowlarks rang out over fragrant green hedges.

On the tall mound, at the girl's head, a red branch with tiny green leaves emerged and grew into a wild rosebush.

And it grows there, all alone, under the glassy dome of the pure azure sky.

There is not a living soul anywhere; only the sun casts its bright eye upon golden fields, green meadows, and the young ears of copious grain.

"And the rose grows; it spreads and grows."

Field insects quietly sing songs in the luxuriant, silky grass. A lizard crawls out from under a lump of earth and stretches towards the warm rays; a mosquito hums; and a butterfly flutters its wings, alights, pauses thoughtfully for a moment, and flutters away over the boundless fields.

"And the rose grows; it spreads and grows amidst its fallen petals."

The rain washes it, and the wind dries its tender wet leaves, combs its long, slender branches, and shakes off the trembling tear of the early morning dew.

And it raises high its wistful, pale blossoms and gazes far into the distance, beyond the sun and the azure sky.

The Monstrosity
A Folk Tale
(1898)

It was dark and quiet in God's world. Night, settling on the earth, covered itself with an immense, black hempen cloth; from under it protruded terrifying, dark apparitions. Some of them were stretching upwards, reaching for the heavens; others were doubled over or kneeling silently on the ground, as if waiting in ambush; and still others seemed to have gathered for a secret council and were now furtively scurrying away.

During the day, these objects looked different. They were the houses, barns, haystacks, ricks, orchards, willows, poplars and roadside crosses of a small Podiliyan village. But now, they were all transformed into such threatening shapes that when you saw them your soul fainted, and you quaked with fear.

At one end of the village there were sharp retorts, as if gunpowder had been scattered in a fire, and it seemed that a ferocious dragon was wheezing, snorting, clanging its teeth, and spewing columns of sparks through its nostrils. Suddenly, the door opened in a low blacksmith shop that had sunk into the ground, and a still brighter blaze burst forth, as if from the mouth of an enraged beast.

A huge blacksmith's bellows, blowing on searingly hot embers, tossed about red flames and whooshed air on a blacksmith who was standing upright, plying a hammer energetically on an anvil wedged into an oak block. All around stood wheels, ploughs, ladders, and harrows. And among them, bayonets, scythes, and axes glittered ominously in the blazing light of the furious fire.

On some of the implements sat property owners and young men from the village. Staring fixedly at a wall covered with a tar-like soot, they were laughing uncontrollably.

Beyond the red flames, an elongated shape was visible; its wings—huge, naked, and serrated—stuck straight up, and its shaggy head ended in a pointed, goat-like beard.

"Look! Just look!" various voices called out. "Look at the horns growing on him, and his slanted eyes, and that funny, turned-up tail! The blacksmith is really something! Where'd he get such a good look at him? The wings are just like a bat's. And look at those fingernails! Ha-ha-ha! And horses' hooves—honest to God, he's got horses' hooves," the people laughingly remarked.

"Maybe I should give his wings another twist and touch up the tuft of hair on his head," the blacksmith commented.

He threw down his hammer, picked up a sharp tooth from a harrow, and began scratching the wall with it. Large white features emerged from under the tooth.

The men finally left, but the blacksmith continued scratching away on the wall with the tooth. He made the hair more dishevelled, raised the eyebrows, and nicked away at the mouth, causing the devil to bare his teeth even more.

Exhausted, he sprinkled some water on the fire and stretched out on his bed to rest. It was then the devil spoke to him: "What have I ever done to you, that you've made me look so ugly? Now, as soon as people walk into the smithy, they make fun of me, and you egg them on by twisting my wings or baring my teeth. Where have you actually seen me, that you depict me as being so ugly and ridiculous? Why are you poking fun at me in this way?"

The blacksmith didn't know where he'd actually seen the devil; this was how the devil had been born in his soul, and this was how he portrayed him.

He felt the urge to draw most strongly after he'd drunk some whiskey—whiskey that the devil surreptitiously slipped him.

A blacksmith's job is a difficult one; swinging a hammer all day long is no fun, so the blacksmith always kept a little flask handy. He'd take a swig now and again, fortify himself a bit, and then get back to work.

Although he never ran out of whiskey, there were times when his throat would turn dry before he could get to the tavern, or send someone else. And, there were also times when the pub owner wouldn't give him any whiskey until he'd put his money down on the table.

"Oh! If only there were a flask on the table as soon as I opened my eyes," the blacksmith thought more than once, sighing deeply.

Well, one morning, he opened his eyes and saw a flask of whiskey standing before him on the table. He was so overjoyed that, without giving the matter any thought, he emptied the flask then and there. The next day, the same thing happened and, on the third day, a flask of whiskey once again stood on the table.

"Where can all this whiskey be coming from?" the blacksmith thought more than once; he'd shudder, push away the bottle, and go back to his work.

But with every swing of his hammer, he'd glance at the flask. It was just standing there. The whiskey, clear as a tear, could be seen through the transparent glass, and it was so aromatic that the blacksmith would stick his nose up in the air and sniff, inhaling as much of the pleasant aroma as possible. When he couldn't stand it any more, he'd grab the flask and drain it to the bottom.

He could feel the devilish drink coursing through his veins, heating up his blood, and throbbing in his temples—and a terrifying figure would arise in his imagination. At first, it would seem far away, as if it were emerging from behind a thick cloud; then, it would draw nearer and grow brighter, until finally, it was so near and so bright, that he'd throw down his hammer, grab a pointed piece of steel, and begin scratching the wall; and the steel would outline more sharply the shape and the details of the terrible monstrosity that the people had named the devil.

Word about his creation spread throughout the village. Even if they had no reason to go the smithy, people would drop by just to take a look at the devil. If a curious young married woman came by, she'd quickly turn her eyes away from the monstrosity: "I hope to God that looking at it hasn't affected my unborn child." If an old woman crept in to see it, she'd be badly shaken, and she'd cross herself to prevent him from possessing her soul.

As for the girls—well, they ran in bevies to the blacksmith's shop, and they certainly had more than their fill of amusement at the devil's expense. "How terrifying and ugly he is! What funny eyes he has, what crooked eyebrows! His hand is like an old thief's! And look how he's spread his claws! And he's stamping his horses' hooves as if he were dancing. Yes, sir! He's one fine lad, there's no doubt about that! You wouldn't regret giving him the eye and joining him in a dance!"

The devil would wait until he was alone with the blacksmith to have another go at him: "You're a wicked man! You've depicted me as loathsome, but you're no better than I am! I'm good to you, and I give you what you like best, and this is how you treat me, how you pay me back! You go to church, listen to the words of the holy evangelists who say you should give bread in return for stones, and then you publicly vilify and make fun of me in return for what I do for you!

"What do those people do for you? You work, pump the bellows, and pound with a hammer until you're all out of breath, and yet you're close to dying of hunger in their midst. Don't you know what they're like? Don't you know how nasty these people are, how abominable? You warm your heart and chase away your worries with my whiskey and, in return, you make a laughingstock of me? You know how much I like to woo young women, but you've made me seem so ugly that they turn their eyes away. Even if I transformed myself into the most handsome lad, no girl would want me, because now they all know that I have horse's hooves! And you know how much it pains me, how it infuriates me, when some old woman provokes me by crossing herself. What makes her better or worthier than me?"

"Perhaps it's true," the blacksmith thought. But all the same, he couldn't refrain from putting finishing touches on the devil's figure. His head burned, his chest seethed, and he experienced an overpowering need to reveal clearly what was hidden within him. The more he applied himself to his work, the more he felt a compulsion to do it—a compulsion that, like a mighty flame, aroused his passions, resonated in his soul, pounded in his heart, and pulsed through his veins.

More than once, he stood and stared at his creation until it came to life, nodded its head, waved its arms around, and shouted angrily: "So, you've been provoking me once again, adding lines here and there to make me even uglier! Come to your senses, my good man! There's nothing in it for you, just some kind of malicious joy—but as for me, I'm wronged."

Sometimes, the blacksmith felt sorry for the devil. Could it be that he really wasn't as evil, terrifying, and black as he'd portrayed him? But then an even greater urge would possess him, and he'd make him uglier still—giving his horns an extra twist, and making his beard more pointed, and his toe-nails longer.

"Go ahead—touch it up, touch it up, my little brother! After all, what wouldn't you do for the sake of your glory and your pride? What do you care about how you're hurting me, as long as you're satisfied? Just take care that you don't regret it!"

Fear would overcome the blacksmith; he'd take a broom and dip it in soot to rub the devil off of the wall; but when he looked into the eyes of the monstrosity and carefully examined all the features he'd worked at so diligently, he'd cast aside the broom, as if it were some evil temptation threatening to destroy the image of his soul.

His trade as a blacksmith was suffering; people came to the smithy not to have any work done, but just to get a good look at the devil.

And they came not only from his village, but from neighbouring ones, as well. No one going to market or to town on business would pass by the smithy without dropping in; and there were times when they came expressly to view the devil.

Word about the devil spread to the lord's manor, to the lord himself. One day, the blacksmith looked up and saw that a carriage, drawn by four horses, had stopped in front of his smithy; the lord got out and headed straight for the door.

"Blacksmith, what kind of a devil have you painted, that everyone goes to see it and talks about nothing else?" the lord inquired.

"Here he is, right over here," the blacksmith pointed at the wall.

The lord looked at the devil, and the devil stood there—just as the blacksmith had painted him—baring his teeth as if he were grinning. And when the lord saw him, he split his sides laughing.

"Blacksmith," he said, "you really do have a devil in you. And if you didn't have to sit here in this smithy eking out an existence, you wouldn't have an equal in the whole world."

When the blacksmith heard this, he became puffed up like his bellows.

This was too much for the devil; it irked him that the blacksmith was all puffed up with pride, and that a good-for-nothing lord was laughing at him.

"So, now that ugly lord is going to be laughing at me, as well!" he raged. "In what way is he better than me? Who gets rich and lives off the work of others? Whose cudgels tear open the peasant's skin and make his blood flow in torrents? Isn't it because of you, O lordling, that people are rotting in dungeons, girls' braids are being shorn in shame, and young men are sent off to carry carbines, while their women are taken to the manor? He's laughing at me and praising the blacksmith, but what would he say if the blacksmith did him a great injustice? Wouldn't he fly into a rage worse than any devil? We'll see!"

At night, after the blacksmith—sitting with a harrow's tooth in his hand in front of the devil's picture—had nodded off, the devil tore himself off the wall, whistled like the wind, and whirled high up into the air. His huge wings spread out like a black cloud and, like a cloud, he slowly descended on the lord's manor.

The lord was a very rich man with an immense fortune—gold coins that he measured in quarter barrels, mouldy copper coins that he dried in bowls, and paper bills that he kept in rolls of cloth. And there was ever so much fine clothing, gold, silver and other wealth!

The lower the devil descended over the lord's courtyard, the deeper the sleep that enveloped everybody. Not only the lord, the lady, and the servants fell asleep, as if someone had placed stones on their heads, but even the dogs and the guards who stood watch in the courtyard both day and night fell into a deep slumber.

The devil dropped to the roof with his transparent body and penetrated the manor to its depths. Removing from his back the coal sack he'd taken from the smithy, he began to stuff into it everything he could find—all the money, silver dishes, gold rings, earrings, silk dresses, and other expensive attire: in a word, he stuffed absolutely everything into the sack, a sack that kept growing bigger and fuller.

When he'd cleaned out the whole place, he put the sack on his back and, returning to the smithy, buried it under the wall on which his likeness was depicted.

In the afternoon, the blacksmith heard a racket outside his building. A dog was barking, people were talking loudly, and it sounded as if they were digging in the ground with spades. The blacksmith came out of the house and couldn't believe his eyes—

they were pulling out his coal sack from under his smithy, and it was full of money and all sorts of other riches!

They seized the blacksmith, chained him, and led him to the dungeon. The poor blacksmith didn't know why, or for what.

He asked the people why they were putting him in chains and taking away his freedom.

"You mean, you don't know why?" the people said. "Isn't this your sack? Don't you recognise it? Wasn't it found under your smithy? Wasn't it you who wanted to steal the lord's possessions? Wasn't it you who set your sights on the lord's wealth and tried to make it your own?"

The blacksmith sat in the dungeon, and he couldn't see anything. It was cold and damp, and toads and other abominations crawled over his body. There was nothing to lie down on, nor to cover himself with; he'd been thrown only a thin bundle of straw to put under his head.

"O merciful God! Why has this happened to me?" the abandoned blacksmith wept. "What sin have I committed that I'm being treated so harshly, that I'm suffering such punishment? I was a man no worse and no better than others, except, perhaps, that I drank the devil's whiskey, and it fired my brain and inflamed my heart; but that's the sum total of my sins!"

The blacksmith didn't know when it was night or day—it was dark all the time, as if he'd been buried in a grave.

"There, you see! Why did you provoke me! Now you've got what was coming to you!" the words rustled over him in the dungeon.

"O you satanic power! So you won't give me any peace even here! You're still torturing me! You say that I provoked you—but who's to blame for it, if not you? Who pumped more blood into my brain, who gave me the satanic whiskey? Wasn't it you? And now you say that I was provoking you! If it wasn't for that satanic whiskey, I would have stayed where I was and kept on forging with my hammer! It's your whiskey that tore me away from my anvil, and when it overpowered me, I began to draw."

"I'm not a fool to take away your whiskey from you—if you didn't drink my whiskey, I wouldn't have any power over you, and I couldn't take revenge on you; but now you've got what was coming to you—they'll hang you on a scaffold and give your soul to me."

"Take me, torture me, kill me, chop me into pieces, let me hang on a scaffold, let the ravens pluck at my body—only don't let my soul perish in hell," the blacksmith pleaded.

A great despair sapped his strength. He hardly knew what was happening to him, or whether he was alive or dead. He lay there for a long time, resting his head on the bundle of straw.

Suddenly, a sliver of sunlight penetrated the dungeon; it brought with it the freshness of tender green leaves and field flowers. From somewhere in the distance, wondrous sounds—like the warbling of birds, like joyful, quiet laughter, like the murmur of a stream gurgling over stones—drifted towards him. And these enchanting sounds were echoed by the forests, mountains, valleys, meadows, groves, streams, and clouds, and all of them blended into one mighty melody: "Glory to God in the highest, and on earth, peace and good will to men!"

The radiance was so blinding that the blacksmith covered his eyes. What was happening? Was it broad daylight? Was the bright sun flooding his dungeon? An angel of God—white as snow, sparkling like the rays of a silver star, and shimmering with the glitter of early morning dew—was standing illuminated before him.

"God has sent me to you, O blacksmith," the angel said, "Rise up and come with me!"

"Oh! God, what have I done to deserve having You send Your emissaries to me?" the awe-struck blacksmith asked.

"You were always a good man; it was only the devil's whiskey that destroyed you. But because you've annoyed the devil, provoked him, and ridiculed him publicly, God has ordered me to lead you out of this dungeon."

The angel touched the chains, and they fell away with a clang; he touched the steel door, and its locks came apart.

"Go home, live quietly, and do not anger God with that satanic whiskey," the angel added, and he flew off to heaven, leaving behind a long white road—a stream of shining stars.

The next day, word spread through the village that the blacksmith was going to be hanged. The lord had erected a large scaffold and sent for an executioner.

And this is exactly how it happened.

They led the blacksmith out of the dungeon and hanged him.

The people began returning home—and there was the blacksmith, standing at his anvil, pounding away at a piece of steel.

"You've just been hanged! And you're still forging?" the people were amazed.

"But how could I have been hanged, if I'm here!" the blacksmith said.

The people returned to the scaffold and found, not the blacksmith, but the bundle of straw that had been placed under his head in the dungeon.

Next to the bundle of straw, hung a horse's bone and hooves—a sign of God's power and of the devil's strength.

Nothing changed in the smithy. The bellows wheezed heavily, the hammer banged, and the ploughs, harrows, and wheels stood as they always had—but, there was no devil on the wall.

The blacksmith didn't even so much as taste the devil's whiskey, and he lived as the world says you should live: "Do not anger God, and do not provoke the devil."

But did the blacksmith enjoy living like this? The folk tale has nothing to say about that.

The Tempest
(1904)

The sun was blazing in the glowing, inert azure of the sky. It had been flaming since early morning, and the farther south it went, the more penetrating it became, burning with a scorching, golden fire. A sultry heat wave flooded all corners of the earth; the clear blue sky, like a searingly hot glass dome in a glassworks, stretched in all directions and pressed down upon the heavy, torrid, unmoving air.

Grainfields, an endless sea of molten gold, stood transfixed in quiet trepidation; crimson poppies drooped their heads in sombre contemplation; and blue corn-flowers looked around silently and timorously, with widely opened eyes.

The mountains, as if wishing to hide from something menacing in the air, receded behind a hazy mist.

A dreamy lake, overgrown with reeds, languished, torpid and spiritless. Swallows folded their wings, and the shrieks of noisy seagulls died in their throats.

On the broad meadows, clusters of clover blossoms, their petals faded and curling, listened attentively; the air was heavy with a numbing desolation, an alarming stillness. Exhausted by the heat, a man wiped his brow with his sleeve and gazed fearfully at the sun; the cattle in the pasture grew restless and scattered in all directions.

The sun was baking, burning, searing. The cracked ground was disintegrating, fracturing into wheels and stars; the grass was wilting, turning yellow; and, through the wilted leaves of the trees, the sun etched the earth with brilliant, fiery, patterns.

And then, on the western horizon, there loomed a huge, dark, threatening mass.

Lightning fragments flashed like arrows. The air was ominously calm and stifling, and a black bulkhead, growing and expanding, forced its way across the sky.

Everything stirred.

A strong fiery wind wrinkled the surface of the water, snatched at the mown hay, tore off leaves, and carried away dust and coarse sand.

It grew dark.

Thick clouds stretched over the entire horizon and covered the sun. Reverberations of mighty thunder rolled in from afar, and lightning slashed the black layers of clouds with increasing frequency.

Over the mountains, the pendulous cloud, crowned by a glowing blood-red aura, hung in grey and yellow streaks.

The thunder's roar drew nearer. The crimson glow faded and was replaced by dark blue and black pillars that rolled in, one after the other, dissolved, disintegrated, and swirled in a fiendish dance.

Birds cowered under branches; panic-stricken cattle raced from the fields, leaving their herdsmen in vain pursuit; people secured windows and doors, and extinguished the fires in their stoves.

Mykhaylo Fediw never went to sleep at noon, but now, as fate would have it, he was sleeping soundly, as if someone had struck him on the head with a stone. He was also called Debrovy, because his house stood at the edge of the village by a *debra [a dale overgrown with thickets]*, and everyone was aware that he knew how to deal with thunderstorms.

This was why more than one householder in the village thought of him now. He, however, was sleeping soundly, oblivious to what was happening.

His terrified wife grabbed him by the shoulder and shook him awake.

Mykhaylo leapt to his feet and glanced out the window.

Beyond it, fire flashed, and a deafening clap of thunder roared with laughter.

"You may laugh if you want to, but you won't be allowed to do what you want to do," Mykhaylo muttered angrily and determinedly.

A dense, muddy darkness was descending, sinking ever lower and lower, swelling, and thickening.

Suddenly, as if the bottom of a lake had been shattered, the darkness was torn into dirty, jagged fragments, and thick, frozen lumps of ice, like clover blossoms, pelted to the ground.

Mykhaylo reached behind the icons, grabbed a priest's ceremonial belt, ran out of the house, and dove into the darkness.

He raced to the old bell tower that stood, seemingly supported by a tall forked maple, alongside the church.

He undressed, girded himself with the belt, and pulled at the rope of the large bell.

The bell would not budge. He tugged at it a second time; the bell's clapper struck the rim of the bell, but there was no sound. It was only after the third attempt that it shouted: "Stop! Stop! Stop!"

The cloud swirled in a pillar of grey smoke, opened up wide with fire, and roared with thunder: "Let go! Let me go!"

"I won't! I won't!" the bell tolled solemnly.

"Let go!

"I won't!"

"At least, let me pass over a small field!"

"No, not over a field, over the forest!"

"I want a field!" the storm cloud roared.

"Over the forest, the forest," the bell replied.

"The field, the field," the dirty yellow pillars rumbled.

"The forest, the forest," the bell tolled.

"Let me advance at least a little; my army is rebelling," the storm cloud pleaded. Behind it, thunderbolts, clattering like an inferno, wound themselves like snakes and, with open jaws foaming with blood, slithered forward to devour, destroy, annihilate.

But the bell rang out its orders loudly, sharply, inexorably: "Over the forest! The forest! The forest! The forest!"

Its breast shattered, its arms shrivelled, its fingers twisted, and its innards shredded, the storm cloud rose and fell, stretching out its head like a bird about to take flight.

Suddenly, whistling like the wind and making the ground shake, it slowly raised its heavy, leaden wings and turned sideways, over the mountains.

With a din, a roar, and a cry like the neighing of a herd of horses, countless heads, bellies, arms, legs, and wings tangled in a single ball, threw arrows, and flew after the storm cloud into the abyss of the murky horizon.

The forest rustled and groaned. Trees bent down to the ground. There was a screeching, roaring, flashing. Flaming arrows split centuries-old oaks, and frozen pellets cracked branches and stripped them of their leaves. Amidst the shrieking, the crashing of the thunder, and the roar of the wind, the clear voice of the bell reverberated ever farther and farther.

The storm caught Matiy, Mykhaylo's neighbour, along with his horses and wagon, in a field abutting the forest. The wind swept dust into his eyes and tried to turn his wagon around; the lightning and thunder terrified the horses. He had to resign himself to God's will. He unharnessed the horses, tied them to the wagon frame, and sat down under it to wait out the storm.

Then he heard the forest groaning—the wind was rushing through it, and the trees were bending like stalks of wheat in a field.

A crashing, deafening roar struck terror in his breast, and his heart stopped beating. Thunderbolts took unerring aim, clouds jostled one another, and then, suddenly, the clouds, the forest, and the fields all disappeared, and there was only the noise, the roaring, and water . . .

The rain slowly weakened; it became quieter, and a cool, clear, transluscent brightness flooded the air.

Water flowed in the ditches, soft white clouds drifted over the sky, and the sun wiped its tearstained face. From the fields wafted the freshness of grass and flowers. The grainfields luxuriated in the pristine water, happy that the hailstorm, having passed them by, had exhausted and mocked the forest instead.

Broken branches and torn leaves, mixed with ice, lay in piles. Trees, torn out by their roots, were leaning on their stronger companions, pressing heavily down upon them.

Others, the ones at the forest's edge, were lying uprooted in ditches, and water was angrily, noisily, and laboriously breaking through the obstructions placed in its path.

It took Matiy a long time to regain his senses; he looked around as if he could not believe that he was still living, and that nothing had happened to him.

He sighed deeply and crossed himself.

It was so quiet, so peaceful, that if it were not for his wet clothing, the terrified horses, and the forest that had been shattered and pounded by the hailstorm, he would have thought it was all a terrible nightmare.

Just then, something struck him on the forehead.

A lump of ice—blue like a dove's egg—was lying at his feet.

He picked it up and bit into it; inside were four leaflets—from a poplar, a maple, an aspen, and a fir.

In the Cemetery
(1916-17)

The brilliant sun, half hidden by the mountain tops, was bathing in the crimson blood billowing along the western horizon. Small, isolated white clouds sailed like boats over a carmine ocean, and the darkened, jagged mountains stretched like the black road of humanity's common fate—its grievous struggle with the fiery-red flames, with which almost the entire world was ablaze.

Above the mists of the vast moors could be seen the roofs and chimneys of a small hillside village, over which the metal-plated towers of churches flashed with a scarlet brilliance.

A wide circle of fantastically traced trees loomed like a black shadow out of the mists, and among these trees were hidden the crosses and monuments of those who had departed to the land of eternal peace.

These uninvited guests had come to the circle of trees from the depths of the forest. They had marked their way with droplets of blood and positioned themselves in straight rows, just as in life they had stood against death, which was their enemy, and which had brought them eternal sleep, peace, and quiet, before their time had come.

The sun rose and set in a sea of blood.

The mist slowly lifted and, pierced by an ochre light, remained suspended over the graves with a rosy reflection—like the dreams, the hopes, and the desires of youth.

This was the day that an important ceremony was to be held in honour of the fallen young soldiers. To commemorate them, the military authorities had constructed a large stone monument. Two mighty figures, representing the two allied armies, held intertwined braided laurel wreaths.

At the appointed hour, the ceremony to consecrate the monument began. Everything was being done properly. The military men were on one side, while the representatives of the civic authorities stood on the other side; the rest of the people took up positions wherever they happened to be.

A tall military dignitary spoke in an affected voice, devoid of emotion, about the virtues of the deceased. At the same time, he extolled the merits of the living army that was honouring their memory. After finishing his address, he turned the ceremony over to the army chaplain, who also gave a speech. There was more warmth in what the chaplain said, but he also stressed that all those who had died had conscientiously fulfilled their civic duty. It was only the wilted flowers on the monument that opposed these assertions with their sad little heads and spoke about life for its own sake.

Quite by accident, the grouping of those who were present was ideally suited to the taking of photographs. A young lieutenant was doing the photographing. He was one of the greatest Don Juans in the military, and he had won more women's hearts than he had taken enemy positions. This was why many rumours were circulating about him.

These rumours were very interesting, and the entire little town was intrigued by his courting of a young married woman who apparently had cuckolded her husband. There were also rumours that one girl from a good home had fallen desperately in love with him. However, in addition to girls from the intelligentsia, the lieutenant did not scorn women from other levels of society; this fact pained the enamoured young lady greatly, and she gave him up completely.

Before long, however, another, more wordly, young lady was found who did not find anything disturbing. And, once again, the people began buzzing. They talked about the inevitable marriage of the military man and the clever young lady.

This was why, even though the mood, in general, was serious, and the sad ceremony absorbed the attention of all who were present, some noticed that the lieutenant was not himself today, that he seemed self-conscious. This surprised everyone who knew his arrogant and proud nature. It was unlikely that this conqueror was lowering his eyes before the women who were looking at him; more likely, it was an involuntary humility in the presence of those whose life had been shortened by cruel fate—a life that he took advantage of to the utmost.

These same women were simultaneously casting glances at the figure of a woman in the prime of her life—a woman with dark, flaming eyes. This was the mother of the girl whom the lieutenant was to marry. She was standing amidst the graves of the deceased with a proudly elevated head, and her feet were placed firmly on the ground. Three-leafed clovers crept out from under them, blades of grass covered with dew struggled to escape, and tiny daisies strained to extricate themselves. With broad hips and uplifted chest, she stood as if embedded in the ground for, with her strength and her fertility, she was the eternal earth mother, life triumphant over the victims of death. She was the giver of life, the everlasting power of rebirth that is transmitted from generation to generation.

The ceremony was proceeding item by item in accordance with a predetermined program.

Behind the military dignitaries stood a handsome young ensign. His gaze kept sliding from the monument to the people gathered there, as if he were gauging the impression that the monument was making on them. His eyes came to rest most often on a girl nestling on her mother's shoulder. From under her lowered eyelashes, she was glancing shyly at one of the symbolic figures of the monument—a Valkyrie—that bore the outlines of her face. The young ensign was the author of the monument, and a second lieutenant was publicly thanking him on behalf of the army.

Unexpectedly, harmonious singing—sounding as if it were emanating from under the ground—could be heard from far off in the distance; it poured through the air that enveloped the earth with a transparent sea of luminous azure. Only a single dark cloud—a blotch of infinite pain, bitterness, or misfortune—hung ominously over the beech forest. The distant, muffled singing was coming ever nearer and, with a resonant echo, was losing itself in the sombre cloud.

There was one more item in the commemorative program: the military authorities were handing over the monument to the town, with the request that both it and the graves of the dead soldiers be looked after.

The people had already begun to disperse, when a church procession appeared at the entrance of the cemetery. The military men, as if under orders, immediately returned to their posts, and in this way forced the others to remain as well, even though it was evident that many of the gentlemen were greatly perturbed by the oncoming crowd.

After a brief prayer, the old priest sprinkled the monument with holy water and, with his entire flock, turned to face the graves of the deceased. The ladies, who had positioned themselves in such a way that their backs were turned to the graves, were forced not only to make way for the procession, but to turn around, as well. They were not at all pleased by this development; haughtily defiant, some of them expressed their dissatisfaction openly by refusing to budge.

A commemorative service, conducted in the traditional Eastern Rite, was begun.

The army, which initially reacted with an official expression of recognition, began to be influenced by the unsympathetic nobility's deprecating stance—the stance that has had such a painful effect on our country, on those very people who were now approaching the graves of the victims of the terrible raging plague that was inflicting more wrongs on their nation than on any other in the world. Because, in addition to its sacrifices of blood, this nation has had to endure such moral suffering that the very thought of it makes the blood in one's veins congeal.

"Lord, Lord, have mercy!" The voice of the elderly priest quavered tremulously, and the national soul wept over its painful misery; it wept because of those who lived off its sweat and blood, while inflicting so much suffering and derision, causing so much misfortune, and provoking so many tears of hopeless parting.

"Lord, Lord have mercy!" The sorrowful plea spread over the charred ruins of villages, fields furrowed by shrapnel, and the homelss, uprooted by war, who were dying a slow death on the roadsides and in the forests of foreign lands.

"Lord, Lord have mercy!" The heartrending entreaty caused the clouds to shudder, and the earth uttered mournfully in reply: "I will rest lightly, like a feather, on their graves . . ."

The Cripple
(1916-17)

There was not a finer young man in the village than Lukyn Maksymyshyn. Tall and slender, he was like the elm that stood by the stream near his widowed mother's house.

On Sundays, when Lukyn put on a white shirt with a broad band of embroidery, girded himself with a wide leather belt, flung a new wool coat over his shoulder, and donned a hat adorned with peacock feathers, all the girls gazed at him in awe. No matter where he was—at a dance, in church, or at work—he invariably stood out among the other young men, and he always took the lead. His face was bright like the sun, his eyes were as blue as the sky, his curly hair was thick and black, and he sported a splendid, youthful moustache.

Even his mother could not help smiling when she glanced at him. "Who does he take after?" she would ask herself. Her daughters were all comely—they resembled her and her husband—but they could not hold a candle to him! It seemed he looked more like some other kinsfolk—especially her elder sister Frasyna who, at one time, had been so attractive as to have no equal. If she had not carried him under her heart, God knows what she would have thought. Her sister had the same blue eyes, the same hair, and was of similar stature.

Her daughters were older than Lukyn, and she had seen to it that all of them had married men who were well-off; she only wished that she could find as good a match for her son.

But Lukyn was capable of finding a better fate for himself; he could marry the richest girl in the village, and even then she would scarcely be a match for him.

"It will probably be necessary to ask around elsewhere and bring home a daughter-in-law from another village," the widow Maksymyshyn often thought.

The widow Maksymyshyn was not among the wealthiest in the village. She could not even begin to compare herself to her sister Frasyna, who had married a very rich man and was swimming in wealth, with more than enough of everything.

Frasyna had not wanted to marry this wealthy man—she had been angry at her father and mother for forcing her into the marriage—but, as a result of that match, she had become the richest woman in the village and had much to be proud of. Even though the widow Maksymyshyn did not have the kind of wealth that her sister possessed, she still was well off, so a daughter-in-law could be brought into her home without anyone losing face.

Her house was shingled and among the best in the village; her garden was a delight to behold; and she had her own land, horses, and cattle. If Lukyn could find a wife who had a dowry equal to what she owned, then even Frasyna would not be able to compare herself to them.

Being the only man in the family, Lukyn had been excused from military service; therefore, as soon as he finished his schooling, his mother began to look around for a daughter-in-law. Whenever she joined a group of women in the street or near the church, she immediately turned the conversation around to say that, although she had asthma, there was so much to do at home that she had to keep working and could not find time to look after herself.

"Are you saying you don't have any help? Don't you have a man at home?" the women said to her. "You're going to make God angry by saying such things. If only everyone had a son like that."

"Well, a son won't do woman's work."

"She's right. A man has his work to do, and a woman has hers. What you need is a daughter-in-law."

This was just the opening that the widow Maksymyshyn was waiting for. "If only God would send us a decent, hardworking one," she would say in her deliberate way.

"You don't have to worry about that; he'll find himself a good housekeeper. He's the kind of young man who only has to set his eye on something, and it's as good as his. You don't have to worry—anyone would marry him."

When the widow Maksymyshyn came home after a conversation like this, she would tell her son everything. Lukyn would just smile; he was pleased with himself, and happy that people spoke about him in this way. But really, why should they speak differently about him? He knew there was not a girl alive who would not marry him, and that any girl he courted would be his. And he scrutinised the girls one after the other in his mind's eye, as if they were ducks swimming along in a straight, narrow line.

There were many girls who were beautiful, and many who were wealthy and came from good families. Marunya had sultry black eyes, Sofiya was tall and blond, Iryna had rosy cheeks like little apples, and Erstyna had long tresses; nevertheless, none of them could compare to Malanka, who served at the home of his Aunt Frasyna.

He did not know why he thought that Malanka was the most beautiful girl he had ever seen. It all began one day when he drove to the stream to water his horses, and she was there, washing clothes on a stone. He crept up softly and, wanting to scare her, embraced her around the waist.

She truly was frightened. Blushing, her nostrils flaring, she raised herself to her full height and faced him.

"Have you gone mad?" she finally managed to say.

"I wanted to frighten you."

"Go to the devil!" she shouted and, turning on her heel, stalked away.

It seemed to Lukyn that, up to that moment, he had not noticed her; it was as if he were seeing for the first time how tall she was, what a fine figure she had, and how passionately her eyes blazed. And from that moment on, she was always in his thoughts.

In order to see her, he began to find some pretext or other to go to his aunt's place more frequently—he needed some rope, or he had to borrow a crossbeam that happened to be mislaid just when it was almost time to mow the hay for the cows. Of course, he did not need a reason to visit his aunt, but he always came up with some plausible excuse, so it would not seem that he was going there to see Malanka.

His aunt loved him. Whenever he came, he talked and joked with her. If he happened to be in a hurry, she would laugh and say that work was not like a rabbit—it would not run away.

Even though his aunt always made him welcome, he often became annoyed with her when she engaged him in conversation. He was happier when he found only Malanka at home, but this happened infrequently. His aunt's husband, even though he was a truly avaricious man, cared for his wife, and rarely sent her to work in the fields. It was Malanka, therefore, who had to do all the more strenuous tasks.

Lukyn was a hard worker himself, and he praised Malanka for knowing how to do everything quickly and efficiently. More than once, however, he was angry at his uncle for making her work too hard.

"The man who weds her won't be sorry," he thought, watching her wield a fork as she pitched sheaves on the hayrack. Her supple figure curved ever so attractively, and her cheeks were as rosy as cranberries!

"Perhaps I should wed her myself?" This idea appeared to jump at him out of nowhere, and then, just as suddenly, it broke off. From that time on, however, it kept recurring.

At first, Malanka considered his courting to be nothing more than a young man's flirting, so she kept her distance. But when he promised to marry her, she gave herself to him, body and soul.

At first, the widow Maksymyshyn wept and was very angry. This was not the daughter-in-law she had been hoping for; she was ashamed that her son was marrying a servant.

But Aunt Frasyna immediately took the side of the young couple. She had no children of her own, and she loved Malanka as if she were her own child. "The young woman is a good worker," she comforted her sister. "If he loves her, let him marry her."

Aunt Frasyna sighed heavily as she said this. She was recalling her youthful years, her youthful love. The widow Maksymyshyn knew that her sister had been passionately in love with the neighbour's son, but her parents had not wanted to hear anything about it. He owned only half a house and two small garden plots; moreover, he had a sister for whom he had to provide a dowry.

Her parents had not waited long—they had married her off to an only son who owned land. His parents had died soon afterwards, and their daughter became the sole mistress in the house. She had more than enough of everything, but there were times when something would come over her, and she would weep in front of her sister, saying that she would give up all her wealth for just one kiss from the neighbour's son.

So now the widow Maksymyshyn looked at her somewhat obliquely. Frasyna noticed this and smiled bitterly. "It's true I'm no longer young, but my heart still remembers. I'm telling you, my sister, do not part the children. Do not cause them to weep and spend their lives in misery."

The widow Maksymyshyn did not stop grumbling, but she did not have the power to turn Lukyn away from Malanka. He scarcely paid attention to what his mother was saying, and he was overjoyed that his aunt was championing his cause.

There was no point in putting off the wedding. And so, after the Feast of St. Peter, Lukyn brought his young wife into their home.

The widow Maksymyshyn did not have any empathy for her young daughter-in-law.

"He's certainly brought me a daughter-in-law with honour and a dowry," she muttered angrily to herself.

She did not say anything to other people, however, for she did not want them to laugh at her. But there was no peace in their home.

No matter what Malanka did, she could not please her mother-in-law. The quarrelling and the cursing kept escalating. The mother complained to Lukyn as to a son, while the wife complained to him as to a husband, and there were times when such an inferno raged in the house that he had to flee from it.

But the widow Maksymyshyn was not fated to live for a long time with her daughter-in-law. She caught a cold and, being an asthmatic, became very ill and was gone within two weeks. She fell into her eternal sleep so quietly that no one was even aware of it. As fate would have it, she died when everyone was out of the house.

Lukyn grieved for his mother, but he was bothered most by the fact that she had died so quietly, as if she had never existed. She had not said one word before her death. It would have been easier for him if she had at least complained, instead of going away so silently.

When she was laid out on the bench, he gazed at her and would have given anything to hear her say at least a single word. She remained silent, however, and her lips were closed tightly, as if they had been sealed by a curse, perhaps even by the words that

he himself had shouted in anger at her at times—"Shut up!"—
words that now came back to haunt him.

But even though he bitterly reproached himself, it was as if
angels had flown over their home. It was quiet and peaceful now,
and there was shouting in the house only when they were chastising
their children. And there were quite a few children—one came
along every year.

One day at twilight Malanka was hurrying to finish hilling the
potatoes. A child was crying in the cradle, and supper had to be
prepared, because Lukyn would soon be home from town, but she
was anxious to finish her work in the garden. Just after she entered
the house and started the fire, Lukyn walked in.

"Aren't you fixing supper yet, my good woman?" he asked her
gently, seating himself on the bench.

"I'm a little late, because I wanted to finish hilling the potatoes.
They're all overgrown with weeds as it is, and if they weren't
hilled on time, what good would they be?"

"That's fine, that's fine; but hurry, because I'm hungry."

"Supper will be ready in a moment; there's borshch left over from
lunch, and I'll cook up some cornmeal. But you were in town for
quite a while. I thought you'd come home, and the two of us would
finish the work more quickly."

"I met up with some people, and we got talking."

"So, what are they saying?"

"Apparently, the newspapers are saying there's going to be a
war."

"Oh, what's a war! If only the potatoes yield well. People were
already talking about a war when I was still small."

"They talked about it, and now they've brought it on."

"Well, they certainly have talked about it long enough."

"It's no joking matter. They're saying that there has to be a war.
But let there be one; I'm exempted, so they won't take me."

It was quite soon after this that the young men began to be called
up; and, before long, almost half the village was taken away to
the army. After a while, others were called up as well. Hearts
always grieve when men are taken away to join the army, but it
is even sadder when there is talk of war.

Mothers cried for their sons, sisters for their brothers, and young women for their lovers. The fathers were worried too, even though they did not yet know that they would have to follow their sons.

There really was a war.

Many people were alarmed, but others did not even think about it. There was no time to think. In the village, there was not enough time to do the work that had to get done, let alone worry about what might or might not happen.

God's will would be done.

As long as a man is still alive, he has to eat, and if he wants to eat, he has to work.

The work did not let up. There are those who take the easy way out, but Lukyn and Malanka were determined to do things right, and their work paid off. Their farm was growing. There was a new shed and a lean-to that had not been there during his mother's lifetime. They were beginning to build a barn; the frame was already completed, the rafters were in place, and only the roof had to be thatched; but first, the grain had to be harvested, so there would be straw bundles for the thatching.

Poor Lukyn did not know that he would not gather his own grain. The war, about which he had heard so little at first, kept drawing nearer. In the fields, one could often feel the earth tremble from the din. But the people still thought that the war would not reach them. They were alarmed mainly by the fact that more and more men were being called up to join the army.

A rumour began to spread that even those who were exempt would be called up. When Malanka heard this, she clutched her head in despair, but Lukyn still did not believe that such a thing could happen. People said a lot of things, but this did not mean that what they said would actually come to pass.

One day, however, just after he had harnessed the horses to the wagon and was about to go into the fields, the bailiff informed him that he was to appear in the village.

Malanka, in the yard at the time, asked: "What does this mean?"

"They're calling me to join the army."

Malanka, covering her face with her hands, wept bitterly.

"Don't be afraid; I'm exempt, so nothing will come of it. But I have to put in an appearance; it can't be helped."

Lukyn was recruited, and in two weeks he had to leave. At first, it seemed to him that nothing had happened, but almost immediately thereafter, it was as if everything had turned upside down. Everything looked strange to him, as if it were not his. He looked at his house, but it no longer seemed the same, and his wife no longer seemed to be his wife, and his children no longer seemed to be his children. If a child ran out of the house and clutched at the hem of his coat, it was as if he did not recognise it. And to make things worse, his wife's weeping was tearing at his heart.

He was to be at home for one more week. Every day, every night, brought him closer to the terrible day. There was no way of putting it off, of pulling away from it. The days and nights passed by swiftly. There were only two days left, but it no longer mattered to him—he could have left immediately; it made no difference—he had to go sooner or later.

These two days also passed by.

On the day he was supposed to leave, he felt numb all over. He sat down on a stump by the shed and stared fixedly at the garden. Large red poppies were blooming in the garden, and smaller white poppies were waving their heads among them. The poppies absorbed all his attention, as if nothing else in the world existed— just the large red poppies with their black centres, and the other poppies with their little white heads.

Suddenly, everything flipped over. "No, no!" something said within him, and he squeezed his fist tightly. "What right do people have to tear me away from my land, my house, my family?"

Once again, a strange rebelliousness surged through his breast. His arms fell to his sides, his head bent down, and he began to cry—he wailed like a little child.

Nearby, someone else began to sob despairingly. It was Malanka. She had seated herself behind him on some brushwood near the house. He did not know when she had come. He turned around.

"What's with you?" Speaking as if he were angry, he rose to his feet, went to the stable, and drove the cattle to the stream.

It was not yet time to water the cattle, but he drove them anyway, just to avoid being at home—to avoid seeing his wife, his children, and the red poppies that had suddenly become so odious.

When the moment came for him to leave the house, he glanced at the icons, swept his eyes over his yard, and looked at the unfinished barn. Malanka gathered up the children and trailed after him, wailing as if she were walking behind a corpse. The soul of a corpse is already on the road of truth—it no longer cares about its body; but this was a living death, a funeral for the living.

When they came to a stop and sat down, Lukyn pressed Malanka, faint from weeping, to his heart. The children lamented in unison.

Quickly, very quickly, the men were herded into the train, like cattle into a stable. Some were shoved into the middle of the cars; others were pushed up on top. There was confusion, shouting, and crying; everything was all mixed up, and the hubbub was like the tumult in hell. Lukyn wanted to see his wife and children once more, but he could not make his way to the side of the car. Suddenly there was a whistle, and they were pulled away, like a string, into the unknown.

When Malanka stepped into her yard, she understood that she was now a widow. She sat down on the earthen embankment abutting the house and raised her arms to the heavens. If it were not for the children, who were crying that they wanted to eat, she would not have come to her senses.

Three weeks later, she received a card from Lukyn, He asked about her health and how she was getting along. He wrote that he was learning military drills, and told her who was there with him from their village. Then another letter came. He asked her to send him some money, because he could not make do with what he had.

There was some talk that the women whose husbands were taken away would receive some money for them, but things turned out differently.

The shots that had been heard all around the village, and which had frozen people's hearts, were silenced. Some thought the war was over, but suddenly people began shouting: "It's the army! The soldiers are here!"

But the soldiers were not alone; tired, bedraggled, and grimy as if covered with soot, they were leading horses and dragging cannons. And they were so hungry, that God forbid! They begged for bread, and people brought them what they could, but it was not enough to even begin feeding them.

Some villagers hoped they would see their kin, but even though there were large numbers of people, there were none that they knew. They said that the men from this village had been sent to fight the French.

For three days and three nights, the soldiers crawled along like dark clouds. All this time, Malanka strained her eyes searching for Lukyn; she did not sleep or eat. She threw the children some scraps of food, and took everything else she could find in the house to feed the soldiers.

A rumour spread that the enemy was almost in sight.

"The enemy will be here tomorrow, no later than tomorrow!" The people were numb with fear.

But the first day, and the second one, and the third passed by, and everything remained quiet. They were beginning to forget their fear, when suddenly there was a great outcry: "The enemy! The enemy's coming!"

Some villagers began to flee blindly; others fled even though they were sorry to leave their work; still others seemed to have lost their minds and did not know what to do.

All the while, the enemy soldiers flowed onward like a river. They occupied the entire countryside. Nothing more was heard about the local soldiers. The enemy was everywhere. And it seemed that everything had sunk into an abyss. There were no rumours, no news, no help of any kind. No one knew what would happen. The possessions of the housholders were pillaged by the enemy. Misery smothered the land.

Malanka was alone in the house with her small children. Often, just as she lay down, there would be a banging at the door: "Open up!" And as many as ten soldiers would walk in, and she was all alone in the house with her little ones. All she could do is hope that they would not harm or rob her. At times, there were soldiers whose language she could understand, and these even invited her and the children to share their food. But there were also those who ate up everything they found in the house.

There was one time when enemy soldiers came and took away an entire hayrack. She pleaded and cried, but they only laughed at her. The villagers began to whisper among themselves that they were taking cows away. If there was only one cow in a family, they might leave it, but if there were two, they would take one. Malanka had a cow and a heifer. The villagers advised her to get rid of the heifer as quickly as possible, because even if she had to sell it cheaply, it was better than getting nothing at all for it.

One day, after she had gone to see a neighbour, she heard her children bawling at home. She ran up just in time to see some

soldiers leading her heifer out of the enclosure. Nothing helped—
not her crying, nor her shouting, nor her curses; they took it as if
it belonged to them.

She grieved sorely for that heifer. The neighbours tried to talk
her out of her grief, and Aunt Frasyna tried to calm her down,
saying that it looked as if she wanted to lay down her life for that
heifer and leave her children as orphans. But she kept repeating
over and over again, that if Lukyn had been here, he would not
have given it up—he would have defended it.

"Lukyn, my dearest Lukyn, why don't you send us any news
about yourself? Maybe you're no longer alive, maybe ravens are
scattering your bones . . ." she lamented as she wept.

The villagers were confident that their soldiers would come and
rout the enemy, but as month after month went by, and they heard
nothing about them, they began to lose hope. There were even women
who, forgetting that their husbands were fighting and shedding their
blood in the war, carried on so shamefully with the enemy, that
Heaven forbid!

"May God's wrath come down on them!" Malanka cursed them
more than once.

"Just listen to her! What a saint she's become! Instead of minding
her own business, she's sticking her nose into everyone else's!"
retorted the women who thought she was pointing at them.

Then, suddenly, something strange began to happen. The enemy
appeared to thin out. The villagers could not believe their eyes—
but they finally were convinced when they saw the enemy soldiers
packing everything on wagons, dashing into homes to pick up
clothing they had left there to be washed, and leading their horses
away. And, among them, there were those who said: "Your soldiers
are coming; you'll have them here in a week."

It seemed that more and more enemy soldiers were coming down
from the mountains. They began digging ditches and assembling
cannons until, finally, a trench had been dug across the entire
village. The villagers, working in the fields, grew faint with fear
as they watched.

The enemy soldiers taunted them: "Why are you afraid? Our
cannonballs will land far beyond the village. And surely you don't
think that your soldiers will fire at you, do you?"

"They'll be aiming at you," the villagers remonstrated, "but we're the ones who may be hit. A bullet doesn't know or care who its victim is—if it's a soldier or someone else."

One day, just before evening, there was a great hubbub and whistling. Everything began clacking as in hell—iron hail pelted the ground, and black smoke billowed in thick clouds.

All who could, tried to save themselves. Carrying whatever they could lay their hands on, some villagers ran away on foot, while others rode off in wagons. Everyone fled, either into the forest, or to more distant villages.

Malanka scarcely managed to get away with her children. Throwing on Aunt Frasyna's wagon the few things she was able to grab from her cottage, Malanka followed the wagon on foot with her children. When the shots came thick and fast, the villagers fell to the ground and lay there until there was a pause in the shooting. Then they got to their feet and continued fleeing.

A prolonged whistle pierced the air. There was a boom and a roar, and then the ground shuddered, and clouds of smoke rose in billows. Malanka clutched at her children and fell to the ground. One child slipped out of her grasp. As she tried to hang on to it, she realised she had fallen into a ditch. It was dark, and she began to grope for her little ones. Three of them were near her, but two others were crying somewhere, farther away. There was no wagon, and there were no other people nearby. She managed to find the other two children, and they sat there, all huddled together.

It began to rain, and water poured into the ditch. The children wanted to eat. She recalled the sack of bread she had tossed on Aunt Frasyna's wagon. What was she to do all by herself? The older children could manage somehow, but what about the younger ones? What did a child know? It wanted to eat, and that was that.

All around, it was so dark that one may as well have been blind. Then she saw something flicker—something like a light in a cottage. As she stared at it, she realised that it really was a cottage, and that there was a light in it.

"Well, my little ones, we'll go to that cottage," she said. Taking the smallest child in her arms, she set off in the direction of the light, with the older children walking alongside her. They waded through water and picked their way over stones and stumps.

The door to the house was open, and a fire was burning in the stove. Some soldiers were drying their drenched coats. On the shelves there were a few overturned pots and dishes; a pillow and some pieces of clothing were strewn on the floor. It was clear that the owners had not had time to pack.

Malanka stood dumbstruck in the doorway.

"What do you want, young woman?" one soldier asked her.

"Do you have at least a crust of bread? The children are hungry, and there's nothing I can give them to eat."

"We don't have anything to eat ourselves. The owners left behind only empty pots," one of them said, smiling bitterly.

She was about to turn away, when one of the soldiers picked up a bag and began searching for something. Finally, he took out two dry crusts.

"You're lucky I found these," he said, giving them to her.

The children stretched out their hands for the bread, but the crusts were very hard, and she could not crumble them. She glanced around the house to see if there was some water, but she could not see any. Well, she would soak the crusts somehow or other. She thanked the soldiers and left. Not far from the house, she sat down under a forked tree, drew her children around her, and stayed there until daybreak.

When it turned light, she rose to her feet and tried to figure out which village the road led to. She could not return to her own village; she had to follow the villagers from whom she had been separated—but in which direction should she go? Well, there was no point in just thinking about it; she had to be on her way.

She started out. There was a village up ahead, but its inhabitants had fled. It was deserted, and all the doors and gates were wide open.

An old woman was sitting by a fence, clutching her chest in a terrible fit of coughing. She told Malanka that all the villagers were probably three villages away by now. She had been told this by a woman who had returned to find a child that had been lost along the way.

Malanka glanced at her own children, as if she were counting them to see if they were all still with her. After asking the old woman which way the villagers had gone, she set out in the same direction.

When she reached the third village, there were so many people in a big pasture that not even a needle could be fitted in among them. She finally managed to find out where the people from her village were, but she spent a long time searching for Aunt Frasyna. The aunt, along with her husband and a servant, was crouching under the wagon—the way people crouch out in the field when hail catches them unexpectedly. Fortunately, she found some of the food she had managed to take from the house, and she was able to give the children something to eat.

They suffered through three days in this manner. Some villagers went to see what was happening. Some even got as far as their own village. The braver ones said that people could return home, because the army had gone off in another direction. But there were corpses all along the road, and on one side of the village some cottages had been torn apart, while others had been burned down.

On their way home, the villagers used forked branches to pile up the corpses, because they were already decaying. The stench was so bad that it made you choke.

At the upper end of the village where Malanka lived, her cottage had withstood the onslaught. There were many wagons near the house, and enemy soldiers were milling around it. Inside the house, she found only a broken bed and one bench. There was no cupboard, and pottery fragments were ground into the straw on the floor. A broken plough lay out in the garden.

She went into the garden, and had just bent over, when something rattled above her; she did not hear anything more.

The people saw a fiery trail stream out of the plane. A deafening roar followed it, and then everything was covered with smoke.

Many people were wounded. A few soldiers were killed, and Malanka was blown to bits. There was nothing left to put into a coffin. They knocked together a small box—no bigger than one intended for a child—and buried her without any funeral rites. There was no one to seal the grave.

II

For a long time, when the unfortunate Lukyn—after leaving behind his home, his wife, and his children—trudged down the road of his sad fate, he was not aware of what was happening. Nor was he the only one. People were being herded like a flock of sheep. At first, they were sent to one command post, then to another. They went without thinking, without any will of their own, as if they truly were just a flock of sheep.

Lukyn was walking like a dead man. He did everything that the others did—he got up in the morning, walked, ate, and slept, but it seemed to him that it was someone else doing these things.

Day after day passed by in this manner. Some of the men complained about the food, or that they had not slept well, but he was indifferent to everything. His thoughts were not focussed on the present—he had left them behind in the past, with his house, his yard, his wife and children.

The men were not kept long in any one place. They were led off somewhere else to learn military drills.

Even though he was obedient and did everything he was told to do, he still could not avoid being reprimanded and punished. At first, it seemed to him that he was being singled out for no reason at all; later, however, he realised that he sometimes did not hear what was being said to him.

But all this did not amount to anything, when compared to the terrible something that was still to come, and in anticipation of which everyone was trembling. Exactly when it was to happen, no one knew, but everyone was preparing for it.

If it were not for this uncertainty, things would have been tolerable. It is always easier to take things in stride when one is part of a larger group. At first, Lukyn did not like being part of a group, but he gradually became accustomed to it. Everyone shared the same fate—nothing but anxiety and sorrow.

The day arrived when, by noon, even though no one had heard anything about it in the morning, the order came to leave. By evening, everyone was at the train station.

It was raining, and so those who had to sit on top of the coaches had it the worst, even though it was so crowded inside that it was impossible to turn around. Lukyn leaned against a wall. His thoughts were fixed on his home, which seemed to be emerging out of a fog.

A few of his companions were singing lively songs. Were they happy? They sang without stopping. Someone began a song about an eagle and a grey falcon: "O eagle, were you in my native land?"

Lukyn joined in—the words seemed to be bursting from his chest. He sang for a long time, without thinking about what he was doing. Even after everyone else had stopped, he kept on singing—asking the eagle over and over again if it had been in his native land.

He did not know how long he had been travelling. He had stopped reckoning time long ago. There were times when he did not know what day it was. In the army, it made no difference if it was Friday or Sunday—every day was the same. Days and nights alternated once or twice, and then it was day again, and then night, and then they suddenly came to a stop in an open field. It was noon when they were told to come out of the coaches. "Have we arrived already?" they asked themselves, and chills ran up their spines, even though the sun beat down on them mercilessly, and perspiration beaded their foreheads.

They had not completed digging the trenches and ditches, when enemy cannons began roaring. Lukyn and the other soldiers responded with fire, and there arose such a racket, such a din, and such confusion, that it seemed the end of the world had come.

Bullets flew, and explosions thundered, tearing up the ground, flinging mud, and ripping out bushes and trees by their roots. People were toppling over like straw. A terrible shrieking joined the booming of the canons and the whistling of the bullets. "It's death, death, living death!" flickered through Lukyn's head. And suddenly, it was as if all of his thoughts broke off, and Malanka stood before him. What was happening to her? Did she know . . . He did not finish his thought. Something struck him powerfully in the back, and he toppled to the ground.

He lay there for a long time, without moving. Was he truly no longer alive? So, death had mown him down as well! It had cast a bullet, or perhaps a full handful of bullets at him, and he had parted with life, for almost no one was left alive around him.

After some time, he sensed that a hand was lying next to him, and that it was spreading its fingers. Whose hand was this? Why was it opening and closing its fingers? Perhaps it was his hand? Yes, it really was his hand. He opened it once more, and then squeezed it into a fist. He raised himself and leaned on an elbow. Was he alive? Nothing hurt, but he no longer had a cap on his head, and his knapsack had been blown away. He felt himself grow stronger, and he sighed deeply. He felt hope stir within him, a hope he had not known before.

The battle was over. The difficult days, however, were not over. He had to spend the winter in the snow. More than once, the soldiers waded through water when it thawed, and then, when there was frost, their coats froze solidly to the ground when they slept. And there was so much work, that God forbid! They dug trenches and carried trees from the forest—there was never a free moment.

Amidst all that suffering, he felt some relief only once, when he received a letter from Malanka, the first in a long time. The news was not cheerful, but at least he knew what was happening back home. She told him not only about herself and the children, but about what was going on in the village; for some reason, however, this no longer concerned him—he only wanted to know about Malanka. He would have given half his life to see her.

In the springtime, rumours again spread among the soldiers that the enemy was beginning to advance. Everyone had thought that the war would end soon, but now it seemed to be starting up again.

Even though everything was ready, the enemy struck at a time when they were least expecting it. The firing began in the morning and continued, almost without a break, for several days. With their intensive onslaught, the enemy soldiers destroyed the front trenches and the wire barricades. Almost nothing was left of the trenches—everything turned into a vast, endless mire. Infernal roaring, shrieks, grenade bursts, confusion, a crush of people and horses, cannons—everything whirled about in a hellish dance.

The army was being decimated; horses kicked their hooves at the sky. Lukyn watched as a soldier next to him, struck by a deadly bullet, faltered and fell. Another one was finishing off a soldier with the butt of his rifle.

Suddenly, everything blurred into a red fog; the world darkened, and he saw nothing else.

When he regained consciousness, he was lying in a bed, and there were people walking around him. He could clearly see a woman in a cap.

"Malanka!" something cried within his soul, but an excruciating pain severed his train of thought. He did not know how long he lay unconscious, but when he came to, he once again saw the woman in the white cap. But now he took a better look and realised it was not Malanka.

She carefully lifted his head, bound it in white cloths, and then did the same thing with his feet.

After some time, he regained control of his senses and began moving his hurt foot. For some unknown reason, in addition to the pain, he experienced another unpleasant sensation.

One day he found out what this sensation meant, and a terrible pain stabbed his heart. His leg had been cut off at the knee. His heart contracted painfully. What was he to do without a leg? How was he to live? How was he to earn a living?

He grabbed at his head, which was wrapped in bandages, and flung the white cloths to the floor. Blood spurted out, but he did not care. Let his life end! What reason did he have for living? He was a cripple!

Once again, he lost consciousness. When he came to, it seemed to him that he had fallen into a dark abyss that he was unable to climb out of.

This was not the end of his misfortune. He had not yet become accustomed to the idea that he was without a leg, when he became aware of something that hurt him even more profoundly.

One day, the nurse left a metal container with a mirror-like shiny lid beside him. He glanced at this lid and went numb. One of his eyes was smaller than the other, his lips were cut open, and his entire face was twisted.

This was more terrible to him than the loss of his leg.

He thought back to when he was a vigorous, agile youth; he recalled how all the girls in the village had chased after him, and he remembered how he had charmed Malanka with his good looks. But now, wouldn't she be frightened if she saw him? Wouldn't she be repulsed by him? He was so ugly now, and without a leg as well. Wouldn't it have been better if he had died—if the bullet had penetrated his heart, and his life had ended?

However, no matter how much he longed for death, he still wanted to live. Of what use is beauty, when there is no life? No matter what he looked like, he was still alive. But what would she—Malanka—say? Perhaps other people would also be frightened, but he did not care about them—only about her, Malanka!

After some time, he was transferred from that hospital to another one. Here he was fitted with a leg and given a card that excused him from further military service.

He was free. He could return home. But, even though he longed to go home, and would have gladly flown there, there was no joy in his heart.

When the time to leave came, and the steam of the train's engine carried him homewards, his heart trembled strangely. Had he ever expected, ever thought, that he would return, that he would come out of the war alive?

But when he neared his village, he was overcome by increasingly sad thoughts. How would he face Malanka? What would she say? And would he be able to take care of his farm as he once had?

His village came into view, and then his cottage.

For the first time in his life, he did not approach his house happily and eagerly. The nearer he came, the more he was gripped by an unknown fear, and the heavier his heart felt in his chest.

When he drew quite close to his home, his heart began beating violently.

Suddenly, he felt as if he had been hit on the head with the butt end of an axe. The windows of his house were boarded up, the door was propped shut and locked, the thatched roof was ragged, the fences were all taken apart, and the plough was broken.

He came up to the windows. The house was deserted. Like a mown blade of grass, he collapsed on the earthen embankment by the house and wept bitterly. What had happened? Where was his wife? His children?

He did not know how long he sat there. He could only feel that his heart was contracting ever more strongly with pain.

"Is that you, Lukyn?" Someone was speaking to him.

Lukyn looked up with haggard eyes.

"Don't you recognise me?"

"It's Ivanykha," he mumbled, as if he were talking to himself.

"I'm your neighbour. God, what's happened to you? I kept looking and looking—is it Lukyn or isn't it?"

"Where are my wife and children?" he managed to ask.

"So you don't know?"

"Where are my wife and children?" He was shouting in an almost insane voice.

"So you don't know? Malanka is dead."

"Malanka! Where? When? How?"

"There was a big battle here. She fled with the children, but no one can flee from death—it will find a person everywhere. It found her as well, right in front of the house, right here, where I'm standing. A bomb from a plane dropped on her and shattered her on this very spot. The children could not stay here alone, so the community gave them to their Aunt Frasyna."

Lukyn uttered only one word: "God!" And he began wailing once again, like a little child.

Someone else must have seen him and recognised him, for while he still sitting in a shocked stupor by the house, Aunt Frasyna walked up with his children.

The aunt struck her hands together in despair when she saw him. The children did not recognise him at first, and the youngest one had no idea that it was his daddy who had come home.

After some time had passed, Aunt Frasyna wanted to return Lukyn's children to him, but she saw he could not cope.

Lukyn walked around as if he were half dead.

"Oh, what haven't I tried, what lengths haven't I gone to in the hope of helping him at least partially regain his senses," Aunt Frasyna was talking with her neighbours by the church.

"He's mourning her so deeply, he's so devestated, that may God help him!

"To make things easier for him, so he wouldn't grieve so much, I told him that she forgot all about him and carried on with the soldiers.

"And when he heard this, my good women, he wailed in despair and began to lament so wildly, that his grief spread through all the ravines and forests."

And truly, when Lukyn heard the words of his aunt, he felt as if he had been thrown off a horse. His chest contracted, and his heart went numb with pain.

He was a cripple—a cripple, ugly, and without a leg! And, what was worse—with a heart that was gored and bloody . . .

Brothers
A fairy tale
(1916-17)

Winter—that white-haired Granny—came and lulled to sleep the weary earth exhausted by the burning sun and enervated by the summer, placed a soft pillow under its head and, with a downy white covering, shielded it from her fierce son, the Frost.

She protected people from him as well. She brought peace into a snug cottage, clothed its inhabitants in cosy garments and, stoking a fire, warmed fingers numbed by the cold.

Every time she came, she greeted the people like old acquaintances, and she always found that nothing much had changed.

There were those who had gone into the ground, and those who had just come into the world; some were happy, while others wept and worried about their usual human troubles. She knew all this very well, and she gazed at everything with a compassionate eye, as the elderly gaze on children, as eternity gazes at fleeting existence.

In the reckoning of Time, the terrifying thirteenth year passed. Old Granny Winter, who had gone away, returned.
She returned and found . . .

Fields, once covered with white down, were now strewn with corpses and with the wounded; a dreadful groaning and shrieking issued from a thousand chests. People were continually moving in throngs from one place to another, as if someone had cursed them with a terrible imprecation, as if they were being pursued by an invisible power. They walked mindlessly, without hoping for anything better; they walked because they had to walk; they walked even though they had no idea why they were walking. They had left behind everything that gave meaning to their existence and was its very essence; they had left everything behind as a thing of the past, as something that no longer belonged to them and remained with them only as a painful memory. They walked towards death, thrusting their chests out to meet it. They walked without questioning why, what for, or of what benefit it was to anyone.

Granny Winter knew the people. She knew their jealousies, angers, ambitions; she knew how hard they had persecuted one another, so that more than once blood had flowed; but that was long ago and, over time, all that had lessened, abated. So Granny was more than surprised when she once again found such fury on the earth. But she consoled herself that it would not last long, for with today's inventions, technical contrivances, and perfected devices, the entire world would surely become a depopulated desert if such killing and slaughter were to continue.

Granny Winter was losing her strength; she had to depart.

When she returned once again, she hastened to tuck the earth in white swaddling cloths and heal its wounds.

But the wounds kept breaking open, spurting fresh blood. She could hear, from afar, the roar of cannons and the whistling of guns. Humaneness was bankrupt; it had disappeared from the face of the earth, and only brute strength and its iron laws remained.

The dumbstruck soldier was no longer in his right mind. With a deadened heart he was fighting his way through thickets of barbed wire, poisonous fumes, and a hail of bullets.

Frenzied horses were dragging their dead masters.

Death was indiscriminately mowing down masses of people.

At every step, life was struggling with death.

All around, death rattles, screams, and wailing were tearing the heavens apart.

For several days now, the infernal fire had not abated, not even for a moment. People were attacking one another like wild animals.

A young rifleman came crashing out of the forest, his bayonet raised high. He was running as if he were totally demented, rushing forward mindlessly, without seeing anything, without hearing anything.

He was blind to everything around him, deaf to the death groans of his comrades, to their screams and pleas for help.

He knew only one thing—that he had to pierce the chest and shed the blood of the young man who was running towards him in the same manner.

They came face to face—stopped—and took measure of one another . . .

"Brother?" The word burst forth from the chest of the one in the foreign uniform.

"Brother!" the rifleman shouted. The extended bayonets fell from their hands, and they embraced each other fervently.

At that moment, two other soldiers from the two hostile camps rushed up and dropped both of them to the ground . . .

They toppled over like broken flints. Their bodies grew rigid, their faces turned ashen, and their eyes became glassy, but it seemed that a thought lingered on their brow, and that their staring eyes were asking: "Why did it happen this way? What is the reason for it? What turned a brother against his brother? Who sent them out against each other? Who divided them, and why has cold steel ripped open their hearts?"

And the cold winter night covered the corpses with white sheets. The moon glanced out dimly from behind the clouds, and its green face was reflected in the widely opened and strangely penetrating eyes of the two brothers—eyes that seemed to be seeing not what they had looked upon during their lifetime, and not what surrounded them now, but something different, more distant, its form only vaugely hinted at by the future . . .

Weighing heavily on their lives, on their souls—on the soul of their entire nation—was the oppressive hand of the past, the past which was telling them to forget about what used to be and who they had been, and to give up all hope for a happier fate. Subjugation had placed heavy shackles upon them—had restrained them with massive chains and cut them off from the whole world. And with every deliberate act, with every groan, the trammels of thraldom were squeezed more tightly.

Those confined within the narrow boundaries were forbidden to look out at the wider world, and so the world forgot about the millions who were dying in chains, who were struggling in vain to free themselves . . .

When Granny Winter once again gazed upon the poor earth, a dreadful plague was roaming over it, laughing wildly, roaring and howling, leaving behind nothing but graves and a desert gouged by grenades. The wind rustled in the desolate forest and whistled through the windows of the abandoned houses. The earth stirred; whole armies were rising without arms, without legs, without heads, while others formed a faceless mass. Muddy, in rags, and carrying—instead of weapons—heavy crosses on their backs.

They went forth in countless rows; they went across the continents, the seas; they remained suspended in the air.

In the field where the two brothers fell, the ploughed land spread far and wide. And whoever walked on the path among these fields saw two grey doves—saw them fly from clump to clump, alight on bushes, sway on trees, and vanish suddenly, without a trace, only to reappear and disappear once again.

When Granny came back the third time, she found that nothing had changed. Grief contracted her heart, and pearly tears flowed from her rheumy eyes.

"Do not grieve!" departing autumn whispered in her ear. "Something new is coming about, something great is suspended in the air . . ."

And it truly was!

A hubbub that was unlike that of the confusion of war was being added to the roar of the cannons from the north-east.

A mighty tempest was sounding ever closer and closer.

A red flag was raised—the red echo of the fire was striking and encompassing ever wider circles.

Waves of people followed—one after the other. Groans, screams, and the scraping of weapons could be heard, but the people were no longer moving along like a herd; they had a definite goal, defined strivings; life was no longer being wrenched away from them—they were willingly giving it up themselves.

Thunder . . .

The sky shook—the earth shuddered. Age-old chains were rent asunder, human suffering was cut short, the national soul was freed.

The rosy stars glittered, the rays of the sun of the resurrection rose high; three stars blazed in a brilliant azure sky. A mighty lion raised his head, a Zaporozhian kozak appeared with a musket, a golden plough emerged on a blue field, and above it, two doves, with wings widely outstretched in the heavenly expanse, carried an olive branch.

But a wing of the younger brother was hanging limply . . .